HOW TO USE LEVERAGE TO MAXIMIZE YOUR REAL ESTATE INVESTMENT RETURN

sensible finance techniques for real estate investors

by
John T. Reed

REED PUBLISHING

342 BRYAN DRIVE • DANVILLE, CALIFORNIA 94526 • 415 / 820-6292

To my son
Daniel Tunnell Reed

OTHER MATERIAL BY JOHN T. REED

- *Aggressive Tax Avoidance For Real Estate Investors*
- *Apartment Investing Check Lists*
- *How To Buy an Office Building*
- *Real Estate Investor's Monthly*
- *How To Manage Apartments for Maximum Cash Flow and Resale Value*

For more information, see the order blank elsewhere in this book

THANKS TO...

Alan Crittenden for sharing his knowledge of real estate finance...Bill Ogorzalek for his typesetting and graphics.

Typesetting and graphics: Oakland Graphics, Oakland, CA
Cover design: John T. Reed
Cover graphics: Diablo Direct Mail and Graphics, Concord, CA
Printing: Delta Lithograph, Van Nuys, CA

Published by Reed Publishing
342 Bryan Drive, Danville, CA 94526
Manufactured in the United States of America
Library of Congress Card Number: 85-090486
ISBN 0-939224-12-7

ABOUT THE AUTHOR

I am a real estate investor and Editor of *Real Estate Investor's Monthly.* My real estate work experience includes property management and real estate sales. I've worked with every type of property except retail. And with sizes ranging from $2,000 building lots to multimillion dollar apartment complexes.

Initially I invested in New Jersey; now in Texas. And I own a home in California. I'm somewhat familiar with real estate in the rest of the nation through contact with readers of *Real estate Investor's Monthly* and my travels as a real estate speaker and seminar giver.

I have a Bachelor of Science degree from West Point and a Master of Business Administration degree from Harvard Business School.

Contents

PART ONE
LEVERAGE

1
Your Leverage Strategy

lev• er• age (lev'er• ij) *noun.* The use of borrowed money to magnify return.

Leverage magnifies return. There is no more important real estate investment technique. Especially during inflation.

But as Charles Dickens pointed out in *David Copperfield,*

"Annual income twenty pounds,
annual expenditure nineteen and six,
result happiness.

Annual income twenty pounds,
annual expenditure twenty pounds ought and six,
result misery."

A double-edged sword

Borrowed money is a double-edged sword. It will magnify your return. But there is no guarantee that the return will be ***positive.***

Borrowed money ***made*** nearly every modern real estate millionaire. And borrowed money ***broke*** nearly every modern real estate failure.

If there were a real estate investor Hall of Fame, and you could ask the members how they got there, they'd say, "Leverage."

And if you could ask those buried on real estate investment's Boot Hill how ***they*** got there, they'd give the same answer—-"Leverage."

Like the gas pedal on your car

Leverage is to real estate investment what the gas pedal is to your car. Let's say you're about to take a car trip. It's over a road you've never travelled before. You want to get to your destination as fast as possible. But you also want to "arrive alive."

If you floor it, you'll get there quickly. . .if you don't crash first. If the road turns out to be relatively straight, high speed is no problem. But if it turns out to have sharp curves, high speed can kill you. In this analogy, no road map is available.

Same is true of real estate investment. You have a "destination." Maybe a net worth of a million dollars or some such. You want to get there as fast as possible. You quickly learn that the more leverage you use, the greater the possible speed (return on investment). But if you are highly leveraged, and you encounter a recession which causes a drop in property net income, you will suffer Dickensian misery. You may "crash" financially.

Paying it back

There are a lot of books and seminars on how to borrow money. But none on how to pay it back. This book is about ***both.*** That's why it's subtitled *Sensible Finance Techniques For Real Estate Investors.*

Can you buy real estate with no money down by using your Visa card?

Yes.

Should you?

Very rarely. Because the annual constant on credit card loans is in the 48% range and the capitalization rate on investment real estate is in the 10% or less range. I'll explain what annual constants and capitalization rates are later in the book. For now, suffice it to say,

"Annual capitalization rate 10%,
annual loan constant 9.5%,
result happiness.

Annual capitalization rate 10%,
annual loan constant 48%,
result misery."

The finance books I've read, and the finance seminars I've attended all pay ***lip service*** to paying the money back. They toss in a, "Now make sure you can afford it," every so often. So they have an out if someone goes bust following their advice. A not unlikely occurrence.

I pay more than lip service. I regard keeping a promise to pay money back on the appointed schedule as a ***sacred*** duty. That attitude pervades this book.

And I'll give you the ***biggest*** "secret" of all for borrowing money right now. The best way to get the loan you want ***tomorrow*** is to pay back the money you borrowed ***yesterday. . . on schedule.***

Few "creative finance" ***techniques*** can help you overcome a history of not keeping the promises you made to your previous lenders. So before you learn the ***techniques*** of borrowing, make sure you learn ***respect*** for the need to pay back the funds the techniques get for you.

A reputation is like fine china. . .

Someone once said,

"A reputation is like fine china; easily cracked, and never really repaired."

So stack loans up as high as you would stack fine china you're about to carry.

Slight imperfections in your credit history are especially important if the loan is to be sold to FNMA or FHLMC. According to Vince Bigone, Chief Loan Officer at Continental Savings and Loan in San Francisco, "If a loan applicant has had two late payments in any one year, investors [like FNMA and FHLMC] won't buy the loan...even if someone is putting $50,000 down on a $100,000 house."

The 15-day grace period

Many mortgage borrowers notice that their loan documents do not call for a late penalty until the 15th day after the due date. So they pay the monthly payment so it arrives just before the end of the grace period. ***DO NOT DO THAT!***

For starters, you often ***miss*** the date and end up ***paying*** the late penalty...which is substantial on a mortgage. And you argue with the lender about whether it arrived before the end of the grace period.

But more important, many if not most mortgage lenders will record you as having paid ***late***! Late ***each and every month***! That, in turn, may result in your being turned down on future loan applications.

Now I know many of you will argue that the payment is not late if you don't pay a late penalty. I disagree. The loan documents state the due date. Typically, the first of the month. Your payment is late if it arrives after the ***due date***. The late penalty date is simply a tradition to make you feel warm and fuzzy about what nice guys the savings and loan people are.

However, taking advantage of the grace period deliberately and systematically does not make the lender have warm and fuzzy feelings toward ***you***. Nor is it likely to make a good impression on the next lender you approach if they find out about it.

I don't want to overstate here. Some lenders will not record you as being late unless you trigger the late penalty. And even if your old lender ***does*** report that you were late every month, some lenders will still make you a loan upon hearing your explanation that you thought the loan wasn't late until the grace period was up. But a high percentage of lenders will ***not*** make you a loan if they learn you're a take-advantage-of-the-grace-period guy. Especially if money's the slightest bit tight.

The big picture on the grace period game

Let's look at the big picture. Playing the grace period game gets you use of the money for 15 extra days...***once***. If you have the money in a money market checking account, you're earning about 7% on it. Seven percent on a $1,000 payment is $70 a year. You only benefit the ***first*** month you do it. And that benefit is worth only 15/365 x $70 = $2.88.

Thereafter, your payments are 30 days apart same as if you were paying on the first of the month. So there's no further benefit of waiting until the end of the grace period. But you must play the grace period game ***every month*** thereafter in order to ***keep*** your $2.88. Because if you ever switch back to paying on the first of the month, you ***lose*** 15 days use of the money...and the $2.88 it represents.

And what about late penalties? My home mortgage has a 4% of the payment late penalty. On a $1,000 payment, that'd be $40. There's goes your $2.88 and a lot more.

Are you going to risk triggering $40 late penalties...not just once but many times...and risk having trouble getting future loans...to pick up a measly $2.88 in interest per $1,000 of payment? That's idiotic. Waiting until the end of the grace period to pay your mortgage is street corner real estate. Don't do it.

If you suffer a financial setback, but keep your credit record clean throughout, you can get the money back. But if you miss payments, it will take you ***seven years*** to clear that out of your official credit records. (So says the Fair Credit Reporting Act. It's ***ten*** years for bankruptcies.) That's time lost which you can ***never*** recover.

And although your ***official*** credit records may be clean seven years after missing a payment, the ***individuals*** involved will remember forever.

Bad credit *can* be repaired

As a ***practical*** matter, good credit ***can*** be restored. Even after bankruptcy. Howard Ruff, the best-selling author (*How To Prosper During The Coming Bad Years*), newsletter publisher (*The Ruff Times*, now *Howard Ruff's Financial Survival Report*), and TV show host ("Ruff House") is a case in point. He declared bankruptcy in his early years. But I suspect his credit rating is pretty good now.

And as Ruff himself is quick to point out, restoring your credit doesn't happen overnight...and it's no fun.

So I don't want to exaggerate the consequences of marring your credit. Time can cure most credit problems. Some lenders...most notably sellers...have hardly any credit standards at all. And ***all*** lenders' credit standards are inversely proportional to the amount of money the lender has to lend.

But don't let any "creative finance" pusher convince you missing payments is OK because

- "The lender can only take the property. He can't make you pay if the property value doesn't cover the loan." (That's true in some situations. But it doesn't prevent your credit history from being marred.)

- "You can always declare bankruptcy."(You ***can*** if you meet the legal requirements. But that's hardly the road to riches.)

- "You can put everything in your wife's name." (Not if the item in question has been pledged as security for a loan.)

- Or any other reason.

Make ***all*** your payments on time. Every single one of them. If leverage is a gas pedal, good credit is a drivers license. With***out*** it, you don't drive ***at all.***

Honest loan applications too

Your payment history isn't the only thing that affects your credit. Your loan applications have to be honest, too.

Finance ***books*** rarely suggest fraudulent finance techniques. But I've been to at least one "creative finance" seminar where ***most*** of what was said was illegal. The classic dishonest "technique" is to sign two purchase agreements. A ***real*** one which shows the real price. And a phony one which shows a phony, higher price. The purpose of the technique is to get the lender to make a larger loan than they would make if they knew the true sale price.

Two investors tried to play that game with President Reagan's Pacific Palisades home. They agreed to buy it for $1,030,000. But they later applied to a federally insured savings and loan association for a $1,200,000 mortgage and told the s & l that the purchase price was $1,900,000.

A federal grand jury charged them with making a false statement to a federally chartered and insured institution, conspiracy, and mail fraud. They pled guilty to making a false statement. The U.S. Attorney dropped the other charges. On November 22, 1982, the U.S. District Court judge sentenced one to two years in jail and fined him $5,000. The other was sentenced to one year in jail and a $5,000 fine.

Lying about occupying the property

Owner-occupants usually get better terms from lenders than investors. That creates a temptation for investors to lie about whether they will occupy the premises or not. To some, lies like that are a finance "technique." As far as I'm concerned, they're just lies. Don't do it.

Someone once said, "Never insult an alligator until after you've crossed the river." Applying that principal to real estate finance means, "Never cross a lender unless you're absolutely positive you'll never need anything from that lender again." Some of the things you may need from a lender in the future:

- reference
- more money
- forebearance

The keys to success in real estate finance

I've done a lot of research on real estate finance. Through my own experience. Reading. Attending seminars. Work in real estate brokerage and property management. And by teaching a seminar on the subject for two years.

It may sound funny to you for me to claim I learned a lot about real estate finance by ***teaching*** it. But if you've ever been an instructor you know just what I mean. All teachers learn from their students.

Based on what I learned from all those sources, here's what I believe are the keys to success in real estate finance.

- good credit
- knowledge of real estate finance
- negotiating skill
- personal characteristics

I've already discussed good credit. I'll say more about it later in the book.

Knowledge of real estate finance

Knowledge of real estate finance is what most books and seminars are about. Including this one. But don't think that knowledge is all you need.

Knowledge helps. In some cases, it can make the difference. But in general, the most successful real estate borrowers are ***not*** successful because of their knowledge. They are successful because of their personal characteristics. . .for the want of a better phrase. Things like persistence. I'll explain that shortly.

So knowledge is important. But not as important as the "creative finance" pushers would have you believe. Simply knowing some fancy technique won't get you high leverage acquisitions. As a matter of fact, ***fancy*** techniques get in the way more than they help. The typical high leverage deal results more from ***per***spiration than ***in***spiration.

Negotiating skills

Negotiating skills are important in real estate finance. But less important than most people think. Trying to "win" a negotiation does more harm than good.

Real estate agents have the right goal. They are vitally concerned with ***doing*** the deal. They couldn't care less what the terms are as a general rule.

Buyers and sellers, on the other hand, tend to be hypersensitive to price and terms. They forget that the profit in real estate comes from doing deals. Not from negotiating a "great" deal.

Think about your last couple deals (if you're not a novice). Did you make or lose a lot of money because of what happened in the negotiation? Or did you make the vast majority of your return simply from the fact that you bought property?

I'll bet it was because you bought property. Because you ***did*** the deal. Not ***how*** you did it. Don't get so wrapped up in "winning" the negotiation that you forget the big picture. If you're buying, your goal is to buy. Not to buy at the best possible price.

If you're selling, your goal is to acquire the next property. Not to get the best possible price on the old one. (When I say "sell" I really mean exchange. See the chapter on taking back a loan when you sell for more information on that. Also see the installment sale and exchange chapters of my book *Aggressive Tax Avoidance For Real Estate Investors.*

"Parking space proximity phobia"

I have some friends who suffer from a psychology problem I call "parking space proximity phobia." Parking space proximity phobia is the fear that the space you park in when you go to a shopping mall is not the absolute closest one there was at the time you parked. People who suffer from that phobia drive slowly around for extended periods scanning the parking lot for empty spaces, back-up lights, or returning shoppers.

There's a similar phobia in real estate. It is the fear that you did not get absolutely every single buck you could out of the other party. I'll call it "last dollar phobia." It's similar to the attitude Woody Allen expressed in the movie "Annie Hall."

Annie: "In my family, raising your voice was the worst crime you could commit."
Woody: "In my family the worst crime was to pay retail."

My advice to you on negotiating is to read up on the subject. Be thorough in your preparation. Be alert to opportunities. But don't get so wrapped up on "winning" the negotiation that you fall prey to last dollar phobia. Your mission is to ***get the next property***. Not to win the "Tough Negotiator of the Year" award.

Personal characteristics

I used to take a poll in my finance seminar. (I don't do the seminar anymore.) I asked the attendees to give me the details of the highest leverage deal they ever did. I was looking for techniques.

I was disappointed. There were many high leverage deals. (I define high leverage as a down payment of less then 20%.) But the techniques used were mundane. Usually an institutional first mortgage and a seller second mortgage. Who needs to attend a seminar or read a book to learn that technique?

Ask

But when I questioned them on the deal I learned there was something unusual about it. For starters, they ***believed*** it could be done. Most investors don't even ***try*** to do high leverage deals. They assume the seller would say no.

I'll remind you of something you've almost certainly heard before. ***You never know until you ask.*** So ask. . .if high leverage is your goal.

Determination

The second unusual thing about their approach was their determination. Where others had floated the idea of a small down payment as a ***trial balloon***, the high leverage guys had ***insisted*** on it.

Actually, determination is just one of the personal characteristics that determines success in real estate finance. And I don't mean to define success in real estate finance as only high leverage. I define success as simply getting the loan you want.

The key to doing better than average in real estate finance efforts is bringing to bear characteristics like these:

- perseverance
- persistence
- courage
- tenacity
- patience
- grit
- diligence
- boldness
- audacity

You get the idea.

The difference between the guy who gets high leverage and the guy who settles for low leverage is ***not*** knowledge of real estate finance techniques.

The difference between the guy who gets the loan when money is tight and the guy who doesn't is ***not*** knowledge of real estate finance techniques.

The difference between the guy who gets the loan he wants and the guy who doesn't ***is*** "invincible determination of purpose once fixed and then death or victory." (apologies to Sir Thomas Buxton)

Searching for the Fountain of Youth

I suspect that most nòvice real estate investors have the same desire when it comes to real estate finance techniques. They want techniques which will let them do deals which

- require little or no money down
- have payments low enough for positive cash flow
- and which are easy to arrange

To find such techniques, these investors endlessly attend "creative finance" seminars and buy "creative finance" books. They remind me of Ponce De Leon searching for the Fountain of Youth. He never found it. Neither will they.

Pick one. . .and *only* one

I can tell you how to accomplish any ***one*** of those three things. In some cases you can combine ***two*** of them. But all three in one technique? Forget it.

Finance techniques that allow low-down payment, positive cash flow, easy-to-arrange deals are about as numerous as Fountains of Youth. The "creative finance" pushers imply that if you just take their seminar or read their book or listen to their cassettes, such techniques will be revealed to you.

Let me remind you of one of the most basic laws of economics.

"There is no free lunch."

High leverage, low payments, and ease of arranging are all valuable. You can get them. But you must pay.

Real estate deals are made up of many terms. What you ***get*** in one part of the deal, you will ***pay for*** elsewhere in the deal. Pushing the down payment percentage down, for example, is like pushing down one end of a see saw.

Can it be done?

Sure. But not without making the other end go ***up*** the same distance.

Do the "standard" deal. . .or pay

In any market at any given time, there is a more or less "standard" deal. For example, the average apartment building sale in the Seattle area in 1984 had these terms:

- gross rent multiplier: 7
- down payment: 23.5%
- term of seller loan: 10 years
- seller loan interest rate: 10.5%

That's according to Cain & Scott's annual *Apartment Market Study*. Cain & Scott is a real estate brokerage firm specializing in apartment house sales in the Seattle area. Their address is 3005 First Avenue, Suite 302, Seattle, WA 98121.

If that's the standard deal, most sellers and real estate agents know it is. Now let's say you just took a "creative finance" seminar and you want to buy with zero down. Zero down would be a significant deviation from the "standard" 23.5% down.

Can you do that?

Yes.

Will it be easy?

No.

How will the difficulty manifest itself?

Sellers and agents who know they can get 25% from the market at present will either refuse your offer or they will demand to be compensated elsewhere in the deal. Usually it's the price. Or it may be the term of the seller loan. Or a blanket mortgage on all your other property and enslavement of your first-born son. I can't predict ***where*** in the deal you'll be required to pay. But I ***guarantee*** you'll pay.

So you may find someone willing to sell to you on a zero down basis. But don't expect to pay the same price as if you had put 23.5% down.

The "Law of Large Numbers"

College boys delight in telling about the mythical guy who strolls down a crowded beach asking every unaccompanied woman to go to bed with him. "He gets slapped a lot," they say. "But he scores a lot, too."

I don't doubt it would work...if you didn't get arrested or killed by a returning boyfriend first. That's the Law of Large Numbers.

You can apply the same Law to real estate investing. "Didja hear about No Money Down Don? He makes a zero down payment offer on every piece of real estate that's for sale. He gets turned down a lot. But he buys a lot of property, too."

No doubt in my mind that would work, too. I ***do*** wonder if it would be worth the effort required and the ***dis***advantageous ***other*** terms you'd have to agree to.

If it fits your strategy, do it

I'm putting down "creative finance" here. But I don't mean to tell you that deviations from the "standard" deal are always bad or ill-advised. I ***do*** want to make sure you understand that don't get "Super Deal" by simply waving your "creative finance" seminar diploma or by chanting some magic words like, "wraparound sale leaseback land contract paper out."

No money down, for example, can be a sensible strategy for some people. So can 30% down. Or 14% interest rate loans. It's just that each approach has its advantages and disadvantageous.

The market rules

The market ***always*** dictates the fundamentals of the deal. All you can do with finance techniques is ***rearrange*** those fundamentals fit your strategy more comfortably. That is worth doing. But it's not the wonder drug the "creative finance" pushers would have you believe.

Risk and reward

All investments have two dimensions:

Risk
Reward

You knew that. But did you know that lenders call loans "investments?" Shocked me first time I heard one use that term. When he mentioned his investments, I thought, "I didn't know these guys had investment property. I thought they only made loans."

They ***did*** only make loans. But to a lender, a loan is an investment. That's important for you to know. Because real estate finance is much easier to understand if you do.

"Technique Number 476"

"Creative finance" pushers are fond of impressing you with the ***number*** of "new" techniques they are going to give you. To make their techniques sound as new and as numerous as possible, they give each a separate, exotic sounding name.

One of the things a writer should guard against is writing to ***im***press rather than to ***ex***press. But that's exactly what the "creative finance" pushers are doing with their zillions of "different" techniques. Trying to ***im***press rather than ***ex***press. And since they try to wow you rather than communicate to you, they wind up confusing you.

How much? When? How sure?

The lender has just three basic questions.

How much do I get?
When do I get it?
How sure am I to get it?

The first two are his ***reward***. The last one is his ***risk***. In the real estate finance seminar I used to teach, I called these two ingredients:

payment pattern and
security instrument.

Every loan, real estate or otherwise, has a specified payment pattern and a specified security instrument or instruments. Sometimes the payment pattern is dependent on an external event. For example, payments on a variable rate loan depend on an interest rate index.

Examples of security instruments include mortgages, trust deeds, leases, land contracts, etc. The security instrument is simply the written guarantee the lender gets from someone that the loan will be repaid.

That guarantee may be signed by someone no more financially secure than you. As in the case of a signature loan. Or it may be guaranteed by someone as solid as a private mortgage company or even the federal government as in the case of FHA or VA insured mortgages.

Payment patterns

Any pattern which can be reproduced on a moving graph paper can be used to finance real estate. You've seen those moving graphs in electrocardiagrams and polygraphs and such. The ink pen can stay steady, or go up, or go down, or wobble. You name it. About the only thing it cannot do is loops. Same thing is true of real estate finance.

For example, since the depression, the main payment pattern in real estate finance was the 25 or 30 year fixed-rate, fixed payment, self-amortizing loan. A $100,000, 30 year 13% loan would have a payment pattern that looks like this

Figure 1

Payment Pattern of Traditional Mortgage

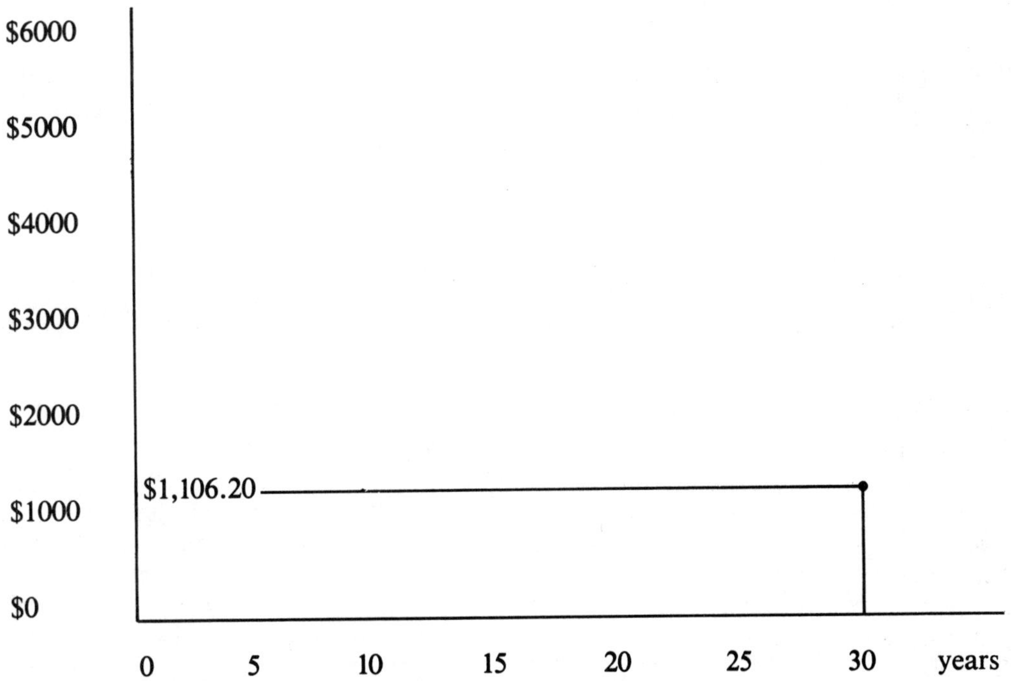

The monthly payment is $1,106.20

Payment patterns don't always have to be level. They can also be

- ascending
- descending
- irregular
- or any combination of the above.

Here's an *ascending* pattern. Graduated payment mortgages and growing equity mortgages among others have this payment pattern.

Figure 2

Ascending Payment Pattern

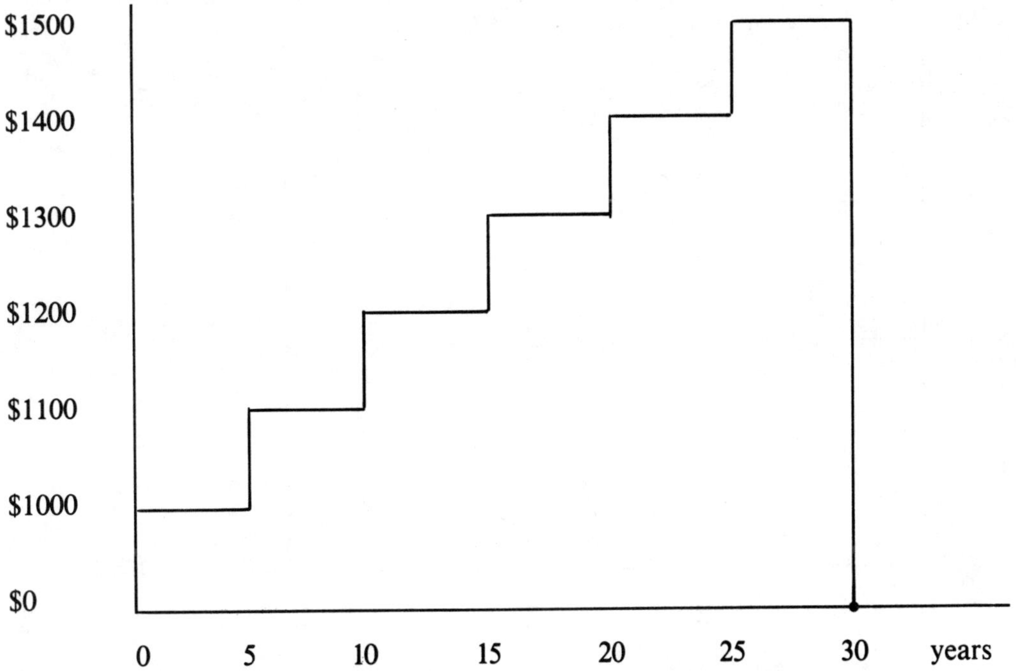

Here's a ***descending*** pattern. It's not common. The only example I can think of is a credit card loan. My Visa card, for example, has a minimum payment of 4% of the unpaid balance per month. Since the balance goes down every time you make a payment, so does 4% of the balance.

Figure 3

Descending Payment Pattern

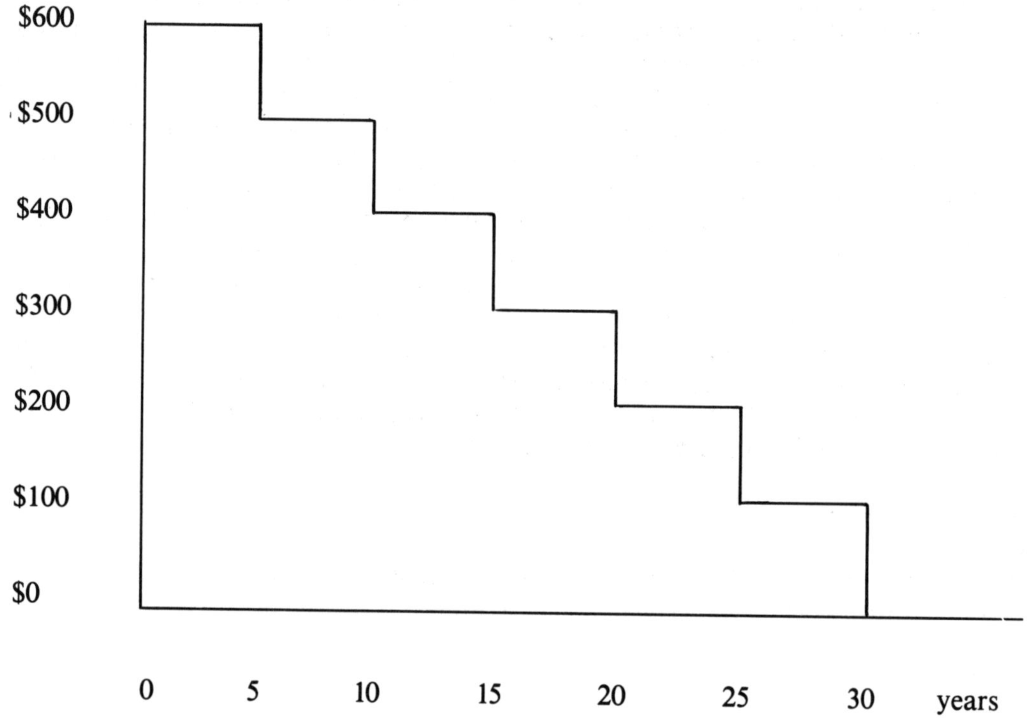

Here's an ***irregular*** pattern. This is a seller second mortgage I had to pay on an apartment building I bought. Terms were $10,000 at 8% simple interest. Only two payments. One at the third anniversary of the accrued interest only. And one at the fifth anniversary of the principal and two years additional accrued interest.

Figure 4

Irregular Payment Pattern

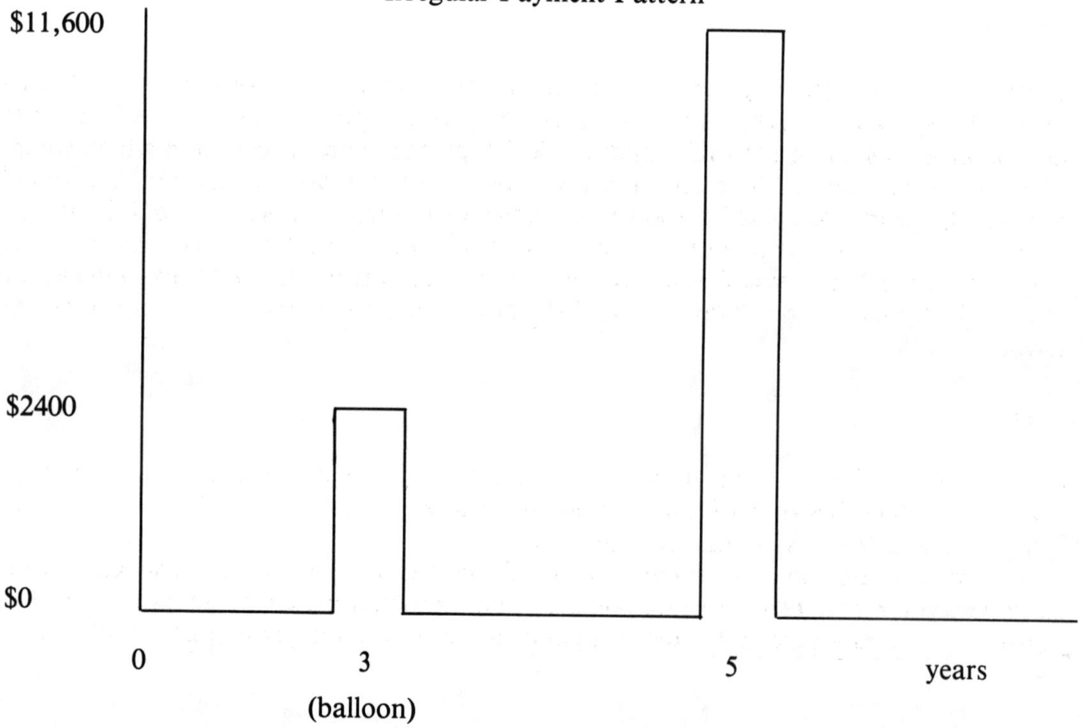

Balloon payment mortgages are common examples of an irregular payment pattern.

Fixed or contingent

Your duty to make a payment can be fixed or contingent. By ***fixed***, I mean that every payment you'll ever make is spelled out in the original loan documents. By ***contingent*** I mean that some or all of the payments depend on some outside event. The word "contingent" has too many syllables. So I prefer to call contingent loans or contingency clauses "if loans" and "if clauses."

An example of a ***totally*** fixed payment pattern would be a ***locked-in*** loan. Most small investors have never heard of such a thing. A locked-in loan is one which you ***may not prepay at all***. Not if you sell the property. Not if you inherit enough money to pay it off. Not for any reason. Insurance companies prefer locked-in loans on large commercial projects.

In some loans, you don't know in advance what your payments will be. Those are "if loans." For example, an adjustable rate mortgage typically spells out your ***initial*** payments. But after six months or a year, your payment amount depends on what happens to some interest rate index. There's a clause in the loan which says, "***If*** the index goes up, your payment goes up. If the index goes down, your payment goes down." That's an if clause and it makes the loan an if loan.

Nearly all loans have if clauses. The most common is a due-on-sale clause. It says, "***If*** you sell by deed or land contract or lease option the property, you must pay off the loan."

I'll go into more detail on if clauses and if loans later in the book.

Security of the loan

The security of the loan is how sure the lender is of getting the agreed upon payment pattern. Lender have what they call "The Three C's Of Credit." They are

- Character
- Capacity
- Collateral

This book is about getting loans. In order to get a loan, you must persuade the lender that the combination of risk and reward your deal presents is acceptable. The lender's reward is in the payment pattern. The lender's risk is in the Three C's. So in order to get the loan, you must convince the lender that ***your*** deal has an adequate combination of character, capacity, and collateral.

Character

I've already discussed the importance of a clean credit history. That's ***one*** aspect of character.

But it's not just ***your*** character that matters. In many cases, you have a ***co-signer***. I'm not talking about parents co-signing for their children. Although that's one situation in which someone else's character is pertinent. More common is the case where a mortgage insuror "co-signs."

Private mortgage insurors like Mortgage Guarantee Insurance Corporation (MGIC) are, in effect, co-signers. So are government mortgage insurors like FHA and VA. Since their character is so high quality, their "signatures" can get you many loans which you could not otherwise get.

So it's not just ***your*** character that counts. It's the character of ***everyone*** who promises to pay the loan.

Capacity

Capacity refers to your having the ***income*** to make the payments. The co-signer technique I just mentioned works because of the additional ***capacity*** it means as well as the additional character. FHA and VA have enormous capacity.

In any event, you must at some point convince the lender that you and any co-signers you get have the capacity to make the payments. Some techniques focus on convincing the lender of that. For example, any technique which alters the payment pattern to make the loan more affordable improves your capacity to make the payments.

As a general rule, you want to make the payment pattern fit your ***income*** pattern as closely as possible. The graduated payment loan, which is relatively uncommon, probably does that best in most cases.

Here's a graphic picture of the typical real estate investment income pattern.

Figure 5

Typical Income Pattern of a Real Estate Investment

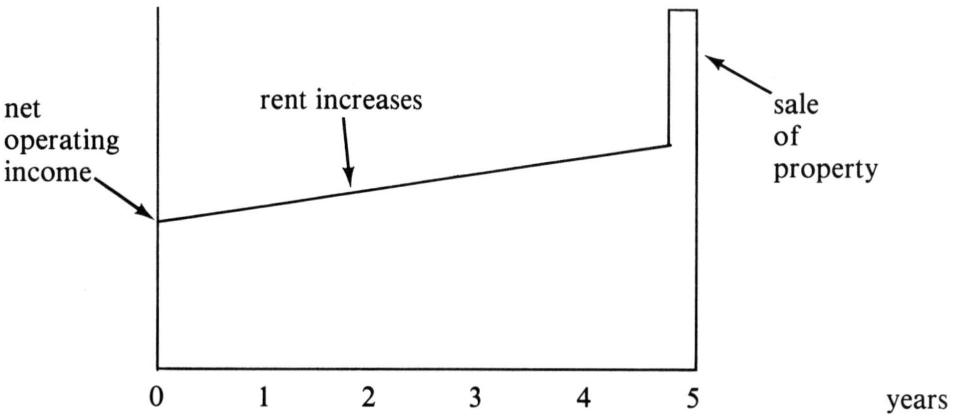

The net operating income goes up gradually each year due to rent increases. And in the year of sale you get a large burst of income from the sale proceeds.

The typical due-on-sale clause fits the sale proceeds income well. But the typical level payment loan does ***not*** fit the rent income pattern well. In the typical deal, you are stretching to the limit to make the payments the first year or two your own the property. Then it becomes progressively easier to make them. Figure 6 shows how the level payment loan fits the typical investment property's income pattern.

Figure 6

Level Payments Loan and Typical Income Pattern Fit

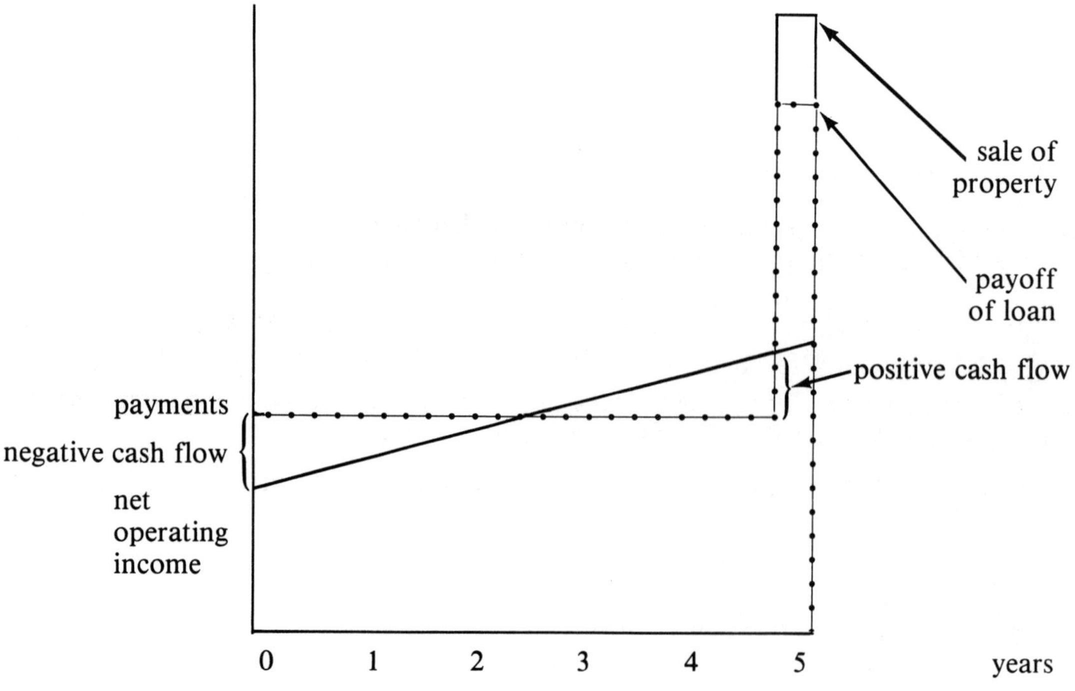

This "stretch-then-slide" effect makes no sense. The graduated payment loan makes sense. Lenders can shift from level payment loans to graduated payment loans without sacrificing yield. But few have done so.

Nevertheless, I urge "graduates" of this book to seek graduated payment patterns whenever possible. The more flexible institutional lenders will probably go along. As will most sellers. The fit between your income and your payments will look like this then.

Figure 7

Graduated Payment Loan and Typical Income Pattern Fit

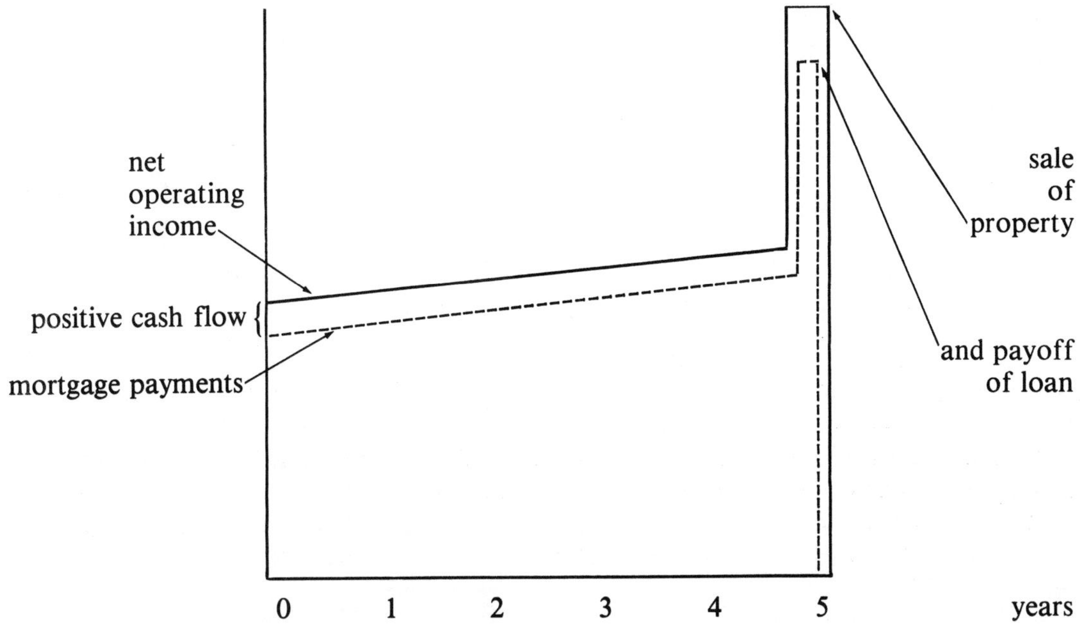

Improving the *fit* between net operating income and mortgage payments is one of the most important finance techniques.

Collateral

Collateral is the last of the Three C's. It involves

- *What* property, if any, is pledged as security for the loan and
- *How* the lender gets at that property in the event of a default.

What property is pretty straight forward. In the typical real estate deal, the property you're acquiring is the collateral for the loan. If you're buying a car, the car is the collateral.

You can get a little tricky with the answer to the "What property" question. Examples include blanket mortgages, substitution of collateral, and hypothecation.

How the lender gets at the property is determined by the security instrument you use. Security instruments include

- mortgages
- trust deeds
- land contracts
- leases
- options.

That's all there is

Believe it or not, that's virtually the entire gamut of real estate finance techniques. This box sums them up in the form of the six lender questions.

Figure 8

THE LENDER'S SIX QUESTIONS

REWARD	RISK
1. **How much** do I get? 2. **When** do I get it?	3. What is the **Character** of those who have promised to pay? 4. What is their **Capacity** to pay? 5. **What Property**, if any, is pledged as security? 6. **How** do I get at the property if they default?

All you have to do to get the loan you want is to answer those six questions to the satisfaction of the lender.

All the techniques in the world

When it comes to ***payments patterns***, you have an ***infinite*** number of choices. Try to get the one that fits your situation best.

When it comes to ***signers***, you can get ***anyone or any organization*** you can persuade to guarantee your making the payments. (Usually, it's someone who benefits from the deal being done.)

When it comes to ***collateral***, you can pledge ***any property you own***...tangible or intangible...real property or personal property...as long as the lender will accept it.

When it comes to ***security instruments***, you can use ***any instrument which is recognized by the law in the state in question.***

Detent versus continuous dials

One of the few things I learned in my days in Army communications was the word "detent." That's not *detente*. *Detente* is a French word usually meaning to get friendly with the Russians.

No I'm talking about "detent"...without the final "e." The dial on your TV is a detent dial. It clicks. You can set it on channel two. Or channel three. But not channel two and a half.

The dial on your FM radio is *not* a detent dial. It is a *continuous* dial. You can set it on *any* frequency. 98.7 or 98.75 or 98.734472590 or whatever.

When a "creative finance" teacher gives you a whole bunch of separate finance techniques with different names and/or numbers, he's making real estate finance out to be a "black box" with a detent dial on it.

"You can use Technique 98, the Wraparound Mortgage," he says. "Or you can use Number 99, the Land Contract. Or you can use..."

He has a Technique 98 and a Technique 99. But no Technique 98.7.

Folks, I've got news for you. There *is* a Technique 98.7. And a Technique 98.734472590, too. The "black box" of real estate finance does *not* have a detent dial. It has a *continuous* dial. That's why I break it down into

- payment patterns
- signers
- collateral and
- security instruments.

It's more of a soup

Maybe a better way to describe real estate finance techniques is that they are like soup recipes. You have ***four ingredients***: the payment pattern, who signs, what, if anything is pledged as collateral, and how the lender gets at the collateral. You can mix those four ingredients in an infinite number of ways. Each recipe will produce a different "soup" or finance technique.

Confusing and misleading

Trying to learn 312 different finance techniques will only confuse you. What's worse, it will ***mislead*** you. Mislead you into believing that there are ***only*** 312 different techniques. Heinz may have only 57 varieties. And there may be only eight million stories in the Naked City. But the number of finance techniques is limited only by your imagination.

Some definitions you need to know

Before I go any further, there are some terms you need to know. This income statement shows the definition of several.

Gross annual income		$40,000.00
Less operating expenses		
Utilities	3,800.00	
Taxes and insurance	4,000.00	
Maintenance	4,000.00	
Payroll	4,600.00	
Vacancies and collection losses	1,600.00	
Total operating expenses		-18,000.00
Net operating income		22,000.00
Debt service (mortgage payments)		-20,000.00
Before-tax cash flow		2,000.00
Tax savings or (tax payable)		+9,000.00
After-tax cash flow		11,000.00

"Return"

When most investors talk about return, they mean "return on original investment." Typically, their "original investment" is their down payment when they bought the property. You can usually talk them into adding closing costs.

"Return" can mean a couple of different things. There are potentially four returns in real estate investment.

- appreciation
- cash flow
- tax shelter
- amortization

When an investor talks about "return," he may mean ***cash*** return only. That would be his ***before-tax cash flow*** divided by his investment. Sometimes called "cash on cash."

Or the investor may mean ***overall*** return. That includes all four returns. Some experts feel using overall return is misleading because it treats cash and non-cash returns the same. Cash is the only real return according to these experts. So they don't count appreciation and amortization until the property is sold.

I use overall return

I believe overall return is the proper one. The typical investor is pursuing a net worth goal. He wants his net worth to be X dollars by such and such date. He does not require that net worth to be in cash. He feels just as good about it in the form of real estate equity.

Furthermore, much of his equity can be converted to cash at any time by borrowing. So the fact that it has not ***yet*** been converted to cash seems unimportant to me.

It's true that not ***all*** of his equity can be converted to cash by borrowing. Lenders don't lend 100% of value generally. (They will in some cases.) But not all of his equity can be converted to cash by ***selling*** either. If he sells, part will go for ***income taxes***. Some may go to a real estate agent as ***commission***. And some may remain in the form of a ***mortgage taken back*** by the seller. So only the appreciation which the investor could convert to cash should be counted as return. In other words, the ***net*** appreciation after sales costs are taken into account.

It's current equity not original investment

Your original investment is irrelevant, ancient history. ***Current equity*** is the only denominator to use when figuring return. Return on ***original*** investment typically goes ***up*** every year. That tends to make you feel you're doing well and shouldn't change anything.

Return on ***current equity***, on the other hand, typically goes ***down*** every year. That's because your equity grows faster than your return. Leverage magnifies return, remember?

But with each passing year, your leverage declines. As a result the magnification due to leverage declines. That's why return on equity goes down. Here's an example.

Example

You buy a $200,000 building. Inflation is 4% per year. Your down payment is 20% or $40,000. The $160,000 mortgage is for thirty years at 13%. Gross annual income is $40,000. Net operating income is $22,000. Sales costs are 5%. I'll assume you're exchanging and therefore not paying any taxes when you dispose of the property. The "tax savings" figure assumes an 80% improvement ratio (80% building; 20% land), accelerated cost recovery system, January purchase, and a fifty percent tax bracket investor.

Here's what your overall return would look like as a percent of the original investment and as a percent of current equity.

balance sheet

	beginning of year 1	beginning of year 2	beginning of year 3	beginning of year 4	beginning of year 5	beginning of year 6
market value	200,000	208,000	216,320	224,973	233,972	243,331
sale costs	10,000	10,400	10,816	11,249	11,699	12,167
net value	190,000	197,600	205,504	213,724	222,273	231,164
mortgage balance	160,000	159,561	159,065	158,504	157,871	157,155
loan-to-net value %	84.21	80.75	77.40	74.16	71.03	67.98
net equity	30,000	38,039	46,439	55,220	64,402	74,009
change in net equity		8,039	8,400	8,781	9,182	9,607

income statement

net operating income	22,000	22,880	23,795	24,747	25,737	26,766
debt service	21,239	21,239	21,239	21,239	21,239	21,239
before-tax cash flow	761	1,641	2,556	3,508	4,498	5,527
net operating income	22,000	22,880	23,795	24,747	25,737	26,766
less interest	20,800	20,743	20,678	20,606	20,523	20,431
depreciation %	8.8	8.4	7.6	6.9	6.3	5.7
depreciation deduct	14,080	13,440	12,160	11,040	10,080	9,120
taxable income	-12,880	-11,303	-9,043	-6,899	-4,866	-2,785
tax savings	6,440	5,652	4,522	3,450	2,433	1,393
after-tax cash flow	7,201	7,293	7,078	6,958	6,931	6,920
overall return from after-tax cash flow and change in equity as of end of year	1	2	3	4	5	
	15,240	15,693	15.859	16,140	16,538	
return on investment	38.10	39.23	39.65	40.35	41.35	
return on net equity	50.8	41.26	34.19	29.23	25.68	

The "new car" effect

The return is low the first year due to the "new car" effect. When you drive a new car off the dealer's lot, it instantaneously drops in value. That's because it's no longer new. And because you're not a dealer.

A similar thing happens when you acquire real estate. If you immediately turned around and sold the property, you would not be able to get out all the money you just paid to buy it. The transaction costs—-attorney fees, recording fees, and such are gone forever. In fact, you'll have to pay similar fees again to sell. And you'll probably have to pay a commission or at least incur the costs of marketing the property if you don't use an agent.

So in the short run, acquisition of a property is a ***step backward***.

Return on equity declines

As the numbers show, return on ***equity*** goes down every year after the second year. I point this out so you'll understand that leverage is important ***every day*** of your investment career. Not just on closing day.

Most investors are leverage conscious when they acquire property. They try to buy with the minimum down payment. But ***after*** closing, they more or less ignore leverage. This results in a condition called "bloated equity" or "lazy equity."

As the years pass, the typical investor is vaguely aware that his situation is deteriorating. The building throws off less and less tax shelter each year. Cash flow and amortization get better. But not spectacularly so. And both are taxable at ordinary income tax rates. He starts to think about the fact that his equity is large enough to move up to a bigger building. A bigger building which would provide much larger depreciation deductions.

According to Bruce Makar of Coldwell Banker, the typical real estate investor sells his property after four to six years. If that typical investor were more aware of his deteriorating leverage and return on equity, he would probably sell sooner...or at least refinance.

Target loan-to-value ratio

Ideally, you would select a target loan-to-value ratio...and keep your leverage there at all times. For example, you might select an 80% loan-to-value ratio as your target. Then you would constantly adjust the value of your portfolio to keep the overall loan-to-value ratio at 80%.

That would mean every time your equity went up, the total value of the properties you owned and the total value of the mortgages you owed would go up too. If you did that, your return on equity would stay relatively constant. And high.

Since 80% is not an unusually high loan-to-value ratio, you would not be taking undue risk. Maintaining a constant loan-to-value ratio is analogous to maintaining a constant speed on a long car trip. The speed which would offer the best combination of safety, legality, and driving time would be 55 miles per hour. If you're speed gradually slowed to say 30 miles per hour, then jumped back up to 55 every hour, you would arrive much later. Yet you would not get any meaningful safety benefits.

That's exactly what happens over the life of the typical real estate investment.

Practical problems with "keeping speed up"

Of course it's a lot easier to hold a gas pedal down than it is to releverage a real estate investment portfolio. There are transaction costs nearly every time you get a loan. (Unsecured loans often have no transaction costs.)

Refinancing generally cannot take you all the way up to 80%. That's because lenders tend to be more conservative on refinancing than on purchases. And because appraisers tend to be conservative, too, when there's no sale price to work from.

You can generally get your highest loan-to-value ratio from sellers. So you'd almost have to buy every year to maintain a relatively high loan-to-value ratio. The lower your target ratio, the easier it is to maintain. Unfortunately, the lower the ratio, the lower the return.

Since it's hard to maintain a target loan-to-value ratio with pinpoint accuracy, how about a ***range*** of ratios instead?

Target loan-to-value ratio range

You could say, for example, that you wanted to keep your loan-to-net value ratio between 75 and 80 percent. In the example above, you would be within that range for years 1, 2, and 3. At the beginning of year four, your loan total would be $158,504 and your net value $213,724. That's a loan-to-net value ratio of 74%.

In order to get back within range, your $55,220 of net equity would have to be in at least $55,220/25% = $220,880 of real estate (after sales costs). And you would need $220,880 -$55,220 = $165,660 of mortgage loans. That's an increase of $220,880 - $213,724 = $7,156 in property value and $165,660 - $158,504 = $7,156 in loans.

To releverage up to ***80%***, you'd need to own $55,220/20% = $276,100 of net value. That would mean acquiring $62,376 more of net value and loans.

Big, little, little, big

During the first three years in the example above, you collected a cumulative total of $7,201 + $7,293 + $7,078 = $21,572 in after-tax cash flow. How's about you invest that cash in another property. If it's 20% down, that $21,572 will buy $21,572/20% = $107,860 worth of real estate.

That would give you ***two*** properties. This table shows the value of each and the total overall value.

	old	new	overall
market value	224,973	107,860	337,628
sale costs	11,249	5,393	16,882
net value	213,724	102,467	320,746
mortgage balance	158,504	90,124	248,628
net equity	55,220	16,898	72,118
loan-to-net value	74%	84%	78%

Voila! By adding an 84% (higher than 80% due to the 'new car' effect) ratio to your 74% ratio you end up with an ***overall*** ratio of 78%. . . which is ***within*** your target range of 75% to 80%.

So you can keep your overall ratio within a fairly narrow range by buying smaller properties in between buying large ones. The out-of-pocket transaction costs on ***purchases*** are pretty small. So acquisitions are a low cost way to keep your equity lean.

The out-of-pocket transaction costs on ***sales*** are usually higher. There are income taxes if you don't exchange. And marketing costs like commissions. Low leverage depresses return. But so do transaction costs. So the big-little-little-big pattern may be the best way to keep your loan-to-value ratio where it should be.

It's *overall* loan-to-value ratio

Real estate investors usually think in terms of ***one property*** when they think of leverage. That can cause you to overestimate the value of some "creative" finance techniques.

For example, one technique for borrowing 100% of your purchase price is to get a second mortgage placed on a low leverage property you already own. You use the proceeds of that second to make the 20 or 25% down payment on the property you acquire.

That no money down technique looks good if you ***only*** look at the new property. But if you look at the investor's ***entire*** portfolio, you get a less impressive, more accurate view.

Let's say you own a $200,000 building. The mortgage balance on it is $100,000. You agree to buy another building for $100,000. Down payment will be 20% or $20,000 which you'll get from a second on your $200,000 property. And you'll get an 80%, $80,000 mortgage from a savings and loan. Here's what your portfolio will look like before and after.

	before	after
market value	200,000	300,000
mortgage bal.	100,000	200,000
equity	100,000	100,000
loan-to-value	50%	67%

Is your overall loan-to-value ratio higher?

Yes.

Is your new loan-to-value ratio spectacular?

No. 67% is relatively ***low***. It's better than 50%. But you don't need to buy a book or go to a seminar to learn how to achieve a 67% loan-to-value ratio.

75% to 80% loan-to-value ratios are standard in real estate. Anything lower is fairly easy to get. If someone can teach you how to get your ***whole portfolio*** above 80% and keep it there, he's got some valuable information. But the part of the "creative" finance seminar where they tell you to borrow against low leverage real estate you already own is not worth paying for.

The risk of high leverage can be reduced

Most people equate leverage with risk. The more leverage, the more risk. As a general rule, that's true. But risk can be reduced through payment structure.

Lenders are trained to identify a ***primary*** and a ***secondary*** source of repayment of the loan. When you buy a home, the primary source of repayment is your income. The secondary source is foreclosure and sale of the house.

With investment property, the primary source is the ***property's*** income. In smaller investment properties, (four units or less, 3,000 square feet or less) ***your*** non-real estate income is important, too. The larger the property, the more the lender relies on the property's income and not yours. Foreclosure and sale of the property is the ***secondary*** source of repayment.

The primary source of repayment

Since the property's income (and yours if the property's small) is the primary source of repayment, it's also the primary indicator of risk. Loan-to-value ratios measure the safety of the ***secondary*** source of repayment. ***Debt-coverage*** ratios measure the safety of the ***primary*** source.

The debt-coverage ratio is the net operating income divided by the debt service. Debt service is another phrase for mortgage payments. In the example earlier in the chapter, the net operating income the first year was $22,000. The mortgage payments were $21,239. In that case, the debt-coverage ratio was

$$\text{Debt-coverage ratio} = \frac{\text{net operating income}}{\text{debt service}}$$

$$\text{Debt-coverage ratio} = \frac{\$22{,}000}{\$21{,}239}$$

$$\text{Debt-coverage ratio} = 1.04$$

Debt-coverage ratios

A debt-coverage ratio of 1.00 means the net operating income and debt service are the same. That, in turn, means the building is just breaking even. Before-tax cash flow is zero.

A debt-coverage ratio of ***less than 1.00*** means the building has ***negative*** cash flow. A debt-coverage ratio of ***more than 1.00*** means the building has ***positive*** cash flow.

Single-family houses generally have debt-coverage ratios of less than 1.00. A friend of mine has a single-family house with this income statement.

Rent	8,100.00
Expenses	-1,577.00
net op. income	$ 6,523.00
debt service	-8,640.00
before-tax c f	$ 2,117.00

The debt coverage ratio on this property is

Debt-coverage ratio = $6,523/$8,640 = .76

After-tax is all that counts

The only numbers that count are ***after***-tax numbers. Unfortunately, most lenders deal with ***before***-tax numbers. Showing them the after-tax numbers is an important technique you should learn.

In my friend's case, the after-tax debt-coverage ratio is better. He paid $96,800 for the property.

I'll assume that 80% of the purchase price is depreciable building and the other 20% undepreciable land. 80% x $96,800 = $77,440. The first-year depreciation deduction under the Accelerated Cost Recovery System is 8.8% (if you by the property in January). That would give him a first-year depreciation of $77,440 x 8.8% = $6,815. I'll guesstimate that his interest expense is $8,600 for the first year. That gives him the following after-tax cash flow.

net operating income	$6,523
less interest	-8,600
less depreciation	-6,815
taxable income	-8,892
tax savings 50% bracket	4,446
before-tax cash flow	-2,117
after-tax cash flow	2,329

When tax savings are taken into account, my friend has $2,329 more than he needs to make the mortgage payments. So his ***after***-tax debt-coverage ratio is

($2,329 + $8,640)/$8,640 = $10,969/$8,640 = 1.27

That, in case you don't recognize it, is a very comfortable debt-coverage ratio.

The above 1.00 part is a buffer

Lenders like, often demand, debt-coverage ratios above 1.00. That's because they want you to have a buffer. Not out of concern for ***your*** welfare. It's out of concern for ***their*** welfare.

A 1.41 debt-coverage ratio means the property has 41% more income than the owner needs to make the payments. That, in turn, means that if the income decline by 41% of the debt service, the owner could ***still*** make the payments. Since investment property income ***does*** fluctuate, some buffer amount makes sense for all concerned.

The above 1.00 part is also part of your return

The amount above 1.00 is positive cash flow. Positive cash flow is one part of your overall return. The lender doesn't care about ***that*** reason for having a greater than 1.00 debt-coverage ratio. But you do.

Property income *does* fluctuate

The net operating income of your properties ***will*** fluctuate in almost every case. Real estate is a cyclical business. Roughly speaking, there are good times every three to five years and bad times in between. There were, for example, recessions in 1949, 1954, 1958, 1961, 1970, 1975, and 1980. According to the National Bureau of Economic Research (Cambridge, Massachusetts), the average peacetime business cycle is 52 months long. That's 4 1/3 years.

I started investing in real estate in 1969. So I've been on the front lines to see three of those recessions and their effect on real estate. If 1970 had an effect on me, it was too small to see.

But I didn't miss the '75 recession. The vacancy rates on properties I was managing went from near zero to near 20%. At the same time, interest rates and expenses rose and property values declined. Look at what a 20% vacancy rate does to your net operating income.

	Boom	Recession
Gross rents	40,000.00	40,000.00
Vacancy loss	-2,000.00	-8,000.00
Op. expenses	-16,000.00	-16,000.00
net op. inc.	22,000.00	16,000.00

And look what that does to your debt-coverage ratio.

	Boom	Recession
net op. inc.	22,000.00	16,000.00
debt service	21,239.00	21,239.00
debt-coverage	1.04	.75

Your before-tax cash flow would go from $761 to -$5,239. To an extent, your loss would be softened by a reduction in your income taxes. And if you had another source of income, you'd probably be able to weather a $5,239 a year storm.

But having enough buffer to withstand such a drop in your net operating income becomes much more important when you move into bigger properties. For example, if your holdings were ***ten times*** as big as this example, your negative cash flow would be $52,390, not $5,239. There's a good chance your other income would be inadequate to weather that storm. That could mean financial disaster.

Recession effects vary

Recessions are not as uniform as my comments above may suggest. Different areas suffer at different times. Some early; some late. The severity of the recession varies from area to area also. And individual properties can escape most of the effects in some cases. But no matter how good you think your area or your property is, don't forget that real estate is cyclical.

That means be sure you can make the payments in both good times and bad. Don't overdo the worst case though. If you try to structure your portfolio so as to withstand a ***depression***, you'll have to forego most of the benefits of leverage. You ought to be able to withstand a ***recession*** without defaulting...but not a depression.

You would have needed a 40% loan-to-value ratio in 1925 to have had a 1.00 debt-coverage ratio at the bottom of the Great Depression.

Overall debt-coverage ratio is what's important

Just as ***overall*** loan-to-value ratio is more important than the loan-to-value ratio on a given property, so is ***overall*** debt-coverage more important than the debt-coverage ratio on a given property.

If you had a debt-coverage ratio of .70 after taxes on a property you might think you'd be in trouble. But you wouldn't be in any trouble at all if all your other properties had debt-coverage ratios of 2.2. Nor would you be in trouble if you owned one property with a sub-1.00 debt-coverage ratio if you had substantial non-real estate income.

The main debt-coverage ratio you need to worry about is the one which divides ***all*** your net income from ***all*** sources by ***all*** your fixed payments. ("Fixed" payments includes both debts and lease payments which have at least one year remaining.)

Lenders may not have that same overall view

Although ***you*** need only be concerned with your ***overall*** debt-coverage ratio, lenders tend to worry more about the ***property's*** debt coverage ratio. That's because they often only have access to one property.

For example, you may say to a prospective lender, "Sure, it's true that I can't make the payments on this mortgage from the property's income. But look at all the income I have from my other properties."

To which the lender replies, "Yes, but if there's a problem, we can only foreclose on ***this*** property."

That situation—adequate ***overall*** debt-coverage ratio but inadequate ratio on the property in question—gives rise to a number of finance techniques. Techniques like blanket mortgages (in which you pledge more than one property for a loan) and agreeing to personal liability.

What's an adequate debt-coverage ratio?

Now that I've explained what a debt-coverage ratio is, and why it's important to both you and the lender, you're probably wondering, "What's the ***right*** debt-coverage ratio?"

It depends on the steadiness of the income source. If you have more than one type of income source, you need to have more than one debt-coverage ratio. Nearly all of us do have more than one type of income source.

The most steady income source would be a long-term U.S. Government bond. Since it's guaranteed, most lenders would accept a debt-coverage ratio as low as 1.00. And you should feel 1.00 is OK too. Although I said ***after***-tax debt-coverage is the important one. I'll talk about ***before***-tax debt-coverage ratios in what follows. That's because before-tax debt-coverage ratios are what lenders use. And because calculating the after-tax ratios would turn the book into a blizzard of numbers.

Suffice it to say that after-tax cash flow is usually better than before-tax in the first several years of an investment. After-tax cash flow is usually worse than before-tax in later years or in any year when you make substantial capital expenditures.

In any event, the point I want to make is the relationship between recessions, debt payments, and survival. That relationship is essentially the same whether you use before-tax or after-tax numbers. Do the laborious ***after***-tax calculations when you suspect they may give you better ammunition to use with a lender.

Lenders generally regard salary income in the same category. Their standard home buying rule says that your mortgage payment cannot exceed 25% to 33% or so of your gross income. That rule assumes the balance of your income goes to pay taxes, auto, clothing, food, and so forth.

In other words, if you think of yourself as an income property, the amount you have left after paying for non-housing necessities is your "net operating income." And the typical mortgage lender will let you take on a payment which equals that "net operating income." In other words, when it comes to salaries, lenders will accept a debt-coverage ratio of 1.00. And so should you unless you know that your job is unsure.

Net leases to credit tenants

Suppose instead of a government bond you lease a building you own to the U.S. Government on a long-term basis. Is the income from that lease any less guaranteed than the income from a government bond?

No.

In fact, long-term leases to tenants with excellent credit are often called "bond leases." That's because they resemble bonds from the lessee so much. So what's an adequate debt-coverage ratio for income from a property leased to a high credit tenant?

1.00 is adequate. There are some institutional lenders who will loan up to 100% of value and presumably allow a 1.00 debt-coverage ratio on property which is leased to high credit tenants. That's because the tenant's credit renders the real estate nearly irrelevant.

Not all bonds or "bond leases" would warrant a 1.00 debt-coverage ratio though. WPPS defaulted in 1983. Obviously, no one would lend you money against the income from those bonds on a 1.00 debt-coverage basis.

By the same token, not all ***tenants*** are high credit. Your lease to IBM may justify a 1.00 debt-coverage ratio. But your lease to Joe's Hardware may not justify less than 1.30. The reason being that Joe's Hardware may move or go bust. Then you'll have to find another tenant. Since vacancies are a real possibility with Joe's Hardware, you need the buffer of a greater than 1.00 debt-coverage ratio.

Note that there are long-term leases and there are long-term leases. Whenever possible, consult the lender as to the wording of the lease before you sign the lease. This is especially important in shopping centers.

Example

Here are some examples which show that high leverage doesn't necessarily mean high risk. By combining high leverage with a prudent debt-coverage ratio, you can have a relatively low risk investment.

80% loan-to-value, 1.10 debt-coverage

You buy a building on the following terms:

Down	$100,000.00
Total debt	$400,000.00
Price	$500,000.00
Cap rate	10%.
Net operating income	$50,000.00
Existing first mortgage	$300,000.00
Payments on first	$2,700.00/month
Seller second mortgage	$100,000.00
Payments on second (13%)	$13,000.00/yr

I'll assume you have a recession the second and third year of ownership. The recession causes a 10% drop in your net operating income. NOI stays level for one year then grows at 4% per year.

	1	2	3	4	5
NOI	50,000.	45,000.	45,000.	46,800.	48,672.
1st mtge	32,400.	32,400.	32,400.	32,400.	32,400.
2nd mtge	13,000.	13,000.	13,000.	13,000.	13,000.
BTCF	4,600.	-400.	-400.	1,400.	3,272.

Note that in year two and three you would suffer a small negative cash flow. But given the assumptions in this example, you could probably handle that without difficulty. Even if the property was much larger, you could probably handle a negative cash flow which was less than 1% of your NOI.

80% loan-to-value ratio, 1.00 debt-coverage ratio

Let's take the same example. but this time we'll assume you had to get a new first mortgage at 12.2% for 30 years. That makes the annual payments $50,000.

	1	2	3	4	5
NOI	50,000.	45,000.	45,000.	46,800.	48,672.
1st mtge	50,000.	50,000.	50,000.	50,000.	50,000.
BTCF	0.	-5,000.	-5,000.	-3,200.	-1,328.

Now the negative cash flow in the recession years is 10% of the NOI. And it has not climbed back to positive after even four years. Cumulative losses by the end of year five are $14,528. Depending on your financial situation, that could cause you difficulty.

Size is also a factor

In this case, the total loss is $14,528. Most people could deal with that with no great strain. So it's not just the ***ratio*** but also the amount of money involved that are important. The more real estate you own, the more important the overall debt-coverage ratio becomes. In other words, the more real estate you own, the more conservative you'd better be on your debt-coverage.

You can come up with a couple thousand bucks by cutting back on eating out and movies. But if you're *forty* thousand in the hole, peanut butter sandwiches and TV won't solve your problem.

90% loan-to-value ratio, 1.10 debt coverage ratio

Note that I've jacked the loan-to-value ratio up to ***90%***. But note also the financing.

Down	$100,000.00
Total loans	$900,000.00
Price	$1,000,000.00

Cap rate	10.0%
Net operating income	$100,000.00
Existing first mortgage	600,000.00
Payments on first	$66,000.00
Seller second mortgage	$300,000.00
Payments on second	$25,000.00

In this case, the seller wants 13% interest on his second. That would result in second mortgage payment of $39,000 a year. But you the buyer insist on a 1.10 debt coverage ratio, so the seller agrees to collect only 8.3% interest on a monthly basis. The remaining 13% - 8.3% = 4.7% will ***accrue*** to be paid in a balloon payment on the seventh anniversary.

	1	2	3	4	5
NOI	100,000.	90,000.	90,000.	93,600.	97,344.
1st mtge	66,000.	66,000.	66,000.	66,000.	66,000.
2nd mtge	25,000.	25,000.	25,000.	25,000.	25,000.
BTCF	9,000.	-1,000.	-1,000.	2,600.	6,344.

Note that although the debt coverage ratio is ***higher***—-90% versus 80%—-this deal is ***safer*** than the 80% deal where there was a 1.00 debt coverage ratio. You only lose a total of $2,000 during the recession years. And you own twice as much property. The trick here is a higher debt-coverage ratio due to accruing part of the interest to the seller.

You say you want more 'realistic' numbers

The 10% cap rate in this example is what you ***should*** get when you buy. I do. But most of you don't.

In this book, I will generally use cap rates in that range because that's sound investing. But in order to make the point on debt-coverage ratios, let me use some "realistic" numbers.

Remember earlier when I recited the details of the "standard" deal as reported by Cain & Scott? They said the gross rent multiplier was 7. That means the selling price was 7 times the annual rents. In the typical case, the total expenses are 45% of the gross income. So with a 7 gross rent multiplier, a building with a 45% operating expense ratio would have a cap rate of .55 x 7 = 8%.

Now I'll run the 80% loan-to-value ratio numbers with that cap rate. And you'll see that those of you who buy on these "realistic" terms had better be even more concerned about debt-coverage ratios than the rest of us.

Down	$100,000
Total loans	$400,000
Price	$500,000
Cap rate	8%
Net operating income	$40,000
Payments on first	$32,400
Payments on second	$13,000

Year	1	2	3	4	5
net op. inc.	40,000	36,000	36,000	37,440	38,938
first mtge.	32,400	32,400	32,400	32,400	32,400
second mtge.	13,000	13,000	13,000	13,000	13,000
BTCF	-5,400	-9,400	-9,400	-7,960	6,462

The cumulative loss here is $38,622, due mostly to the lousy cap rate. If you're going to buy properties with cap rates like that, you'd better master the techniques for improving the debt-coverage ratio. Techniques like accruing interest.

Suggested debt-coverage ratios

As I said, you need a different debt-coverage ratio for each type of income you have. Here are the ratios I suggest. They are based in part on what lenders demand for these income sources. I'm a bit more aggressive than the lenders.

Income source	Debt-coverage ratio
AAA net leased property	1.00
Salary	1.00
Commissions	1.00 (what's your history?)
Income from your business	1.00+ (same as commissions)
Apartment building	1.10
Multi-tenant office/retail	1.20
Multi-tenant industrial	1.25

These are not ***comfortable*** margins. But then as Justice Oliver Wendall Holmes said, "Certainty generally is illusion and repose is not the destiny of man." Nor is comfort the destiny of real estate investors.

You want comfort? Demand that sellers sell you apartment buildings on terms which would give you debt-coverage ratios of 1.30. How do you do that? You'd probably have to make down payments in the 30% to 40% range.

The debt-coverage ratios I recommend represent prudent levels of risk. They do ***not*** represent ***absence*** of risk.

These debt-coverage ratios also will not please the typical seller. Sellers would rather you had a debt-coverage ratio of .85. In other words, they want you to overpay for the property. That's why real estate deals are full of tension. The seller is trying to pull your debt-coverage ratio down. You and any lenders involved are trying to pull it up.

But I never said real estate finance was easy. If it was, everybody'd be doing it.

Calculating your debt capacity

Your capacity to carry debt is the sum of your various net incomes divided by the debt-coverage ratio which is appropriate for each. Let's look at the case of a typical, fictitious real estate investor.

Clifford Mahler is self-employed. He's also married. His wife Debra works as an executive with an advertising firm. Her income is salary. That means a 1.00 debt-coverage ratio would be adequate for it. She makes $34,000 a year.

Cliff's business income varies according to the economy and other factors. In 1984, he netted $51,000. He figures he'll net $55,000 this year. But a 10% variation one way or the other would not surprise him. They figure they spend 67% of their non-real estate income on necessities other than real estate.

They own an 8 unit apartment building. Bought it four years ago. Gross income is $33,600 a year. Net operating income is $18,500. Loan payments on the property are $16,000 a year.

They also own a home. Payments are $9,000 a year.

Here's their debt carrying capacity.

Income source	Net Amount	DCR	Capacity
Debra's salary	11,220.00	1.00	11,220.00
Cliff's business	18,150.00	1.10	16,500.00
8-Unit	18,500.00	1.10	16,818.00
Total			44,538.00

The net amounts of Debra's and Cliff's non-real estate income are 33% of their gross incomes. The other 67% I said goes for non-real estate necessities like taxes, food, etc.

Their total annual debt service capacity is $44,538.00. At present, they are carrying debt service of

8-Unit	$16,000.00
Home	9,000.00
Total	$25,000.00

So they have $44,538 - $25,000 = $19,538 worth of debt capacity lying idle. What should they do? If maximum return on equity. . .consistent with a prudent level of risk. . .is their goal, they should leverage up. Exchange up to larger properties. And they should keep in mind that the larger properties will also bring ***still more income***. That means even more debt capacity.

"But is it wise to leverage up to the hilt?" Cliff and Debra ask. The "hilt" is determined by the debt-coverage ratios you choose. I believe the 1.00 I've used on Debra's income and the 1.10 I've used on their other income represent livable risk levels. If you believe those debt-coverage ratios are too low, say why. If you can't say why, leverage up to those levels.

Again, *after*-tax is the best way to calculate your capacity. I've used before-tax here to avoid a numbers blizzard. The figures above should be adequate to teach you the point I'm trying to make.

The "proper" risk level is a matter of expertise *and* taste

The debt-coverage levels I've recommended in this book are not the ***right*** ones. Since I wrote this book, readers will tend to think of me as an expert. And indeed, what I write about loan-to-value ratios and debt-coverage ratios is ***partly*** based on my expertise. For example, I know that lenders will make high loan-to-value ratio/low debt-coverage ratio loans on property leased to credit tenants. You may not have known that before you read the book.

But the ratios I recommend are based on both my expertise ***and*** my taste for risk.I'm thirty-nine now. When I was younger, I chose higher loan-to-value ratios and lower debt-coverage ratios. I was single then. And heck-bent on making a million while I was still young.

Now I'm married and have two sons. I've made a few bucks and I'm confident I'll make a few more. I don't ***need*** to set any records anymore. So I'm content with twenty or twenty-five percent down.

I foresee that in another couple years, I'll crank my loan-to-value ratio down still further. By holding properties longer and by making down payments in the 30% range. By the time I'm a "senior citizen," I may be amenable to free and clear ownership.

The ratios I recommend in this book are for maximum return on equity consistent with a prudent risk level.

High leverage versus low leverage

In the world of real estate, high leverage is macho. By high leverage I mean less than 20% down. And low leverage is for sissies. By low leverage I mean more than 25% down.

I don't see it that way.

Seems to me that high leverage is for ***beginners***. And low leverage is for people who have made theirs.

High leverage for beginners

Poor people ride the bus. Affluent people ride in their cars or taxis or whatever. Did you ever think about why?

The bus stops at every corner. That takes time. And most bus trips require transfers. Waiting for the second bus also takes time.

An affluent person's time is valuable. He can't afford the extra time it takes to wait for other stops or making connections. The car costs more out of pocket to drive and park. But it saves time. And time is money. Poor people don't have much cash. But they've got plenty of time. So the bus is cost effective for them.

So it is with leverage.

High leverage takes more time

"Creative" finance pushers leave you with the impression that all you need to do high leverage deals is learn some techniques. Not true.

To do a high leverage deal, you have to find a seller who doesn't need ***all*** of his equity converted to cash. Actually, there are a few ways for you to get in on a high-leverage basis with the seller getting all his equity in cash at closing. One group of techniques which allows that is the owner-occupied mortgage insurance programs. The other would involve the afore-mentioned high-credit tenant, long-term leased properties.

But aside from those techniques, which have limited application, high leverage generally requires a seller who is willing to wait for part of his equity.

If you ask ***me*** to sell you a property in which I'm required to wait for some of my equity I'll turn you down. I want all my equity into the next property ***now***. Most other sellers ***will*** wait for part of their equity. But not enough to make the deal a high leverage one. As I said earlier, the typical deal as I write this is 25% down (investment property). And that's ***after*** seller financing.

An untypical seller

So the typical seller wants you to put up 25%. If you won't someone else will. So in order to do a high leverage deal, you have to find an ***untypical seller***.

Can that be done? Yes. But it takes ***more time*** than finding the typical seller.

I usually make an offer on one property when I buy. Sometimes I have to make an offer on two different properties because I don't get the first one for some reason. Contrast that with the high leverage investor. In his book *How To Write A Nothing Down Offer*, Richard Allen says, "...the average Nothing Down investor will have to make five different formal offers—-usually on five different properties—-before achieving one purchase."

And far more informal "would-you-sell-for-nothing-down?" inquiries.

Making offers takes time

Making offers on different properties takes time. You have to find out what properties are available. You've got to inspect the property. You've got to evaluate the community and neighborhood. You've got to analyze the income and expenses. You've got to analyze the financing available. You have to negotiate...longer if it's high leverage. You have to confer with your attorney.

How much time does it take? In an article I wrote for the *Real Estate Investing Letter*, I estimated it takes a total of 50 man-hours to make an acquisition. ("The Value of a Real Estate Investor's Time" January 1983 edition)

The Chicago firm of Schlaes & Young Information Systems, Inc. did a survey. They asked professional investors how long it took to analyze a 12 year old 250,000 square foot office building with 45 tenants and different lease terms. The answer: two to seven "person" days. Most said at least five "person" days. Five "person" days is forty man hours. And that's just for financial analysis. That doesn't count negotiating, looking for properties to analyze, and so forth.

What's your time worth?

If you make $50,000 a year at a forty hour a week job, your time is worth $50,000/(50 weeks x 40 hours per week) = $50,000/2,000 hours = $25 an hour. At that rate, 50 man hours is worth $1,250. So a "Nothing Down" deal in which you make five offers is really a 5 x $1,250 = $6,250 down deal if you make $50,000 a year.

Admittedly, $6,250 is still a high leverage deal when the average home sells for $74,800. But it's 8% down. Not nothing down. Unless...

Unless you make *less* than $50,000 a year. If you make $20,000 a year, your time is only worth $20,000/2,000 hours = $10 an hour. At $10 an hour, an offer costs you 50 hours x $10 an hour = $500. Five offers cost you $2,500. That's not nothing down on a $74,800 house. But it's pretty close.

How do you want to spend your time

There's also a question of ***how*** you want to spend your time. Being a New York City garbage collector pays well. But I'd pass the job up myself. I don't like collecting garbage. I also don't like trudging around looking at buildings. And in order to make five formal offers, you have to look at many more than five buildings.

I suspect some of you reading this will say, "Oh, I ***like*** looking at property!"

I don't believe you. I would have said that myself a few years ago. In retrospect, I was so excited about becoming a success in real estate investing that I was blind to the drudgery of parts of it.

In addition to not liking driving around looking at properties, I'm also not very fond of negotiating. It's stressful. Don't be too quick to dismiss me as a Casper Milquetoast. I've been in a lot of negotiations. I'm a "battle"-tested, "battle"-hardened veteran. That's how I got to know negotiations are stressful.

So high leverage not only takes time, it also requires you to spend time in ways that many would find less than appealing.

Higher leverage means higher risk

You can ***reduce*** the risk of high leverage with techniques like accruing interest. But no matter how you structure the deal, if you are forced to sell, high leverage puts you in a more precarious position than normal or low leverage does.

A beginner's strategy

In the movie "The Spy Who Came In From the Cold," Richard Burton refers to a girl he had spent some time with. "She believed in free love. At the time, it was the only kind I could afford."

The same could be said of zero down payment investing. "He preached zero down investing. At the time, it was the only kind I could afford."

High leverage investing requires

- more time
- drudge work
- more risk

than investing with 20% to 25% down. Who would put up with those things? People who have no choice.

Rich man; poor man

Let's suppose you've just graduated from college and you have a net worth of ***minus*** $14,000. Your balance sheet contains a tiny bank account, a '75 volkswagen, a half of a rent security deposit on the apartment you share with a roommate, and a large education loan. What's your leverage strategy?

You don't have much choice, do you?

Now let's suppose you're 40. You've been investing in real estate since you were 25. You're net worth is $1,500,000. Your annual income from your job and investments is $180,000. Do you want to have to make five offers in order to buy a property? Does a millionaire with $180,000 in income do drudge work?

And why should you take risks? Taking risks is a necessary evil for those at the bottom to climb out. But a millionaire has no meaningful place to climb.

The American Dream

The American Dream consists of a nice home, a reliable car for every driver in the family, a quality education for the kids, and enough money left over for vacations, clothes, restaurant meals, and so forth. A lot of people use the phrase "American Dream" as a put-down. Not me.

It's a worthwhile dream.

I figure the American Dream, as I've just defined it, requires about $100,000 a year income at most. The main cost factor is the nice home. Here in California, the highest priced market, a nice home can cost $300,000. That's about a 2,500 square foot home on a one-third acre lot. Nice, but not a mansion. If you're not from California, just figure our prices are about double yours. A $300,000 California home is a $150,000 home in Southern New Jersey, which is where I used to live.

The income required to qualify for a $300,000 home is about $100,000. And if you can afford the house payments, you can afford the cars, education, and so forth. Of course, if you live in Southern New Jersey or some other area where homes are cheaper, the American Dream might cost $75,000 or $50,000 or whatever.

After the Dream, then what?

You don't start with a negative net worth and get to the American Dream without taking some risks and making some effort. In my early years, I bought one property with a VA no money down loan. I bought two others with 10% down private mortgage insurance loans. (Yes, I lived in both.) I also bought a twelve-unit apartment building with about 17% down. The rest of the properties I bought were 20% down.

So I struggled, took risks, did the drudge work, made the multiple offers, and so forth to rise up from my humble beginnings. (My net worth when I graduated from college was about ***positive*** $1,500. That's because I graduated from West Point. Tuition there was free and cadets were paid a salary.)

But once you've got the money you need to afford the American Dream, then what? Sure you can show off by buying ***expensive*** cars and replacing your nice home with an ***estate or mansion***. And you can take up some expensive hobby like flying your own plane or buying a yacht or raising quarter horses. If you've got the money to do so, enjoy. But busting your back to ***get*** the money to do those things...that's another question.

Somebody once said, "I cried because I had no shoes...until I saw a man who had no feet." But the next level up sounds silly. "I cried because I had no Guccis...until I saw a man who had no Florsheims."

The leverage counterpart would go like this. "I took risks, did drudge work, and made offer after offer because I wanted to own my own home." Makes sense. But it sounds silly to say, "I took risks, did drudge work, and made offer after offer because I had no 380 SL."

Seems to me that additional money is beyond the point of diminishing returns. Or to put it another way, an ***additional*** dollar does not have anywhere near the same value to a millionaire as it does to a negative net worth 22 year old.

That changing value of the dollar due to your changing financial situation dictates a changing strategy when it comes to leverage. You use high leverage at the ***beginning*** of your investing career...because it's the only kind you can afford. But since high leverage deals are risky and a pain in the neck to arrange, you don't bother with them when your net worth and income approach the American Dream level.

Net worth of $500,000 ought to do it

I figure a net worth of about $500,000 is about all you need. If you earn 15% on it, that's $75,000 a year. The other $25,000 you need to total $100,000 can easily come from whatever work you do. If your net worth were $750,000, you wouldn't need to work at all. But that can get boring.

Can you earn 15%? Sure.

Even those of you who believe negative cash flow is unavoidable (it's avoidable) should agree that your ***overall*** return will be at least 15%. If not, what the heck are you investing in real estate for? You can get 14% in mortgages.

$500,000 in equity, if invested at a 75% loan-to-value ratio, will buy you $2,000,000 worth of real estate. Let's say that $2,000,000 were spread over five properties...each worth $400,000. Each year, ***all*** five properties throw off cash flow and tax shelter. And each year they appreciate and the mortgage balances decline through amortization.

To get at the appreciation and amortization, simply refinance ***one*** property every year. Every ***five*** years, you start over. That means each time, you would be refinancing a property which had accumulated five years worth of appreciation and amortization. With a 4% inflation rate, appreciation alone would total $86,661 on just one of those properties after five years!

The habit of making money

The typical real estate investor doesn't slow down when his net worth hits $500,000 though. By then, making big money has become a ***habit*** for him. He keeps accumulating the stuff even though he has no plans to spend it.

If you fit that description, do the following. Go to the drug store and buy a bottle of Mennen Skin Bracer. Pour a small amount into the palm of your hand. Then slap yourself in the face with it and say, "Thanks, I needed that."

William Nickerson did something like that. He's the guy who wrote the book, *How I Turned $1,000 Into $5,000,000 in Real Estate In My Spare Time.* One day in the fifties, he had to fill out a loan application. In doing so, he discovered that his net worth had risen to $500,000. That'd be a couple of million in today's dollars.

That made him wonder what he was doing still working for the phone company. He didn't wonder long. He quit. Said it was one of the most fun things he ever did. He had always wanted to be a writer. So that's what he did. The rest, as they say, is history.

So I urge you to use real estate finance techniques as a ***means*** to an end. . . namely, financial independence. But don't fall into the Silas Marner/Scrooge McDuck habit of making money for the sake of making money.

It's hard to turn the darn thing off

Did you notice that I said William Nickerson quit work to become a writer when his net worth was ***$500,000***. . . and that he is the author of the book, *How I Turned $1,000 Into **$5,000,000** In Real Estate In My Spare Time*? Did you wonder how a guy who spent his day writing got from $500,000 to $5,000,000?

The answer is that once your net worth gets to $500,000 it doesn't stop just because ***you*** do. Like Old Man River, it just keeps rolling along. With 4% inflation, your $2,000,000 worth of real estate grows to $2,080,000 in one year. ***Five*** years later, it will have grown to $2,433,306. Counting the cash flow, tax shelter, and amortization, that means your net worth will have about ***doubled*** in those five years.

I suggest this pattern

Net worth	Leverage strategy
zero to $100,000	20% or less down
$100,000 to $400,000	20% to 25% down
$400,000 or more	25% or more down

If you're one of those who cringes at the thought of putting down more than 25%, get over it. All that macho high leverage stuff is beginner talk. With a 30% down payment, sellers, lenders, and real estate agents roll out the red carpet for you. You have positive cash flow even if you invest in properties which typically have negative cash flow. When something big breaks, you have it fixed and write a check to pay for it. When balloon payments fall due, you have so much equity that it's no big deal to get a loan.

30% down is real comfortable. Like a pair of Guccis or a 380 SL.

You say you want to be a star

Some of you probably will not be satisfied with $100,000 a year. You want $200,000 a year. Or $500,000 a year. My tastes are too plebeian, you say. You won't be satisfied until you have a penthouse apartment on Park Avenue, a Rolls in the basement, *pied-a-terres* in San Francisco, London, and Paris. Not to mention a summer place on Cape Cod complete with sailboat and a cabin in Vermont. And you're thinking of buying yourself a seat in Congress.

No problem. If you have a conspicuous consumption tapeworm to feed, high leverage real estate investing is the way to do it. This book will help ***you*** as much as it will help readers who agree with my advice to cool it after you reach $500,000 net worth.

To return to the gas pedal analogy, I recommend that beginners do the limit. . . or even "four miles per hour" over the limit. I recommend that intermediate level investors ease off the gas a bit. And I recommend that people who have arrived, get out of the investment rat race and relax. If you won't be satisfied until you're a zillionaire, just keep doing the limit.

2
How To Measure The Time Value of Money

Time value of money

To understand real estate, you must understand the time value of money. Stated simply, a dollar to be received in the future is worth less than a dollar to be received now. And a dollar to be received ***five*** years from now is worth less than a dollar to be received ***two*** years from now.

When it comes to ***receiving*** money, sooner is better than later.

Why money has time value

Most people know that a dollar to be received a year from now is worth less than a dollar to be received now. If you ask them, "Why?" they'll probably say, "Inflation."

Inflation is only ***part*** of the reason. The main reason is ***opportunity cost.***

If I give you $10,000, you can invest it. In a money market fund, you can earn about 8% these days. Since you have an ***opportunity*** to earn 8%, ***not*** putting the money in a money market fund has an opportunity cost of 8%.

You can also invest the money in mortgages. These days, they earn about 14%. If the risk of mortgages is acceptable to you, your opportunity cost is not 8% but 14%.

You're a real estate investor. I believe real estate investors can earn an overall return of at least 25% in moderately leveraged real estate. So a real estate investor's opportunity cost is 25%.

Where do I get 25%?

Whenever I say you can get 25% people say that's ridiculous. Not at all.

Let's say you buy a property for $200,000. You put down 20% or $40,000. The $160,000 mortgage is at 13% for 30 years. Real estate generally keeps pace with inflation. Some years it's behind. Some years it's ahead. But over the long term, real estate keeps up or even moves faster.

The median existing home sale price was $20,100 in 1968. In 1985, it's $74,500. In 1968, the Consumer Price Index was 104.2. In 1985, it was 320.1. Real estate prices went up 3.7 times. The Consumer Price Index went up 3.1 times.

The increase in prices for 1984 was 4%. If your $200,000 building goes up 4%, it will increase in value by $200,000 x .04 = $8,000. The mortgage balance will drop from $160,000 to $159,534. That's $466 more.

Let's say the property were 75% depreciable improvements and 25% undepreciable land. The depreciable improvements portion would be worth $150,000. IRS tables allow you to claim a first year depreciation deduction of 8.8% (if you buy in January.) 8.8% x $150,000 = $13,200.

You've already earned $8,466 through appreciation and amortization. That's a $8,466/$40,000 = 21.2% return. A 25% return would be $10,000. So you need to get $10,000 -$8,466 = $1,534 in return from cash flow and tax shelter to achieve 25%.

The lowest tax bracket is 11% (over $3,400 for a married couple filing jointly). 11% x $13,200 (depreciation deduction) = $1,452. So you only need $1,534 - $1,452 = $82 in cash flow for the year to achieve a 25% return in the lowest tax bracket.

Appreciation	$8,000.00
Amortization	1,452
Tax savings (lowest bracket)	82.00
Cash flow	49.00
Total return	$10,000.00

Percent return $10,000/$40,000 = 25%

If you were in the ***highest*** tax bracket, your tax savings would be $13,200 x 50% = $6,600. That would give you an overall return of $8,000 + $466 + $6,600 + 82 = $15,148/$40,000 = 38%.

I didn't mention cash flow in this example. With a 13% mortgage, there probably wouldn't be any. But you ***should*** be able to get positive cash flow. No great mystery. It's mainly a matter of avoiding high priced areas, small properties, and high payments. If you did have positive cash flow, your return would obviously be even higher. I'd guess the average investor with a 75% to 80% loan-to-value ratio earns an overall return of 30% to 50%.

Lenders have different opportunity costs

You need to know ***your own*** opportunity cost in real estate finance. You also need to know the ***lender's*** opportunity cost. The lender's opportunity cost is well publicized. It is the market rate on the mortgage in question.

As I write this, for example, the FNMA rate on a 30-year fixed-rate conventional mortgage was 12%. Therefore, any lender who lends money on a similar mortgage at less suffers an opportunity cost.

Computing the discounted value

The main mathematical exercise in time value of money is computing present values of future payments. For example, how much would you pay me for $100,000 to be paid to you five years from now?

To get the answer, you need to know two things:

- the discount rate
- the payment pattern

The discount rate is the lender's opportunity cost. If you are paying me money now in return for money to be paid to you later, you're a lender. I'll use the discount rate I recommended above: 25%.

The payment pattern is whatever the borrower and lender agree on. In this case, let's say the payment pattern is simply one lump sum payment of $100,000 at the end of five years.

Skip the formulas and tables

You can't compute the present value with any math you learned in school. Unless you took a course in mathematics of finance.

There *is* a mathematical formula for calculating present value.

$$P = S(1 + i)^{-n}$$

S is the sum due in the future. i is the interest rate per period. n is the number of periods until the money is due. Shall we do an example? Nah. It's a waste of time.

Before about 1972, people used ***financial tables*** to do these calculations. With those tables and a ***regular*** calculator, you could compute present values. You still see those tables around. . . in the appendices of some real estate finance books among other places. But you won't find any financial tables in this book.

Get a financial calculator

Formulas are a waste of time. So are the tables. They're obsolete. The way to do financial mathematics is with a financial calculator. A financial calculator is one which has the following keys

Key	Meaning
n	number of periods
i	interest rate per period
PV	present value
FV	future value
PMT	payment amount

You can buy a financial calculator wherever calculators are sold. Twenty bucks ought to be enough. Status conscious real estate agents often sport more expensive, fancy calculators like the Hewlett Packard 12C. Either plain or fancy is fine.

When I have heavy duty calculating to do I use my Radio Shack Model II. The Model II is a desktop computer.

To answer the problem I posed above simply put the following into your financial calculator:

n	5
i	25
FV	$100,000

Then push PV to get the answer. My Texas Instruments 'MBA' says

PV	32,768

That means the present value of $100,000 to be received five years from now is $32,768 when discounted at a rate of 25% per year. In other words, if you could put $32,768 into a bank account paying 25%, your balance at the end of five years would be $100,000.

You can test that statement with a regular calculator. Just multiply $32,768 by 1.25. Then multiply that answer by 1.25. Do that five times. My 'MBA' gives these answers: 32,768 x 1.25 = 40,960 x 1.25 = 51,200 x 1.25 = 64,000 x 1.25 = 80,000 x 1.25 = 100,000. Ta da!

To compute a mortgage payment

To find the monthly payment on a 30 year, $160,000, 13% mortgage

n	360 months
i	13%/12 months = 1.0833333
PV	$160,000

Then ask for the PMT.

PMT	1,769.92

To compute a future balance

To find what $10,000 will grow to in three years at 13%

n	3
i	13
PV	$10,000

Then ask for the FV (future value).

FV	$14,428.97

To compute a mortgage balance

You borrow $160,000 at 13% for 30 years. What will the balance be after one year? After two years? After five years? We already calculated what the monthly payments would be—-$1,769.92.

n	348
i	13/12 = 1.0833333
PMT	$1,769.92
PV	$159,533.91

This is a little tricky. You may be wondering where the 348 came from. Shouldn't it be 360?

No. I said find the balance ***after one year***. If we put 360 in n, the PV would be $160,000. . .the ***original*** loan amount. $160,000 is the present value of 360 payments of $1,769.92 discounted at 13%/12 per month. Present value and loan balance are the same thing.

To get the present value after one year, just subtract one years worth of payments from n. In this case, 360 - 12 = 348. The present value (loan balance) of 348 payments of $1,769.92 discounted at 13%/12 per month is $159,533.91.

To do the other balances on my calculator you do ***not*** need to reenter the i or PMT values. Just enter a new n.

n	336
PV	$159,003.41

That's the balance after ***two*** years. After five years it's

n	300
PV	$156,930.71

Feel free to check those answers with your old fashioned tables if that's the way you do things. But keep in mind that I got those answers about as fast as it took you to read them.

Suppose there's a balloon payment involved.

What if there's a balloon payment? How 'bout finding the present value of this one. You're selling a property. The buyers have agreed to a mortgage for $200,000. They insist the loan be at 10% for 30 years. . .although they will accept a seven year balloon payment.

You know you can't get them a 10% interest rate. But that's what other sellers are offering in your area so you agree to pay whatever points are necessary to get a lender to make the loan.

After calling around, you find that 13.5% is the lowest yield any lender will accept.

The buyers have agreed to the payments required by a $200,000 10%, 30 year mortgage. That is

n	360
i	10%/12 = .833333
PV	$200,000
PMT	$1,755.14/month

At the end of seven years, they will also pay

n	360 - (7 x 12) = 276
i	10%/12 = .833333
PMT	$1,755.14
PV	$189,298.39

$189,298.39 is what the loan balance will be after seven years. It's also their balloon payment. So their payment pattern looks like this.

Month	Payment
1 thru 83	$1,755.14
84	$1,755.14 + $189,298.39 = $191,053.53

A financial calculator can calculate the present value of an even payment stream or the present value of a single future payment. But it cannot calculate the present value of a combination of both. Maybe the Hewlett Packard 12C can. But it's simple enough to just do three steps.

Step one

Calculate the present value of the first 83 monthly payments. The discount rate is 13.5%. That's the yield the lender you found demands. He couldn't care less that the buyers will only pay 10%. That's ***your*** problem. What we're about to find out is how big of a problem it is. To calculate the present value of the first 83 payments, do this.

n	83
i	13.5/12 = 1.125
PMT	$1,755.14
PV	$94,367.02

Step two

Now calculate the present value of the final payment.

n	84
i	13.5/12 = 1.125
FV	$191,053.53
PV	$74,651.43

Using Visicalc to do time value of money calculations

Visicalc is the brand name of the most popular computer program. The generic name for Visicalc is "spreadsheet program." There are a number of other spreadsheet programs. SuperCalc, CalcStar, MultiPlan to name a few. I'm not interested in getting into the "Which is best?" debate.

I use Visicalc. Since the different spreadsheet programs are pretty similar, what follows applies to all of them. There may be slight variations in some commands. But you should be able to figure them out without my putting a translation table in this book.

Do you need a personal computer?

A lot of investors already have personal computers. If you don't, you may be wondering if you should get one. I don't think you ***need*** one. It's nice. It's a help. But they aren't free. So don't feel that you should rush out and buy one just because I'm writing about them here. Reading what follows may help you decide. It'll give you an idea of what the computer can do for you.

Visicalc amortization table

You may want an amortization table. You might want it for general reference. Or it may be a part of a multi-year projection you're doing in an investment analysis. Visicalc can do it for you. Here's how.

Visicalc is a blank TV screen. Across the top are lettered columns. They start at "A" and go to "BK." 63 columns if you're counting. Down the side are numbered lines. . . 1 through 254.

As a result, there are grid coordinates for every location on the screen. For example, the upper left corner is A1. The lower left corner is A254. And so forth.

Annual amortization table

You can do either a monthly or an annual amortization table. Monthly would be appropriate for general reference purposes. . . to see where you stand at any given point. Annual would make more sense for a multi-year investment analysis. First I'll show you an annual table.

	A	B	C	D	E	F
1	Amount	500000				
2	Interest	13				
3	Payment	66707				
4						
5	Balance	500000	498293	496363	494183	491720
6	Interest	65000	64778	64527	64244	63924
7	Principal	1707	1929	2180	2464	2784

A couple of Visicalc tips. I gave the command /GFI. That means "global format integer." In plain English: "Forget the decimals." The reason is I'm using columns which are nine spaces wide. 500000.00 plus a space on either side to distinguish it from other numbers won't fit in nine spaces. And who cares about decimals anyway?

The original loan amount is labelled at coordinates A1 and entered into B1. B2 is the interest rate in percent. And B3 is the annual payment. I figured it out with my financial calculator.

The amortization table is rows 5, 6 and 7 starting with column B. Row 5 shows the loan balance at the beginning of each year. Row 6 shows the interest paid that year. That's important because only interest is deductible. And row six shows the principal amount paid each year.

The math is simple. To get the interest paid the first year, multiply the interest rate by the loan amount. 13% x \$500,000 = \$65,000. To get Visicalc to do that you put the following formula at location B6.

+B2/100*B5

You put a + in front of B2 because Visicalc will think B2 is a word instead of a location otherwise. You divide B2, the interest rate, by 100 to change it from 13 to .13. You *could* have avoided that by putting .13 in B2 to begin with. But we tend to think in terms of percents rather than decimals. And Visicalc doesn't mind. So let *it* put the decimal in. That's what it does when you tell it to divide by 100.

An asterisk is a multiplication sign. You can't use x because Visicalc thinks x is a letter...which it is. You and I can tell from the context whether x means multiply or just "x." But Visicalc isn't that smart.

+B2/100*B6 means (13/100) x $500,000. That equals $65,000, so 65000 appears in B6.

The formula for B7 is

+B3-B6

Makes sense. If the payment is $66,707 and the interest portion is $65,000, the principal portion must be what's left over. +B3-B6 means $66,707 - $65,000 = $1,707. Which is why 1707 appears in location B7.

To calculate the balance at the beginning of year two, just subtract the principal paid in year one from the original balance. So the formula for C5 is

+B5-B7

Or $500,000 - $1,707 = $498,293.

The replicate command

To get the rest of the table, you don't need to type in all those formulas. You use the "replicate" command. To generate row five ("Balance"), just replicate the formula in C5 as far across the screen as you want. Visicalc will ask you if each component of the formula is to be "relative" or "no change." For row five, both components are "relative."That means the letters will advance one each column. It would look like this if you could see the formulas.

	A	B	C	D	E	F
5	Balance	+B1	+B5-B7	+C5-C7	+D5-D7	+E5-E7

Row six ("Interest") is a replication of the formula at B6—+B2/100*B5. Only when the computer asks whether the components are "relative" or "no change," say "no change" on the B2 part. (You do that by typing "N" when asked.) "Relative" on the B5 part. By doing that, you're telling Visicalc, "The loan balance (B5, C5, D5, etc.) changes every year. But the interest rate, B2, is always the same."

Row seven ("Principal") is a replication of the formula at B7—+B3-B6. Say "No change" on B3. B3 is the annual mortgage payment. It's the same every year. And say, "Relative" (by typing "R") on the B6 part. B6 is the interest paid that year. It changes every year.

A	B	C
Interest	+B2/100*B5	+B2/100*C5
Principal	+B3-B6	+B3-C6

And so on.

The points problem

A few pages ago I showed you how to calculate points. Then, I used a financial calculator. Now I'll show you how to do it with Visicalc.

The borrower agreed to pay $1,755.14 a month for 84 months. And a balloon payment of $189,298.39 at the 84th month. Lender wants a 13.5% yield. The *face* amount of the loan is $200,000. How much would the points be.

To get the answer from Visicalc you use the NPV command. NPV stands for net present value. First you set up the screen. Like this.

	A	B	C
1	Face amount of loan	200000	
2	Interest rate	.135	
3	Net present value	@NPV(B2/12,B6...B89)	
4	Points	+B1-B3	
5	Month	Payment	
6	1	1755.14	
7	2	1755.14	
8	3	1755.14	
and so on until month 84			
89	84	191053.53	

To write the number of each month, just enter 1 at A6. Then put 1 + A6 in A7. Then replicate A7, answering "R" for "relative" from A8 to A89.

To enter the payment, just enter 1755.14 at B6. then replicate B6 from B7 to B88. Enter 191053.53 manually at B89. $191,053.53 is the combined total of the $1,755.14 monthly payment and the $189,298.39 balloon payment due at month 84.

NPV

To do the actual calculation, enter @NPV(B2/12,B6...B89) at B3. "@" just means "here comes a command" to the computer. NPV has a particular format. The amount after the left parenthesis and before the comma is the interest rate. In this case, B2/12 or .135/12 = .01125. .01125 is the ***monthly*** interest rate converted to decimals.

B6...B89 means "from B6 to B89." The three periods mean "from-to."

So when you enter the command @NPV(B2/100*12,B6...B89), you are asking the computer to give you the net present value of the income from B6 to B89 discounted at the rate located at B2.

The points

The points are the difference between the present value and the face amount of the loan. So to get them you simply subtract the present value of the payments from the face amount of the loan. In other words, +B1-B3.

When the computer does the calculation, you will see the following on the screen.

	A	B
1	Face amount	200000
2	Interest	.135
3	Net present value	169018.45
4	Points	30981.55
5	Month	Payment
6	1	1755.14
7	2	1755.14
8	3	1755.14
and so on		

Note that this is exactly the same answer my calculator gave. Other calculators might give slightly different answers.

The calculator is probably quicker is you just want one answer. But if you want to try ***different*** numbers to see how they come out, Visicalc is the only way to go. That's called "playing 'what if'?." Computers are great for playing "What if?"

For example, if I change the face amount, the points at B4 will instantaneously recalculate. If I change the interest rate, the net present value and points will recalculate in a few seconds. Same thing if I change the payments or the balloon payment.

This would be a great advantage in a negotiation where you are going back and forth between the borrower and lender trying to find the best compromise to do the deal.

Understanding time value of money is crucial

You *must* know how to do time value of money calculations to really understand real estate finance. I won't spend any more time on it here. A whole book could be written on the time value of money calculations pertinent to real estate investing. But I will *use* time value of money calculations throughout the book.

The *true* sale price

According to the National Association of Realtors, sellers have been using a lot of "creative" finance in the recent recession. Or "people-to-people" financing as the NAR has taken to calling it...since "creative" financing got a bad name. Here are the percentages of deals which used various forms of "people-to-people" financing in January of 1982.

- Assumption 43%
- Seller second mortgage 32%
- Seller first mortgage 22%
- Relatives, friends help 21%
- Land contract 18%
- Wraparound 15%
- Buy-down of interest rate 11%
- Lease option 8%
- Realtor takes comm. as note 3%

By the way, I don't like these categories. Some duplicate others...like a seller second and a wraparound. The two are not always synonymous. But they often are. "Relatives and friends" are not a ***technique***...they're ***sources***. Anyway, you get the idea that funny money real estate financing is widespread when interest rates are high.

Before I move on, let me draw your attention to the low percentage of deals in which the ***real estate agent*** took his commission in the form of a note. Real estate agents think "creative" finance is good for ***you***...but ***they*** don't want any part of it for themselves. That's because they can't pay the bills with notes. And neither can you. Sellers should not take back mortgages of any kind. What's good for the Realtor is good for the seller.

Funny money deals; funny money prices

In the real estate business, seller financing is called "funny money" or "Chinese money" or "paper." An old real estate industry line is, "I'll let you set the price if you'll let me set the terms."

If you took someone up on that offer, the dialogue would go something like this.

You: "I want a million dollars for my two-bedroom bungalow in a push-the-lock-buttons-down neighborhood."

Sharpie: "Sold. I'll give you a dollar a year for a million years...binding on our heirs and assigns, of course."

Who got the best of that deal? I haven't seen your bungalow. But I suspect a dollar a year is below market. If you were the seller in a deal like that, would you brag about selling your bungalow for a million dollars?

I doubt it.

But that's only an extreme case of what the typical seller does. He names a price which is too high. Then, in order to get his too-high price, he gives the buyer a mortgage at a too-low interest rate. I call it the "Santa Claus Conspiracy." You give me a Santa Claus price and I'll give you a Santa Claus mortgage.

In Communist countries, workers say, "The government pretends to pay us so we pretend to work." In that same vein real estate sellers pretend their property is worth a lot of money and real estate buyers pretend the mortgage is worth its face value.

Is a $100,000 mortgage worth $100,000?

Is a $100,000 mortgage worth $100,000? Probably not.

Any long-term investment is worth ***the present value of the payments to be received.*** That means the $100,000 written on the face of a $100,000 mortgage is meaningless when it comes to valuing that mortgage. Remember what I told you lenders want to know about the loan you want them to make?

How much do I get?
When do I get it?
How *sure* am I to get it?

The same applies to a mortgage you're trying to sell. The prospective buyer of the loan will discount the payments he'll receive to their present value at whatever discount rate he feels is appropriate.

Example

Clifford Mahler sells a 10 unit apartment building. The sale price is $250,000. There is an existing, assumable mortgage. The balance is $70,000. It was originally $80,000 at 9% for 30 years. A little less than 19 years remains.

The buyer puts down 20% or $50,000. Clifford hasn't read this book (or my other book *Aggressive Tax Avoidance For Real Estate Investors*) so he takes back a second mortgage for the balance. At 11% which is the going rate for seller seconds in his area. The second is interest only with a balloon payment in seven years. Here's a recap.

Down payment	$ 50,000.00
Cliff's second	130,000.00
Existing first	70,000.00
Price	250,000.00

At the time, the ***market*** rate on commercial second mortgages like the one Cliff took back is 14%.

How much did Cliff get for his 10 unit?

Not $250,000.

What Cliff got is the ***present value of what he received plus the present value of the debt he was relieved of.***

The present value of what he received

What did Cliff receive?

He received $50,000 in cash and a promise to pay 11% x $130,000 = $14,300 a year for 7 years and a balloon payment of $130,000 at the end of seven years.

What are those three things worth?

The present value of $50,000 in cash is $50,000.

You calculate the present value of the second the same way we did the points calculation a while back. The appropriate discount rate is 14% because that's what a prospective mortgage buyer could get elsewhere.

So what's the present value of $14,300 a year for 7 years. Actually, it would more likely be $14,300/12 = $1,191.67 a month for 84 months. Discounted at 14%.

n = 84
i = 14/12 = 1.166666666667
PMT = 1191.67

PV = 63589.61

And the present value of the balloon payment?

n = 84
i = 1.1666666666667
FV = 130000

PV = 49068.00

So the *total* present value of Cliff's second mortgage is

PV of monthly payments	$ 63,589.61
PV of balloon payment	49,068.00
Total PV	$112,657.61

Cliff's "$130,000" second mortgage is really only a ***$112,657.61*** second mortgage. And he'd be lucky to get that for it.

The present value of the debt he was relieved of

What about the ***existing first*** mortgage? A lot of people who will concede that the second isn't really worth $130,000 will balk at discounting the first, too. "Why!?" they ask. "You owed $70,000 on that loan when you sold the property. Now you owe nothing. So you're $70,000 better off."

Not so.

Was the lender demanding that Cliff pay him $70,000? Of course not. He did not have that right in the mortgage. The existing first mortgage lender is stuck with that loan for the duration. He can't demand a $70,000 payoff (assuming there's no due-on-sale clause).

What Cliff really owed on that loan was $643.70 a month for 225 more months.

What's that worth?

At present, first mortgages are going for about 12%. The present value of 225 payments of $643.70 discounted at 12% is

n = 225
i = 12/12 = 1
PMT = 643.70

PV = 57509.21

Cliff sold for $220,167; *not* $250,000

If Cliff tells his friends he got $250,000, he's misleading them. If ***he*** thinks he got $250,000, he's kidding himself.

He got

- $50,000 in cash
- a piece of paper worth $112,657.71 if he's lucky
- let off the hook on an obligation with a present value of $57,509.21.

That adds up to $220,166.92. Not $250,000.

To put it another way, the ***true*** sale price of a piece of real estate is the cash the seller received plus the ***market*** value of any loans, existing or new, on the property. In this example, Cliff could sell his loan for $112,657.71 tops. And the existing first mortgage lender could sell their loan for $57,509.21 tops. The ***face*** value of the loans is utterly irrelevant unless the loan is paid off at closing.

Cash value is all that matters

The ***cash value*** of real estate is the only one that matters. When the seller gets all cash for his equity and there's no loss of a below market interest rate loan, the sale price and the cash value are the same.

But most income property deals are done with funny money. In good times and bad.

Single-family deals use funny money less often. There, the percentage of funny money deals tends to go up when interest rates go up.

It is imperative that you know how to calculate the ***true*** price of property.

The cash equivalent movement in loan appraisals

Since the first edition of this book came out, a number of major mortgage lenders have complained about appraisers using comparable sales prices without noting the effect of below-market seller financing. They have called for "cash equivalent" appraisals. Cash equivalent appraisals are the same as the true sale price I advocated in both the first edition of this book and this edition. So this true sale price idea is not just my idea. It is now accepted by the industry as a necessity.

Why funny money is used

You may wonder why funny money is used at all. Good question. I don't think it ***should*** be used at all. I don't take back mortgages when I ***sell.*** Although I will take the best financing I can get when I ***buy.*** And that's often seller financing.

Sellers take back loans because they are unwilling to sell for fair market value. They are especially unwilling to sell for fair market value when values fall.

Do real estate values fall?

A lot of people think real estate always goes up in value. The statistics on sale prices seem to support that. Here are the median sale prices of existing single-family homes as reported by the National Association of Realtors.

Median Sale Prices of Existing Single-Family Homes

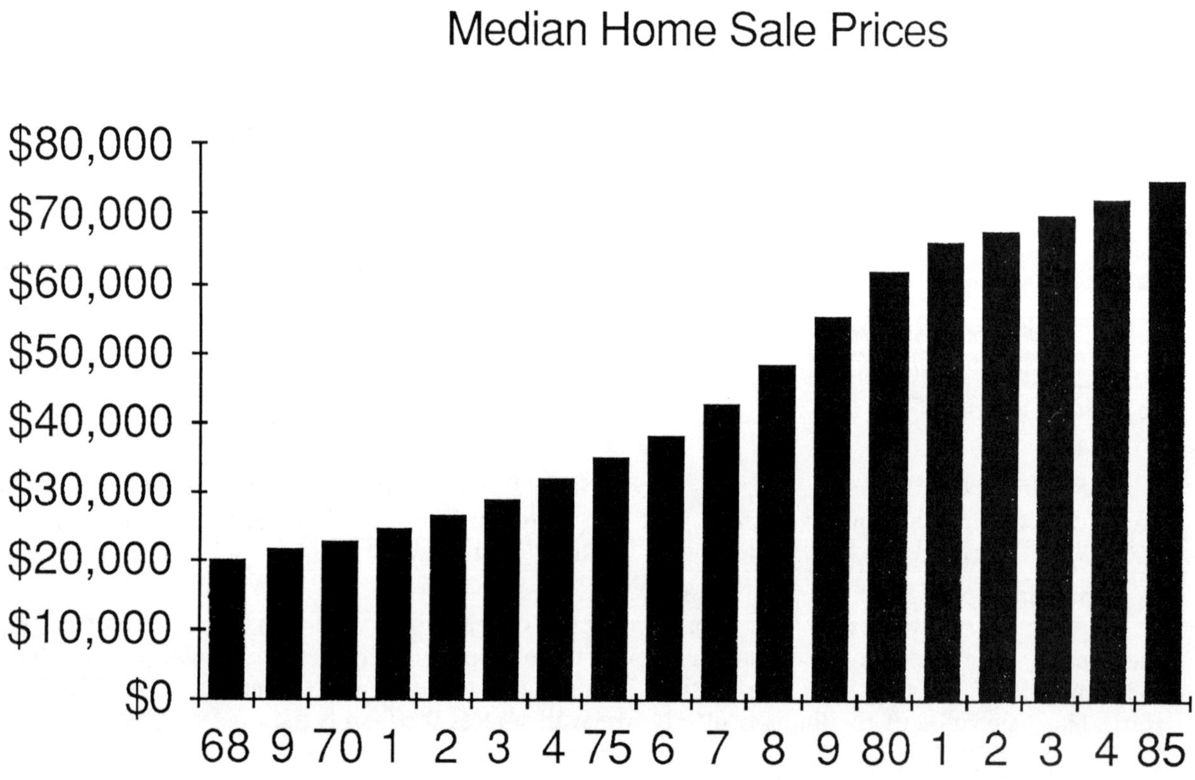

Do you see any price drops in those figures?

Me neither.

But we had three recessions during that period. One in '70, one in '73, and one in '80. There were no ***price*** drops during those recessions. But would you believe me if I told you that the percentage of deals involving seller financing went ***up*** during those recessions?

I don't have year by year statistics on seller financing. But the NAR statistics on "people-to-people" financing I cited earlier showed that 54% of deals in January 1982 included seller mortgages. When I was a real estate salesman in the early seventies, the percentage of seller loans went from zero to a much higher percentage when the '73 recession hit.

Increase in interest rates equals drop in values

When interest rates go up, real estate values drop.

Note that I said "***values***"; not "***prices.***" Prices rarely drop. The '68 through '82 home prices above show that. But ***values*** do drop.

Sellers cover up the drop in values by offering loans at below-market interest rates. (The other terms of seller loans are also usually better than commercial lenders give.) Sellers also cover up the drop in values by withdrawing their properties from the market and by letting them sit on the market for extended periods.

So if you want a ***complete*** picture of the market, you need to know

- sale prices
- sale terms
- number of properties on the market
- time to sell
- market interest rates

The IRV formula

You can see the relationship between interest rates and values in the IRV formula. The IRV formula is

$$I = RV$$

where

I = income
R = rate (capitalization rate)
V = value

If you remember your algebra, you know that if $I = RV$, then $V = I/R$. Or value equals income divided by the capitalization rate. If you have a property with a net operating income of $100,000. . .and the going cap rate is 10%. . .its value would be

$$V = I/R$$

$$V = \$100,000/10\%$$

$$V = \$1,000,000$$

Cap rates are not the ***same*** as mortgage interest rates. But they are such close "cousins" that I won't bother to distinguish between them here.

So what happens to the value of the building with the $100,000 net operating income if interest rates go up? Let's say they go up two percent.

That would make the rate ***12%*** instead of 10%. And the value would be

V = I/R

V = $100,000/12% = $833,333.33

So when the interest rate goes ***up*** from 10% to 12%, the value of the building in this example drops from $1,000,000 to $833,333.33. But if the seller ***insulates*** the buyer from that interest rate increase by offering a 10% loan, there will be ***no*** drop in ***price***. And that's exactly what typically happens.

Other forces at work

Of course, other forces are at work. Interest rates are just ***one*** factor. Changes in ***income*** affect values. Anticipated value increases cause investors to settle for less income or even negative income. So it's possible for both values and interest rates to go up at the same time. . .if the other forces at work more than compensate for the adverse effect of the increased interest rates.

During the seventies, for example, mortgage interest rates rose from 7 1/2% to 12%. But values, not just prices, rose too. That's because personal and rental income rose and cap rates fell. Mostly falling cap rates.

In 1970, real estate investors expected positive cash flow. That requires high cap rates.

But by the late seventies, value increases had become so big and so consistent that investors were willing to accept negative cash flow. The change from positive cash flow to negative cash flow represents a large drop in cap rates.

An engineer would see the forces on real estate values as a bunch of vectors. Some push values up. Some push values down. The ***net*** strength of all of those vectors determines whether values go up or down. ***Any*** increase in interest rates is a value-reducing "vector." Whether values ***actually*** go down depends on whether the vectors pushing ***up***. . .baby boom, growth in the economy, and so forth. . .are more powerful or not.

Figure 12

Some Value Changing Vectors

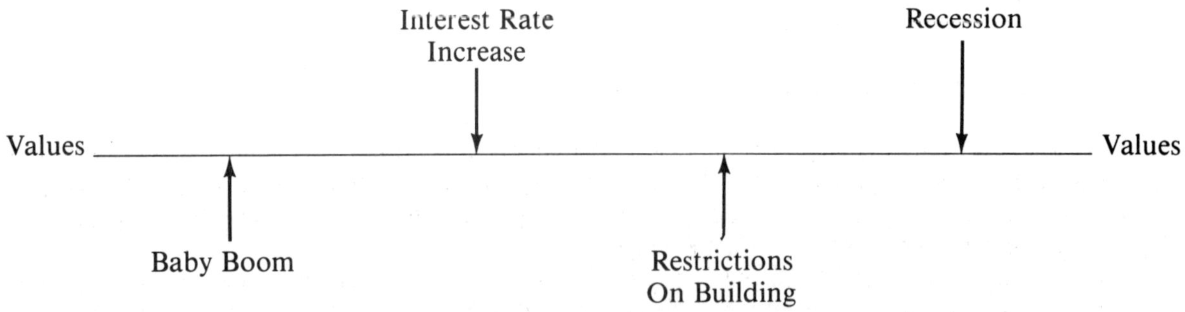

"Sellers' markets" and "buyers' markets"

There is no such thing as a "sellers' market." Never had one. Never will.

And what's normally called a "buyer's market" is really ***nobody's market***. Here's what's ***really*** going on.

The phenomena known as "buyers' markets" and "sellers' market" are both caused by the same thing. The slowness and reluctance of sellers to react to changes in real estate values. In other words, sellers are always ***behind the market***.

That's not hard to understand. They haven't been ***in the market*** since they bought their last property. In the typical case, that was several years ago. So they're out of touch.

Buyers, on the other hand, are in the market right now. They don't know real estate values when they start. But after a day or so, they're up on what property is worth in their area. I'm not saying they feel confident. They don't. ***All*** buyers wonder if they overpaid for the property. Even pros. But the fact of the matter is that buyers quickly acquire a working knowledge of local real estate values during their search for a property.

The so-called "sellers' market" is really a "buyers' market"

When values go ***up***, sellers are behind the market. As a result, they ***under***price their properties. In other words, they sell them for ***less than fair market value***.

Sure the sellers are happy. And sure the sellers are raising prices in a "sellers' market." But they aren't raising them ***enough***. That's why properties sell so ***fast*** in a "sellers' market."

What would ***you*** call it if properties were being sold for ***less*** than market value. I call it a "buyers' market." The fact that sellers are ***happy*** in such a market just proves that "Ignorance is bliss."

The so-called "buyers' market" is really "nobody's market"

If sellers are selling for ***less*** than market value when values go ***up***, what do you think they're doing when values go ***down***?

Sellers are ***behind*** the market, remember? So when values go ***down***, as they did after the October 1979 increase in interest rates, sellers are slow to ***reduce*** prices accordingly. Heck...slow ain't the word. They ***refuse*** to reduce the prices.

So where sellers sell for ***less*** than market value when values are going up, they try to sell for ***more*** than market value when values are dropping. It can't be done...by definition.

'Market value' is defined as

"the highest price a property will bring when exposed to the market for a reasonable period of time."

Selling for ***more*** than market value means selling for more than the "highest price the property will bring." It is impossible to sell for more than market value.

But that doesn't stop millions of sellers from trying. So in a so-called "buyers' market," you've got zillions of properties for sale for ***more than market value***. Buyers will not and should not pay more than market value. So I'll be darned if I'll call that situation a "buyers' market."

But it isn't a "***sellers'*** market" either. Not when you've got a zillion sour-pussed sellers grousing about their property not selling.

It's ***nobody's*** market. That's who's selling. Nobody. And that's who's buying. Nobody.

Seller finance is nothing more than a price cut

How do you sell a property which is being offered for more than market value? Cut the price to market value. That's the only way. But most sellers have so much ego wrapped up in their sale ***price*** they can't bring themselves to do that. So they accomplish the same thing by cutting ***terms***. That's far more palatable to the typical seller.

Let's go back to Clifford Mahler's $250,000 10 unit. Suppose it was worth $250,000 on a ***cash*** value basis. Then interest rates went up. About that time, Cliff put it up for sale. Like the typical seller, he asked $250,000. What it ***used*** to be worth. He insisted on all cash and that the buyer pay off of the existing first mortgage so Cliff's released from liability on it.

Result? No offers. The real estate agent bugs Cliff to "help" with the financing. Translation: "***Provide*** the financing."

Finally, Cliff agrees to take back the $130,000 11% second mortgage we used in the earlier example. And he agrees to let the buyer buy ***subject to*** the existing loan. The asking price stays at $250,000.

What has he done? He has, in effect, cut the price by about $30,000. Remember we said that the ***present value*** of the benefits of that deal was $220,167 not the $250,000 selling price.

Result? The property sells. Its fair market value was $220,167. When Cliff insisted on $250,000, it wouldn't sell. It wasn't ***worth*** $250,000 after the increase in interest rates. It was worth $220,000.

Property will sell for market value in *any* market

It is ***never*** hard to sell anything. . . for its fair market value. If you're having trouble selling real estate or anything else, it's almost always because the present value of what you are asking is greater than the market value of the property in question.

It is not "buyers' markets" or high interest rates or scarcity of money or any of that nonsense that keeps people from selling real estate. It is simply sellers trying to get more than their property is worth.

High interest rates cause values to drop. They do ***not*** cause selling difficulty. Selling difficulty arises when interest rates cause value drops which sellers refuse to accept.

Nuff said.

3
Reed's Rules of Real Estate Finance

Real estate finance can be complex. Complexity can confuse. To help you avoid confusion, I offer these simple rules.

1. Simple is better than complex.

"Creative" finance pushers like to impress you with the quantity of "new" techniques they're teaching you. There aren't many truly new finance techniques. So they ***create*** "new" techniques by combining several old ones in one complex "new" one.

Then you trot out to the real world and try to persuade a seller to do a double wraparound inside-out subordinated ground lease-option.

The seller says, "Huh?"

The agent says, "Huh?"

Your attorney says, "Huh?"

Since a confused mind says no, the seller usually says that too.

Avoid complex techniques. The best way to finance real estate is a first and maybe a second mortgage or trust deed. Deviate from that pattern only as a last resort. Use more complex arrangements only when there are compelling reasons to do so.

A number of real estate organizations give awards for the "Deal of the Year." Usually, the

"Deal of the Year" is incredibly complex. Indeed, the complexity seems to be what the organization is rewarding.

In my book, the "Deal of the Year" is the one which is the simplest, the quickest, the smoothest. Pursuing those complex "Deal of the Year" awards is a good way to see deals fall through. KISS is not my creation. But I'll repeat it here because it's a useful mnemonic. KISS stands for Keep It Simple Stupid. It's good advice. . .especially in real estate finance.

2. Familiar is better than exotic.

Another way "creative" finance pushers make you think you're learning a lot of new things from them is to emphasize exotic techniques. For example, a land contract is exotic in most areas of the U.S.

In New Jersey, land contracts are exotic. Deals are hardly ever done using land contracts there. The reaction you get from sellers, agents, and attorneys will be similar to the reaction you get on double wraparound inside-out subordinated ground lease-options.

"Huh?"

And another "No."

Clutching at the unfamiliar

They say a drowning man will clutch at a straw. So will a real estate investor desperate for a way to finance a deal clutch at an unfamiliar technique. Every three to five years we have a recession. In most cases, recessions are accompanied by high interest rates. High interest rates kill real estate deals. That makes the people in real estate desperate for salvation.

Then along comes a "new" technique. They may read about it in the Sunday real estate section. Or in a new "creative" finance book. Or hear about it at a "creative" finance seminar.

Because they're desperate, they ***want*** to believe this "new" technique is the solution to all their problems. Because they are ***unfamiliar*** with the technique, they have no reason to ***doubt*** that it's the answer to their prayers.

I'm going to cover virtually every real estate finance technique there is in this book. I'll explain the advantages and disadvantages of each. So check the section on the specific technique you're considering to see whether you should use it.

But I can probably give you the answer right now.

No.

No, the unfamiliar finance technique is ***not*** the answer to your prayers. In the vast majority of cases, the unfamiliar technique will only ***worsen*** your problems. Only in rare situations will you find that an unfamiliar technique is better than a familiar one.

I thought about wording this rule, "When in Rome, finance as the Romans do." I decided the broader familiar versus unfamiliar was better. But, "When in Rome, finance as the Romans do" is still good advice.

I attended a finance seminar in 1974. One technique which excited me was using a land contract to get around a due-on-sale clause. So I promptly made an offer using that technique. The seller didn't even respond.

In some parts of the country, the midwest and northwest, land contracts are quite common. But I was trying to buy a property in Southern New Jersey. Land contracts are unheard of there.

In general, you should not deviate from the common local practice. That means use trust deeds in the states where trust deeds are common and mortgages where mortgages are common. Use ground leases if you're in one of those areas where they are common like Maryland or Hawaii. But avoid them elsewhere. Use land contracts for secondary financing if you're in one of the areas where that's the common practice like the Midwest or Northwest. But don't expect much if you try to use a technique which is unfamiliar to sellers and agents in your area.

3. You *always* pay the current market interest rate when you finance real estate.

High interest rates always increase the demand for "creative" finance. People want ways to get around the high rates. "Creative" finance appears to do that.

It doesn't.

Nothing gets around high interest rates. Repeat, ***nothing***.

Many "creative" finance techniques ***appear*** to get around high interest rates. They don't. What they ***really*** do is one of two things:

1. ***Hide*** payment of all or part of the current market rate or

2. ***Postpone*** payment of all or part of the current market rate.

In the section of this book where I explained how to calculate the ***true*** sale price of a property, I explained that the lower the interest rate the higher the price. That applies to both seller loans and assumptions.

So you may ***think*** you're getting below-market interest rate loans when you assume an old loan or get a seller loan. You're not. You're simply paying the additional interest in the form of a higher price and therefore a larger mortgage amount.

Example

For example, you own a $100,000 property. One offer says the buyer will get a new $80,000 mortgage at 13% for 30 years. His payments will be $884.96 a month. That will give you all cash.

Another offer asks you to take back an $80,000 mortgage at 11% interest only for ten years. That buyer's payments would be $733.33 a month.

Which offer would you take? One gets you $100,000 in cash now. The other, $20,000 in cash now, $733.33 a month for 120 months, then a balloon payment of $80,000. . .you hope.

No contest. But if the buyer who wants you to take back the mortgage were to increase his price to, say, $120,000, you might accept.

What would the buyer's payments be if he paid $120,000 and put 20% or $24,000 down? His mortgage amount would be $96,000. At 11% interest only his payments would be $880.00 a month.

Did the buyer get around today's high interest rates? ***He*** probably thinks so. After all, the market rate is 13% and he's paying 11%.

But what's his payment? $880. What would his payment have been if he had paid $100,000 and got a new 13% mortgage? $884.96. Practically the same amount.

All the buyer has done is hide 2% of the 13% he's paying in the price and mortgage amount. The interest rate written on the mortgage may be 11% instead of 13%. But he's paying almost the exact same payment as if he were paying 13%. So who's kidding whom?

Here are some common techniques where you pay all or part of the current market interest rate by hiding it in a higher price:

- seller loans
- assumptions or "subject to"
- buy downs
- zero interest loans
- VA (actually a form of buy down)

Postponing it

Some techniques actually ***do*** reduce the payments over what they'd be if you got a new loan at current rates. . .but only temporarily. Like the mechanic in the Fram filter commercial says, "You can pay me now, or you can pay me later." And I'll add, "But don't ever think you can ***avoid*** paying me at all."

Here are some examples of techniques in which payment of all or part of the current market interest rate is postponed:

- accruing interest (to be paid in a later balloon)
- negative amortization (ditto)
- graduated payment mortgage (later payments are ***higher*** than they would have been with a level mortgage)
- interest only loans (principal is paid in a balloon)

Only three choices

You have only three choices when it comes to current market interest rates.

1. You can pay the current market interest rate up front and out in the open by simply getting a ***new mortgage*** from a lender (other than the seller).

2. You can put a below market interest rate on the loan document but end up in effect paying market interest by paying a ***higher price*** for the property.

3. You can ***postpone*** paying all or part of the current market interest rate by using a technique which allows lower payments now in return for higher payments later.

THERE IS NO FINANCE TECHNIQUE WHICH WILL ENABLE YOU TO AVOID PAYING CURRENT MARKET INTEREST RATES! Every time rates go up, millions of Americans search frantically for such a technique. It doesn't exist. It cannot exist. It violates immutable laws of economics.

The law of supply and demand

Everybody knows the law of supply and demand. But most forget it from time to time. Everybody knows there's no free lunch, but every now and then, someone figures he's discovered a free lunch.

If the market rate for first mortgages is 13%, no one is going to make a first mortgage loan for less. When 13% is the market rate, that, by definition, means that he can ***get*** 13%. He doesn't have to accept less. So why should he?

Free lunch in assumptions?

A lot of people think there's a free lunch in assumptions, "subject to's," and wraparounds (which are a form of assumption or "subject to"). "Only the lender gets hurt," you hear them say.

Baloney.

Only the seller benefits is more to the point. The moment the market interest rate goes above the rate on an existing loan, the value of that loan drops. It makes no difference whether the property is sold or not.

The lender is worse off the moment his interest rates falls behind the market. Who's ***better*** off. The owner of the property. He's better off whether he sells the property or not. And if he can sell the property to another buyer without having to pay off the loan, he's better off yet.

A property with a below market interest rate assumable loan is ***more valuable*** than an identical property which a buyer would have to finance at current market rates. When you buy a property and take over an existing below market interest rate loan, the seller does not ***give*** you that loan. He ***sells*** it to you. You pay more for the property than you would if it did ***not*** have that loan.

So the notion that "only the lender is hurt" in an assumption is nonsense. Assumptions and "subject to's" do not affect lenders at all. Increasing interest rates are what hurts them. The notion that the ***buyer*** of a property with a low interest loan is getting a good deal is ***also nonsense***. The buyer is ***paying for*** everything he's getting.

Sticking your fellow citizens with part of the bill

I once got a 7 1/4% VA loan which was subsidized by a state government program. At the time, market rates were over 8%. Did I get a good deal?

Yes.

Did I avoid paying current market rates?

Yes.

How does that square with my saying it's impossible to avoid paying current market rates? If you include ***subsidies*** which are sometimes available from government or relatives, my rule would have to be changed to say that ***someone*** will pay the current market interest rate when you finance real estate. . . although it may not be you in some cases. In the absence of subsidies, ***you*** pay the full market rate. With subsidies, your relatives or fellow citizens pay part of it.

I am against subsidy programs as a taxpaying citizen. But if you're eligible for a government subsidy, and it fits your investment strategy, and the red tape doesn't cost more than the subsidy, by all means take advantage of it. . . as I did on that 7 1/4% VA deal.

When it comes to family subsidies, I go back to the "There is no free lunch" rule. If you accept a favor from someone. . . relative or otherwise. . . you ***owe*** them. For that reason, I recommend that you keep dealings with friends and relatives on a business basis. They can be a useful source of loans. . . because you don't have to waste a lot of time convincing them you're a trustworthy person. But accepting more than you give in the long run will only chase away your friends and alienate your relatives.

4. Face-to-face negotiating is almost always better than through a third party.

Real estate agents are taught that you must always have a third party negotiator. The reason is buyer and seller have too much ego involvement in the deal. As a result, they tend to flare up and kill the deal.

I used to be a real estate agent. I was taught that. And I believed it. Matter of fact, it was taught to me with such unequivocal conviction that I never doubted it for a second.

It ain't true. At least not in the vast majority of cases.

I highly recommend that you meet the other party face-to-face to negotiate the deal. The reason is simply communication.

Face-to-face is far and away the best way to communicate. Telephone is second best. Writing is third best. And through a third party is worst of all.

Party game

We've all seen that party game where a sentence is whispered from person to person. Inevitably, the last guy's version is a ridiculous mangling of the original.

So why would a buyer telling an agent who tells another agent who tells the seller be any different? It isn't. Things get lost in the "translation." And when you're negotiating a $50,000 or $150,000 or $500,000 or $1,000,000 deal, you can't afford to have things lost in translation.

The pros go face-to-face

I've interviewed a lot of professional real estate investors. I've yet to meet one who didn't prefer to negotiate face-to-face.

Agents have a vested interest in the third party approach

I should have realized when I first heard an agent say you need a third party that he had a vested interest in saying it. Real estate agents are ***in the business*** of being third party negotiators. If the public gets the idea that face-to-face is possible or even preferable, they're liable to make less use of agents.

One of the lessons I've learned in life is that it's possible to brainwash yourself. The way to do that is to repeat something over and over. Eventually, you start to believe your own propaganda.

Brainwashing oneself is an occupational hazard of political activism and sales. Both political activists and salespeople have a viewpoint they're trying to sell. "My idealogy is best," says the activist. "My product or service is best," says the salesperson. Over and over.

As a result of this brainwashing, salespeople are totally sincere when they tell you a third party negotiator is best. They could take a lie detector test and pass. They really ***believe*** you have to have a third party.

Don't believe them. Not that they're lying. It's just that they've numbed a portion of their brain so that they are no longer capable of objective analysis on that subject.

Take the agent with you

I have no qualms about taking an agent ***with you*** when you negotiate. Matter of fact, it's probably better than going alone if there is an agent involved in the deal.

The typical experienced is a skilled negotiator. The typical investor is less so.

The typical experienced agent has knowledge of standard local lending practices and local lenders. Although even many experienced agents are ignorant of nonstandard techniques.

The other party may believe something that ***both*** you and the agent say, or something the agent says, where he would ***not*** have believed the same thing from you alone.

Sometimes third parties ***are*** best. Remember that I never said that you are ***always*** better off negotiating face-to-face. Sometimes, the agents' line about emotions running too high is correct. When that happens, you should turn the negotiation over to a third party.

Jay Kaplan was the head man at Consolidated Capital. They are one the nation's biggest syndicators and buy lots of income properties. Jay says he prefers to negotiate face-to-face. But he told of one time when the seller seemed hung up on beating Jay Kaplan. The seller knew that Jay Kaplan was one of the most experienced property buyers in the country and seemed out to prove he was tougher than Jay. So Jay turned ***that*** negotiation over to someone else

So the rule is, "Face-to-face is almost always best, but keep alert for those times then a third party is better."

By the way, the third party doesn't have to be an agent. It can be an attorney. But as a general rule, agents are better than attorneys. That because agents are deal oriented. Like you, they want the deal to go through.

5. Real estate is a cyclical business.

Don't you forget it. Real estate is a cyclical business. That means the cost and availability of money fluctuates widely every three to five years. It also means the market goes from high vacancy to low vacancy every three to five years.

Forgetting the cyclicality of the market has been the downfall of many an investor. There's a saying on Wall Street: "In a bull market, everyone thinks he's a genius."

In real estate, everyone thinks he's a genius during the upswing portion of the cycle. Everyone thinks he's turned into King Midas and that every property he touches will turn to gold. Investors start to think that high appreciation rates are permanent, that low vacancy rates are guaranteed,

and that money will always be available on the same terms as now.

As a result, they agree to dangerously high leverage, dangerously low debt-coverage ratios, and dangerous balloon payments.

Write it on the blackboard 100 times

If this were grade school and I were your teacher, I'd make you write "Real estate is a cyclical business" on the blackboard a hundred times.

"Wouldn't that be brainwashing?" you ask.

Darned right it would. But it's brainwashing you *need*.

It's temporary! Temporary!

I'm the editor of *Real Estate Investor's Monthly*. And it seems I spend half my time trying to convince my readers that the *current* situation is not permanent.

When things are going well as they did in the late seventies, I was telling them it won't stay like this. Used to get into arguments on the subject at cocktail parties. The other guy would tell me that real estate would keep going up because of the Baby Boom or some such. And I'd say recessions are almost as regular as the seasons.

And when things are going badly, as they did in the beginning of the '80s, I spend a lot of time trying to convince people that the world has not come to an end.

Real estate is a cyclical business. Cycle means up then down then up then down ad infinitum. The only thing as predictable as the cycles is that every upturn and downturn will bring forth people who claim *this* one is permanent.

It happens with weather, too. When I first moved to California in 1977, we were having a drought. When the drought went into its second straight year, "experts" began to appear who said this was a *permanent* change. They had erudite analyses to prove their theories.

California weather returned to normal for a few years. Then in the winters of '81-'82 and '82-'83, we had record rain falls. There were slides all over and brim full reservoirs. And sure enough, "experts" appeared to prove that *this* was permanent.

6. Don't take back a loan when you sell.

There's a whole chapter on this later in the book. So I won't elaborate on it now. But since about half of all investors disregard that advice, I'll also tell you the "right" way to take back a loan.

The short answer to why you shouldn't take back a loan is that you are a real estate investor, not a lender. Real estate investors earn higher returns than lenders. Taking back a loan depresses your overall return. It does that through tax payments, opportunity costs, and the costs of taking action in the event the borrower defaults.

7. Don't agree to a large balloon payment which falls due in less than seven years.

A "large" payment is one which requires you to refinance or sell the property. A balloon payment you can make from your checking account or via a quick loan can fall due *any* time.

I had a balloon payment due in 1983. It was only for $34,000. I made that from cash on hand. When I bought that property, the balloon was five years off.

I had rejected a property that same year because the *entire first mortgage* of several hundred thousand dollars was due in five years. And I'm glad I did. Otherwise, I'd have been scrambling around in a 14% market trying to get a mortgage to pay that balloon.

Some of you reading this have probably violated this rule. If so, I suspect your nodding your head in agreement as you read this.

Beginners violate this rule

Cain & Scott's annual *Apartment Market Study* revealed that *seasoned* investors negotiated much longer balloon dates than first-time investors. Here's the breakdown.

	1-5 yrs	6-9 yrs	10+ yrs
First time investor	44%	31%	25%
Seasoned investor	18%	44%	38%

Some of the difference between the seasoned and first time investor are due to smaller properties. In other words, the first time investors are buying smaller properties. That, in turn, means smaller balloon payments. In many cases, the balloon payment probably is so small that refinancing or sale of the property would not be required.

But *most* of the difference between the seasoned and first time investor is probably due to experience. Today's seasoned investors were yesterday's first timers. I suspect they suffered either discomfort or financial pain due to their short balloon due dates. As a result, they hang tough on that subject when they negotiate. . .and they tend to ask for a longer due date to begin with.

I recently negotiated with some buyers. I came down to having two lenders willing to make the loan. One wanted 17% but was willing to accept a seven year balloon. The other only wanted 14 3/4%, but would not accept a balloon longer than five years. The 14 3/4% would cost me fewer points so I offered to split the points savings with the buyer if they'd accept the five year balloon.

Their answer was they wouldn't agree to the five year balloon if they got *all* the savings in points. They were doing the right thing.

If you're a first-timer, save yourself the pain or discomfort. Don't violate Reed's Rule Number 7. Don't agree to a large balloon payment which falls due in less than seven years.

8. Tell the truth.

Already covered earlier.

9. Keep your promises.

Ditto.

10. Interest rates are totally unpredictable.

More about that later.

11. Lender's loan criteria are inversely proportional to the amount of money they have to lend.

The more money lenders have, the more they lower their standards to try to get the stuff out the door. If you and/or your property are relatively unattractive to a lender, one way to increase the probability you'll get a loan is to wait until the lenders are flush to apply.

How do you tell when their flush? Read the trade journals carefully. When lenders have *little* money, they demand kickers on commercial deals, cut out rental houses at the low end, demand perfect credit history, etc. When they have a *lot* of money, they will do a deal without kickers, loan to investors, accept borrowers with problems in their credit history, etc.

4
Tax Ramifications

Real Estate Finance And Income Taxes

Most real estate finance transactions have a silent partner. The IRS. (Some deals have *no* tax effects. For example, a deal in which a tax exempt lender loaned money to a tax exempt borrower.)

Most "creative" finance pushers know little about tax laws pertaining to finance. Ask them about the tax ramifications and they'll say, "See your accountant." But for some of the finance techniques they advocate, that's like this conversation:

Pusher: "And in conclusion, you should jump off the Golden Gate Bridge."

Pushee: "Won't I get hurt?"

Pusher: "See your doctor."

A "multidisciplinary" field

Steve Roulac is a well-known real estate consultant. He says, "Real estate is a multidisciplinary field." In addition to being a consultant, Steve is a user of big words. "Multidisciplinary" being a prime example.

The word "discipline" usually refers to marine drill sergeants and such. Not here. The discipline Roulac refers to is definition number 8 in my *Standard College Dictionary*. "A branch of knowledge or instruction."

So what Steve means by "multidisciplinary" is that in order to understand real estate, you have to know *several* fields. He's right.

And one of the most important related fields for a real estate investor to know is tax law. Roulac spent his youth getting a law degree, an MBA degree, a CPA, and a PhD in economics. So he's a multidisciplinary kind a guy. Me too. Although I did not gather such high-powered merit badges. I have worked in various jobs to learn about the different related fields. And I've studied them via seminars, books, and periodicals.

But the typical "creative" finance pusher has not done a similar quantity of "homework." Typically, he's a real estate agent who has gathered a basketful of techniques and put together an act. His knowledge of the tax ramifications of the techniques he advocates is summed up by the phrase, "See your accountant." That doesn't cut it.

Taxes and real estate

Taxes are *very* important in real estate investment. Tax laws affect the structure of most deals. Installment sales are a prime example. When a seller does an installment sale, he usually claims it's for tax reasons.

Sellers are one of the prime sources of investment real estate finance. . .even in good times. So knowing the tax laws can help you negotiate seller financing.

I wrote for the *Real Eastate Investing Letter.* We took a poll of our readers periodically. We always asked the readers to rank the four benefits of investing. Here's how they ranked them.

1. Appreciation
2. Tax shelter
3. Cash flow
4. Amortization

The *Cain and Scott Apartment Market Study* asks a similar question. In 1980 and '81, Seattle apartment investors ranked tax shelter second after "inflation hedge" as an objective. But in 1982, tax shelter moved into first place.

If tax shelter is the first or second most important investment objective of the people you're dealing with, you'd better know more about it than, "See your accountant."

How you can use tax knowledge

You can use tax knowledge four ways in real estate finance.

1. More accurate pre-deal analysis
2. To persuade lenders to approve the loan
3. To persuade sellers to go along with you
4. Avoid tax pitfalls in some techniques

I already mentioned that you should watch your debt-coverage ratios. And I added that *after*-tax debt-coverage ratios are the ones that matter. Ignorance of how to compute after-tax numbers will lead you to unnecessary conservatism. And that conservatism has a high opportunity cost.

Lenders and tax law

Lenders are also concerned about your debt-coverage ratio. But they deal in ***before***-tax figures. They're wrong to do that. *After*-tax is all that matters. By carefully computing the after-tax numbers and showing them to the lender, you can often persuade them to make a loan which they would otherwise rejected. A friend of mine bought a $125,000 house he "couldn't afford" that way. By taking them a neatly typed projection showing how his ***after***-tax income was more than adequate to make the payments.

Sellers and tax law

Sellers are *very* tax conscious. After all, that sale usually hurls them into a high bracket. The typical seller has owned the property for five years. Five years worth of appreciation means he's selling for 50% to 100% more than he paid for the property. Plus his tax basis is not what he ***paid*** for the property. It's what he paid ***less*** all the depreciation he's claimed.

Let's say the sale price is $100,000. That'd be the low end of the investment real estate market. The seller probably bought that property five years ago for about $60,000. He claimed maybe $12,000 in depreciation. So he's got a gain of $100,000 - ($60,000 - $12,000) = $52,000. The tax on that gain will be in the $10,000 range.

So on the typical ***low end*** investment deal, the seller is staring down the barrel of a $10,000 tax bill. The bigger the deal, the bigger the seller's tax problem. If you've got a way to reduce that tax, he's all ears. And there ***are*** a number of ways to reduce the seller's tax bill. Ways which help also ***you***, the buyer/borrower.

Avoid pitfalls

Do you know how to avoid the ***excess loans over basis*** problem in an installment sale? Do you know the tests you must meet to have ***lease*** financing payments be fully deductible? Do you know how to make sure the sale of an ***option*** is not taxed as the sale of the ***property*** itself? Did you know that ***wraparounds*** are invisible to the IRS? Do know what ***imputed interest*** is? Do you know how the tax doctrine of "***substance over form***" affects real estate finance? Do you know the tax effect of ***points***? Do you know how ***mortgage*** amounts affect basis? Do you know how ***personal liability*** for the loan can affect tax deductions?

You didn't hear about any of these things at that "creative" finance seminar, did you? The seminar leader said, "Charge!" And many an investor charged.

Now here I come and ***my*** conversation with the investor goes like this.

Reed: "Freeze!"

Investor: "Wassamatter?!"

Reed: "You just charged into a tax mine field."

Investor: "I did?! Where are the mines?"

Reed: "You'll know where most of them are by the time you finish reading this chapter. The guy who told you to charge in here didn't tell you about the mines, did he?"

Investor: "No. Well, he ***did*** say to see your accountant on tax matters."

Reed: "Did you?"

Investor: "Well, I ***meant*** to. I mean I didn't know that so many finance techniques had tax ramifications."

Reed: "So the 'creative' finance guy told you to see your accountant on tax matters. But he did ***not*** tell you how to recognize all the 'tax matters' in real estate finance?"

Investor: "I guess not."

Interest

Interest is deductible. ***Usually.***

Section 163 of the *Internal Revenue Code* says you can deduct interest. But it's more complicated than that.

For one thing, you have to be ***obligated*** to pay it back to deduct it. If Mom and Dad pay your mortgage payments, they may ***think*** they can deduct the interest on their tax return. They can***not*** unless they ***signed*** the mortgage, too.

Construction period interest

You can deduct construction period interest on your principal residence. But not on other property. You have to amortize construction period interest over ten years. That is, deduct 10% of the total interest each year for each of ten years. Like straight line depreciation.

Family "loans"

One common source of money to buy real estate is relatives. When one relative borrows from another, and pays interest, he expects to deduct that interest. The deduction may be disallowed. If IRS claims there was no real loan. . .that it was a gift in reality.

Investment interest

I did not mention the investment interest limitation in my tax book, *Aggressive Tax Avoidance For Real Estate Investors*. I didn't mention it because it generally does not apply to real estate investments. But I get so many calls and letters about it that I plan to include it in that book in the future. And I'll cover it here.

Believe it or not, real estate investments are not "investments" in the eyes of the tax law. That's right, they're not investments.

The property you own and rent out is generally "trade or business property" in the eyes of the tax law. The investment interest limitation does not apply to trade or business property.

The investment interest limitation

The investment interest limitation is pretty convoluted. I'll try to translate into English.

You May Deduct

1. $10,000 plus
2. "net investment income" plus
3. negative cash flow plus amortization on "net leased" property

Number 1 changes to $5,000 for each spouse if you are married and file separately.

What is "net investment income?"

The phrase "net investment income" has a special meaning. "Net investment income" is

INVESTMENT INCOME
dividends
interest
rent
royalties
net short-term capital gain
recapture
less
INVESTMENT EXPENSES
operating expenses
straight line depreciation computed using the appropriate *useful life*; not a 19 year recovery period (no matter whether you actually use accelerated or not and no matter whether the property is eligible for the Accelerated Cost Recovery System or not)

Use Form 4952

In many cases, it's easier to just get the appropriate form and fill it out. Schedule G (Income Averaging), for example, is a heck of a lot easier to understand than Sections 1301 through 1305 of the Internal Revenue Code.

The form for investment interest is Form 4952 "Investment Interest Expense Deduction." You can get it by calling the IRS forms number listed in your local phone book.

Postponed, not lost

You don't go to jail if you have "too much" investment interest. You don't even lose the deduction. But you *do* have to postpone deducting it until some future year when you do *not* exceed the investment interest limitation. Because of the time value of money, that means you *do* lose *part* of the present value of the deduction.

How many years can you carry the "excess" interest forward?

Forever.

What is "investment property?"

"Investment property" is property which is *not* held in a "trade or business." It refers to "passive" income. Raw land is generally considered to be passive and therefore "investment" property.

"Net leased" property is "investment property," too.

What is "net leased" property?

A property is "net leased" for purposes of the investment interest limitation if it meets *either* of the following tests:

1. Owner is guaranteed a specified return or guaranteed that he will not lose money or
2. Owner's operating expenses (not counting property taxes) are less than 15% of rental income.

A single-family rental house *could* trigger the investment interest limitation through the 15% net lease test. That's because the typical rental house lease is largely a net lease. Owner pays taxes, insurance, and the mortgage. But the tenant pays all other expenses.

An actual single-family rental house case I used in the March '83 issue of *The Real Estate Investing Letter* had this income statement.

income	8,100.00
taxes	1,000.00
insurance	172.00
repairs	405.00

Property taxes don't count for the purposes of the 15% expense test. That leaves $172.00 for insurance and $405.00 for repairs for a total of $577.00. $577 is only 7.1% of the gross rental income of $8,100. That means this particular rental house is "net leased" property. That, in turn, means that it is "investment property" (as opposed to "trade or business property"). All of which means that the interest on the mortgage on that property is subject to the investment interest limitation.

The 15% test does not apply to construction period interest.

Example

The example property cost $100,000. 80% of the value is improvements. Straight line depreciation on that property would be $100,000 x 80% = $80,000/20 years = $4,000.00. So the "net investment income" would be

income	8,100.00
less op. expenses	1,577.00
net op. inc.	6,523.00
less s/l depreciation	4,00.00
"net invest. inc."	2,523.00

Remember that the investment interest limitation consists of

1. $10,000 plus
2. "net investment income" plus
3. negative cash flow plus amortization on "net leased" property.

The third part of the calculation in this example would be

negative cash flow	-2,117.00
amortization	500.00
net total	-1,617.00

So the total investment interest this investor can deduct on this property is

1. $10,000 plus
2. -$ 2,523.00 plus
3. -$ 1,617.00

or $10,906. His actual interest for the year on this property was $8,140.

The 15% expense test doesn't apply after five years

Section 163(d) of the Internal Revenue Code covers the investment interest limitation. Paragraph (6)(B) of that section says the 15% expense test does not apply to "real property of the taxpayer which has been in use for more than five years."

Does "been in use" mean in use by you or in use by ***any***body, including previous owners? I suspect it means in use by you.

Beware of escalation clauses when you are the owner

Real estate investors often swagger. And one of the things they brag about when they are swaggering is that they "always get escalation clauses on long-term leases. . .escalation clauses on ***every***thing."

That may be a good way to swagger yourself right into losing part of your interest deduction.

Proposed regulation 1.57-3 contains several examples. One says that if you have leases with escalation clauses, the expenses which escalate will not be counted in the 15% expense test. Nor will that part of the rent be counted as "gross rent." That makes it harder to ***pass*** the test.

That same proposed regulation has an example which says that escalation clauses tied to the ***Consumer Price Index*** or some such will not disqualify any expenses from the 15% test.

Proposed regulations are not law

As readers of my tax book know, IRS regulations are not necessarily law. ***Proposed*** regulations are ***definitely*** not law. And this proposed regulation is weaker than most because it's twelve years old and it relates to the Minimum Tax On Tax Preference Items. . .which is no longer in effect.

Proposed reg 1.57-3 ***does***, however, indicate how IRS thinks about the net lease issue. And it contains a position which is arguably correct. So you should try to abide by it when you can.

That means you try to tie any lease escalation clauses to the Consumer Price Index (CPI) rather than to the expenses of the property. Tenants will tend to prefer the other way. But if you show them proposed reg 1.57-3 they may relent.

Run the numbers before you get excited

Run the numbers first. Your property may not run afoul of the 15% expense test even *with* escalation clauses tied to specific expenses. If not, you can write your escalation clauses any way you like. But if they cause you to drop below 15%, and the tenant will agree, it would probably be wise to use CPI.

How do you tell which loans are for 'investments'?

You may have assumed that investment interest is interest on a loan secured by a net leased property or raw land only. Not necessarily.

Any loan you have...personal loans, car loans, you name it...may be considered a "debt incurred...to purchase or carry property held for investment."

For example, you buy an "investment property" and pay all cash for it. No loan at all. Next month, you buy a vacation home that costs slightly more money than the "investment property." You borrow 80% of the cost of the vacation home.

Interest on a loan incurred to purchase a vacation home is definitely *not* investment interest. But IRS may claim that the purpose of the loan on the vacation home was to buy the "investment" property.

Harking back to proposed regulation 1.57-2 we learn that

"The determination of whether the purpose of incurring or continuing an indebtedness is to purchase or carry property held for investment must be made on the basis of the facts and circumstances of each particular case."

The proposed reg further states that IRS will look suspiciously on "...substantially identical amounts [which] are borrowed and expended simultaneously..." Example 2 of proposed reg 1.57-2 says that where "...the taxpayer is unable to show that the loan was for business or personal as opposed to investment use. It will be inferred that the loan was incurred for the purpose of purchasing or carrying investment property." In other words, any loan you have while you own "investment property" is subject to challenge as being an "investment" loan.

The lesson? If you own "investment" property, try to keep non-investment loans as separate as possible. Separate in time. Separate as to how they are secured. Separate lenders from those who make your investment loans.

Summary on the investment interest limitation

Raw land is "investment property." Therefore, interest on loans to buy and hold raw land is subject to the investment interest limitation. That could reduce the present value of the interest deductions.

Single-family rental houses and similar property like rental condos, duplexes, and so forth may flunk the 15% expense test. That would make them "net leased" or "investment" properties. Same problem as with raw land. But it can be fixed by writing the leases so that you ***pass*** the 15% expense test. To do that, just make more and more expenses the responsibility of the owner until they total 15% of the rental income.

Neither the Internal Revenue Code nor any court decision says that escalation clauses alter the way you compute the 15% expense test. But proposed reg 1.57-3 does. So you should try to tie escalation clauses to the CPI or some index other than the specific property expenses.

Net leased commercial property may also flunk the 15% expense test. Run the numbers before you sign the lease and allocate responsibility for the expenses accordingly.

If you've owned the property five years or more, you don't have to pass the 15% expense test.

In multi-unit buildings, the owner typically pays expenses totaling about 40% of the rent. So these do not flunk the 15% expense test. That means they are "trade or business" properties. And that means the interest on their loans is fully deductible.

No zero interest loans

There is no such thing as a zero interest seller loan in the eyes of the tax law. The law has ***minimum interest rates.*** If you do a seller-financed deal with a ***lower*** interest rate, you have to report it at the ***minimum*** interest rate for tax purposes. "What's the minimum rate?" you ask. Nine percent or the "applicable federal rate," whichever is less if the seller loan is for $2.8 million or less. The applicable federal rate (AFR) if the seller loan is more than $2.8 million. And there is no blending. The ***entire*** loan amount must be reported at the same rate. That is, the first $2.8 million of a larger than $2.8 million loan only gets the 9% rate if, by coincidence, the AFR happens to be 9%.

There are ***two exceptions***:

- AFR only, not 9%, if the property in question is eligible for the investment tax credit
- 110% of AFR if the deal is a sale-leaseback

Don't try to get around the $2.8 million limit on larger loans by breaking up the loan into more than one loan. Treasury regs will nix that.

Accrual method versus cash method

Cash basis taxpayers report income...like loan interest...only when they ***receive*** it and deduct expenses only when they ***pay*** them. Accrual basis taxpayers report income when they ***earn*** it...whether they have received it or not. And accrual basis taxpayers deduct expenses...like interest...when they ***incur*** them...whether they have paid them or not.

When a seller loan is made, both the seller and the buyer must report that loan for tax purposes using the ***same*** method. You may only use the ***cash*** method if

- the seller loan is $2 million or less (not $2.8 million)
- the seller is not a dealer
- the seller was already a cash basis taxpayer

If the property is later sold subject to the seller financing, the ***new owner*** must also use the same method as the original seller and buyer.

If the seller loan is ***more than $2 million***, not $2.8 million, they must both use the ***accrual*** method

Imputed interest

All of this is called "imputed interest." Also known as the Original Issue Discount rules. An IRS official recently described the entire Tax Reform Act of 1984...which applied these rules to seller financing...as understood by "neither man nor beast."

Different rules apply depending on *when* the deal was agreed to. The key dates are

- Prior to 7/24/75—-below 4% must report as if 5%
- Prior to 7/1/81—-below 6% must report as if 7%
- 7/1/81 to 1/1/85—-below 9% must report as if 10%
- 1/1/84 to 6/30/84 for deals closing after 1/1/85—-OID Rules
- 7/1/84 to 12/31/84 for deals closing after 1/1/85—-OID Rules
- 1/1/85 to 6/30/85—-H.R. 5361 rules

I will not go into the OID Rules or H.R. 5361 here. My tax book, *Aggressive Tax Avoidance for Real Estate Investors* covers those subjects.

Assumptions, subject tos and wraparounds

The imputed interest rules (9%, AFR, and all that) do ***not*** apply to loans assumed or taken subject to after June 30, 1985. But wraparounds are *not* considered to be assumptions or subject tos for this purpose. That is, the imputed interest rules *do* apply to wraparounds.

IRS does not impute interest, *you* do

Many people are under the impression that IRS imputes interest when appropriate. That's incorrect. *You* will impute the interest when required. When you fill out your tax return, you must report interest income or deductions in accordance with the law. That means you must recalculate the deal using the legal rate when the actual rate was below the legal rate. You may *not* simply report the actual rate and wait for IRS to recalculate it. That's negligence at best and fraud at worst.

What the imputed interest rules mean for structuring deals

Seller financing should be done at the ***lowest interest rate*** allowed by law to minimize the tax bite to the buyer and seller. By using a lower interest rate, a higher percentage of the seller's receipts are taxed at long-term capital gains rates instead of the ordinary income rates applied to interest income.

But the lower the seller's interest rate, the lower the value of the paper he receives for his property. So he should trade off the lower interest rate for a ***higher price.*** A higher price increases the buyer's depreciation deductions...which lowers his tax bill.

Prepayment bonus

Finally, the buyer should insist on a ***prepayment bonus*** if he's going to pay a higher price than the property's is worth if sold on a cash basis. Otherwise, if he ***prepays*** the loan for some reason, he's cheating himself.

That is, he paid a ***premium*** over market value in return for seven to ten years of below-market rate seller financing. But if the below-market rate seller financing only lasts three or four years, the premium is too high. By prepaying the loan, the borrower is, in effect, buying the loan from the seller. Any other loan buyer would get the loan at a discount reflecting its interest rate, remaining life, and so forth. So the borrower should be able to buy it at a discount, too. The prepayment bonus gives the borrower that right.

On a ***non-business*** property like a residence or vacation home which is not rented out, the prepayment bonus is ***ordinary income*** in the year you receive it. Revenue Ruling 82-202.

On ***business*** property like rental houses, apartment buildings, etc., you can ***either*** pay ordinary income tax on the prepayment bonus in the year you receive it or you can reduce your basis in the property by the amount of the bonus. That, in turn, will reduce your future depreciation deductions. Internal Revenue Code sections 108 and 1017.

The ***seller*** must recalculate their "gross profit" in the year of the prepayment bonus. The gross profit is part of the calculation the seller does each year to figure out how much tax to pay on their installment sale. Internal Revenue Code section 453.

Wraparound mortgages

Wraparound mortgages are a favorite of the "creative" finance crowd. But I've yet to hear a "creative" finance pusher even mention the tax ramifications of wraparounds.

There are two tax ramifications.

1. Which interest is deductible?
2. Are "excess loans over basis" a payment received in the year of sale?

Definition of a wraparound

Wraparound is an *adjective* not a noun. You can have a wraparound mortgage, a wraparound trust deed (often called an "all-inclusive deed of trust"), or a wraparound land contract.

The wraparound concept is best explained by example. You're buying a $500,000 building. There is an existing loan with the following terms:

Original rate	$260,000
Interest rate	9%
Term	30 years
Payments	$2,092.02/mo.
Call	15 years
Current balance	$243,465.33

Terms of *your* deal are as follows:

Price	$500,000
Down	$125,000
Total loans	$375,000
Total payments	$3,857.30/month
Call	8 years

Note that I did ***not*** specify the nature of the loans or the interest rate. That's because you could do this deal two ways. It could be a ***wraparound*** loan at 12% or a purchase subject to the existing first mortgage and a ***straight second*** mortgage at 16.1% interest only. Here's the way each would look.

Buyer's eye view	Wraparound	Straight 2nd
1st mortgage payment	0	$2,092.02
2nd mortgage payment	$3,857.30	$1,765.28
Total payments	$3,857.30	$3,857.30

Seller's eye view	Wraparound	Straight 2nd
Income	$3,857.30	$1,765.28
Outgo	$2,092.02	0
Net income	$1,765.28	$1,765.28

The income and outgo numbers in the seller's eye view show the special payment pattern usually used in wraparounds. The wraparound mortgage is actually a ***junior*** mortgage. . .usually a second. But when a wraparound is used, the first mortgage is "wrapped up in" the wraparound loan amount. In this case, the wraparound loan would be $375,000 at 12% with a 30 year amortization schedule callable in 8 years (to coincide with the call date on the existing first mortgage).

"Callable" means the lender has the right to call the loan or make the borrower pay it all off. If the market interest rate is higher than the mortgage rate when the call date arrives, the lender will almost certainly call the loan. In that case, the call is the same as a balloon payment due date.

The borrower makes a single payment of $3,857.30 to the wraparound lender. The wraparound lender then makes a $2,092.02 payment to the first lender. The wraparound lender gets to pocket the difference. . .$1,765.28 in this case.

IRS wants to ignore wraparounds

The IRS wants to ignore wraparounds for tax purposes. In other words, they want to tax the transaction as if the seller had sold the property subject to the first mortgage and taken back a mortgage with payments equal to the difference between the wrap payments and the payments on the existing first.

What difference does it make?

It makes a small difference on how the monthly payments are taxed. In this example, the borrower either gets to deduct the 12% interest on first year of the wraparound loan or the 9% interest on the eighth year of the first and the 16.1% interest on the second. Here are the numbers.

Interest paid	Wrap	1st and 2nd
First mortgage	0	$21,776.84
Second mortgage	$44,927.07	$21,183.36
Total interest deduct.	$44,927.07	$42,960.20

As you can see, the borrower in this example gets a slightly better deal on interest deductions in the first year with the IRS approach. . . ignoring the wraparound structure and taxing the deal as if it were a straight first and second.

The seller is also better off with the IRS approach. Under the wrap approach, the lender would have to report as interest income the same as the buyer deducted. . . $44,927.07. But the lender could only deduct the ***interest portion*** of the payments on the first mortgage. . . $21,776.84 in the first year. So the lender would have ordinary net interest income of $44,927.07 - $21,776.84 = $23,150.23 that year with the wrap. But only $21,183.36 with the straight second mortgage.

So why ever do wraps?

Good question. I wrote an article on wraps once. The title tells the story. "Another Look At Wraparound Mortgages: Benefits Are Purely Psychological" (*The Real Estate Investing Letter* August 1981).

There are two reasons to do wraps.

1. Psychology can be darned important.
2. "Excess loans over basis."

"Excess loans over basis"

It's possible for the amount you owe on a property to be greater than your basis. Your basis is generally what you paid for the property less all the depreciation deductions you've claimed. More loans than basis. . . called "excess loans over basis" in tax talk. . . is especially likely when you've held a property for more than a few years and you've refinanced.

If you do an installment sale, you pay tax on money as you receive it. ***Unless*** you have excess loans over basis. Tax law says that excess loans over basis constitute a ***payment received in the year of the sale.***

The law figures your property is worth what you paid less depreciation. After all, every year you've been claiming depreciation deductions. . . in effect, claiming the property value has been declining. So when you sell a property with a basis of, say $225,000, the tax law says you are $225,000 worse off.

If the buyer takes over a loan you owe, either by assuming it or taking the property subject to the loan or by paying the loan off, you are ***better*** off. . . by the amount of the loan. For example, if before the deal you owed $350,000 and now you no longer owe it, you are $350,000 better off.

So if you give up a property with $350,000 worth of loans and a basis of $225,000, tax law says you're better off to the tune of $350,000 - $225,000 = $125,000.

Real tax on paper *income*

When you sell and have excess loans over basis, you can have ***paper income*** that you have to pay tax on. Suppose in the example above The sale price was $500,000. The buyer is making a $150,000 down payment and is taking over your $350,000 loan balance.

You will receive $150,000 cash in the year of the sale. And you'll pay tax on the long-term capital gain. That's what you would expect. But you'll also have to pay tax on the $125,000 of excess loans over basis. In other words, you ***receive*** $150,000 in cash, but you must ***pay tax*** as if you had received $275,000 in cash.

It's possible that the tax payable could exceed the amount of cash you receive. Although that would only happen if you gave the buyer a loan representing a high percentage of the value of the property.

But whether the tax payable exceeds the cash proceeds or not, most investors would like to avoid paying tax on excess loans over basis.

The Stonecrest case

That's where wraparounds come in. In particular, wraparound ***land contracts***. If the buyer takes over your loan, the amount of the loan is considered income. So the trick is to convince the IRS and/or the courts that you ***still owe the money***. Stonecrest Corporation did. Here's how.

Stonecrest sold their property on a wraparound land contract. In a land contract, the buyer doesn't get the deed until he has made specified payments. Typically, he gets the deed when he pays off the land contract.

The Tax Court was impressed with five aspects of the deal.

1. Stonecrest Corporation ***continued to make the payments*** on the underlying first mortgage.

2. The deal was a ***land contract*** instead of a sale.

3. The buyer did not ***assume*** the existing loan.

4. Stonecrest Corporation ***remained liable*** on the underlying first mortgage.

5. Stonecrest's payments to the underlying first lender were ***not dependent*** on the buyer's making his payments to Stonecrest.

In the Stonecrest case (*Stonecrest*, 24 TC 659), IRS said the excess loans over basis was a payment in the year of sale. IRS wanted the tax that would be due on the excess loans over basis. The Tax Court decided in favor of Stonecrest. The Court said that Stonecrest's duty to continue to make the loan payments was so extensive that they had not been relieved of the loan by the buyer.

Unfortunately, *Stonecrest* is a 1955 case. The more recent, the better. Taxpayers also ***won*** similar cases in *Estate of E.P. Lamberth*, 31 TC 302 (1958) and *United Pacific Corp.*, 39 TC 721 (1963), and *Hunt*, 80 TC 62 (1983).

In *Hunt*, the taxpayer used a ***mortgage***, not a land contract. So the land contract is apparently not necessary for the *Stonecrest* method of avoiding excess loans over basis taxes.

The IRS "nonacquiesced" on those decisions. "Nonacquiesced" means they said they didn't like the decisions and they planned to ignore them. Civics students may wonder what right the IRS has to ignore court decisions. Good question. But the fact is they claim the right to ignore any court decisions other than those of the U.S. Supreme Court.

In more recent years, the IRS has been more successful at attacking attempts to avoid tax on excess loans over basis. IRS ***won*** these cases.

Waldrip, 429 F 2d 1216 (5th Circuit, 1970)
Ledford, 492 F 2d 1186 (9th Circuit, 1974)
Voight, 68 TC 99 (1977)
Maddox, 69 TC 854 (1978)
Lichtman, TC Memo 1982-630

Temporary Regulation 15A.453-1(b)(3)(ii)

In addition to winning these cases, IRS has issued Temporary Regulation section 15A.453-1(b)(3)(ii). It says

"The wrapped indebtedness shall be deemed to have been taken subject to even though the title to the property has not passed in the year of sale and even though the seller remains liable for payments on the wrapped indebtedness."

In plain English, the temporary reg says IRS plans to ignore both the wraparound structure of a deal and the *Stonecrest* decision. In the spring of '81, the CPA firm of Laventhol and Horwath issued a news release which said Temporary Reg 15A.453-1(b)(3)(ii) was illegal. Many tax people, myself included, agree with them.

What to do on wraparounds

If you have an excess loans over basis problem, you ***may*** be able to avoid it by mimicking *Stonecrest*. IRS says no. Others say yes.

But don't forget that you can and should do an exchange. In that case, there will be no tax at all. See my book *Aggressive Tax Avoidance For Real Estate Investors*. There's an order blank for that purpose in this book.

Secondly, both selling and buying on wraparound land contracts are undesirable from a practical, real estate standpoint. . .tax aspects aside. When I sell, I ***don't want*** to remain liable on the loan. Nor do I want to worry about making some guy's mortgage payments. Nor am I interested in taking back mortgages. . .wraparound or otherwise.

And when I buy, I want the deed. And I'm very leery about relying on someone else to make the payments on my first mortgage.

In other words, man does not live by tax avoidance alone. Taxes are just one aspect of a deal. Not the overriding aspect in most deals. So be aware of the tax controversy over wraparound land contracts. But don't lose sight of the disadvantages of wraparound land contracts for both buyer and seller.

Financing with leases

A lease is not just something landlords use to keep tenants in line. It's also a financing device.

As a general rule, you finance real estate with mortgages or trust deeds. You only use leases in unusual situations. I'll discuss those situations later.

Sometimes, investors try to use leases to ***get around*** problems regarding mortgages. What they ***really*** want is a mortgage. But for some reason, they can't get a mortgage. So they try to get a mortgage by ***calling it*** a lease.

If that's what you're doing, it's probably illegal.

What's a lease?

The legal definition of a lease is ***not***

"a form with the word 'lease' at the top."

In most questions, the law values ***substance over form***. If your document "walks like a mortgage, talks like a mortgage, and associates with mortgages, it's a mortgage," in the eyes of the law. . .no matter what form you use.

Forget law for a minute. Just tell me in your own words what a lease is. I suspect you'd say something like this.

"A lease is an arrangement in which a tenant gets to use someone else's property in return for rent. When the specified period is over, the owner gets the property back."

Fine. Now let's say I own a house. I could get $675 a month rent for it if I wanted to. Suppose I tell you that you can move in and live there for twenty years if you pay me rent of one dollar per year. Is that a lease?

I suspect you'd regard that as more of a ***gift*** than a lease. So would the IRS and the courts. So you have to add to your definition of a lease the requirement that the rent amount bear a ***reasonable resemblance to the fair market rental value*** of the property. Adding that to your definition we get

"A lease is an arrangement in which a tenant gets to use someone else's property in return for fair market rent. When the specified period is over, the owner gets the property back."

Lease option

Let's combine the lease with an option. . .a common arrangement. Suppose the house I just mentioned is worth $100,000. It has an existing mortgage of $50,000 at 9% with monthly payments of $442.54. You, the buyer, would like to take over that loan. But, alas, it contains a due-on-sale clause.

But clever fellows that we are we hit upon a way to get around the due-on-sale clause. A lease option. I will lease you the property for $442.54 a month. The term of the lease will be the same as the number of years left on the loan. You will give me a $50,000 leasing fee up front. And you have the option to buy the property for one dollar at the end of the lease.

Is that a lease?

It ***looks*** like a sale subject to the existing mortgage, doesn't it? Since it looks like a mortgage, it ***is*** a mortgage. . .in the eyes of the law.

Just as rent must be at fair market rental value, so must option prices bear some reasonable resemblance to the market value of the property. . .at least as well as the parties were able to determine that value when they signed the option.

What do you think the chances are that my property will be worth one dollar 23 years from now? That's about what the IRS and judges think, too.

They would also ask why I rented you the property for almost $200 a month less than market rental. And they would want to know why you the tenant were willing to pay a $50,000 leasing fee when the going rate was in the zero to $200 range.

In other words, the IRS and judges aren't stupid. Nor does the law slavishly follow the words people put on paper. Your deal will be taxed according to the "walks-talks-associates" formula.

If it walks like a lease, talks like a lease, and associates with leases, it'll be taxed as a lease. Otherwise, it's a mortgage, gift, or whatever it ***does*** walk like, talk like, and associate with.

Miscellaneous finance/tax questions

Q: "Are points deductible?"

A: On your principal residence, yes. As long as charging points is an "established business practice" in your area and the amount is no more than usual and it's for purchase or improvement.

But points you pay to buy any other kind of property are ***not*** deductible. You have to amortize them over the life of the loan.

When a ***seller*** pays points, he can deduct them from his gross sale price to get his net sale price. That would reduce his capital gain. But he can***not*** deduct the points as an expense.

Q: "Can you deduct prepaid interest?"

A: No. Amortize it over the life of the loan.

Q: "Can you deduct a prepayment penalty?"

A: Yes. It's deductible as interest in the year you pay it. Doesn't matter whether it's your principal residence or not.

Q: "Can you deduct the fees you pay to get a loan?"

A: No. Amortize them over the life of the loan.

Summary on tax ramifications of real estate finance

The typical "creative" finance book or seminar is abysmal when it comes to telling you about tax ramifications. I have tried to correct that problem here.

But don't go gonzo in the other direction. In other words, don't run around structuring deals as if tax avoidance were the be all and end all of existence. Tax avoidance is ***a factor***. Sometimes, an ***important*** factor. But rarely a ***decisive*** factor.

Tax ramifications are neither as unimportant as the typical "creative" finance pusher would let you believe...nor as all important as the typical tax avoidance pusher implies.

PART TWO:
LENDERS

5
Loan Sources

The following list covers just about every category of lender who might help a real estate investor.

- savings and loan
- mutual savings bank
- life insurance company
- commercial bank
- mortgage broker
- real estate broker
- individual
- credit unions
- real estate investment trust
- pension fund
- finance subsidiary of manufacturing firm
- fraternal association
- finance company
- second mortgage company

- venture capital firm
- factor
- trust fiduciary
- investment club
- endowment fund
- foundation
- investment banking firm
- title insurance company
- Federal Land Bank
- FHA and VA when other lenders not available
- pawnbroker
- employer

When you want to leave no stone unturned

That list is not meant to be used every time you need a loan. Rather use it when you are having trouble finding a loan. Use it when you want to leave no stone unturned. It's a list of virtually all the "stones" there are.

Where to locate them

That was a list of ***categories*** of lenders. Now here's a list of places to look to find the names of ***specific*** lenders.

- Yellow Pages under
  - Real Estate Loans
  - Banks
  - Credit Unions
  - Financing
  - Savings and Loan Associations
  - Pawnbrokers
  - Real Estate
  - Pension and Profit Sharing Plans
  - Factors
  - Title Companies

Look at the Yellow Pages both in the area where you live and the area where the property is located if different.

- Local newspaper classified under
  - Loans
  - Mortgages

Look at papers from both where you live and where the property is if different.

- *Wall Street Journal* (Friday "Real Estate Corner" under "Mortgages")

Get the regional edition for both where you live and where the property is if different.

- Display ads in trade journals:
  - *National Real Estate Investor*
  - *Real Estate Review*
  - *Southwest Real Estate News*
  - *Southeast Real Estate News*
  - *Real Estate Forum*
  - *Buildings*

- Directories for borrowers:
  - *Crittenden Directory Real Estate Financing* (subscription combined with weekly newsletter, quarterly updates to directory—500+ lenders in income property and residential development)
  - *Novick's Income Property Finance Report* (111 John Street, Penthouse, floor NY 10038 212-233-7360)
- Trade association directories:
  - U.S. League of Savings Associations
  - American Bankers Association
  - Mortgage Bankers Association
  - American Conference of Real Estate Investment Trusts
  - National Association of Real Estate Investment Trusts
  - United Mortgage Bankers of America
  - Credit Union National Association, Inc.
  - National Association of Federal Credit Unions
- Recently closed transactions reports

Most metropolitan areas have a company which produces weekly or monthly reports on transactions which recently closed. One that I'm familiar with is DRESCO. DRESCO publishes the *Roddy Report* in Austin, Dallas, Denver, Miami, and San Antonio. The *Roddy Report* lists transfers of development land and income properties. In the Dallas *Roddy Report*, one column is labelled "AMT OF D/T PAYABLE TO." Which means amount of deed of trust (mortgage) and to whom payable. To whom payable is the lender.

So lenders are often coy about what they're doing. But when they make mortgage loans, they insist that the mortgage be recorded. That reveals it to the public...or at least to those who pore over the deed and mortgage recordings to compile reports like the *Roddy Report*.

So these transaction reports show who, if anyone, is making what loans at present.

Your area and property type

Lenders generally restrict themselves to one or a few ***property types*** and one ***geographic area***. If the loan you want is over $1,000,000 to $1,500,000, there are many lenders who will lend anywhere in the U.S.

So the starting point for finding a lender is to find out which lenders make loans on the property type you have in the location you have it.

Usually no mystery

Usually, there's no mystery to finding a lender. In the typical single-family rental house deal, the agent points you toward the lender they use most often. The agent and the lender work together constantly. So the agent can predict fairly accurately whether your loan will be approved before you even fill out the application.

A little digging can help sometimes. I bought my first duplex in 1969. The agent pointed me toward their favorite savings and loan. But I wanted no prepayment penalty. That particular savings and loan had prepayment penalties.

The agent checked with one other savings and loan. Then they told me I'd have to accept a prepayment penalty because they couldn't find a lender without one.

My mother was in the mortgage business at the time. She made a few calls and easily turned up a lender who agreed to make the loan with no prepayment penalty.

LESSON LEARNED: Shop around.

You've heard that many times regarding loans. But it, like many other finance lessons, bears repeating.

Loan source opportunities

Several of the early purchases I made were the result of pouncing on finance opportunities. I bought one duplex on a 7 1/4% VA no money down loan. That's noteworthy because at that particular time, the fall of 1973, the market rate was above 8%, the New Jersey usury limit was 8%, and FHA's charter had expired and Congress failed to renew it for several months. In other words, for a month or two, VA buyers were the ***only*** ones who could get loans.

I also pounced on a brief "window" of conventional money also in the fall of 1973. And I later bought two homes, each time pouncing on "windows" of especially favorable financing.

The lenders in these cases were traditional lenders—savings and loans, mortgage companies, and banks. The only unusual aspect of the transactions were that the terms were significantly more favorable than were available before or after the month or so when I got the loans.

They made it once

My fifth property was a beat-up 12-unit apartment building. Most savings and loans don't make loans on beat-up 12-units. So I went to the savings and loan which had the existing loan. They also had a relationship with the seller and he promised them he'd put the sale proceeds in their s & l if they make me the loan I needed. They did.

Work for a lender

My seventh property was a single-family house for my wife and I to live in. We were generally thinking about buying, but not yet. My wife worked for a large bank at the time.

Then interest rates began to increase dramatically. But her employer had a special low rate for employees. She heard through the grapevine that the employee ceiling would be lifted soon. So we immediately looked for and found a house. We beat the lifting of the employee ceiling by only a day or two. And saved a substantial amount of money each year as a result.

Real estate agents aren't the only ones whose inside knowledge helps them leap through temporarily open "windows" of favorable finance terms. Employees of other real estate related firms also benefit.

What am I supposed to do, work for a lender?

You might think that's not very helpful. On the grounds that you can't go work for a lender. You might think again on that. Especially if you're young.

The six year plan

I entered civilian life with the following plan. I was going to work two years in real estate brokerage, two years in real estate management, and two years in real estate finance. My goal was simply to be an investor. I had to work somewhere. And I felt that six year program would be excellent preparation for my ***real*** career as an investor.

It was a good plan. I ended up only doing the first three years. Then I went to Harvard Business School. I excused myself from working two years as a lender, because I married a banker.

Since you and/or your spouse have to work somewhere, consider working for a real estate lender for several reasons:

- you'll learn about real estate finance
- inside information on financing opportunities
- favorable employee loan benefits

Savings and loans

Savings and loans have traditionally been the number one source of mortgage money. In March of 1983, for example, s & ls loaned $5,877,000,000 on one to four-family homes. That was 41% of the $14,216,000,000 total. Mortgage companies were second largest with $3,879,000,000 (27%).

Figure 14

Where Home Mortgage Money Came From In March 1983

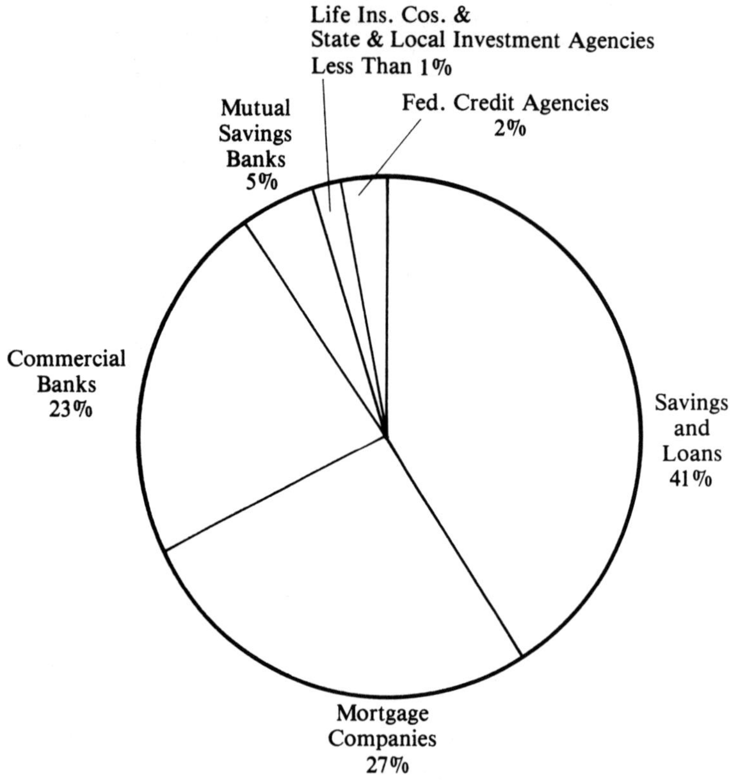

Source: HUD   1 to 4 Family Structures Only

Savings and loans are also the main construction lenders. In March of 1983 they had 50% of that market.

Figure 15

Where Construction Money Comes From

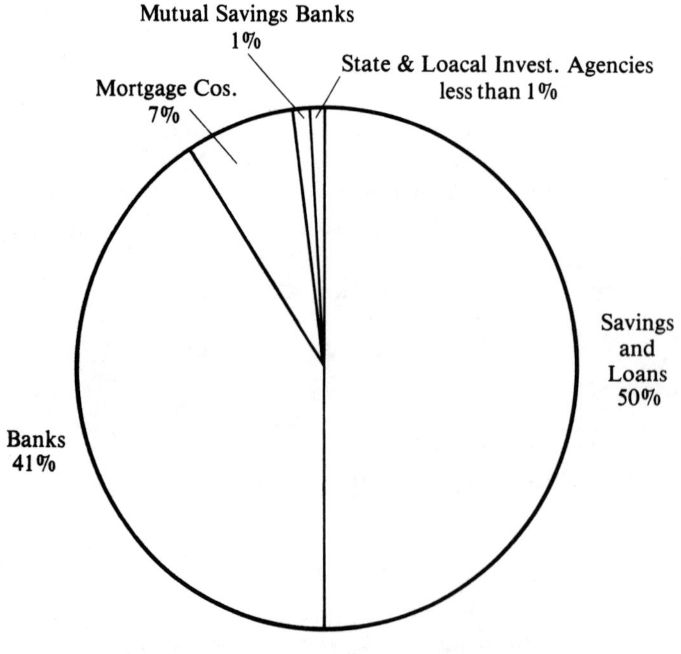

Source: HUD   1 to 4 Family Structures Only

Savings and loans made 52% of the apartment building mortgage loans in March of '83.

Figure 16

Where Apartment Mortgages Come From

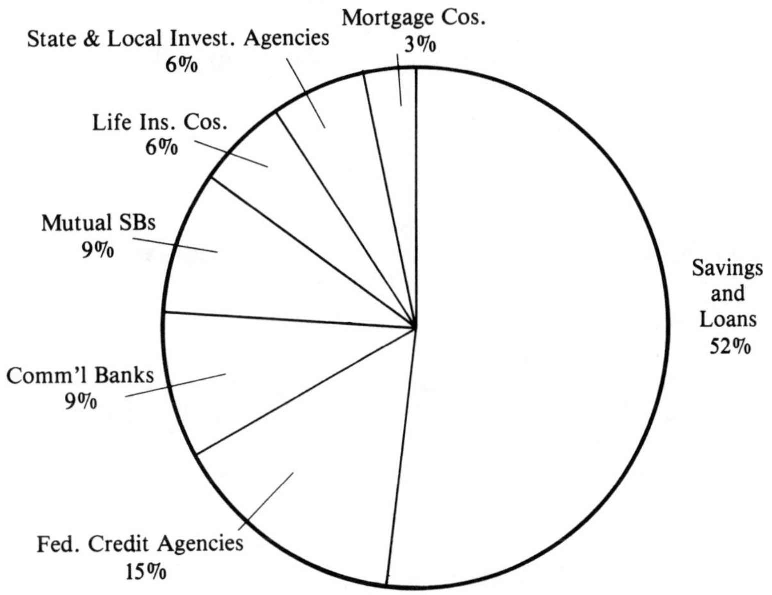

Source: HUD Multi-Family Residential

Only on commercial mortgages (non-residential) do the s & ls come in second. . .to the commercial banks.

Figure 17

Where Commercial Mortgage Money Comes From

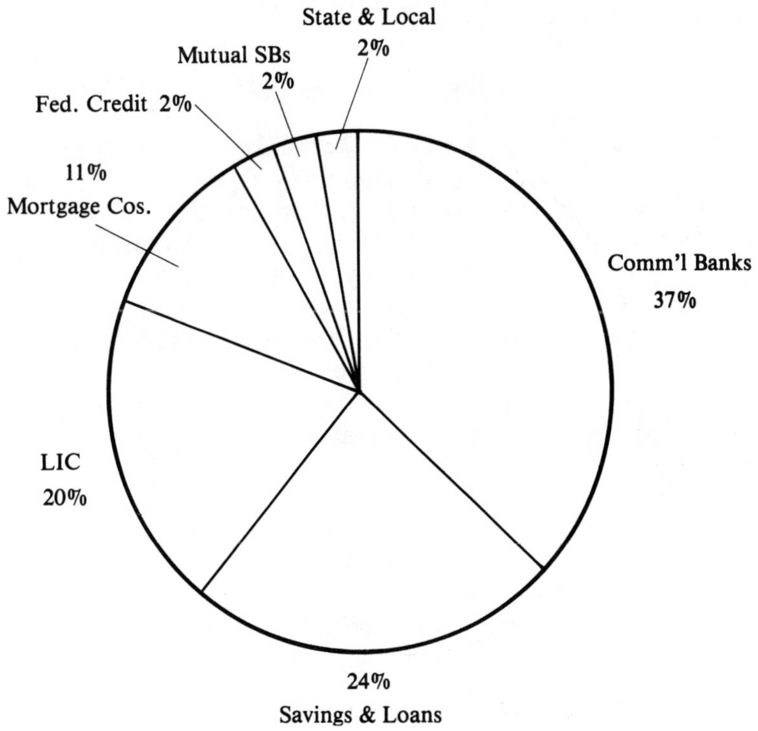

Deregulation

Deposit institutions have been, and continue to be, deregulated. It used to be that savings and loans were ***required by law*** to put most of their deposits into home mortgages.

The Garn-St. Germain Depository Institutions Act of 1982 eliminated loan-to-value ratio ceilings on residential loans. It also allowed deposit institutions to put up to 40% of their assets into *non*-residential mortgages. And up to 30% into ***consumer loans***. And up to 10% into ***loans to businesses*** (starting in '84).

Furthermore, previous laws have allowed more or less unfettered competition for deposits.

In transition

All of which labels the savings and loan industry as one ***in transition***. That makes it hard to say where it's going to end up. I suspect that s & ls will continue to specialize in home mortgages. . .partly because the law still requires it to an extent. . .and partly out of habit.

In the longer run, I suspect deregulation will result in s & ls behaving more like banks. That does not mean there will be less mortgage money, however. While s & ls will behave more like banks, banks will behave more like s & ls.

They can't ***both*** make ***only*** consumer and business loans. The market for consumer and business loans is only so big. The loan "pie" will always be made up of roughly the same pieces as now. Those who favor deregulation call it a "level playing field" move. And level is what will probably happen to the mortgage market share. Instead of one type of lender dominating, each type will have a similar market share of each loan category.

I can't make a table of lender characteristics

I would love to make a table showing the characteristics. I would love to. . .but I can't. I've tried. So have many others. But there are too many exceptions to whatever rules you use.

For example, there's a temptation to say that s & ls make single-family home mortgages, life insurance companies make big commercial mortgage loans, and so forth. Unfortunately, it's not that simple.

Constant change, many exceptions

Not only is the deposit industry in a transition, market interest rates constantly change which makes the criteria lenders use change on a daily basis. The lender who wouldn't make loans on non-owner-occupied property last week may do so this week. The guy at ABC Savings and Loan with a hang-up against master-metered apartment buildings may have retired so now that lender will consider them. And so it goes.

You say you want to know what loans an s & l will make? I can only respond by asking you, "Which s & l? When? And under what circumstances."

Football players and coaches are fond of saying, "On any given day, any team in this league can beat any other team." By the same token, at one time or another, any savings and loan you want to name has probably made any kind of loan you want to name. There may have been some special circumstances on the unusual loans. . .but they made them just the same.

So I can't neatly categorize any type of lender. That information is available only from your local lenders. And its accuracy lasts about as long as fresh fish.

You got a property you want to finance?

Get on the telephone and find out what's available.

Mutual savings banks

Mutuals are common in New York state and Massachusetts. Most real estate finance books spend space analyzing the differences between mutuals and savings and loans. And monks used to argue about the number of angels that could stand on the head of a pin. Suffice it to say that mutuals are like s & ls. And with deregulation, they'll be even more so.

Life insurance companies

Life insurance companies get their loan money from whole life policies. A whole life insurance policy is one in which a cash value builds up over the years.

The other kind of life insurance is term insurance. Term has no cash value. And it costs a lot less.

Whole life policies are less popular than they used to be. Reasons include:

- increased prevalence of pension plans
- increased pension benefits
- increased social security benefits
- increased home equities
- decreased purchasing power due to inflation
- increased sophistication regarding returns
- money market funds

But the life insurance companies still have a bunch of money to invest. Life companies tend to favor multi-million dollar income properties. They'll typically invest in any metropolitan area although they're usually averse to small isolated towns. Some prefer their region or side of the Mississippi. They often work through correspondents...mortgage bankers and brokers in the area where the property is.

Because they analyze deals on a case by base basis, life insurance companies are more "creative." That is the terms they offer vary with the market. During tight money, they often demand ***equity kickers*** (a share in the increased rents and increased income of the property). When money is plentiful, they offer fixed rate loans on longer and longer terms. Single-family home mortgage lenders, on the other hand, tend to stick with a few standardized mortgage types and change slowly.

Commercial banks

I am originally from southern New Jersey. I worked there as a real estate salesman for two years. During that time, I never heard of a commercial bank making a permanent mortgage loan (construction loans, yes, but not permanent loans). Our loans came from savings and loans and mortgage companies.

I now live in northern California. I am writing this in a home mortgaged to a commercial bank. My old house had a loan from a commercial bank. And the builder who built my current house arranged a seven-month blanket second on my current home's lot and my old home...also from a commercial bank.

So the importance of commercial banks as permanent mortgage lenders varies around the country. I don't know why, but it does. You can find out whether they are active lenders in your area in a one minute phone call to a local real estate agency.

Other than that geographical variation, I see no great difference between banks and savings and loans when it comes to home mortgages.

Mortgage brokers

Mortgage brokers provide processing expertise. As a result, they tend to specialize in mortgages which require more than ordinary processing efforts. That would include ***insured mortgages***, both FHA/VA and private mortgage insurance. And it includes life insurance company income property loans.

Mortgage brokers also act as a sort of "manufacturer's rep." Some lenders are too small to have their own soliciting, underwriting, and servicing staffs. (Underwriting means checking out the borrower and property to make sure the risk is acceptable. Servicing is collecting the payments and paying the taxes and insurance after the loan is made.) A rich individual would be an example. These lenders "subcontract" the solicitation and underwriting to mortgage brokers.

Certified Mortgage Banker

The Mortgage Bankers Association of America awards a professional designation—CMB or Certified Mortgage Banker. Professional designations usually require advanced study and experience. I have generally been impressed with those who hold professional designations. All other things being equal, you should go to a CMB when you need a mortgage broker.

Higher fees

Mortgage brokers are middlemen. They expect to be paid for what they do. As a result, you usually pay more in fees for a loan you get through a mortgage broker than you do for a loan you get direct from a lender.

That's not to say they don't earn their fees. As a general rule, they do.

A mortgage broker's role is like a real estate broker's. But instead of finding a buyer for your real estate, he finds a buyer for your loan. If you can sell your property on a for sale by owner basis, and not sell it for much less than a broker could have got, you'll do better. Same goes for selling your mortgage.

But you'll do some of the work the broker would have done. And avoiding a big discount over what a broker could have obtained is easier said than done. . . in both property sales and mortgage lending.

Real estate brokers

Real estate brokers make two categories of loans:

- taking all or part of commission in the form of a note and
- acting as a mortgage broker.

Brokers hate taking back a note for all or part of their commission. But they often do. Usually they will refuse to agree to such a thing at the listing stage. But often they will agree at the final stage of negotiation.

When the deal is within their grasp, but the parties are a little bit apart, brokers often reluctantly agree to become lenders. Especially when the broker is running back and forth between the parties asking each to give. When they finally turn to the broker and say, "What about ***you***? How much are you willing to give? You're making money on this deal, too."

What's good for the goose. . .

When mortgage money is expensive, real estate agents persuade a lot of sellers to take back below-market rate loans for part of their equity. I have advised investors to make the agent take the same medicine.

If the agent convinces you to take, say, half of your equity in the form of a seven year, 10% interest only mortgage, you pay him his commission on exactly the same terms. . . half in the form of a seven year, 10% interest only mortgage.

Furthermore, your obligation to make your monthly payments and balloon payment to the real estate agent should be ***contingent*** on your receiving the same payments from the guy who bought your property. After all, your obligation to pay the commission in cash is contingent on the deal closing. So if you have to wait on the buyer for part of your money in an installment sale, the agent also should have to wait on that same buyer.

Wait til final negotiations

I recommended this course of action in a newsletter I used to write for. One reader told me he tried to list a property with several real estate companies on those terms and they all refused.

I'd like to hear their explanation of why they refuse to take back a loan but recommend that their clients do so. I mean what's all this about what a great investment it is? If taking back a loan is such a great idea, why won't the brokers do it?

The solution is to agree to pay a cash commission as usual in the listing agreement. But don't say in the listing agreement that you'll take back a loan. Then when the agent tries to switch you to taking back a loan, you tell him to do the same. With the commission in sight, and his urging you to take back a loan having occurred seconds before, I suspect he'll find it harder to be Mr. Tough Guy.

What's good for the client is good for the Realtor.

Real estate agents as mortgage brokers

Individuals with money to lend sometimes approach real estate brokers. They set up an informal relationship. The selling broker on the first property I bought made occasional second mortgage loans for a single man. Somewhere along the line, he had met this man, impressed him, and become his mortgage broker.

Relationships with local lenders

Real estate brokers also often have more subtle but possibly very important relationships with institutional lenders. Lenders like banks and savings and loans use real estate brokers somewhat the way life insurance companies use mortgage brokers...as solicitors.

When money is plentiful, the lender relies on real estate brokers to channel the borrowers their way. And when money is scarce, the brokers rely on the lenders to help ***them***. Some real estate brokers have very special relationships with important local lenders. When things are tough, working with such real estate brokers can mean the difference between getting the loan and not getting it.

The difference between getting the loan and not

The broker who owned the company where I was a salesman often told how he could get mortgages during the '70 money crunch because of his relationship with a certain big savings and loan. It got to the point where other companies were steering their buyers to our listings because they knew if anyone could get financing, we could.

I think the existence of, and importance of, special relationships between real estate brokers and local lenders is ***the best kept secret in real estate finance.***

How do you find such real estate brokers? The lenders will rarely tell you. Lenders talk like diplomats. The best way to find such brokers is deal with the ***most successful*** brokerage companies. Because it's hard to become a successful real estate agent ***without*** establishing such relationships.

Individuals

As I've said, some individuals invest in mortgages through brokers. Some advertise in the newspaper. Other than answering those ads and calling the brokers, I wouldn't recommend that you do anything to seek out individual lenders.

The biggest category of individual lenders is ***sellers.***

Credit unions

My car insurance company was USAA. USAA only insures military and state department officers. Plus they have a once a member, always a member policy. Their motto is "Serving you best because we know you better."

Credit unions operate on the same principle.

You probably know that credit unions are generally cheaper than other lenders. But you may not know why.

Lending and insurance are similar industries. Both have underwriters. An underwriter's job is to evaluate risk. Insurance companies do it with actuaries and actuarial tables. Those tables use experience to forecast future losses.

USAA can be a little cheaper on car insurance than most companies because of the homogeneous nature of their policyholders. Military and state department officers have a more narrow claims history and probability of future claims than the population in general. So USAA can forecast its claims more accurately than most insurors. Furthermore, it has fewer claims.

The same is true for credit union loan losses. Credit unions are made up of employees or members of an organization. As a result, they tend to be somewhat homogeneous. That, in turn, means they can forecast their losses more easily and they typically have fewer loan losses than a bank or other lender would. So they can afford to charge less.

By borrowing from a credit union, you avoid paying the "penalty" which the many good borrowers pay for the sins of the few bad borrowers at other institutional lenders. So as a general rule, if the loan you need is available from a credit union, you'll probably do better there.

Federal credit unions have been allowed to make mortgage loans since April 1977. State chartered credit unions have been able to do so even longer. Unfortunately, credit unions don't make many mortgage loans. But they do make loans for cars and other similar purposes. Since ***all*** your loans appear on your balance sheet, they are all related to your real estate investments.

Real estate investment trusts

There are three kinds of real estate investment trust (REIT):

- equity
- long-term mortgage
- short-term mortgage

Equity REITs buy property. They are of no interest in a finance book. But the short- and long-term mortgage REITs are your basic mortgage lenders.

REITs are hard to categorize. There aren't a great many of them. But what they lack in numbers they make up for in diversity. There's a REIT doing virtually every kind of real estate lending.

Consolidated Capital

Consolidated Capital, for example, has three REITs. They make income property second mortgages, wraparounds, and such. Their minimum is relatively low—$300,000 last I heard. And they claim to be able to close in seven days. Plus they are willing to be "creative."

Consolidated Capital started as a real estate syndication outfit. They buy and manage income properties around the country. So they are real estate investors and claim to be able to understand real estate investors' needs better than lenders who are just lenders.

One manifestation of this is that they often make loans in which part of the interest accrues. As a result, your payments would be like those on a 12% mortgage even though Con Cap's ***yield*** would be higher. ***Much*** higher, actually. That's one of the ***dis***advantages of Con Cap. They ain't cheap.

Other REITs make construction loans, land development loans, subordinated sale-leasebacks, long-term permanents and so forth.

Where to find REITs

The REITs who make loans generally advertise in the same places as other mortgage lenders. Con Cap, for example, usually has an ad in the Friday *Wall Street Journal.* But if you're in a no-stone-unturned mode, you may want to get a directory of REITs. Write the National Association of Real Estate Investment Trusts, 1101 17th Street, N.W., Washington, DC 20036.

Pension funds

Pension funds have a lot of money. As a result, they are the subject of much talk in the real estate industry. But the fact that they have a lot of money doesn't mean they're going to lend any of it to you.

The head construction lender of a major bank said pension fund trustees were horrible people to deal with. He was referring to their extreme conservatism.

Pension funds come under the Employment Retirement Income Security Act of 1974 (ERISA). In twenty-five words or less, ERISA says that any pension fund trustee who isn't "prudent" is in big trouble. I read one quote from a pension fund trustee who said that the ***return*** you got didn't matter as long as you were "prudent."

Conservative and cheap

So pension fund trustees are the kinds of guys who were suspenders ***and*** a belt.

Only time I've ever encountered them in the marketplace is when I contracted to have my home built. The builder had a commitment from a pension fund. It was for loans of up to $250,000 on single-family homes with a loan-to-value limit of 60% and a favorable interest rate. The 60% loan-to-value limit is suspenders and belt conservatism; the favorable rate, the price the pension fund has to pay to get people to accept the 60% loan-to-value limit. Like the man said, they care more about prudence than yield.

That suggests that you turn to a pension fund for a loan when the loan-to-value ratio or other aspect of the lender's risk is low. Because pension funds are one of the few lenders who place such a high premium on safety that they would give you credit for safety above and beyond the norm. Most lenders charge the same for 80% loan-to-value ratio loans as they do for 60%.

I presume the pension funds generally make their loans through intermediaries like life insurance companies. I have never seen a pension fund ad.

Finance subsidiaries of big corporations

Finance subsidiaries are very interesting lenders. Also relatively new. Westinghouse Credit Corporation's Real Estate Group is one. General Electric Credit Corporation (GECC) is another.

Like Consolidated Capital, these finance subsidiaries claim to be willing to do "creative" loans. Last time I checked, GECC was doing all sorts of off the wall stuff. Like basing the loan-to-value on what the rents on a to-be-acquired building would be ***after*** a projected rent increase, condo conversion loans based on the post conversion value, lending against receivables on recreational lots, hospital loans.

The finance subsidiaries I'm familiar with tend to prefer the bigger loans—a million dollars or more. Although in the lending business it seems there's always an exception.

How do you find these guys? Ads. They advertise in the major real estate publications like *National Real Estate Investor*. They're also listed in the *Crittenden Finance Directory*.

Fraternal associations

Fraternal associations are a tiny segment of the market. To find out what, if any, loans are available, contact the fraternal associations you're a member of and ask them. Don't expect to find commercial wraparounds or any of that. Expect them to be somewhat like credit unions if they make loans at all.

Finance companies

Finance companies used to be makers of small consumer loans only. Nowadays, they, too have minimums. And they like to make home equity loans—second mortgages on homes. Beneficial Finance Corporation, for example, advertises in my Yellow Pages that they make first and second mortgages of from $5,000 to $200,000. They also make personal loans and loans secured by personal property as low as $500. The interest rate gets better the more you borrow.

Finance companies are known for high rates. And there's a connotation of financial trouble to dealing with them. While that may be true of some of their customers, there's nothing wrong with finance companies *per se*. While their rates may be high, they also loan on small amounts. The difference between a 14% rate and a 20% rate is 6%. But on a $50,000 loan, that's only $3,000 a year.

But finance companies move faster than deposit institutions. They'll make small loans that other lenders won't. And they typically have lower front end fees. Some make house calls.

In the San Francisco Yellow Pages, I find companies under "Loans" who will

- make ***third*** mortgages
- approve loans in ***two days***
- take applications ***by phone***
- loan on ***income property***
- buy existing mortgages
- make loans with ***no prepayment penalty***
- make ***assumable*** loans
- make loans for ***any purpose***
- loan against existing mortgages you own

Of course, finance companies are also known for making loans to those with bad credit. I hope you don't need that particular aspect of finance companies. But if you do, it's available.

Don't let the negative reputation of finance companies throw you off. A finance company may well be the ***best choice*** of a lender if your situation requires what they do best.

Second mortgage company

A second mortgage company is just a specialized version of a finance company. You find them through the Yellow Pages or through newspaper ads.

Venture capital firm

I have never heard of a venture capital firm making a real estate investment loan. They want to get a piece of the action in some hot company of the future. Some make loans; others, *convertible loans*. Convertible means a loan which can be converted into equity at some future date.

But harking back to my statement that ***all*** the loans on your balance sheet are related to your investments, venture capital is relevant.

You might use venture capital if you have your own business. . .and that business might increase dramatically in value. To the extent that venture capital frees up capital for your real estate investments, it is, in effect, real estate finance.

Venture capital is a whole 'nother subject. You could write a book on venture capital alone. Several people have:

- *Up Front Financing* 1982 by A. David Silver (Ronald Press, 605 Third Avenue, New York, NY 10158)
- *How To Raise Venture Capital* 1981 by Stanley Pratt et al (Scribners)
- *Where The Money Is And How To Get It* 1980 by Ted Nicholas (Enterprise Publishing, Inc., 725 Market Street, Wilmington, DE 19801)
- *Guide To Venture Capital Sources* 1982 by Stanley Pratt (Prentice-Hall, Inc.)

The National Association of Small Business Investment Companies, 512 Washington Building, N.W., Washington, DC 20005 can give you information on venture capital.

Shrewd guys

A lot of screwballs think their ideas for new businesses warrant a venture capital firm putting up a million or two. They're whistling Dixie.

Venture capitalists are probably the shrewdest money people you'll ever run into. They usually have highly ***educated*** people on the staff. . .a lot of my Harvard Business School classmates work for venture capital firms. Plus they have ***experienced*** people. Often a successful entrepreneur or two. Furthermore, the experienced venture capitalists have seen a lot of would-be Henry Fords come and go. They will not be dazzled by your footwork.

So if you plan to pitch a venture capital firm, you'd better have your act together. Not only a sound idea, but also evidence that you can get things done, know how to finance growth, and so forth. They also like to see total dedication so it'll be hard to invest in real estate on the side. And any real estate you own will draw the question, "Why aren't you getting the money you need by selling that?"

Factors

Like venture capitalists, factors are not real estate lenders. But as with venture capitalists, any source of money you find may help you with your real estate investments.

Factors purchase accounts receivable. They typically also lend money against accounts receivable. If you have a business, you usually have accounts receivable. You provide a product or service, then send the buyer an invoice. After thirty days or so, he pays. . . or at least you ***hope*** he pays.

By using a factor, you

- get the money ***now*** instead of later
- don't worry about nonpayment.

Of course, factors don't do this for free. They charge a percent or three for doing a credit-check on the buyer. And they charge interest on the money during the period when you've been paid but they haven't.

Some businessmen use factors because they are small and don't want to establish a credit department. By using a factor, they subcontract the credit checking out.

Other businessmen use factors for cash flow. They want to get paid ***quicker***, even if they get ***less*** because of the interest and credit-check commission.

You find factors in the Yellow Pages under "Factors."

Trusts

Bank trust departments hold money for other people. While they hold it, they're supposed to earn a decent return on it. In some cases, the trustee feels real estate loans are an appropriate investment.

I have never run into such a loan. But I am assured they are made. Intermediaries like mortgage brokers probably do part of that business. And if you're in a no-stones-unturned mode looking for a loan, you might call all the trust departments in your area. Most banks have them.

Investment clubs

You've probably heard of investment clubs which invest in the stock market. Well why not invest in mortgages instead. . . or in addition to stocks? Some do.

They represent an infinitesimal part of the mortgage market. But in keeping with the no-stone-unturned approach. . . .

The National Association of Investment Clubs, 1515 East Eleven Mile Road, Royal Oak, MI 48068 may be able to help. I would expect the lending clubs would probably run newspaper ads or deal through intermediaries like mortgage companies or real estate brokers.

Endowment funds

An endowment is a large lump of money given to some on-going institution like a college. The institution is supposed to live off the income from the funds investments. Sometimes the managers of such funds invest in mortgages.

Find through intermediaries like mortgage brokers. . . or as a last resort, call endowment fund managers at colleges, hospitals, and so forth.

Foundations

Foundations are charitable organizations based on a lump of money given by a philanthropist. They have two functions:

- do good
- do well

They give away money to do good. They invest in order to have something to give away (and to pay their own salaries and pensions). In their investments, they expect to do well.

When I was at Harvard Business School, I met one of my fellow alumni who was in charge of investing the money of one of the nation's most famous foundations. When I commented that he seemed awfully return-oriented for someone who worked for a do-gooder outfit he told me he worked for the do-well side of the organization. That the do-gooders had instructed him to earn the maximum prudent return. So he was your basic real estate buyer/lender.

Investment banking firms

Investment banking firms are Wall Street. Companies like Merrill Lynch, E.F. Hutton, etc. They have real estate finance subsidiaries. For example, Morgan Stanley & Company's real estate subsidiary is Brooks Harvey & Co., Inc. which bills itself as offering "Creative Financing and Counseling For Major Real Estate Projects." Generally they do only multimillion dollar deals.

They advertise in trade journals like ***National Real estate Investor*** and they are listed in Crittenden's Directory. In the June 1983 issue of NREI, Sonnenblick-Goldman Corp. (subsidiary of Lehman Brothers Kuhn Loeb Incorporated) ran an ad bragging about their arranging a $35,000,000 second mortgage on a Manhattan office building.

The BIG time

One word of warning. The world is full of young men and women who want to do BIG deals. They salivate over the idea of a $35,000,000 mortgage. Many of these young people have concluded that the only difference between the guys who do the $35,000,000 deals and the guys who do the $35,000 deals is ***guts***. Having the moxie to go to New York City in your best suit and drop in on the folks at Brooks Harvey.

Guts ***is*** one of the things that separates the men from the boys. But it's ***only*** one of the things. You also need a proven track record on deals which bear some resemblance to the one you want to do.

So don't embarrass yourself and me by wandering into an investment banking firm asking for a loan a thousand times bigger than any you've ever obtained before. . .saying, "I read in this real estate finance book that you guys make $35,000,000 loans. That's good because I want one."

Title companies

I have ***heard*** that title companies sometimes make loans. Never saw one first hand though. You know where to find them.

Federal Land Bank

The Federal Land Banks are supervised by the Farm Credit Administration, a federal government agency. They make loans on farm or ranch land. . .which is unusual. Few lenders will loan on raw land.

Federal Land Banks will lend up to 85% of value for up to 35 years. But their appraisals are said to be conservative.

Since this is a book for real estate investors, not farmers, you probably would not have occasion to use a federal land bank. I include it only in the interest of thoroughness. . .just in case you find yourself involved with farm or ranch land.

FHA and VA

Generally speaking, the FHA and VA do not ***make*** loans. They only ***insure*** loans made by others.

But they ***will*** actually make loans when other lenders are not available.

Pawnbrokers

Most people consider pawnbrokers to be a joke. I saw a cartoon once in which an executive trying to impress a visitor told his secretary to, "Get my broker on the phone." To which she replied, "Stock or pawn?"

I have never used a pawnbroker, But I see nothing wrong with them *per se*. They loan money against small items of personal property. No other lenders do that. If you need fast cash, and you have a bunch of small items of personal property which you're willing to pledge as security, go to a pawnbroker.

As is the case with almost every other lender, they're not Santa Claus. But they may still be your best alternative in some situations.

It's a mistake to rule out ***any*** category of lender because of image. There's nothing wrong with accepting small items of personal property as security for a loan. Nor is there anything wrong with borrowing against such property. The fact that pawnbrokers are often used by people who don't know how to manage their money is irrelevant.

Employer

You are far more knowledgeable than I about whether your employer will lend you the money you want. All I want to do here is ***remind*** you that employers often make real estate loans.

Computerized mortgage guides

In today's Sunday real estate section of the *San Francisco Examiner* I read about a new service called a computerized mortgage guide. It is a company which gathers up-to-the-minute information on which lenders are making which loans on what terms.

Sounds like a great idea. Now, the only way to find out is to call all the lenders in the area. In some areas, there are already ***printed*** versions of this idea. But they're usually out of date and not as easily searched as a computerized list would be.

First Boston's Shelternet is the biggest computer mortgage network. Planning Research Corp. of McLean, VA has another called "Loan Express." Another is CompuFund, Inc. of Dublin, CA. The National Association of Realtors plans a mortgage network called Rennie Mae.

6
How Lenders Decide Whether To Say Yes

DMP, DMU

There are two aspects to a lender's decision on your loan application:

- DMP
- DMU

DMP stands for the Decision Making Process. DMU for Decision Making Unit.

The decision making ***process*** for buying a pack of gum is usually that you see it next to the cash register and decide on impulse to buy it. The decision making process for buying new living room furniture is usually that you and your spouse and perhaps a parent or other adviser visit a number of furniture stores, agonize over the decision for a while, then buy.

The decision making ***unit*** for the gum is you. The decision making unit for the living room furniture is you, your spouse, and any advisers you use.

Lenders' processes and units vary, too. Depending upon the loan and lender, the unit may be an individual...or a committee. The process may be just a credit check...or pages of application and appraisal materials.

The loan officer

In almost all cases, you deal with a loan officer. There are all kinds. Beginners. Seasoned veterans. Competent. Incompetent.

Since investors usually go hat-in-hand to the loan officer, concerned about what the officer will think of them, they're often blind to the officer's shortcomings. Too self-conscious of their own shortcomings to notice.

Process-oriented

Most real estate investors don't like real estate loan officers. It's not just because the loan officers sometimes say, "No."

Loan officers and real estate investors are very different kinds of people. Real estate investors are entrepreneurs. They are ***goal-oriented.*** Optimistic. They take risks, overcome myriad obstacles, persist in the face of discouragement, drive to achieve big success.

Loan officers, on the other hand, prefer a set routine. They want someone to tell them, "Here's the policy manual that says how we do things. Read it and follow it." In his book *The Bankers*, Martin Mayer told the story of a banker who was retiring a few years ago. At his retirement dinner, someone asked what was the biggest change he had seen in banking in his forty years in it. He thought a minute and said, "Air-conditioning."

Loan officers are generally risk averse. One of the main reasons they chose to work in the lending business was job security. They want to wear a suit, have a prestigious job, and get a gold watch when they retire. They recoil at the thought of taking the kinds of risks real estate investors take. They are pessimistic. They have limited goals.

"Give me your conservative, your methodical..."

The typical loan officer thinks the typical real estate investor is crazy. Always exaggerating his income and the property's prospects. Getting himself into deals where he's stretching to make the payments.

Loan officers wish they could make loans to people like themselves---conservative folks with "realistic" expectations for the future. Slow, methodical plodding types. Unfortunately, few, if any, loan applications come from such people. Seems that the loan officers have to deal with us kooky, hard-chargin', optimistic investors in order to make their loans.

"Creativity" versus policy

Being goal-oriented, investors will attack a problem twenty different ways, if necessary, to reach their goal. For the typical loan officer, the process ***is*** the goal. The investor's goal is to do the deal on good terms. The loan officer's goal is to fill out the forms the way it says in the manual.

When there's a mismatch between the manual and the investor's goal, the investor suggests a solution which attempts to give both the lender and the investor what they want. But the loan officer doesn't listen. "The manual doesn't allow that way of doing it," he says. "But don't you see that it gives you the same yield and safety as the way in the manual?" says the investor. "It's not in the manual," says the loan officer

That's difference between being goal-oriented and being process-oriented. If loan officers weren't working for the savings and loan or bank, they'd be working for the government or electric company.

The wealth gap

Loan officers get all the prestige they can eat. But not much else. It's not a high-paying job. The typical loan officer probably makes a salary in the $20,000 to $30,000 range...and has a net worth consisting of unspectacular home equity, a couple of cars, and some bank accounts.

Real estate investors, on the other hand, are either millionaires or plan to be. So on one side of the table you've got a millionaire of Christmas Present or Christmas Future. And on the other side, you've got Bob Cratchit.

Bob resents your money. You resent having to ask some nickel and dime wage slave to lend you more. You especially resent being ***turned down*** by some guy you could buy and sell a couple times over...because your application "wasn't strong enough!!"

Lending is an art

In spite of all that, the key to succeeding is to find a loan officer with whom you have rapport. Lending is an art, not a science.

Sure, you occasionally run across a lending formula. Every now and then you see one printed in a magazine. Sometimes lenders even print their formula in the paper so you can see if you'll qualify for a loan.

The occasional formula notwithstanding, loans are not made by formulas. Basically, if the lender's decision making unit likes you, you'll get the loan. Unless the loan you want is way out of line.

Rapport

If you have rapport with the loan officer, you have either won or half won the battle. You've won it if that officer is the entire decision making unit. You've half won it if he has to submit it to higher authority.

When the loan officer has to submit the loan to higher authority, ***two*** relationships are important. ***Your*** relationship with the officer. And ***his*** relationship with higher headquarters.

If the loan officer likes you, but higher headquarters doesn't like him, you'll have a tough time getting the loan. You'll succeed when the details of your deal and your personality mesh with the lender's current loan preferences and personalities.

How do you establish rapport?

Rapport is born not made. There's nothing you can do to create it if it's not already there. It's like the friendships you made in school and in the service. You liked some people and didn't like others. And the feeling was usually mutual. You didn't try to change the minds of those who didn't like you...or at least you shouldn't have.

Well, some of those people you didn't like in school or the army grew up to be loan officers. And there's no more point in trying to establish rapport with them now than there was then.

So rapport is more something you ***find*** than something you ***create***. In other words, you just keep looking until you find a loan officer with whom you have rapport.

Sometimes, that means going over someone's head for a loan. I know from both first-hand experience and observations of others that talking to someone else in a lending institution often gets a loan that was first turned down. It doesn't always work. But once you've been turned down, there's little harm in trying it.

Same thing applies to trying another institution. Many an applicant got nowhere at institution A but was warmly received down the street at institution B. Again, rapport was probably at least partly responsible.

So you should ***shop around*** when you're looking for a loan. I wish I could give you more original, more novel advice. But all I can do is to try to give you a better explanation than you've ever heard before as to ***why*** you should shop around.

Lender policy

Lenders ***do*** have policies. I don't want to overstate the rapport issue. If the loan you want doesn't fit the lender's current policy at all, they probably won't make it. That's not to say that policy is ironclad. It's not. And rapport is exactly the ingredient which dissolves policy obstacles.

But your time is better spent trying to get an apartment mortgage, for example, from a lender whose policy approves apartment mortgages then trying to get a non-apartment lender to make a policy exception for you. You should try to apply to a lender whose policy matches the loan you need. But when you can't find one, try to get an exception to policy from another lender.

The reasons for the policy

The main way to get an exception to policy is to find out the ***reasons*** for the policy. . . then show the lender how they can achieve those goals another way. For example, if the lender won't make a loan with a loan-to-value ratio of 85%, ask why.

The answer will probably be security. So you look in the security techniques section of this book and start offering alternative ways to achieve security. . . like mortgage insurance, a blanket mortgage, assignment of rents, a co-signer, a pledged savings account, etc., etc.

In the unlikely event you exhaust all the ways to provide additional security without finding one which satisfies the lender, try trading yield for security. That is offer to pay more points or a higher interest rate or a sooner balloon or whatever.

If, after trying every security and yield trick known to man you ***still*** don't get the loan, you're either talking to a blockhead or they flat don't want to give you a loan and the "policy" line was just a lie.

Matching loan to lender

Theoretically, you should be able to trade risk for reward. In fact, institutional lenders will rarely do that. Rather each institution has a risk/reward mix it likes and rarely deviates from. In order to trade risk for reward, you have to take your deal to a different category of lender.

For example, if your credit history is a little rough, banks generally will not lend money to you at any rate. But ***finance companies*** will. . . albeit at a higher interest rate.

There is also a ***"creativity"*** spectrum. Savings and loans are very ***un***creative. Some REITs and industrial credit companies are very creative. Generally, "creativity" requires either a ***big*** deal. . . so that the loan fees make extra study worthwhile. . . or a dumb lender. . . like a seller.

There's also a ***specialty*** spectrum. If the loan is at all oddball. . . like hotel, miniwarehouse, or single-purpose long-term credit leased property. . . you need to locate one of the few lenders which has decided to make such loans.

The better you ***match*** the deal you want to do and the particular lender's preferences, the greater the probability you'll ***get*** the loan and better its ***terms*** will be.

Lender hangups

I have hangups. You have hangups. Loan officers have hangups. You may run into one who won't make loans on master metered (owner pays utilities) buildings. Or one who hates a particular community. Or one who will have nothing to do with private mortgage insurance.

Did you ever try to talk someone out of a hangup? It ***can*** be done. But unless talking a loan officer is the ***only*** way, your time is better spent finding another officer with***out*** the hangup that's stopping you.

If it's the only way, marshall your facts and try to convince the nay sayer why his hangup is incorrect. For example, I wrote an article called "What's Wrong With Master Meters" in the June 1983 *Real Estate Investing Letter*. In it I set forth facts, figures, and logic to convince the reader that the "Post Energy Crisis" fear of master metered buildings is a bunch of nonsense.

I suspect most of those who refused to consider master metered buildings ***before*** they read the article ***still*** refuse to consider them. But I also suspect I opened a few minds.

Loan size

Lenders' loan policies vary with the size of the loan. The smaller the loan, the less flexibility, the more they stick to the policy manual. The larger the loan, the more flexibility, the more they do what's needed to do the deal. So you improve loan terms by ***shopping*** when it comes to smaller loans. You shop less on the larger loans. . . and negotiate more.

Lenders have loan limits. The closer your loan is to their limit, the harder it to get a yes. So on large loans, go to even larger lenders.

Like courting

Many a writer has compared seeking a loan to courting. It's an apt comparison. As with the pursuit of the opposite sex, you can't appear too eager and you can't appear to take the other person for granted.

Getting someone to say, "Yes"

When you apply for a loan you're asking someone to say, "yes." You're also asking someone to say, "yes," in sales, seduction, labor negotiations, diplomatic negotiations, etc. You could become a better real estate loan getter by reading books on ***those*** subjects.

How do you get someone to say, "yes?" It comes down to what they ***say*** they want (loan policy), what they ***really*** want (psychology), the relationship between you and them (rapport), and other similar factors.

Books on negotiating

I'd love to send you to a few good books on negotiating. Unfortunately, the only one I like at all is *Getting To Yes* by Roger Fisher and William Ury (Houghton Mifflin Company). Neither Gerard Nierenberg's *Art of Negotiation* nor best seller *You Can Negotiate Anything* by Herb Cohen (Lyle Stuart, Inc.) has much substance. But then the ***whole subject*** of negotiation is hard to get hold of. Even the authors of *Getting To Yes* admit in their conclusion, "There is probably nothing in this book which you did not already know at some level of your experience."

Negotiating tricks

Don't use negotiating tricks. By tricks I mean making the other guy sit in a shorter chair, face the sun, etc. That's childish nonsense.

Fisher and Ury call them "dirty tricks" and say they fall into three categories:

- deception
- psychological warfare (like a short chair)
- pressure tactics (the old close-the-briefcase-and-walk-out technique)

Canned tactics

Also, be careful of canned negotiating tactics. For example, you might hear a seasoned investor say, "I like to make the lender wait before I respond...sweat a little bit."

That's fine...unless interest rates go up in the interim. Sometimes canned tactics succeed. Sometimes they blow up in your face.

Another canned tactic is ***finding fault*** with the other guy's property. Sometimes it works. You point out faults and the other guy reduces his price out of shame. Don't try it with me, though. It makes me mad.

I sold a car once. One dealer offered me $1,200 after lecturing me on all the things wrong with the car. I ended up selling it for $1,200...but not to him. I'd have probably taken $1,150 from someone else after his insulting attempt to humiliate me into selling at his price.

A real estate saleswoman started to use the fault-finding tactic on me while presenting a counter offer on my house recently. I cut her off in mid-sentence with, "The two agents I had appraise the property saw all of those faults. They took them into account in their appraisal. I priced the house accordingly. If I lowered the price ***again*** for those things I'd be paying for them ***twice***. I'm not going to pay for them twice."

It's a circular process

One of the things that makes getting a loan difficult to explain in a how to book or seminar is that it's a ***circular*** process. ***Linear*** processes are easy to explain. For example, in my book *Aggressive Tax Avoidance For Real Estate Investors*, I explain the process by which you can fight IRS. First you refuse to sign the IRS agent's Form 870, then you appeal within IRS, then you can go to Tax Court or District Court or Claims Court, etc.

The process of fighting IRS is linear, sequential. Real estate finance doesn't work that way.

What do you want? What have you got?

Try putting a property on the market. One of the first questions a prospective buyer will ask is "What financing is available?"

I say never take back a mortgage. So if you're going to provide a buyer with financing it'll be through a buy down.

So let's say you anticipate the "What financing's available?" question and approach a lender before putting the property on the market to see what loan terms they'll give. Know what they'll say? "Let us see the deal."

Fake it

Here's how I handled a recent sale of an apartment building with a buy down. In my offering brochure, I offered to buy a second mortgage which would, in effect, be a 12% wraparound with a five year balloon. No lender told me they'd sell me such a loan. But I had to start somewhere.

Then I found a buyer who wanted the 12% wrap, but for ***nine*** years not five. I told them I didn't think I could get nine, so we compromised at seven.

Then I went looking for a lender. Had a heck of a time finding one. Finally found one which would make the loan, but only up to 64% of value. . . not the 75% of value we wanted.

I wondered if we could find a ***third*** mortgage lender for the difference between the 64% second and the 75% total we needed. We did.

The the second mortgage lender demanded that the buyers be personally liable. At first they refused. But when the lender said, "No," the buyer agreed to personal liability on the second but not the third.

Along the way, the second lender also increased the number of points I had to pay from one to four.

Hard to diagram

So you can see the process would be hard to diagram. It's more of a back and forth dialogue with the only basis being the common goal of each of the participants. The lender wanted to make the best loan they could. The buyer wanted to get the best terms they could. And I wanted the highest net I could get.

I tried to diagram the process of getting a loan for the finance seminar I used to teach. I couldn't do it. In his "Nothing Down" seminar, author Bob Allen diagrammed the "Nothing Down System of Creative Financing." His diagram covers two pages and looks like the organization chart of the Department of Health and Welfare.

Small loans are a bit linear

Actually, the process for getting a standard mortgage on a single-family house is pretty linear. You call around to get current loan terms, pick the best, apply, credit check, appraisal, commitment. But on income property loans and seller loans, there's a sort of "You go first" syndrome.

Be reasonable

Although lenders generally do not give out much information on terms until they "see the deal," you *can* get a general idea of what they will and will not do. Sometimes you can cajole it out of the lender with a series of pointed questions

"Will you go ten years?"

"Well, I can't comment without seeing the deal. But I doubt we'd *ever* go ten years. Five is probably the best you could get."

You can also get an idea of what's reasonably possible by asking real estate agents active in the market what they've heard lenders are doing these days.

And you can get a feel from the real estate finance trade journals like *The Crittenden Report*.

It will do you no good to ask for a loan which an institutional lender would never do. You just antagonize the lender and destroy your credibility with them. It's OK to ask for more than you think you'll get. But just a bit more. If you ask for a *lot* more, you make them think you don't know what you're doing.

Relationships

Bank loans to businesses are generally part of a ***relationship***. That's less true of real estate investment loans. But you should be aware of the value of a relationship in the mind of the lending institution.

A better than average relationship with the lending institution warrants better than average terms. So where a relationship exists, you should make sure the loan officer doesn't forget it.

Deposits

The most common aspect of a relationship with a lender is ***deposits***. Deposits you have had with the lender in the past. . . or will have in the future. Sometimes loans are made on the promise that the sale proceeds will go into the lender's institution.

I got a loan on an apartment building that way. The seller promised to put the sale proceeds in the savings and loan in question.

From a strategy standpoint, you should ***not*** have enough deposits to have clout with a lender. Any money you have in bank accounts above and beyond what you need to pay your monthly bills should be withdrawn and invested in real estate. . . if you're still in the making-your-million mode.

But if you're in the I've-made-mine mode, and you've got plenty of deposits, by all means use them to get better loans.

Also, keep in mind that ***your*** deposits aren't the only ones that matter. I've already mentioned the ***seller's*** deposits. Deposits belonging to those on the "People Check List" below can swing a loan, too.

Insurance policies

Life insurance companies make mortgage loans. You don't have deposits with them. But you ***do*** have policies.

Now I'm not talking about ***individual*** policies. Life companies make ***big*** loans. They are not going to make you a $2,500,000 loan on better than average terms because you send them $167 a month in life insurance premiums.

But if you have a business, or are connected to someone who does, you may have ***group*** insurance policies. On those, the premiums can be substantial. If so, and you're applying to the company in question for a mortgage, be sure to let the salesman you deal with know so he can pass the word up his chain of command that they should be nice to you.

Other customers you've brought

If you've sent customers to the institution, remind them of that. Backing up a bit, you should always be on the lookout for opportunities to do that. And when you do, send a letter pointing it out. . .or at least make a note for your own reference.

Your tenure

Most lending institutions are impressed by loyalty. So if you've been dealing with an institution for more than a year or so, point that out to them.

Favors you've done

Lending institutions someone times ask investors for favors. One typical favor would be to take some REO off their hands. REO is "Real Estate Owned." It means real estate the lender acquired by foreclosing on mortgages. They don't want it. And the regulators are on them to get rid of it. Sometimes that's hard because the properties that get foreclosed are usually not prime. So they call their local real estate investor for help.

If you've helped one in that way or another way, remind them when you apply for a loan. I got a loan that way once because the seller had taken a doggy REO off the lender's hands once upon a time.

Future business

Lenders will sometimes give you special consideration if they expect to benefit from ***future*** business from you. I worked for a lender briefly. And I was amazed at the amount of consideration which was given to customers for nothing more than the vague promise of future business. I happen to think that's appallingly bad management. But it happens nevertheless

Don't lie. The fact that many institutions will do favors for the possibility of future business doesn't mean you should ***mislead*** them about how much business you're going to give them. But if future business is a genuine possibility, by all means give the lender an accurate estimate of it when you apply for a loan.

Connections

Your connections may help get you a loan or a better loan. Here's a list of possible connections I call the "People Check List."

- **Family**: Parents, children, siblings, in-laws, etc.
- **Friends**: From each place you've lived, school, armed forces, jobs, clubs, teams, etc.
- **Sellers**: Present and past
- **Tenants**: In present building or the building you're acquiring
- **Members**: Of property owners associations
- **Advisers**: Attorney, accountant, broker
- **Partners**: Business,real estate, golf, tennis
- **Dentist**
- **Doctor**
- **Professors**
- **Employer**
- **Fellow students**: At real estate seminars or adult education classes

These folks might help you by

- Providing ***equity*** money either as a general or limited partner
- ***Co-signing*** or guaranteeing an obligation
- ***Lending*** you money
- ***Purchasing assets*** you want to sell for a better price than you could get elsewhere
- ***Pressuring a lender*** with whom they have a relationship
- Transferring ***deposits*** or business to the lender with whom you are negotiating, or threatening to withdraw same.

Nothing is free

Before you ask your connections for favors, remember that nothing is free. If someone does you a favor, you owe them a favor. But some of these are relatively painless favors, like moving deposits.

Two kinds of mortgage application

There are two main kinds of mortgage application:

- standard house mortgage
- income property mortgage

The standard house mortgage almost always requires you to fill out a FHLMC/FNMA "Residential Loan Application." FHLMC stands for Federal Home Loan Mortgage Corporation, known as "Freddie Mac." FNMA stands for Federal National Mortgage Association, known as "Fannie Mae."

FHLMC and FNMA *are* the secondary market for home mortgages. Lenders want their loans to be salable to these agencies. So they use FHLMC/FNMA forms and procedures even when they have no immediate plans to sell the loan to FHLMC or FNMA.

In other words, if you apply for a home mortgage, or a loan on a building with less than five units, you'll probably have to fill out the FHLMC/FNMA form. So let's go over it.

FHLMC/FNMA Residential Loan Application

The form is shown below

RESIDENTIAL LOAN APPLICATION

Any Married Applicant May Apply For A Separate Account **Loan Number** ____________

MORTGAGE APPLIED FOR	☐ Conventional ☐ FHA ☐ VA ☐ ______	Amount $	Interest Rate %	No. of Months	Monthly Payment Principal & Interest $	Escrow/Impounds (to be collected monthly) ☐ Taxes ☐ Hazard Ins. ☐ Mtg. Ins. ☐ ______

Prepayment Option

SUBJECT PROPERTY

Property Street Address	City	County	State	Zip	No. Units

Legal Description (Attach description if necessary) | Year Built

Purpose of Loan: ☐ Purchase ☐ Construction-Permanent ☐ Construction ☐ Refinance ☐ Other (Explain)

Complete this line if Construction-Permanent or Construction Loan	Lot Value Data / Year Acquired	Original Cost	Present Value (a)	Cost of Imps. (b)	Total (a + b)	ENTER TOTAL AS PURCHASE PRICE IN DETAILS OF PURCHASE.
		$	$	$	$	

Complete this line if a Refinance Loan | Purpose of Refinance | Describe Improvements ☐ made ☐ to be made

Year Acquired	Original Cost	Amt. Existing Liens		
	$	$		Cost $

Title Will Be Held In What Name(s) | Manner In Which Title Will Be Held

Source of Down Payment and Settlement Charges

This application is designed to be completed by the borrower(s) with the lender's assistance. The Co-Borrower Section and all other Co-Borrower questions must be completed and the appropriate box(es) checked if ☐ another person will be jointly obligated with the Borrower on the loan, or ☐ the Borrower is relying on income from alimony, child support or separate maintenance or on the income or assets of another person as a basis for repayment of the loan, or ☐ the Borrower is married and resides, or the property is located, in a community property state.

BORROWER	CO-BORROWER
Name / Age / School Yrs ____	Name / Age / School Yrs ____
Present Address No. Years ____ ☐ Own ☐ Rent	Present Address No. Years ____ ☐ Own ☐ Rent
Street	Street
City/State/Zip	City/State/Zip
Former address if less than 2 years at present address	Former address if less than 2 years at present address
Street	Street
City/State/Zip	City/State/Zip
Years at former address ☐ Own ☐ Rent	Years at former address ☐ Own ☐ Rent
Marital Status ☐ Married ☐ Separated ☐ Unmarried (incl. single, divorced, widowed) — Dependents other than listed by co-borrower: No / Ages	Marital Status ☐ Married ☐ Separated ☐ Unmarried (incl. single, divorced, widowed) — Dependents other than listed by borrower: No / Ages
Name and Address of Employer — Years employed in this line of work or profession? ____ years; Years on this job ____; ☐ Self Employed*	Name and Address of Employer — Years employed in this line of work or profession? ____ years; Years on this job ____; ☐ Self Employed*
Position/Title / Type of Business	Position/Title / Type of Business
Social Security Number*** / Home Phone / Business Phone	Social Security Number*** / Home Phone / Business Phone

GROSS MONTHLY INCOME

Item	Borrower	Co-Borrower	Total
Base Empl. Income	$	$	$
Overtime			
Bonuses			
Commissions			
Dividends/Interest			
Net Rental Income			
Other† (Before completing, see notice under Describe Other Income below.)			
Total	$	$	$

MONTHLY HOUSING EXPENSE**

	Present	Proposed
Rent	$	
First Mortgage (P&I)		$
Other Financing (P&I)		
Hazard Insurance		
Real Estate Taxes		
Mortgage Insurance		
Homeowner Assn. Dues		
Other:		
Total Monthly Pmt.	$	$
Utilities		
Total	$	$

DETAILS OF PURCHASE

Do Not Complete If Refinance	
a. Purchase Price	$
b. Total Closing Costs (Est.)	
c. Prepaid Escrows (Est.)	
d. Total (a + b + c)	$
e. Amount This Mortgage	( )
f. Other Financing	( )
g. Other Equity	( )
h. Amount of Cash Deposit	( )
i. Closing Costs Paid by Seller	( )
j. Cash Reqd. For Closing (Est.)	$

DESCRIBE OTHER INCOME

B—Borrower C—Co-Borrower	NOTICE: † Alimony, child support, or separate maintenance income need not be revealed if the Borrower or Co-Borrower does not choose to have it considered as a basis for repaying this loan.	Monthly Amount
		$

IF EMPLOYED IN CURRENT POSITION FOR LESS THAN TWO YEARS COMPLETE THE FOLLOWING

B/C	Previous Employer/School	City/State	Type of Business	Position/Title	Dates From/To	Monthly Income
						$

THESE QUESTIONS APPLY TO BOTH BORROWER AND CO-BORROWER

If a "yes" answer is given to a question in this column, explain on an attached sheet.	Borrower Yes or No	Co-Borrower Yes or No	If applicable, explain Other Financing or Other Equity (provide addendum if more space is needed).
Have you any outstanding judgments? In the last 7 years, have you been declared bankrupt?			
Have you had property foreclosed upon or given title or deed in lieu thereof?			
Are you a co-maker or endorser on a note?			
Are you a party in a law suit?			
Are you obligated to pay alimony, child support, or separate maintenance?			
Is any part of the down payment borrowed?			

*FHLMC/FNMA require business credit report, signed Federal Income Tax returns for last two years, and, if available, audited Profit and Loss Statements plus balance sheet for same period.

**All Present Monthly Housing Expenses of Borrower and Co-Borrower should be listed on a combined basis.

***Neither FHLMC nor FNMA requires this information.

FHLMC 65 Rev. 8/78 FEB-RE-QUA 3 FNMA 1003 Rev. 8/78

This Statement and any applicable supporting schedules may be completed jointly by both married and unmarried co-borrowers if their assets and liabilities are sufficiently joined so that the Statement can be meaningfully and fairly presented on a combined basis; otherwise separate Statements and Schedules are required (FHLMC 65A/FNMA 1003A). If the co-borrower section was completed about a spouse, this statement and supporting schedules must be completed about that spouse also.

☐ Completed Jointly ☐ Not Completed Jointly

STATEMENT OF ASSETS AND LIABILITIES

ASSETS		LIABILITIES AND PLEDGED ASSETS			
		Indicate by (*) those liabilities or pledged assets which will be satisfied upon sale of real estate owned or upon refinancing of subject property			
Description	Cash or Market Value	Creditors' Name, Address and Account Number	Acct. Name If Not Borrower's	Mo. Pmt. and Mos. left to pay	Unpaid Balance
Cash Deposit Toward Purchase Held By	$	Installment Debts (include "revolving" charge accts)		$ Pmt./Mos. /	$
				/	
Checking and Savings Accounts (Show Names of Institutions/Acct. Nos.)				/	
				/	
Stocks and Bonds (No./Description)				/	
				/	
Life Insurance Net Cash Value Face Amount ($)				/	
SUBTOTAL LIQUID ASSETS	$	Other Debts Including Stock Pledges		/	
Real Estate Owned (Enter Market Value from Schedule of Real Estate Owned)					
Vested Interest in Retirement Fund		Real Estate Loans			
Net Worth of Business Owned (ATTACH FINANCIAL STATEMENT)					
Automobiles (Make and Year)		Automobile Loans		/	
Furniture and Personal Property		Alimony, Child Support and Separate Maintenance Payments Owed To		/	
Other Assets (Itemize)					
		TOTAL MONTHLY PAYMENTS		$	
TOTAL ASSETS	A $	NET WORTH (A minus B) $		TOTAL LIABILITIES	B $

SCHEDULE OF REAL ESTATE OWNED (If Additional Properties Owned Attach Separate Schedule)

Address of Property (Indicate S if Sold, PS if Pending Sale or R if Rental being held for income)	⇩	Type of Property	Present Market Value	Amount of Mortgages & Liens	Gross Rental Income	Mortgage Payments	Taxes, Ins. Maintenance and Misc.	Net Rental Income
			$	$	$	$	$	$
		TOTALS →	$	$	$	$	$	$

LIST PREVIOUS CREDIT REFERENCES

⇩ B-Borrower C-Co-Borrower	Creditor's Name and Address	Account Number	Purpose	Highest Balance	Date Paid
				$	

List any additional names under which credit has previously been received ______________________

AGREEMENT The undersigned applies for the loan indicated in this application to be secured by a first mortgage or deed of trust on the property described herein, and represents that the property will not be used for any illegal or restricted purpose, and that all statements made in this application are true and are made for the purpose of obtaining the loan. Verification may be obtained from any source named in this application. The original or a copy of this application will be retained by the lender, even if the loan is not granted. The undersigned ☐ intend or ☐ do not intend to occupy the property as their primary residence.

I/we fully understand that it is a federal crime punishable by fine or imprisonment, or both, to knowingly make any false statements concerning any of the above facts as applicable under the provisions of Title 18, United States Code, Section 1014.

______________________ Date __________ ______________________ Date __________
Borrower's Signature Co-Borrower's Signature

INFORMATION FOR GOVERNMENT MONITORING PURPOSES

The following information is requested by the Federal Government if this loan is related to a dwelling, in order to monitor the lender's compliance with equal credit opportunity and fair housing laws. You are not required to furnish this information, but are encouraged to do so. The law provides that a lender may neither discriminate on the basis of this information, nor on whether you choose to furnish it. However, if you choose not to furnish it, under Federal regulations this lender is required to note race and sex on the basis of visual observation or surname. If you do not wish to furnish the above information, please initial below.

BORROWER: I do not wish to furnish this information (initials)________
RACE/NATIONAL ORIGIN ☐ American Indian, Alaskan Native ☐ Asian, Pacific Islander ☐ Black ☐ Hispanic ☐ White ☐ Other (specify) __________
SEX: ☐ Female ☐ Male

CO-BORROWER: I do not wish to furnish this information (initials)________
RACE/NATIONAL ORIGIN ☐ American Indian, Alaskan Native ☐ Asian, Pacific Islander ☐ Black ☐ Hispanic ☐ White ☐ Other (specify) __________
SEX ☐ Female ☐ Male

FOR LENDER'S USE ONLY

(FNMA REQUIREMENT ONLY) This application was taken by ☐ face to face interview ☐ by mail ☐ by telephone

______________________ ______________________
(Interviewer) Name of Employer of Interviewer

FHLMC 65 Rev. 8/78 **REVERSE** FNMA 1003 Rev. 8/78

The form is mostly self-explanatory. So I won't cover all of it. Rather I'll just cover the parts where you might have a question or overlook something.

Fill out one in pencil

Get two copies of the form from the lender. Fill out one in pencil first. Then type the other. Neatness counts in mortgage applications. And unless you fill them out every day, you'll probably foul it up the first time.

Prepayment

At the top of the front is a block labeled "Prepayment Option." Type "No prepayment penalty" in there. You may not get it. But it won't hurt to ask.

Year built

Try to find out the year built. I hate applications with blanks on them. I suspect loan processors do, too.

The underneath side of the lid of the toilet tank usually has the date that fixture was made. Often it's the date the house was built, too.

Or you may be able to estimate the vintage of the house from construction features. For example, underground utilities came into vogue since the sixties. My last house was on a street with wires on poles. It was built in 1964. It also had mailboxes on sticks by the street instead of on the house. Mailboxes on sticks weren't ***required*** until about 1976, according to my local post office.

My roof on that house was shot. Roofs last about 20 years. So you can get a handle on the age of the building from the condition of the roof. If the roof is either new or shot, the house is probably about 20, 40, or 60 years old. You can usually tell which of those ages from looking at other aspects of the house or street.

Don't waste a lot of time on it. But do try to estimate the age and fill in that blank.

Base Employment Income

This is salary or wages. Be sure to note any scheduled increases.

Overtime, Bonuses, Commissions

If you expect to receive overtime pay, bonuses, or commissions, estimate them. Use last year's pay stubs or W-2 as proof. If ***this*** year's will be much higher, get some sort of proof. . .like a letter from your employer.

Net rental income

This is your positive cash flow from your investment property. If you had extraordinary capital expenditures last year, be sure to not count them. The lender is interested in your "stabilized" net rental income, not what it was in an unusual year.

If you have ***negative*** cash flow, be sure to point out that the loss plus your depreciation deductions provide substantial tax savings. You should calculate your ***after***-tax income and attach the calculation. Point out that your ***after***-tax income is equivalent to that of a person making X dollars a year who did not have real estate investments.

Lenders tend to assume that you are the typical borrower. That your before-tax income is greater than your after-tax income. But you're a real estate investor. You're before-tax income is often ***less*** than your after-tax income. So it's important that you do the numbers for the lender so that you translate your income to its equivalent for a non-real estate investor.

If you fail to do that, you'll lose on two counts:

- Your income will look low
- You'll get no credit for the tax savings which are one of your main sources of investment return.

You make tax benefits a big deal when you invest. Make sure you also make them a big deal when you apply for a loan. You'll have to attach a separate explanation because the standard loan application does not ask about tax shelter.

Other income

Don't overlook any. Use your tax return and check register deposit. Don't forget ***tax exempt bonds.*** They may not show up in your check register. And they surely aren't listed on your tax return.

The FNMA form only has three lines for "Describe Other Income." Don't let that stop you from adding a sheet to fully describe a long list of other incomes. Here's a check list of sources of income to make sure you don't overlook any.

Income Check List

- Interest on bank accounts, CDs, security deposits, pending tax refunds
- Pending tax refunds
- Pending refunds from disputed bills
- Royalties
- Payments you receive on loans you've made like personal loans to friends and relatives, mortgages you've taken back, loans you've taken back when you sold your business.
- Trust income
- Annuities
- Dividends
- Inheritance
- Alimony
- Pensions
- Disability payments
- Insurance claims pending
- Lawsuit settlements pending
- Commissions earned but not yet received
- Condemnation awards pending
- Value of free lodging, meals, car or other perks you receive
- Value of stock options received as compensation
- Christmas bonus
- Severance pay
- Income from sale of property
- Value of gifts you receive
- Strike fund payments
- Unemployment compensation
- GI Bill money received
- Educational aid
- Grants you receive
- Pay for serving on jury
- Mileage or other expense reimbursements by employer
- Income from odd jobs
- Value of prizes won
- Rewards won
- Tips

Assets

You want to show as many assets as possible. But don't exaggerate values. That just makes you look dishonest. The trick is to make sure you don't ***overlook*** or undervalue any assets.

Real Estate Owned

Be sure to attach a separate schedule if you have more properties than will fit on the three lines on the form. "Gross rental income" should be your current gross ***scheduled*** income. That is, your current "street" or asking rent, assuming you have at least some units paying that much.

Under the "Mortgage Payments" column, make sure you put ***only*** principal and interest, ***not*** the additional amounts you usually pay for taxes and insurance. They go under the next column, "Taxes, Ins., Maintenance, and Misc."

Put only your ***stabilized*** operating expenses in this column. That is leave off unusual things you may have had to purchase last year.

"Net Rental Income" is your "Gross Rental Income" less mortgage payments and "Taxes, Ins., Maintenance, and Misc."

Net Worth of Business Owned

This is highly subjective unless the stock in your business is traded in the market regularly. Use the highest value you can reasonably justify. Explain the basis for your figure.

Automobiles

Use the *Blue Book* (*Kelley Blue Book*, Kelley Blue Book Company, 2950 A7 Airway Avenue, Costa Mesa, CA 92626) value. My library has it...in a town of 15,000. Yours almost certainly does, too.

Furniture and Personal Property

This is one area where most people exaggerate. You shouldn't exaggerate. But you should try to make the number come out as high as reasonably possible. And you should attach an itemized list. High furniture and personal property figures are taken with a grain of salt, unless you have a ***list*** of each item and its value. Then it sounds more believable.

The itemized list should be no trouble to come up with. You should already have one in case of theft or fire loss. And if you don't, now's as good a time as any to do it.

Here's a check list of furniture and personal property to make sure you don't overlook any.

Furniture and Personal Property Check List

- Go through each room of your house and list furniture...don't overlook valuables inside cabinets, drawers, and closets
- Inventory your jewelry at home and in safe deposit box
- Inventory your clothing (Sounds silly, but if the house burns down, you'll wish you had. The quickest way is to dictate what you have in your closets and drawers then send the tape to a secretarial service for transcription.)
- Inventory your storage areas...at home and at other locations like a miniwarehouse you rent, your mother's attic, storage areas you use at your investment properties, etc.
- Collections at home and in safe deposit box
- Art works
- Books
- Office equipment and furniture
- Telephones you own
- Check desk drawers for valuables like calculators, recorders, etc.
- Silverware and other silver pieces
- Value of manuscripts not yet published (*I* have those.)
- Value of unused supplies
- Value of cassettes and records
- Inventory items in your garage and in your cars

- Inventory items in your vacation house
- Cameras (35mm, video, etc.)
- Deck or patio furniture
- Food. . .especially if you have more than normal
- Value of vine collection (These days, practically everybody's got a few bucks tied up in wines.)
- Drapes, rugs
- Toys

Now that I've reminded you of the God awful amount of junk you've accumulated, why don't you convert some of it to cash by selling it. An old fashioned garage sale is a finance technique, you know. (For more information on garage sales, try *The Garage Sale Manual*, by Jean Young published by Praeger.)

Lenders may take the value of your furniture and personal property with a grain of salt. But they take ***cash*** at face value. Better to show $50 more in cash than $100 more in the form of a three year old TV set.

Other Assets

Here's yet another check list.

Other Asset Check List

- Descending postage unused reading on your postage meter
- Security deposits you've left with apartment landlord, your business office landlord, your miniwarehouse landlord, utility companies
- Cash on hand. . .in your pockets, purse, and hidden around the house
- Money owed you by friends, relatives, business associates, people who bought property from you
- Insurance company savings accounts (Maybe my insurance company is the only one that has this.)
- Stale uncashed checks you've written
- Value of copyrights you own
- Payments you've received buy not yet deposited

Liabilities

If you ***jointly*** own something, make sure you only list ***your share*** of the debt.

Verifications

To help speed the process, give the lender the account numbers, addresses, and signed authorizations they need to check on your loans, employment, and deposits.

Income property mortgage application

There is no standard income property loan application. Or at least if there is, it is nowhere near as widespread as the FNMA/FHLMC "Residential Loan Application."

There ***is***, however, a more or less standard format which you should know. It has two sections

Summary Section

- Cover letter
- Summary of loan terms sought
- Table of contents
- Photographs of subject property

- Present loan number if same lender
- Numerical summary (rule of thumb calculations)
- Brief description of property
- Income/expense summary
- Map of neighborhood and region (if other than local lender)
- Borrower's resume (To show ability to manage income property)
- Lender's application form (if any)

Documentation Section

- Income support (detailed rent roll, rental comparables, other income proof)
- Expense support (line by line basis for each expense figure)
- Detailed legal description of property
- Survey
- Credit references of borrower
- Appraisal
- Sales comparables with photographs
- Resume of appraiser
- Additional photographs of subject property and neighborhood
- Aerial photograph (on $1,000,000 or higher deals)
- Community data
- Brochure (if one was used to sell the property)
- Site date
- Zoning
- Insurance coverage
- Borrower's financial statements (use check lists for completing FNMA/FHLMC form)
- Property's actual performance figures for last three years
- Cash budget for coming year

Not precise

This list of what you include in an income property loan is not precise. It's probably more thorough than the typical application. My impression is that the more relevant data you give the lender, the faster and more probable the approval.

People tend to mentally fill in blanks with the worst thing. In other words, if you fail to explain the source for your expense figures, the lender will tend to think you probably underestimated them to make the application look good. They'll add some corrective amount which will usually be too much. Better to give the true figures and ***prove*** them with a statement from your utility or copies of bills or tax returns or whatever.

In his book *Selling Income Property Successfully*, John B. Allen said, "More [income property] sales are lost because of inaccurate information or lack of information than for any other reason."

I think the same thing applies to ***financing*** income property sales. Don't try to take short cuts or leave out information which is negative but will eventually be demanded by the lender. It's like pulling off a bandage. Get it over with.

Cover letter

Here's a sample.

John T. Reed
342 Bryan Drive
Danville, CA 94526

Mr. James Arledge
Vice President
Southwest Mortgage, Inc.
1111 Kings Highway
Dallas, TX 75240

Re: Cottonwood Apts.
1500 Beverly Circle
Plano, Texas

Dear Jim:

Enclosed is our application for a $500,000 first mortgage on the above property.

As we discussed yesterday, this is a refinancing. The proposed loan is 74.8% of an M.A.I. appraisal done last month (copy enclosed).

Please call me if you have any further questions, Jim. Thank you for your consideration.

Sincerely yours,

John T. Reed

Proposed loan

Here's a sample.

<u>Proposed Loan Terms</u>

Loan amount.............$500,000

Appraised value.........$668,500

Commitment period.......60 days

Lender's yield..........13.25%

Discount points.........None

Amortization schedule...Thirty years

Term....................Ten years

Personal liability......None

Security................First trust deed on Cottonwood Apts.

Prepayment penalty......Locked in for five years then 1%

Assumability............Subject to lender approving buyer

Fees....................1 point
Lenders title insurance policy
credit application fee $25.00
Escrow fee $50.00
Filing fees approx. $15.00
Document preparation $750.00

THERE WILL BE NO OTHER FEES OR CHARGES.

Numerical summary

Here's a sample.

NUMERICAL SUMMARY

Number of units	28
Unit mix	14 two bedroom 14 one bedroom
Unit size	two br, 875 sq. ft. one br, 675 sq. ft.
Permitted tenants	Adults, no pets
Utility metering	Master metered
Lot size	200 x 220
Building size	22,000 sq. ft.
Net rentable area	21,700 sq. ft.
Density	28.6 units per acre
Parking	42 spaces
Parking ratio	1.5 spaces per unit
Rent per square foot	2 br, $.457/sq. ft. 1 br, $.548/sq. ft.
Operating expense per sq. ft	$2.995/sq. ft.
Operating expense ratio	50%
Capitalization rate	9.7%
Gross rent multiplier	5.14
Per unit value	$23,875
Per square foot value	$30.39
Debt-coverage ratio	0.96

Description of improvements

This is a concise, narrative description of the property. Break it into a sort of list or outline form to make it easy to read. Here's a check list of things to cover.

Improvements Description Check List

- Location of lot (corner, interior, cul de sac)
- Shape of lot
- Terrain
- Drainage
- Paving
- Landscaping
- Utilities available
- Type construction (e.g. brick veneer over wood frame)
- Room count
- Architectural style
- Features of rentable space (e.g. wall-to-wall carpet, illuminated kitchen ceiling)
- Parking
- Recreational facilities
- Laundry facilities (in apartment buildings)
- Appliances
- Equipment details (e.g. Ajax Model WG-900 boiler)
- Security systems
- Architect
- Age
- Glazing
- Type and age of roof

Sample description

Lot: 300' x 220' (1.515 acres)
Parking: 1.81 spaces per unit
Pool: 35' x 16' resurfaced Fall of '81
Roof: Pitched, asphalt shingle installed Spring '79
Construction: Brick veneer over wood frame, two-story, colonial garden type. Slab. Soundproofing concrete between floors.
Finish: Wall-to-wall carpet, ceramic tile baths, individually controlled heat and air-conditioning, walk-in closets, linen and pantry closets, double sink, disposer, two-door frost-free refrigerators, smoke detectors in each unit.
Mechanical: Central two-pipe heating and air-conditioning, Marley Cooling Tower installed new April '82, 40 ton American Standard Versare Liquid Chiller compressor rebuilt Spring '83, Ajax WG-900 gas boiler installed new '76. Swimquip pool filter. Rheem domestic hot water heater installed new September '81.
Laundry: One laundry room on each floor. Two washers and dryers in each room.
Age: 19 years.
Terrain: Level.
Drainage: To street
Paving: Concrete walkways and asphalt parking and driveways installed new November '80
Landscaping: Bermuda grass and hedge, young shade trees on west side
Utilities: Texas Power and Light, Lone Star Gas, City water, sewer, and trash collection.
Glazing: Single-pane aluminum sliding windows.

What to take pictures of

Take pictures of the following to include in the mortgage application:

- Elevations of building(s)
- Landscaping
- Parking
- Recreational facilities
- Typical interior (need wide angle lens)
- Adjacent streets
- Neighborhood landmarks or features
- Rent comparables buildings
- Sale comparables buildings
- Aerial photo

Pictures should be good quality (not instant) and in color. Do not use photocopies of photos. Reproduce photos at a professional photo developer. If you need them in a hurry, there are color print developers who have 60 or 90 minute service. They're listed in your phone book under "Photographic Color Prints."

Neatness counts

Remember, neatness counts in mortgage applications. All of this ought to be word-processed. Performance figures look good when computer generated. Try to avoid 14 inch wide computer paper, though. It doesn't fit in file drawers. Wouldn't hurt to ***bind*** your application materials. But don't try to use fancy packaging to make up for a lousy deal.

Your goal in the neatness area is to convey the image of competence and credibility. . .and to make the materials easy to read and store. Your goal is ***not*** to dazzle the lender with your book publishing skills.

It's time-consuming

You probably think my explanation of how to do a mortgage application is very time-consuming. You're right. You're asking someone to loan you tens of thousands, hundreds of thousands, maybe millions of dollars. Darned right it's time-consuming.

It's midnight oil stuff. I remember the first income property loan application I prepared. Took me several days of full-time work. But I got the loan. And the loan officer was particularly impressed with my application. He said so and noted that the appraiser would probably rely on it as a result.

You ought to be able to knock out a home loan application in an evening's work. But if you spent less than a day or two on an income property application, you probably took too many shortcuts.

Often, the seller is getting more money from the third-party lender than he's getting from the buyer. Yet the typical buyer or seller spends a great deal of time on his dealings with the other party. . .and treats the lender as if he were a side issue, a routine technicality. You should spend as much or more time "selling" the lender on the deal as you spend selling the other party.

7
Special types of loans

Construction loans

A construction loan is usually one used to build a new building on vacant land. But ***renovation*** of an existing building might also be done via a construction loan. Or to put it another way, if extensive renovation is being done to a property pledged as security of a loan, it's a sort of construction loan whether the lender calls it that or not.

I'm not a construction loan expert. Richard Harris is. If you plan to get involved in construction borrowing or lending, I recommend you read his book, *Construction and Development Financing*. I did. And I was amazed at what I did not know.

And I was so impressed with the ***complexity*** of construction lending that I decided I would get a major construction lender to make a construction loan on my property if I ever build again. . . ***even if I can afford to pay all cash.*** That's because I want someone who knows what he's doing protecting me from mechanic's liens and all the other pitfalls in construction.

Construction lending is hairy stuff. Construction lenders generally require personal liability. Depending on local law and circumstances, first mortgages and second mortgages can switch places and mechanic's liens recorded ***after*** a mortgage was recorded can gain priority ***ahead*** of that mortgage!

Construction lenders have been known to send a man out to the site with a copy of the front page of that day's newspaper. Another guy takes a picture of the vacant site including the guy holding that newspaper up to the camera. This is to prove that the site was vacant on the day the loan was recorded. Thereby establishing priority over a mechanic or supplier who claimed he had done work or delivered supplies to the site ***prior*** to the recording date. Craziness.

Land development loans

It's hard to borrow against raw land. Sellers of raw land will usually take back loans. But institutional lenders are extremely reluctant. Institutional lenders ***will*** lend against raw land if it's part of a plan to put ***buildings*** on the land. Here are some thoughts on improving your chances of securing a land development loan.

Both lenders and local governments often require ***surety bonds*** guaranteeing the performance of the contractors (who will grade, install underground utilities, etc.) and bonds guaranteeing ***your*** performance. Be prepared to qualify for and pay for those bonds.

Zoning variances, building permits and such often ***expire*** if the building is not begun by a certain date. Be prepared to convince the lender that you'll make the deadlines.

Hire ***architects and engineers*** with solid reputations. Because the lenders will be very interested in who you're using.

The biggest key to getting a land development loan is to convince the lender that the deal is going to go all the way through. That you have the financing commitments and know-how and equity money to take the land all the way through the process until they are paid off.

Construction loans have floating rates

Floating rate loans are extremely dangerous. But that's what virtually all construction loans are. One to three points over the prime rate. If prime goes up a lot, you could be wiped out. Therefore, you ***must hedge*** the interest rate risk. To do that you either find a fixed-rate loan (the simplest way) or you sell interest rate futures contracts short.

Hedging is a very complicated subject in itself. In essence, hedging in this case is like buying an insurance policy against the prime rate going up. If you're hedged, any increase in the prime rate ***costs*** you money on your construction loan. But you make an offsetting ***profit*** on the interest rate futures contracts you sold short. So you come out approximately even.

If the prime rate does ***not*** go up during the loan term, you lose only the commission you had to pay to sell the contracts short. That's about like paying an insurance premium and not having a loss. It's better to have it and not need it than to need it and not have it.

How to handle margin calls resulting from a *drop* in prime rate

If the prime rate goes ***down*** during the term of the loan, you'll ***lose*** money on the futures contract you sold short. If they go down enough, you'll get a ***margin call***...a demand from your stock broker (who sold the contract short for you) that you bring in additional money. But you'll benefit so much from the prime rate going down on your construction loan that you won't mind.

In order to meet the possible margin call, you need to set up an appropriate size ***line of credit***. The idea behind the line of credit would be, "Look Mr. Line-of-credit Lender, if interest rates go down, I will have ***increased debt carrying capacity*** due to the payments on my construction loan. That's where I'll get the money to pay the payments on your line of credit advance, if any. Also, a drop in interest rates ***raises*** the value of my real estate, so I will have ***increased equity*** to pledge as collateral if you need it."

Hedging is not a suggestion, it's *mandatory*

I'm not just tossing this hedging idea out as a suggestion. It's ***mandatory!*** The only floating rate loan you should accept without hedging is one so small that you could pay it off immediately if interest rates went into the stratosphere. Like a credit card balance.

When my wife and I have credit card balances on which we pay interest, we do not hedge them in the interest rate futures market. Because they're so small that if the interest rate jumped, we'd just pay them off.

But if you are borrowing a ***substantial*** amount of money on a ***floating rate*** loan...like a construction loan on a home you're building...or a construction loan on a subdivision you're developing, you *must* hedge.

The prime rate peaked at 20% in 1981. Suppose it happens again? How long can you afford to pay 20% plus two percent or whatever your deal is with the construction lender? And what if the runup in interest rates causes your permanent lender to renege on his commitment to pay off the construction lender? They're not allowed to do that. But the real world doesn't always operate by the rules. We're talking catastrophic losses here.

All builders ought to hedge their floating rate loans. I surmise that few do. And few builders know any other builders who hedge. But virtually ***all*** builders know guys who ***used*** to be builders but aren't anymore because the prime rate went up and wiped them out. So the typical builder knows the "disease" and many of its victims. But, surprisingly, few builders seem to take advantage of the "vaccine" to prevent them from dying of the "disease," available since October 20, 1975...the date interest rate futures contracts were first traded.

Not just builders...home buyers, too

My hedging advice does ***not*** apply only to builders. It applies to ***anyone*** who has a large, floating rate debt which they could not pay off in a hurry if the interest rate went way up. The most likely *non*-builder example would be a husband and wife who are having a home built. In my opinion, they are behaving ***irresponsibly*** if they fail to hedge that loan.

There's a saying on Wall Street, "If you're not hedging, you're speculating." And neither builders nor home buyers have any business speculating on interest rates with tens of thousands of dollars...or more. Because as Reed's Rule of Real Estate Finance Number 10 says, "Interest rates are totally unpredictable."

How to hedge

I don't have the room in this book or the expertise to give you the details on how to hedge. But on the other hand it's not such a big deal that a home buyer should say, "to heck with it." So I'll point you in the right direction.

Call a *large* stock brokerage firm...like Merrill Lynch. Tell the person who answers that you want to talk to someone about hedging in the financial futures market. They'll probably say the best one to talk to on that is So and So. Then they'll either transfer you to him or her or have them call you back. You may need to call several large brokerage firms before you get the help you need. And if you're not in a major metropolitan area, you'll probably be referred to someone in the nearest major metropolitan area.

For more information:

Chicago Board of Trade
LaSalle at Jackson
Chicago, IL 60604
312-435-3558

When to use standby commitments

A commitment is a promise by a lender to make a certain mortgage. And ***standby*** commitment is the same thing only the lender who makes a standby commitment hopes that you will ***not*** accept the loan. A standby commitment is a sort of insurance policy. It guarantees that you'll have a mortgage if you can't find one anywhere else. But the ***terms*** of a standby commitment loan are usually worse than a normal loan to encourage you to find the loan elsewhere.

You use a standby commitment when a property is being ***changed*** in some way...and the loan you hope to get after the change is not yet available. The typical case is new construction. The ***permanent*** lender (30-year mortgage) says, "We'd probably be interested in making the loan when the building's done and rented. But we won't commit ourselves until then." Or they may only be willing to make a ***smaller*** loan than you think you'll be able to get later.

The ***construction*** lender says, "We'll loan you the construction money now. But only if you have a commitment from a permanent lender."

So you get a standby commitment. That satisfies the construction lender that they will be paid off upon completion of the construction. As construction nears completion, it becomes easier to get a permanent loan because the lender has a building to look at, not just plans. And because the market conditions in which you'll be looking for tenants are better known than they were before you started building. In fact, you may have even pre-leased much or all of the space in the building. . .which helps you get the maximum amount of financing on the best terms.

The basic idea behind a standby commitment is that it's easier to finance a "pig" than a "pig in a poke." A to-be-constructed building is a "pig in a poke."

Not just new construction

The use of the standby commitment is not restricted to new construction or even to ***physical*** changes like renovation. You may benefit from a standby commitment any time you expect to significantly increase the building's value or lower its risk. That might be due to rent increases without renovation, zoning changes, better management, etc.

If you got a new permanent mortgage, ***then*** improved the building greatly, you have difficulty extracting the increased equity due to prepayment penalties, lock-ins, and other payoff transaction costs on the less advantageous first permanent mortgage. Plus you'd be paying the transaction costs of obtaining ***two*** permanent mortgages instead of the cost of obtaining one plus the lower costs of obtaining a standby commitment.

On the other hand, if you used a standby commitment to buy time, you can obtain the ***post-improvement*** permanent mortgage with its superior terms at a minimum of transaction costs.

Forget using standbys because you think rates will come down

All the high-powered finance books list ***dropping rates*** as one time to use standby commitments. Forget it.

The idea is that if interest rates are now 13% and you ***think*** they'll be 12% in the future, you should get a standby commitment now and get your permanent mortgage ***after*** the rates go down.

I remind you of Reed's Rule of Real Estate Finance Number 10. "Interest rates are totally unpredictable." If you can ***get*** a permanent commitment now. . .and its terms are acceptable, ***take it***!

Remember, if you're not hedging, you're speculating. The interest rates you ***think*** will go ***down*** may go ***up*** instead. You can hedge by simply getting a fixed rate loan, i.e. take the permanent commitment you've been offered. Or you can hedge by getting a standby and selling interest rate futures contracts short. Taking the permanent is simpler. And that's Reed's Rule of Real Estate Finance Number 1 "Simple is better than complex."

A hedged adjustable rate is a sort of standby commitment. . .only maybe cheaper

If it weren't for prepayment penalties and lock-ins, you could use a permanent mortgage to buy time the way you use a standby commitment to buy time. But most ***fixed***-rate mortgages have either prepayment penalties or lock-ins or both. ***Adjustable*** rate mortgages, on the other hand, do ***not*** usually have prepayment penalties or lock-ins. So another way to buy time in a value-increasing situation is by placing an adjustable rate mortgage on the property.

Of course, that adjustable rate mortgage must be hedged. If it ***were*** hedged, you'd have the best of both worlds: the advantages of the adjustable rate mortgage without the disadvantages of the exposure to fluctuating interest rates. The advantages of the adjustable rate mortgage include lower initial rate, higher loan-to-value ratio, and lower debt-coverage ratio.

Shopping center construction loans

I recently read two books on real estate finance. Each covered the subject of financing a shopping center in some detail. If I didn't know that shopping centers already exist, those books would have convinced me that financing a new shopping center is so complicated that no mortal man could ever do it.

The problem is too many "750 pound gorillas." You've got the construction lender, the permanent lender, and the anchor tenants. Anchor tenants are usually departments stores. They are "the franchise" as they say in professional sports. A shopping center with no anchor tenants is an empty building. Anchor tenants are essential. And they know it. And so do the lenders.

The construction lender won't make the construction loan until the permanent lender commits to take the construction lender out (pay them off) when the center is complete. And the permanent lender won't commit until the anchor tenants sign long-term leases. And not just ***any*** lease will do. The permanent lender has a whole list of clauses they demand and clauses they will not accept in those anchor tenant leases.

Then there are the anchor tenants. They have real estate experts on their staffs. And their real estate experts ***also*** have lists of clauses they will and will not accept in the leases. And their list often ***conflicts*** with the permanent lender's list. Last but not least in a book aimed at real estate investors is the real estate investor who's building the shopping center. He has a list, too. All he has to do to get his list accepted is persuade the 750 pound gorillas to do it his way. Good luck.

It can be done

Fortunately, all these gorillas need each other. Department stores got to be in ***somebody's*** shopping center. If they overdo the negotiating, they'll never open a store. And permanent lenders got to lend. Their money comes from someone and that someone expects to be paid interest. So the lender has to ***earn*** interest somewhere.

So it obviously is possible to arrange financing for a new shopping center. But I wouldn't recommend it to the faint of heart or the inexperienced. Someone once noted that the meek may inherit the earth but they won't get the mineral rights. Ditto getting shopping center construction loans.

Future expansion

It's common for an owner of an existing shopping center to find it makes sense to ***expand*** the center. The main thing you need to know is that long-term documents like leases with shopping center tenants and shopping center mortgages frequently contain clauses which give the tenant or lender a lot of power to control expansion. As the developer, you need to keep future expansion in mind when you are negotiating the original documents. If the documents are already signed, you need to check each and every one of them before you proceed with expansion plans.

Condo conversion

Converting an apartment building to a condominium usually requires some fancy financing footwork. The problem is that the existing lender typically will not sit still for a conversion. And he usually has a clause which gives him the right to call the loan if you being conversion. Some existing lenders will agree to stay on for the conversion...although they'll usually want something for their trouble.

But in most cases you have to refinance the building with a loan which will permit condo conversion. The condo conversion loan is a ***blanket*** mortgage on all the little condos in the building. Whenever you hear the word "blanket" you should think "release clause."

You will need a release clause in the new mortgage which will allow you to release each condo as it is sold to the individual condo owner. Since extensive ***renovation*** is also typically a part of condo conversion, a ***construction loan*** fits the situation well. Construction lenders are used to releasing individual home lots as they are sold.

Depending on the rental market and condo conversion laws in your area, the conversion announcement to the tenants might trigger an ***exodus*** leaving a high vacancy rate. That can cause cash flow problems which you must anticipate and plan for. It also means that you must keep the possibility of conversion secret as long as possible.

Some states and communities have ***laws*** severely restricting condo conversion. Make sure you are familiar with them before you start.

Office buildings

Financing office buildings is like financing other properties except for a couple of items. For one thing, you may have long-term leases. As with shopping centers, you must be very careful about what these contain. And you must coordinate the negotiation of long-term leases with the prospective lender if you are building the office building or planning to refinance it. If you don't, you may find that you've let the tenant talk you into some clause which makes it difficult or more expensive for you to get financing on the building.

The other unique aspect of office buildings is the fact that the owner typically installs walls, doors, carpet and such in the tenant's space in accordance with tenant specifications but at the owner's expense. Sometimes the tenant pays all or part of the renovation cost. As a borrower, you must show the prospective lender that you understand and have accurately estimated these costs.

Co-ops

In April, 1984, FNMA announced that they would begin buying co-op loans on individual co-op units. FHA has had a program (213) for co-ops for some time.

PART THREE: TERMS

8
Terms Of The Loan

Minimum requirements

In order to have a valid mortgage (or trust deed. . . I'll use the word "mortgage" to refer to both), you need the following:

- Date
- Signatures of the borrower and lender
- Names of borrower and lender
- Clause pledging the property as security for the loan
- Amount of the loan, interest rate, and payment schedule
- Description of the property

Those are the bare minimum requirements. With today's consumer-oriented judges, you also need to give the borrower various protective clauses. And some state laws require certain clauses which, if missing, would invalidate the mortgage.

Sellers versus institutions

Institutional lenders typically use a standard mortgage document. In fact, where home loans are involved, it's a standard FNMA/FHLMC form.

You should definitely ***read*** an institutional lender's form before you sign it. That's so you know what you're getting into. But don't expect to find any nefarious traps.

Seller mortgages are quite another matter. Sometimes, sellers use a standard form. But other times, they or their attorney draws it up. When that happens, the resulting document can contain some mean stuff.

The same is true of institutional lenders when it comes to income property loans. ***Home*** mortgage lending is a very civilized, consumer-oriented, Marquis of Queensbury realm. When you start doing income property loans, however, you are no longer a consumer. You're on your own.

Note and mortgage

You probably already know, but I'd better make sure, that there are *two* documents:

- mortgage or trust deed and
- note

A note is an IOU. It says the borrower owes the lender such and such an amount and states the interest rate and payment schedule. The mortgage says that such and such property is hereby pledged as security for the note.

Late penalty

Any lender who knows what he's doing will require a late penalty. You may not know, however, that the late penalty must conform to state law. An excessive late penalty can violate state laws...sometimes usury laws. That's a serious matter. If you're the lender, make sure your attorney stays within the law. If you're a borrower, you may want to check the pertinent laws to see if the penalty in your loan violates the law. If it does, you may be able to get substantial amounts from the lender. Some usury laws penalize the lender through ***forgiveness of the debt!***

Prepayment penalty

If prepayment is not specifically permitted by the note, you generally may not prepay at all. Some states have laws limiting prepayment penalties. When I invested in New Jersey, the law said the lender couldn't charge more than three percent the first year, two percent the second, and one percent the third.

I sold a house in California in 1983. I knew the mortgage had a prepayment penalty. But I assumed it would be about the same as New Jersey's. California being pro-consumer. I had lived in the property more than three years, so I expected the penalty would either be passed or small.

Wrong.

It was ***seven percent*** of the balance less 20% of the original amount. Almost eight thousand dollars. The clause reads

"The undersigned may prepay this note in full or in part at any time. If in any twelve month period during the first five years from the date hereof the undersigned shall prepay in excess of an amount equal to 20% of the face amount of this note, the undersigned promises to pay the holder of this note a prepayment premium in an amount equal to six months advance interest on the amount of principal repaid in excess of an amount equal to 20% of the face amount of this note. After said five year period, prepayments may be made without payment of premium."

One way to avoid prepayment

In my case, we required the buyer to buy subject to the mortgage and to pay the penalty himself if he decided to pay the loan off before the fifth anniversary. At the time, the loan was at 14% and the market rate was more like 12.5%. In order to get him to accept the 14% loan, we promised to pay the buyer one twelfth of 1.5% of the remaining balance each month for eighteen months (about $175 a month) and one twelfth of one percent (about $115 a month) of the remaining balance for an additional eighteen months...or until the loan was paid off, whichever came first.

In other words, we made the loan equal to a 12.5% loan for eighteen months and equal to a

13% loan for eighteen months. After that, the borrower will have to pay 14% or refinance if market rates are cheaper then. Actually, the prepayment penalty will be done at the end of the first eighteen months. So it might pay the buyer to refinance then even though it would cost him his $115 a month subsidy for the remaining eighteen months.

In effect, my wife and I will be paying a ***smaller*** "prepayment penalty" to the buyer. Discounted at, say 10%, the present value of $175 for eighteen months then $115 for eighteen months is

n	18
i	10/12 = .833
PMT	175
PV	$2,913.89

n	18
i	10/12 = .833
PMT	115
PV	$1,914.85

Since the second 18 months doesn't start until the end of the first 18 months, you have to double discount it. Once to get the value of the 18 payments. And once to bring ***that*** present value down to ***its*** present value 18 months earlier. To do this, you make the PV of the second 18 months the FV and discount it to its PV 18 months earlier.

FV	1914.85
n	18
i	10/12 = .833
PV	$1,649.16
Total PV	$4,563.05

$4,563.05 beats $8,000. And if the buyer refinances before the eighteen months is up, it'll be even better. And finally, if we can earn more than 10% on the money in the interim, which I think we can, the "penalty" we will have paid will be even less than $4,563.05.

Our buyer was willing to go along with this rather than getting a new 12.5% mortgage for two reasons.

1. We would have held out for a higher price to compensate us for the prepayment penalty.
2. By buying subject to our loan, he avoids the fees he would have to pay a lender for a new loan. . .about $3,000 in this case.

So the buyer saved a little and we saved a little. If I had known the size of the prepayment penalty before I started building our new home, I might have waited another year and a half to do it so we could avoid the prepayment penalty altogether. Then again, we wanted the new house ***now***, so we might have gone ahead even if we knew about the $8,000 prepayment penalty.

Lest you think the bank got off scot-free, my wife worked for the lender for the first two and a half years we lived there. During that time, we paid only 10% (employee rate) on the first $125,000 of the loan instead of 14%. That saved us $12,500. And the bank had waived all the front end charges... which saved us another several thousand dollars.

Shop for a better prepayment penalty

If you think you may want to pay off the loan during the prepayment period, you should shop for the best prepayment penalty you can find. Some lenders have no prepayment penalty at all.

Prepayment penalties and due-on-sale clauses

Sometimes you get a double whammy. You're ***forced*** to pay off the loan by a due-on-sale clause. Then they ***also*** demand a prepayment penalty.

That combination seems a bit much. After all, the lender is the one who's forcing pay off of the loan. Seems unfair for them to penalize you for doing something they forced you to do. Actually, the lender might argue that they didn't force you to sell the property. And there's logic to that.

But it wasn't persuasive logic to a number of courts and legislatures. They have stopped lenders from both enforcing a due-on-sale clause and collecting a prepayment penalty. Furthermore, the Federal Home Loan Bank Board (FHLBB) recently put out a rule saying that federal savings and loans could ***not*** both enforce due-on-sale and collect a prepayment penalty. FHLBB is the agency which regulates federally chartered savings and loans.

You must get a prepayment bonus if below-market interest rate

In virtually all seller-financed deals, the interest rate is below-market. And the sale price is ***above*** the cash equivalent value. In other words, you are paying a premium on the price for the low interest rate. The longer the term of the below-market interest rate, the higher the premium you pay.

But what if you pay the seller loan off ***early***? Then the seller gets to have his cake and eat it, too. And you get the shaft. You paid a high price to get a low interest rate for X years. But you didn't ***keep*** the loan for X years. So you paid for something you never got.

The solution is a ***prepayment bonus***. You absolutely ***must*** get a prepayment bonus in any below market financing whenever possible. As you know, the ***market value*** of a below-market interest rate mortgage is ***less*** than its face value. If the seller who took back the mortgage tried to sell it, he'd have to sell it at a substantial discount.

When you prepay a mortgage, you are ***buying*** that mortgage. Your prepayment bonus should be such that you are not paying more than market value. Why should the borrower be treated any differently than any other mortgage buyer?

The prepayment bonus

Call a guy who invests in discounted mortgages. They run ads in the classified section of your newspaper and in the *Yellow Pages*. Ask a couple of mortgage investors what they'd pay for the loan the seller is going to take back the day after closing. Let's say they'd want a 40% discount. In that case, your prepayment bonus clause should say that your prepayment bonus would be 40% the day after closing, zero the day the loan matures, and prorated between zero and 40% any time in between.

The seller may balk at that. It's a fair clause. But the reason sellers take back mortgages is to pump up the sale price and their ego. If you get the right to buy the mortgage the day after closing for 60% of its face value, the self-delusion contained in the sale price becomes evident. Most seller's egos can't handle that.

Furthermore, the fact that you can pay off the mortgage at 60% of face value may be a "material fact" to any institutional lenders involved in the deal. They may reduce the ***sale price*** for loan purposes by 40% of the seller mortgage to reflect the fact that you could pay off the seller right after closing and thereby buy the property for much less than the stated sale price. This would ***not*** be a problem if there were no new mortgage. But you should disclose it if you are using a combination of new and seller financing.

Selling the seller on the idea

One solution to the seller ego problem might be to get the seller to agree to an ***appraisal clause***. That is, you, the borrower/buyer, have the right to buy the mortgage from the seller at any time. The purchase price shall be determined by an independent appraisal made by an experienced mortgage investor.

Or you might use a ***time value of money formula***. Like you may buy the mortgage at any time for its discounted present value discounted at the then market rate for similar mortgages. You might even specify a certain published mortgage interest rate like the FNMA 30-year fixed-rate conventional mortgage rate.

You may have to accept a delayed prepayment bonus clause

Or you might use a percentage discount but say that it does not kick in until the end of the second year or some such. Prepayment before that must be at face value. I don't like that choice as much as the others.

Impound accounts

An impound account holds your monthly tax and insurance payments until the annual bill comes due. As a borrower, you want to avoid impound accounts. They are an interest-free loan to whoever holds the account.

If you lend, you want them...for the same reason, and to make sure the borrower pays the taxes and insurance.

I would not shop for a lender who doesn't require an impound account. It's not that big a deal. But I would try to talk a lender out of requiring impounds.

Where impounds are required, I would request that the formula for computing the ***amount*** of the impound be specified in the mortgage or note. Normal is to subtract the balance in the account at year end from the total bills expected for the year and divide by twelve.

Inflated impound accounts

Over the years, there have been several occasions where I have caught lenders trying to juice the impound amount up above what's necessary to increase the amount of money they're earning interest on. When I've written them about it, I've usually obtained a reduction. But I've had to fight through at least one initial brush off each time, too.

You have to convey that you know what they're trying to pull and that you plan to fight it. You could, for example, complain to FNMA or FHA or whoever's involved in the loan. The lender's aren't terrified of FNMA or FHA, and FNMA and FHA really don't care whether your impound account is too high or not. But the paperwork you generate usually convinces them to give in.

As a last resort, you could threaten to go to the media, the legislators for your district or small claims court. Again, the issue probably isn't the most exciting thing to happen so don't expect to make the evening news. But you might get it in your paper's ombudsman column. And the fact that it ***might*** end up on the evening news or in court scares a lot of lenders.

Whether they're entitled to hold your tax and insurance money interest-free is arguable. But they're sure not entitled to hold ***more than*** your taxes and interest.

My first lender applied the tax and insurance money to the loan principal. That was the equivalent of paying me interest on the money...at the mortgage interest rate. Then when the annual bills came in, the principal went back up by that amount. Those were the good old days. You probably won't get that deal from an institutional lender these days. But you might get it from a seller.

Lender must pay bills

If the lender *does* require impound accounts, then *you're* darn sure entitled to have the lender promise to pay those bills promptly. And to pay out of the lender's pocket any late penalties or other costs resulting from their not making the payments correctly.

Hazard insurance

Lenders who know what they're doing require borrowers to keep the property insured...and to name the lenders as "additional insureds." The FNMA/FHLMC clause requires the borrower to keep the property insured

"...against loss by fire, hazards included within the term 'extended coverage,' and other such Hazards as lender may require..."

That last "other such Hazards as lender may require" is probably unenforceable because it's too vague.

Amount of hazard insurance

Lenders typically require the insurance coverage to be at least as much as their loan amount. The FNMA/FHLMC clause says

"...that Lender shall not require that the amount of such coverage exceed that amount of coverage required to pay the sums secured by this Mortgage...

Insurors, on the other hand, will pay claims up to the ***replacement cost*** of the structure...and no more. Sometimes, the amount of the loan is greater than the replacement cost. My last home is a case in point.

We bought it with a 90% loan-to-value ratio loan. The land represented about 20% of the value. So the replacement cost of the structure was about 80% of what we paid. but the lender wanted us to buy insurance for ***90%*** of what we paid.

When I tried to order the insurance, the insurance company said, "We'll write the policy for that amount...and we'll charge you the premium for that amount. But we absolutely will not pay out that amount if the house burns to the ground. We will only pay out the replacement cost."

We called the lender and explained that to them and they agreed to let us carry insurance for the replacement cost only...even though it was less than the loan amount. You should check to make sure you aren't paying for "phantom" insurance that you can't collect on because the loan amount is greater than the replacement cost. Again, you might have to argue with the lender over it. But right's right so you'll eventually prevail.

Bob Bruss is a nationally syndicated real estate columnist. In a recent column, one of his readers told of suing a lender in small claims court for the excess insurance premium caused by the lender insisting on the loan amount instead of the replacement cost where the replacement cost was lower. The borrower won the court battle. And the lender changed its policy.

If you can negotiate over it, you should require that the amount of hazard insurance required in the mortgage be

"equal to the loan amount or the replacement cost, whichever is less."

Insurance shenanigans

I sued a mortgage company once. During the suit, I was sending them mortgage payments. Out of spite, they tried to beef up my impound accounts. It didn't work. I complained to FNMA and they had to back down.

Then I got my annual statement. It had a deduction for hazard insurance. But the amount did not seem to be the one I remembered the insurance agent quoting. I investigated. Turned out the mortgage company had gone out and bought another insurance policy without my knowing it. . .through a friend who may have paid them a kickback. Their reason? They said I had allowed the insurance coverage to lapse and they were taking action permitted by the hazard insurance clause to protect the lender.

In fact, I had not allowed the coverage to lapse. They were just trying to punish me. The lesson is that when other people are taking care of your money, you'd better watch them with an eagle eye. A lot of things may be going on that you have no idea about.

What if there's a claim?

What if you have an insurance claim? In the event of a major claim like a fire, the insurance company would typically make the check out to the owners of the property ***and*** the lender. You could either use the money to restore the property, or you could use it to pay off the loan and leave the property as a vacant lot. Your right to do either should be spelled out in the mortgage. . .as it is in the FNMA/FHLMC form.

In some mortgages, the ***lender*** has the right to decide whether the insurance money goes to repair the damage or pay down the loan. Resist such a clause.

You should also spell out that ***small claims***, like less than $5,000, should be paid to the owner only. I got a claim check for $135 once. . .for water damage done when a tenant left his water faucets full open when the water was shut off for repair. When the main valve was turned on, he had left the apartment and the carpet was ruined.

Anyway, the check from the insurance company was made out to the mortgage lender (a life insurance company in another city), my wife and me, and my co-tenant who was working in Saudi Arabia at the time. I threw the check in the trash. Because the hassle I'd have had to go through to get it endorsed by all those parties exceeded the amount of the check.

Zoning insurance

In some states, title companies will provide zoning insurance as an endorsement to a title policy. Zoning insurance protects you and the lender against your being in violation of zoning laws. A good idea whether the lender requires it or not.

You should insist that ***no*** prepayment penalty be due in the event the loan is prepaid due to insurance proceeds. Also, the ***monthly payment*** should be reduced pro rata when you pay the loan down with insurance proceeds. Otherwise, you might find that 25% of your units have been eliminated by a fire. . .and 25% of the rent income along with them. . .but you still have to make the same monthly mortgage payment.

Maintenance

Lenders virtually always require that the borrower "keep the property in good repair." Failure to do so is a default. That's fine. But make sure the lender has to give you ***plenty of written notice*** before foreclosing due to your failure to maintain the building. Otherwise, some shyster seller is liable to use this clause to take the property back or to cause you legal problems for the purpose of extorting "protection" money from you. Plenty of written notice would be a list of repairs and six months to complete them or explain why they are not necessary.

Protection of lender's security

This is the clause which allows the lender or his agent to do things like order the fire insurance you failed to get. Again, you want this clause to require the lender to give you plenty of written notice before they start spending your money for you and taking over the management of the property. This is rarely a problem with institutional lenders. But a seller might abuse this clause. Or a mortgage company.

Condemnation

The standard condemnation clause says that the condemnation proceeds (payment from the government which took the property) will be first applied to reduce the debt. Any left over will be given to the borrower. I'd prefer that ***both*** the lender and the borrower share in each dollar of proceeds. . . allocated according to the percentage of value the loan represented at the time of the condemnation.

For example, if the loan balance was 60% of the condemnation award, the lender ought to get 60% of each dollar and the borrower 40%. In a total taking, it would work out that way anyway. But if only part of the property were taken by the government, it doesn't seem fair to me for the lender to get ***all*** of the money.

You should also insist that no prepayment penalty will be due if the loan is totally or partially prepaid due to condemnation.

Notice

This is a ***very important*** clause. It says how and where notice must be given by either party to the other. The FNMA/FHLMC clause requires the lender to send notice by certified mail to the address of the mortgaged property or other address designated by the borrower. And it requires the borrower to give notice by certified mail, ***return receipt requested***, to the lender's designated address. Nice how you have to get a return receipt but they don't.

That's an OK clause. But you'd better make sure that you keep the lender posted as to your current address. Whenever it changes, you'd better send the lender a return receipt letter informing them.

Foreclosure by Monday

I used to pay a seller payments on a second mortgage. One day, shortly after I had moved, and while I was off teaching seminars, a letter was forwarded to our new address. It was from the seller. . . an attorney. It informed us that the property we had bought from him would be sold at foreclosure the following Monday. We got the letter on a Wednesday.

The letter said the seller was foreclosing due to our default. He did not say how we had defaulted. And we didn't have a clue.

I had informed the seller of our new address when I made my most recent payment. But the change of address had crossed in the mail with his foreclosure notice. We lost precious days while the post office forwarded the letter.

Turned out the seller was off his rocker. When we finally got in touch with him, he said we had not made the last two monthly payments. We told him he was nuts and that we had the cancelled checks with his signature on them. He checked, found that his bookkeeper had screwed up, apologized, and withdrew his foreclosure threat.

But we had only averted our property being posted on the courthouse bulletin board by 24 hours. We probably would not have lost the property given the facts. But having our property appear in the paper as being foreclosed would have done severe damage to our credit in the community. The retraction is always less prominent. And less remembered.

That's where I learned the importance of plenty of written notice. The mortgage in question only required about ten days notice. And it's where I learned the importance of keeping the lender informed of your address.

Use third party collector for wraparound

To protect the buyer/borrower, payments on the first mortgage in a wraparound should be made by a third-party collector, like a bank or title company. Simply because they are more trustworthy than an individual seller.

On my Fort Worth apartment building, we put the rent receipts into a Fort Worth bank account. On the 25th of each month, that bank deducts the wraparound payment from my account and issues two cashier's checks: one to the first mortgage lender for the principal, interest, taxes, and insurance; and one to the guy who sold me the building for the rest. We paid a $125 front-end fee when we set this up. And no further charges.

If the seller is using a wraparound to avoid being taxed on "excess loans over basis," he should have a tax attorney scrutinize the collection arrangement to be sure it conforms to the principles set forth in the court decisions which said you could use a wrap to avoid that tax. Namely, *Stonecrest*, 24 TC 659 and *Hunt*, 80 TC 62.

Due-on-sale

Due-on-sale clauses are a subject in and of themselves. I'll cover them in detail in the chapter on preserving existing financing. For now, suffice it to say that you would prefer ***not*** to have a due-on-sale clause. But unless the mortgage is FHA or VA, you probably ***will*** have one.

Due-on-encumbrance clauses

A due-on-encumbrance clause is like a due-on-sale clause. Except it applies to putting additional ***mortgages*** on the property, not to sales, lease-options, or land contracts. Avoid due-on-encumbrance clauses. You often need to further encumber the property to pay for major capital expenditures like new parking lot surfacing or a new roof. Or, if the first is assumable, it may be cheaper to put a second on the property than to refinance the first in a sale.

If you ***already*** have a mortgage with a due-on-encumbrance clause, take heart. It may not be enforceable. In some states, the courts feel prohibiting junior encumbrances is a bit much. They may apply a standard of reasonableness. For example, if the total of the existing and new loans will not exceed 75% of value, it would be hard for the first lender to argue that it's security is endangered by the new loan. *LaSala v. American Savings and Loan*, 97 Cal Rptr 849

In properties with long-term leases to high-credit tenants, it ***is*** reasonable for the first lender to prohibit those leases becoming ***subordinate*** to the new, junior loan. Because if they ***were*** subordinate to that new loan, foreclosure by the junior lender would wipe out the leases.

Personal liability on second means personal liability on first

It is also reasonable for a ***non***recourse first mortgage to contain a clause which says that it ***becomes a recourse*** loan if you put on the property another mortgage which ***is*** a recourse loan. Recourse, you'll recall, means that the borrower is personally liable on the loan.

The logic is this. If you are personally liable on the ***second*** but ***not*** on the ***first*** mortgage, you will be likely to pay only the ***second*** if there's not enough money to pay ***both*** loans. . .to protect your other assets. That sort of makes the second the first and the first, second. Understandably, the first mortgage lender does not want that to happen.

Borrower's right to reinstate

Most states give home owners the right to cure defaults and stop foreclosure. In many states, the home owner even has the right to get the property back after foreclosure, if he pays the loan and foreclosure charges off. This is one of the problems with investing in foreclosures. The new owner's title isn't totally clean until the redemption period expires. . .often a year or more.

As a borrower, you want as much time to reinstate or cure defaults as possible. Expect to pay whatever charges the lender has incurred starting foreclosure. But you ought to have the right to straighten everything out before the property is actually sold at a foreclosure auction.

Personal liability

Most investors want to avoid personal liability on loans. That annoys me.

At Harvard Business School, I attended a talk where a successful businessman was speaking to student members of the Small Business Club about starting your own business. Come question time, every single question was about how to avoid loan liability. "Should we put everything in our wife's name?" "Should we incorporate to avoid liability for financing?" "Should we only accept non-recourse loans."

After about twenty minutes of, "How can I avoid liability for the failure of my business?" questions, I was on the verge of standing up and saying, "Why don't you guys who are so interested in avoiding responsibility for failing start the Harvard Business School Deadbeats Club? In the meantime, some of us in the room would like to hear about how to ***avoid*** failing."

My fellow students were saved from that speech by the speaker's cutting off discussion on that subject.

Keep your promises

You ought to keep your promises. I said that in the beginning of the book. And if you promise to pay back a loan on an investment property, you darn well better pay it back. If the investment goes ***well***, you sure won't give the lender a nickel of your profits. So you have no right to expect the lender to absorb ***any*** of your loss.

Far as I'm concerned, people who are eager to avoid personal liability have not yet achieved the maturity to become investors.

There *are* legitimate reasons for non-recourse

Having condemned non-recourse seekers, let me now point out when I think it's legitimate and appropriate to seek a non-recourse (also known as no personal liability or property-is-sole-security) loan.

1. Syndicate general partners
2. Multimillion dollar deals
3. Effect on other lenders

Syndicate general partners

The general partners in a limited partnership or syndicate usually try to avoid personal liability on mortgage loans. That because of IRS regulation section 1.752.

Reg 1.752 says that limited partners' basis in the partnership is their equity and their share of any ***nonrecourse*** loans against the partnership property. But if ***any*** partner is personally liable on any partnership loans, ***only*** those personally liable can include those loans in their basis.

In the case of *Raphan v. U.S.*, 83-2 USTC paragraph 9613, the Claims Court created a loophole for getting around regulation section 1.752. But Section 79 of the Tax Reform Act of 1984 overruled ***Raphan*** and slammed that loophole shut.

Example

For example, a limited partnership buys a million dollar property with $200,000 down and $800,000 of loans. Let's say there are eight limited partners who put up $20,000 a piece and two general partners who put up $20,000 each.

If the general partners are personally liable for the $800,000 loan, only they can count it. That would mean the general partners' basis would be $840,000 ($800,000 + $20,000 + $20,000). And the limited partners' basis would only be $20,000 each.

But if the debt is nonrecourse, ***all*** partners get a basis of $100,000 ($80,000 in debt + $20,000 equity).

Multimillion dollar deals

Let's say you and I have a six shooter revolver. I put one bullet in, spin the revolver, point it into the air, and pull the trigger. If the gun goes off, you lose $100. If it does not go off, you win. Would you take the bet?

You probably would. Or at least you should. You've got a five sixths probability of winning. And it you lose you're only out $100. So what the heck.

How about if I offer you the same bet only with $1,000? You'd probably do that, too.

How about $10,000?

You ***should*** take that bet, too. Still five sixths probability of winning. But now you're starting to get nervous about losing. $10,000 is a lot of money. You understand the probability of winning. But you're also aware of how bad you'd feel if you lost $10,000. I mean it would be nice to ***win*** $10,000. But ***losing*** $10,000 would be ***terrible***. The pain of losing would exceed the joy of winning.

How about a million?

No way, huh?

Risk preference

Your reaction to those various bets is called your "risk preference." Every bet I offered you had the exact same probability of winning—-five sixths. You should have taken every one.

But your aversion to losing large sums overrode your ability to calculate probabilities. At the $100 level, you're unemotional...like Mr. Spock of Star Trek. But at $10,000, you lose your Vulcan analytical powers and become just another emotional, fraidy cat human.

When it comes to multimillion dollar deals, the amount you could lose may well exceed your net worth. So you could lose everything you've worked for all your life. For what? The chance to earn more money. You've probably already got a net worth of a million dollars (if you're doing multimillion dollar deals). What are you going to do with another million? You certainly don't ***need*** another million. It'd be nice. But it's not worth risking everything for.

So you don't accept personal liability on multimillion dollar loans unless you have so many millions that you wouldn't miss the amount you're being asked to be personally liable for.

If lenders didn't make nonrecourse loans, there'd be no General Motors, no IBM, hardly any multimillion dollar deals done at all.

Effect on other lenders

The final legitimate reason to avoid personal liability is that it looks better to other lenders. If you have one non-recourse loan, and you apply for another loan, the second lender feels more secure if the first loan is non-recourse. Because it means that first lender will not have a shot at your personal assets. That will keep them available for the second lender to seize if necessary.

By assuming personal liability, you, in effect, pledge your personal assets as security for the loan. So you want to avoid being personally liable on loans because you've only got so many assets to pledge. The fewer you have to include in any loan, the more you have available for the next lender.

You can use personal liability as an *offensive* weapon

Note that personal liability can and should be used as an ***offensive*** weapon at times. If your overall balance sheet (net worth statement) is strong...and you want a loan which is secured by a relatively ***weak*** property, offering to assume personal liability may get you the loan.

Lenders using personal liability more often lately

As a practical matter, lenders have often not made use of their right to go after the non-mortgaged property of the borrower even when they had the right to. But according to the August 7, 1985 *Wall Street Journal*, lenders have become more aggressive lately. They are going after borrower's other assets more often. Especially if the borrower was an investor. That is, the property which was foreclosed was rented out and not the borrower's residence. And the *Journal* said lenders are even more likely to go after the investor personally if the deal was a ***nothing down*** deal.

Fear of failure and its consequences is not a legitimate reason to avoid personal liability

The thing that galled me about my Harvard classmates' desire to avoid personal liability was that it was motivated by fear of failure...and unwillingness to accept the consequences of failure. It is the height of selfishness to ask someone else to put his money into a venture which you wouldn't put your money into because of your opinion of the probability of failure.

If you think the chances of failure are so great that you wouldn't risk ***your*** money, don't do the deal at all. It would be immoral to proceed. As I mentioned earlier regarding venture capital, any lender who knows what he's doing is going to see how much of ***your*** money and assets you're willing to risk in the deal as a measure of your confidence. If the answer is "as little as possible," expect a savvy lender to do likewise.

There's nothing wrong with high leverage...if you are determined to succeed. But there is very definitely something wrong with asking others, whether institutions or individuals, to take risks ***you*** are unwilling to take.

Sometimes you can have partial personal liability on a nonrecourse loan

Let's say your mortgage is ***totally*** nonrecourse. And that you are unable to make the building break even. The negative cash flow is causing you financial problems. And on top of it all, the property does not seem to be appreciating. Then the light bulb goes on.

"Hey," you think, "if I stop paying ***all*** the bills, I can pocket the entire amount of the rent for months...until the foreclosure sale. It's nonrecourse, so what the heck. I'll finally make a profit on this rotten deal."

Because of that temptation, nonrecourse mortgages often contain a clause which requires you to use all the rent money to pay the mortgages and operating expenses of the property before ***you*** take any of it. Furthermore, that clause makes you ***personally liable*** for any operating expenses or mortgage payments which you do not pay to the extent that rent money was available to do so.

So you may want to think several times before you walk away from a property with a nonrecourse loan on it.

High-risk, non-recourse debt is really equity

When debt is non-recourse, and risks are high, the "lender" is really an ***equity partner*** with the borrower. The courts have so stated in a number of cases. An investor who tries to get non-recourse debt because he thinks the deal will fail is trying to give the "lender" the ***dis***advantages of equity (high probability of loss) while keeping for himself the ***ad***vantage of equity (possibility of gain). Like I said, the height of selfishness.

Calls

A call gives the lender the right to receive a balloon payment of the balance then due. It's a sort of option. For example, in 1978, I bought an apartment building subject to an existing mortgage. That mortgage had a call date of December 1, 1991. The clause was worded

"The holder hereof [lender] *shall have the option to demand and receive payment in full of the then existing unpaid principal balance of this note and all unpaid accrued interest at any time after December 1, 1991 by giving the maker hereof* [borrower] *at his last known address written notice mailed no later than thirty days prior to the date upon which payment in full shall be due."*

I recommend that you not agree to any call or balloon due date sooner than ***seven years*** if the payment would be so large as to require sale or refinancing of the property. If the payment is small enough that you can finance it from cash on hand or an unsecured loan, it doesn't matter how soon it is.

The seven year figure is based on gut feel. You'll probably sell (exchange, actually) within two to five years. That gives you another two years at worst. . . in case the property doesn't sell as fast as you thought it would. Or in case money is tight when you go to sell or refinance.

Money is sometimes hard to find or expensive for a year or so. But it usually becomes available within three years. A seven year deadline gives you the breathing room you need to find one of those periods where the market will permit refinancing at reasonable rates or sale for enough cash to pay off the balloon.

Attorney fees

Lenders like to get a clause requiring borrowers to pay attorneys fees in the event of a problem. In mortgages and elsewhere, you should request that it be a ***two-way street***. And that there be some reasonable limit on the amount of the fees. If you can't get a specific dollar amount, at least demand that the word "reasonable" be used. Here's the wording I suggest.

"If litigation is required to enforce this agreement, the prevailing party will be entitled to receive reasonable costs and attorney fees from the other party."

Commitment

Most institutional loans are preceded by a commitment. Principals in the deal ***rely*** on the commitment and spend large sums of money in anticipation of the committed loan.

A commitment is ***usually*** a binding contract. But only usually. You must take care to make sure that it ***is*** binding. Here's how.

- You gotta ***pay*** something for it. No consideration, no binding contract.
- Make sure the person who signs it is ***authorized*** to do so.
- Get it ***in writing***.
- Make sure the entity issuing the commitment is ***substantial and trustworthy***. A small mortgage broker may not be.
- It's best to get the commitment from the ***lender*** to you, ***not*** from the lender to a middleman and from the middleman to you.
- The commitment must be ***detailed.*** The less it says, the more pre-closing trouble you'll have and the more difficult it will be to enforce it in court.

All commitments have ***conditions***. Do not take any action which ***relies*** on the commitment until you are sure you have complied with or will be able to comply with all the conditions.

Do not allow any blank check clauses like "borrower will pay attorney fees." State the fee amount or put a limit on it.

Lender misbehavior on commitments

Lenders renege on commitments in a significant percentage of cases. Especially when rates go up between the commitment date and the closing date. More frequently, lenders come up with ***additional demands at the eleventh hour*** and threaten not to close if you don't comply.

In one of my deals, a nationally known lender issued a detailed commitment letter in August. Then in November, just prior to closing, their attorneys came up with a long list of additional demands and threatened not to close unless they were met.

One was that the holder of the existing first mortgage which was being taken subject to agree to notify the new second mortgage lender in the event of default on the first. The first mortgage lender refused. So were told that we ***must*** do something which we had no power to do.

Another aspect of that incident really galls me. It occurred in November of 1983. A few months before, the U. S. Supreme Court had decided the case of *Mennonite Board of Missions v. Adams* (103 S. Ct. 2706). That case said the due process clause of the Constitution requires a mailed notice be sent to a mortgage lender when a property is being sold for nonpayment of taxes.

Seems to me the same principle would apply to a junior mortgage holder's right to mailed notice in the event of foreclosure by a senior mortgage lender. I pointed that decision out to the attorneys for the lender and my buyer's attorney. None had heard of the decision! And they said it would not apply to a non-judicial foreclosure. I'm not an attorney, folks. But I feel pretty certain that these attorneys ***should*** have known about that decision. And that the due process clause of the U.S. Constitution applies to ***all*** extinguishment of property interests.

The explanation that it would not apply to non-judicial foreclosures was apparently just ***obfuscation by buzzword.*** When a layman finds a fault with the professional analysis of an attorney or accountant, the "professional" often defends himself like a frightened octopus...by squirting "ink" in the form of irrelevant buzzwords like "non-judicial foreclosure." Ultimately, the new lender simply dropped their demand that the first mortgage lender promise to send notice of default.

The August 26, 1985 *San Francisco Chronicle* has two stories on lenders misbehavior at the eleventh hour. One demanded earthquake insurance the day before closing. Another tried to collect a prepayment penalty in violation of the law. Others up the rates and points just prior to closing. Others delay the deal if they think rates will rise.

To try to minimize the number of eleventh hour dirty tricks, I recommend that you send a letter to the loan officer after every conversation with him or her. The letter summarizes the conversation as it applied to the terms of the loan. It should contain words to the effect that there will be no additional demands from the lender prior to closing. If you can have a witness present or on the other phone...disclosed to the loan officer, of course...then both you and the witness sign the letter summarizing the loan terms and conditions. For effect, you might send each letter ***return receipt.***

Try to get the right to substitute bond collateral

You should ask for the right to substitute bond collateral of equal or better quality for the real estate pledged as security for the loan. To increase the probability that the clause is enforceable, specify the minimum Moody's or Standard & Poors bond rating which will be considered equal. And if the seller is unsophisticated, make sure that the quality you specify *is* really equal or better than the mortgage they're taking back.

As a borrower, you want to specify the lowest rating the seller will agree to. CCC if you can get it. If the loan is a high leverage loan...with no prepayment penalty or other niceties of good lending...CCC may be equal or better.

The bonds would also need to have the ***same payment pattern***. That is, the monthly payments and balloon payments on the seller's mortgage would have to be met by the payments and maturity of the bonds.

Substituting bonds may allow a prepayment bonus

When you want to refinance a property...either in a sale or just to take some equity out...an existing low-interest loan is often in the way. Substituting bond collateral is a way to get that loan out of the way without paying it off at face value. You buy bonds with a similar payment pattern, execute documents pledging the bonds as security for the loan, and get the lender to execute documents removing the mortgage from your property. Do this through a title company to make sure you get the mortgage removed.

If the old loan was at a below-market interest rate, you can buy the necessary bonds at a substantial discount. And the lower the Moody's or Standard & Poors rating, the bigger the discount.

So instead of having to pay off, say, a $100,000 low interest mortgage with $100,000, you'd buy maybe $60,000 of bonds. Thus netting $40,000 more from the proceeds of the new loan. This resembles the defeasance technique described elsewhere in the book. But in this case, the lender removes the existing mortgage from the property. So there's no need to convince the new lender to make a second mortgage on first mortgage terms. That is, substitution of bond collateral is a simpler and cleaner form of defeasance.

PART FOUR: SELLERS

Chapter 9
Seller Loans

Seller financing

This is the second edition of this book. My thinking on seller financing has advanced somewhat since the first edition. Plus, the tax laws relating to seller financing have changed dramatically since then.

The primary advance in thinking has been my realization that many of the advantages of seller financing are the result of ***taking advantage*** of the seller's ignorance of prudent loan underwriting. Underwriting means the steps lenders take in setting sound lending policy and making sure each loan conforms to that policy.

Seller loan characteristics

Seller loans typically have the following characteristics:

1. Higher loan-to-value ratio than institutional lenders
2. Almost never an appraisal
3. Rarely a credit check
4. Almost never an origination fee
5. Usually 'porous' documentation
6. Rarely a prepayment penalty

7. Below-market interest rate
8. More flexibility on payment pattern
9. Usually no more than a ten year term

One through six are dumb

Seller loan characteristic number nine is a little bit smart. Institutional lenders generally agree to 25- or 30-year loans.

Numbers seven and eight are not necessarily dumb or smart. You'd have to look at the whole deal to tell.

But numbers one through six are ***just plain dumb***. The "creative" finance gurus say institutional lenders are "inflexible;" that sellers are "flexible." But on numbers one through six, "dumb" is a more accurate word than "flexible."

Why institutional lenders don't act like sellers

Institutional lenders don't refuse to make high loan-to-value ratio (more than 80%) loans because they're jerks. They refuse to make high loan-to-value ratio loans because they know what they're doing.

The mortgage industry has a hundred years experience with loan-to-value ratios ranging from 1% to more than 100%. Yes, I said more than 100%. How did they get high leverage experience if they refuse to make high leverage loans? They ***have*** made them. Sometimes with mortgage insurance like FHA, VA, or private mortgage insurance. Sometimes ***by accident*** because the appraisal they relied on was high.

They've tried it

Institutional lenders have ***made*** high loan-to-value ratio loans...and seen what happened when they did. If they had mortgage insurance, they probably suffered little or no out-of-pocket loss. But they saw first-hand ***how often*** high leverage deals end up in foreclosure.

And since they have to foreclose...then file a claim with the mortgage insuror if the foreclosure proceeds are not enough to cover the loan and foreclosure costs...they see the losses the ***mortgage insuror*** suffers.

In fact, when the loan-to-value ratio rises above 75% for an investment property or 80% for an owner-occupied home, the probability of default, foreclosure, and loss by the lender increases ***exponentially***. ***That*** is why institutional lenders refuse to make high loan-to-value ratio loans.

Sloppiness

The other of the first six seller loan characteristics are simple sloppiness. When a seller takes back a loan, he is ***buying a bond*** for tens of thousands of dollars...often more. Anyone who is sloppy about how they spend tens of thousands of dollars is likely to ***lose*** a lot of money.

Scams

All of this brings me to my point about seller financing. Most sellers are unsophisticated about mortgage lending. That lack of sophistication creates an opportunity for unscrupulous people. They take advantage of unsophisticated people.

You read about various scams...and see them on the evening news... nearly every week. A couple of sharpies are in the area selling cancer insurance to little old ladies. Or aluminum siding they can't afford. Or near worthless gemstones. Etc. Etc.

Those scams are obviously wrong. But is persuading a seller to take back a mortgage on the sale of a property a similar scam?

I think it is...in most cases.

Ethics, morality, and legality

It is unethical and immoral. . . in my opinion. . . for a sophisticated person to take advantage of an unsophisticated person's lack of sophistication. Indeed, I can make a strong case that it is ***illegal.***

The key ethical and moral question is this:

"Is the value of what the other person is getting equal to what the other person is giving up?"

Example

Let's say a retired couple want to sell their home. They are unsophisticated in real estate and mortgage lending. Their home is worth \$75,000. But like many obstinate sellers, they refuse to sell for less than \$80,000. Their first mortgage is assumable but only has a balance of \$30,000.

As a result, no sale. They've already bought a home in Florida to retire to. And they've started making mortgage payments on it. So their need to sell their old home is pressing.

Then along comes a recent graduate of a "creative" finance seminar. He gives them their price. . . \$80,000. They are elated. There's just one catch. They have to take back a second for \$50,000. It's a ***no money down*** deal.

Make that a seven-year second at 10% with no payments until the balloon payment. That is, all interest will accrue.

What they gave; what they got

What did the sellers ***give up***? Real estate equity with a genuine fair market value of \$75,000 -\$30,000 = \$45,000. Remember that the home is only ***worth*** \$75,000. Not the \$80,000 they're selling it for.

What did the sellers ***get***? A piece of paper.

What's the piece of paper worth?

Little or nothing.

Why?

Substandard

A mortgage owed to you is an asset. Normally, mortgages have market value. They can be sold and borrowed against.

What is the market value of a mortgage? Depends on the terms of the loan. . . ***and*** the care that was taken in writing it. . . ***and*** the loan-to-value ratio.

If the loan is at a below-market interest rate, it will sell at a ***discount***. That is, if its face value is \$50,000, a buyer will insist on paying ***less*** than \$50,000. By paying less, he raises his yield on the money he pays up to the market interest rate level.

Most real estate investors know about that.

But there's more. Let's say the retired couple does the deal then decides to ***sell*** the loan. . . maybe to get the money they need to pay for a serious operation. They put an ad in the paper. It says,

"Second mortgage for sale. 10% interest. 7 years. \$50,000 balance. Best offer. 555-1234"

Guys who invest in such mortgages will call. The calls will go like this.

Mortgage buyer: "Are you the one with the ad 'second mortgage for sale'?"

Retired lady: "Yes. We know we have to sell it for less than \$50,000 because of the low interest rate."

Mortgage buyer: "How much equity does the borrower have in the house?"

Retired lady: "None, probably. He just bought it."

Mortgage buyer: "How much did he put down?"

Retired lady: "Nothing. He took over our $30,000 loan and we took back this second for the rest."

Mortgage buyer: "Thanks anyway, Ma'am."

Retired lady: "Wait a minute. I said we'd be willing to sell it for less than $50,000. Why don't you make us an offer?"

Mortgage buyer: "I don't buy mortgages unless the borrower has at least 25% equity in the property. . . and I make sure of that by getting an independent appraisal. I might be interested in this mortgage four or five years from now if the property value goes up so that the borrower has 25% equity."

Retired lady: "We can't wait that long. Surely there must be a price at which you'd buy the mortgage now."

Mortgage buyer: "Not really, ma'am. You might find someone who will buy a mortgage where the borrower has only 20% equity. But zero equity is tough to sell."

Retired lady: "You mean no one is going to offer us anything for this mortgage loan?"

Mortgage buyer: "I'd be very surprised if anyone were willing to buy it, Ma'am. Somebody might give you a couple thousand bucks for it. . . like buying a bunch of lottery tickets. At least 25% equity is the first rule of the mortgage business. Seven years is too long, also. Mortgage buyers like three years or less. I gotta make some other calls, Ma'am. Thanks for your time. Good luck with your loan."

Little or nothing

A mortgage with less than 25% borrower equity is worth little or nothing.
So in this example, the retired couple gave up property worth $45,000 and got property (a note and mortgage) worth little or nothing.
Many real estate investors would say,

"Tough. The buyer didn't lie. He gave them exactly what he said he was going to give them. Nobody held a gun to their heads. Besides the buyer paid them $5,000 more than anyone else was willing to pay. If the mortgage they took back isn't marketable that's not the buyer's problem. It's not **his** *fault they need the money. If they were going to need the money they should have cut their price and sold to a buyer who'd get a bank mortgage. They were greedy. It's their own fault. Besides, in seven years they get $50,000 plus seven years worth of interest accruing at 10%."*

Is that an acceptable answer?
No.

The ethical standard I suggest

I suggest the following ethical standard on seller financing.

Thou shalt not do a high-leverage, seller-financed deal unless the seller is at least as sophisticated in financial matters as you.

Now let me elaborate on what I mean by "sophisticated." The seller is as sophisticated as you in financial matters if:

- He or she has a net worth of at least $50,000
- He or she has a ***net worth*** at least as large as yours ***and***
- He or she ***earned*** that net worth himself or herself (as opposed to getting it as an inheritance or gift)

In the alternative, the seller may have a net worth ***less*** than yours only if the seller's ***profession*** requires expertise in real estate finance. For example, a ***mortgage loan officer***, an ***attorney*** whose clients include mortgage lenders, a real estate ***syndicator***, an ***accountant*** whose clients include mortgage lenders, an experienced ***real estate broker***, certified real estate ***appraisers***, and so forth.

I do ***not*** include in this list secretaries and clerks who work for the people listed above, title company employees, attorneys whose work does not include real estate finance, accountants whose work does not include real estate finance, real estate salespeople (other than experienced brokers), and so forth. In other words, the professional exception is only for ***true professionals in mortgage lending.***

The minimum net worth standard of $50,000 is an idea I got from the securities industry. A solicitation I got recently from USAA Income Properties said you must have a gross annual income of at least $30,000 and a net worth of at least $30,000 or a net worth of at least $75,000 to invest in their partnership.

Minimum income and net worth standards are common in the securities industry. To prevent unsophisticated investors from getting in trouble. And thereby preventing the securities dealer from lawsuits I should add. I think the minimum net worth standard is a good idea. It's a darned shame the real estate brokerage profession won't adopt the same standards as the securities brokerage profession.

Exactly the type who would *not* take back a mortgage

You may be thinking, "Your list is a list of the people most likely to say 'no' to a high leverage, seller-financed offer."

That's right. That's not how I came up with the list. The reason the list of sophisticated sellers is also a list of those most likely ***not*** to agree to a high leverage seller loan is because ***no one*** should agree to such a loan. This is simply a list of the people smart enough to know that.

In fact, some people who would be on my list of sophisticated mortgage people ***would*** take back a high leverage seller loan. That's because sellers...even sophisticated sellers...get emotionally involved with the sale price they get. And when emotions come in, better judgement often goes out.

So if you can find a seller who is sophisticated in mortgage lending...and who still wants to take back a high leverage seller loan...by all means take him up on it if the rest of the deal is OK. I would.

Not even with a signed waiver

But do ***not*** do a high leverage seller financed deal with an unsophisticated seller. He or she does not realize that they are giving up valuable real estate equity for paper of little or no value.

I would not even do such a deal if the seller signed a very thorough waiver acknowledging every possible pitfall of sloppy mortgage lending. Because reading a warning label (waiver) on a mortgage is not the same as knowing from years of experience the probabilities of default and the expense of foreclosure (or trust sale in the case of a trust deed).

As a practical matter, a waiver sufficiently thorough to protect you from a subsequent lawsuit would be more likely to ***inspire*** such a suit...by laying out in detail how terrible a deal it is for the seller. The seller would sign the waiver. Then, after a number of months or years went by, the numerous dangers listed in the waiver would worry the seller. In a semi-panic, he or she gets our their copy of the waiver and says, "What have I done?" Then calls an attorney...who argues his client didn't understand the terminology of the waiver, that the waiver was presented as a mere formality or boilerplate among many other papers to be signed, etc.

Legality

I said I thought high-leverage seller financed deals with unsophisticated sellers were not only unethical and immoral but also ***illegal***. "What law do they violate?" you ask.

I can think of two:

1. Laws against "unconscionable acts" and
2. Laws making a real estate agent a fiduciary of his client.

Unconscionable acts

I suspect the Texas law against unconscionable acts is typical. Here's what it says.

Texas Business and Commerce Code. Section 17.45. DECEPTIVE TRADE PRACTICES ACT

DEFINITIONS. As used in this subchapter:

'Unconscionable action or course of action" means an act or practice which, to a person's detriment:

(A) takes advantage of the lack of knowledge, ability, experience, or capacity of a person to a grossly unfair degree, or

(B) results in a gross disparity between the value received and the consideration paid, in a transaction involving transfer of consideration.

Now, suppose you are convicted under this law. What punishment could you get. That's section 17.50 of the Texas law. It says.

"(b) In a suit filed under this section, each consumer who prevails may obtain:

(1) the amount of actual damages found by trier of fact. In addition, the court shall award two times that portion of the actual damages that does not exceed $1,000. If the trier of fact finds that the conduct of the defendant was committed knowingly, the trier of fact may award not more than three times the amount of actual damages in excess of $1,000;

(3) orders necessary to restore to any party to the suit any money or property; real or personal, which may have been acquired in violation of this subchapter; and

(4) any other relief which the court deems proper; including the appointment of a receiver or the revocation of a license or certificate authorizing a person to engage in business in this state if the judgment has not been satisfied within three months of the date of the final judgment. The court may revoke or suspend a license to do business in this state or appoint a receiver to take over the affairs of a person who has failed to satisfy a judgment if the person is a licensee of or regulated by a state agency which has statutory authority to revoke or suspend a license or to appoint a receiver or trustee. Costs and fees of such receivership or other relief shall be assessed against the defendant."

The plain English translation of that is

(1) actual damages [the difference between the value of the equity and the value of the seller mortgage] plus double that amount up to a limit of $2,000. If defendant acted knowingly, triple the actual damages less $3,000.

(3) deed the property purchased back to the seller for nothing [the decision requiring this could come years after the purchase]

(4) seizure of your business if you fail to pay the damages and fine or fail to deed the property back within 90 days. Possible revocation or suspension of your real estate license.

Probability of conviction

I have never heard of anyone who was convicted of an unconscionable act for buying a property in a high leverage seller-financed deal. It's possible that no one ever has been. There is no easy way to find out.

But there is no doubt that the law is on the books. . . in Texas at least. And I suspect every state has a similar law.

Suppose a seller finds out about this law. A high percentage of Texas apartment owners have the book I got it out of. . . the Texas Apartment Association *Redbook*. And suppose you bought a property from that seller on a high leverage, seller-financed basis.

If he can sue you and win. . . and prove that you ***knowingly*** committed the act. . . he gets the property back or triple the difference between the market value of his equity and the market value of the paper you gave him. In the example above, that'd be 3 x $45,000 = $135,000. And if you have a real estate license, he could use the threat of revocation as an additional club to get you to settle out of court.

That's the bull's eye you sit on if you do a high leverage seller-financed deal. $135,000, in this example, is the prize someone might get for suing you. That's a lot of incentive. Maybe enough to get a hungry attorney to file the suit on a contingency basis (no charge to the seller unless he wins).

Can anyone ***hit*** the bull's eye? I don't know. But then I don't have to worry about it either. I haven't done any such deals. I've done high leverage deals. But always with either mortgage insurance and institutional financing or with sophisticated sellers.

License laws

If a real estate agent receives a commission in a high leveraged seller-financed deal, an argument can be made that the agent has breached his fiduciary duty to the seller. In more cases than most people realize, the ***buyer*** is one of the agents receiving a commission.

Getting a commission for selling a property to yourself is a popular practice among real estate agents. It is ethical and legal. I did it myself when I was an agent on nearly all of my deals. But, again, I did no high-leveraged seller-financed deals except with one high-powered, decades-of-experience, real estate investor who could have bought and sold me many times over.

Real estate agents are required by law to make a full and complete disclosure of all material facts which might influence the seller. California Civil Code sections 2020 and 2230 say that. Every other state has a similar law.

It is well established that this means informing the seller when he is selling for less than market value. One court case that said that in California was *Fisher v. Losey* (1947) 78 C.A. 2d 121.

But does it ***also*** mean that an agent has a duty to disclose that a high-leverage seller loan has a market value far lower than the market value of the equity it replaces? I don't know. But it seems logical to me. The requirement that an agent disclose a below-market sale price to a seller would have little meaning if it could be gotten around simply by substituting a near worthless mortgage for cash.

Note that it is ***easier*** to win a suit against an agent and his broker than to win against a mere buyer. Because an agent holds himself out as having superior knowledge and skills in real estate and is under an obligation to exercise more care than an ordinary person. That is the law in every state.

Also, as a practical matter, most real estate firms have a public image they want to protect. That makes them eager to settle lawsuits quickly. And they typically have errors and omissions insurance policies which offer a good source of payment for a plaintiff and his attorney.

The easiest target of all would be a buyer who ***also*** got a commission in the deal as one of the selling agents (and his broker). . . because of the ***compound*** violation of an unconscionable act committed by a knowledgeable fiduciary against his own client. I mean how rotten can you get?

"He said yes!"

Practically everybody who has been in the real estate business very long has been amazed at what a seller accepted at one time or another. Experienced real estate agents can tell ***a number*** of stories about sellers accepting terms they thought didn't have a prayer.

Nothing ventured, nothing gained.

"Ask" is the only negotiating rule I would generally recommend.

Some risks

Asking for a ***very*** favorable deal is not riskless. It can sour a negotiating relationship which might otherwise succeeded.

A buyer recently offered to buy an apartment building I was selling. But the offer included no cash. . .just a note on a property they were selling. That's a standard "nothing down" technique. Notes like that are called "paper" and this is one of a number of paper techniques.

My response was to let loose a blast against such "mickey mouse, 'creative' finance, seminar nonsense." The blast was so fierce the buyer turned tail and ran, never to be heard from again.

That doesn't mean they shouldn't have made the offer. If they approach ***enough*** sellers with that, they'll eventually find someone dumb enough to take it. . .or someone with a property so doggy that even ***that*** offer is too high a price to pay for it.

If, however, they really wanted to buy ***my*** building, that was the wrong way to start.

Don't give up til the seventh "no"

In his book, *The Five Great Rules of Selling*, Percy Whiting says, ". . .keep on selling until your prospect has said ***no*** seven times." That works. . .in selling and in negotiating with sellers. That is to say the number of *yeses* you get will increase if you persist until the seventh no.

Unfortunately, people you use that on will cross to the other side of the street when they see you coming.

I said earlier that negotiating was like selling. . .that you could learn to be a better negotiator by reading books on sales among other subjects. There's no question that you can make money as a skilled salesman. Whether you apply your skill to traditional selling or to negotiating investment purchases.

But don't forget that skilled salespeople as a group are generally regarded as obnoxious. And skilled seducers (another negotiating-like activity) are generally regarded as cads.

"Win/win" negotiations

I can't get through this section without addressing the "win/win" negotiation. As I understand it, a "win/win" negotiation is one in which both parties win. A number of real estate gurus proclaim themselves to be "win/win" negotiators.

I think "win/win" is a meaningless concept. "Winning" is in the eye of the beholder. It's not a term which can be objectively defined. . .at least in the context of a complex real estate transaction.

For a real estate guru to proclaim himself a "win/win" negotiator is like a politician proclaiming himself to be in favor of "fairness." Both fairness and winning have definable meanings in the context of athletics. Fairness means "according to the rules" and winning is defined in the rules for each sport. As far as I'm concerned, proclaiming yourself "win/win" is about as meaningful as wearing a button that says, "I'm a nice guy." I'll be the judge of that.

The way negotiations *really* are

All negotiations contain two categories of elements:

- elements in which the interests of the parties coincide and
- elements of a zero sum game.

If both parties agreed on everything at the outset, there would be no need to negotiate at all. On the other hand, if there were no elements in which the interests of the parties coincided, there would be no basis on which to negotiate.

In a real estate negotiation the ***coinciding*** interest is that both the seller and the buyer want some one other than the present owner to own the building. At the same time, they are engaged in a zero sum game.

Zero sum game

A "zero sum game" is one in which any gain is at the expense of the other party. For example, there cannot be a "win/win" coin flip. One party's got heads; the other's got tails, and it's only going to come up one or the other. Somebody's got to win. And somebody's got to lose.

In fact, the very word "win" implies lose. You can't have a top without a bottom. You can't have a front without a back. And you can't have a winner without a loser.

The zero sum aspect of every real estate negotiation is the ***price***. The seller wants it to be as high as possible. The buyer wants it to be as low as possible.

Blowing smoke

"Win/win" negotiators can't structure a "win/win" negotiation without seller financing. If the seller owned a free and clear building and refused to take back a mortgage, the "win/win" negotiator would be at a loss for words. Ain't no way he can disguise the fact that the seller wants the highest possible price, and Mr. "Win/win" wants the lowest possible price.

The "win/win" negotiator's forte is to get himself that low price. . . but ***conceal*** that fact from the seller. He typically does this by taking advantage of the seller's lack of understanding of real estate finance. For example, he pays the seller in part with "paper" which is worth less than it appears to be.

I taught you how to blow away such smoke in the chapter where I told you how to compute the ***true sale price.***

There's only one market value

In that chapter I told you the ***true*** sale price is the total ***market*** value of all that you receive.

The market value of ***cash*** is the same as its face value. The market value of "paper" you receive, whether you take it back or its secured by some other property, is ***what you could sell it for***, not its face value. And the value of having someone take over your existing loan is ***what the lender could sell that loan for***, not its balance.

Apply that approach to any "win/win" negotiator and he'll be revealed for what he really is. . . just another guy who's trying to get the best deal he can.

Seems to me that about the only way you could determine who won a negotiation would be to measure the ***sale*** price and terms or their cash equivalent against the ***market*** price and terms or their cash equivalent.

If the ***sale*** cash value is less than the ***market*** cash value, the ***buyer*** won. If it's ***more***, the ***seller*** won. If it's the ***same***, it was a ***tie***.

How do you measure ***market*** value? An appraisal is probably the best. But then appraisers can be wrong. So it's hard to tell who wins in most real estate negotiations.

Most real estate deals are ties

Most real estate negotiations which result in sales are ties. The property sells for the equivalent of its fair market value. I suspect the "win/win" crowd also do mostly ties, too.

If they really push the "creative finance" though, some of their sellers are selling for ***less*** than the cash equivalent of fair market value. In that case, the seller has ***lost***. . . both concpetually and in reality. The buyer has tricked the seller out of some of his equity. "Bilked" would not be an inappropriate word.

Such sellers probably ***think*** they have "won." After all, the buyer told them several times that he believed in "win/win."

Ringer had it right

Robert Ringer wrote *Winning Through Intimidation.* I don't like the title. The book is not as bad as the title makes it sound. And I think Ringer's overly cynical. But I think he presents a more accurate picture of real estate negotiations than the "win/win" crowd.

Ringer says everybody wants to "grab your chips" (take some of your money for themselves). He further says that you can divide the people you meet in real estate into those who honestly admit they are in a zero sum game with you and those who swear they're your buddy and only want what's right. Ringer prefers the honest ones.

As I said, I think the world is not as bad a place as Ringer depicts. But I share his skepticism for those buyers or sellers who tell me they want ***both*** of us to "win" the negotiation.

Unavoidable unpleasantness

Most people find negotiations unpleasant. That's because of the zero sum game aspect of negotiating. I wish it weren't that way. But wishing won't make it so. Neither will some "magic" incantation like "win/win."

If you want to buy or sell real estate you simply have to survive the unpleasantness of locking horns with the other party over how much cash equivalent will be paid for the property.

Arguments to use with seller

Some of the following arguments don't make sense from an investment strategy standpoint. Although all are factual. I would not use these against a widow or an orphan or other "exploitable" classes of people. But if the other party is a rompin' stompin' real estate investor who ought to know what he's doing, they may point out a benefit he would rather have than cash. And in some cases, the seller knows the argument is not sensible but he may glom onto it as a face-saving device.

- Installment sales often mean the gain is taxed at lower rates.
- If you sell on an installment basis, almost all your equity continues to earn a return. But if you sell for cash, a large chunk of it goes to Uncle Sam.
- If the seller wants to buy another property, you might talk him out of it by pointing out the tenant problems he will avoid if he retires to just cashing mortgage payment checks.
- Point out your strong credit history (if you have one).
- Point out that the ***total*** dollars he'll receive over the life of the loan will be far greater than the total he'd receive in a cash sale.
- Point out that most sellers take back mortgages (if true in the market in question) so if he doesn't give you one he'll just have to give one to someone else later.
- Point out that delaying the sale to wait for a mythical cash buyer will exacerbate the "jump ship" problem one has with tenants and managers in a building which is for sale.
- Remind him that ***he*** got a second from the seller when he bought if it's true.
- Offer ***additional collateral*** like a mortgage on other property you own. (See the chapter on security techniques for more on this.)
- Ask why he's so anxious to make a total break with the property. Does he know something about it he's not telling?
- Offer to ***substitute collateral.*** That is if he wants to be done with this property, take a second mortgage on ***another*** property you own.
- Offer a wraparound mortgage and point out that the yield to him will be higher than the face interest rate.
- ***Reverse negotiate.*** That is, after you've negotiated the price ***down***, offer to go back up if he'll give better ***terms***.
- Give ground on other terms in order to get a better loan-to-value ratio and/or debt-coverage ratio.
- In complex deals, offer to pay part or all of his extra attorney fees (always keep a dollar limit on it though).

• Offer to buy a mortgage or other life insurance policy and make him the beneficiary. Check the premium first.

• When dealing with publicly traded corporations, point out that they can put the second in their pension fund or just keep it as a corporate investment. That will make the sale look more profitable since they carry the second on their books at face value.

• Offer a percent of operating profits and/or resale profits (as a last resort).

• Remind the seller that he can borrow against or sell the second mortgage you want him to take back.

• Point out that your seller might be able to find another seller who will accept the mortgage you're asking him to take back as all or part of a down payment on the other seller's property.

• Point out that you'll probably pay the second off early (if that's the case) or that you have always paid off early in the past (if that's the case) or that most buyers pay off seconds early.

• Offer to pay an origination fee or document preparation fee or some other miscellaneous fee that the seller would ordinarily pay.

• Point out that the terms he's asking for leave no cash flow or cause negative cash flow. That, in turn, increases the chances of inadequate maintenance and default. Insist that the debt-coverage ratio be sensible via accruing all or part of the seller's interest.

• Offer to *lease* the property thereby avoiding the tax (if properly drawn). (I'm not fond of leases, though.)

• If seller insists property's performance will be better than you think, ask him to take back a "performance second" in which the payments are contingent on the property's performance.

The seller's decision-making unit

I told you earlier that lending institutions have decision-making units. So do sellers, sometimes. Among the people the seller might implicitly give veto power to are

- Spouse
- Listing agent
- "Uncle Louie" (family "expert")
- Attorney
- Banker
- Accountant
- Partners
- Board of directors (if corporation)

You have to convince ***all*** of the people in the decision-making unit to do the deal.

Sophisticated technique; unsophisticated seller

Finance seminars and books, including this one, often tell you about sophisticated finance techniques. Unfortunately, most of the sellers you meet didn't take the same seminars or read the same books. As a result, they are ***suspicious*** of your technique. People fear that which they do not understand. Or that which their attorney or "Uncle Louie" doesn't understand.

Here are four suggestions for educating and reassuring them:

• Show them copies of ***articles*** or excerpts from ***books*** covering the technique in question. The printed word is more believable to most people.

• ***References***. If you've used the technique in question with a ***previous seller***, and that seller is happy with it, refer the current seller to the previous seller.

• Suggest that the seller talk to someone whose judgment he respects who ***does*** understand the technique in question. That might be an attorney, the author of an article or book on the subject, a local title officer who has handled a similar deal (local title officers have handled an amazing variety of deals).

• Show the seller ***the numbers***. . . from his standpoint. An actual projection of the seller's income and taxes over the life of the loan usually makes the deal easier to discuss than the more abstract version.

What the seller wants

The classic formula for salesmanship is to find out what the buyer wants and tell him why what you have is what he wants. Same goes for convincing a seller to accept your offer.

Listen to him. Not in the passive way most people listen to others. But ***really*** listen to him. Try to understand what he ***says*** he wants. ***And*** try to detect any unspoken wants.

I'm not just talking about ***financial*** needs. Real estate sales like most other human endeavors are far more complex than the surface elements. Sellers have psychologist Abraham Maslow's "Hierarchy of Needs." That is they need air, water, food, rest, safety, love, self-esteem, and self-actualization. . .in roughly that order. Maslow said there is ***no such thing as a money-motivated person.***

So what you're really trying to do is structure the deal in the way that makes the seller feel good about himself. That's not to say he'll sell you his building if you promise to sing three choruses of "For He's A Jolly Good Fellow." But he ***may*** accept less than the best deal from his standpoint if it's structured in a way that makes him feel like a shrewd investor. Others need to feel like tough negotiators.

The junk bond scam

I got a red hot "creative finance" technique for you. The junk bond scam. Here's how it works.

First you find a little old lady who's trying to sell her house. But she's asking about 10% too much. So no takers. She's getting desperate. She's got $100,000 equity by her asking price. Maybe $85,000 as measured by an independent appraisal.

You make her a ***full price offer***. She'll accept won't she? After trying to sell for many months, you're darn right she will.

There's only one catch. Instead of giving her $100,000 in ***cash***, you're offering to give her a $100,000 Buttes Gas & Oil Corporation subordinated debenture. A bond. Says right on the face that Buttes Gas & Oil Corporation promises to pay the owner $100,000. It's listed on the New York Stock Exchange. It pays 10 1/4% interest. And there's a balloon payment of $100,000 due on August 15, 1997.

Why would you pay her $100,000 for $85,000 worth of equity? And why do you prefer to pay her with a Buttes Gas & Oil bond instead of cash?

Because you can buy the Buttes Gas & Oil bond at a ***discount***. In fact, on March 5, 1985, that bond closed at 56 3/8. That means a $100,000 Buttes bond cost just $56,375.

So, in reality, you're getting $85,000 worth of real estate equity for just $56,375! Neat technique, huh?

Your basic unconscionable act

I presume you realize that I offer this "technique" tongue in cheek. If you actually did such a deal, you'd be guilty of unethical, immoral, and probably illegal conduct. Recalling the language of the Texas law for example, we have a sophisticated person entering into a transaction with an unsophisticated person and the unsophisticated person is giving significantly more value than she is receiving. Texas defines that as an unconscionable act. And provides severe penalties for committing it.

If the authorities got wind of such a deal, they'd probably prosecute you. And they'd probably get a conviction.

The respective values are clearly not equal

Honest appraisers might disagree on the value of the lady's real estate equity. But none would rate it lower than $85,000. And there's no disagreement whatsoever about the value of the Buttes Gas & Oil Corporation subordinated debenture. It's listed right in the *Wall Street Journal* every business day. You can look it up yourself...on the "New York Exchange Bonds" page. It's listed as "Butte." I don't know why they leave off the "s." Multiply the price you see by $1,000 to get the cost of a $100,000 bond.

So in this example, giving a lady with $85,000 equity a bond with a market value of $56,375 is a bad deal to the tune of $85,000 - $56,375 = $28,625. Texas, you may recall, allows triple damages as one of the penalties for unconscionable acts. That'd be $28,625 x 3 = $85,875.

If a real estate agent got a commission on the deal, he'd be eligible to lose his license or pay fines and damages or all of the above. Agents, you'll recall, are supposed to protect their clients (the sellers) from taking less than market value for their equity.

Forget Buttes Gas & Oil. Make it a mortgage.

OK. Forget the Buttes Gas & Oil bond. Make it a seller second mortgage instead. The little old lady's got $100,000 equity according to her asking price. Fine. Make her a full-price, nothing down offer.

She's to take back a mortgage for $100,000, interest only for 12 years at 10 1/4%. You'll agree to pay off the principal balance of $100,000 on August 15, 1997.

Anything wrong with that?

Well, let's compare it to the obviously unconscionable Buttes deal.

The ***interest rate's*** the same.

The ***term*** is the same.

The ***amount*** is the same.

So there's no difference at all on the ***payment pattern.*** What about the ***risk*** aspects? Which is a better risk—-a Buttes Gas & Oil subordinated debenture or a second mortgage of $100,000 secured by equity of $85,000 on a house owned by an investor who made no down payment. He may even have ***bad credit.*** After all, those real estate "creative finance" gurus are always saying they're going to tell you how to get rich buying lots of real estate with no money down ***"even if you have bad credit."***

Which is the better risk?

You might get some disagreement from financial experts. But I'd say the Buttes Gas & Oil bond was the better deal. And I think most financial experts would agree.

The Buttes bond is 100% ***liquid.*** You can go to your nearest stock brokerage firm and sell it for cash in a matter of minutes. In contrast, the no-money-down, $100,000 second mortgage secured by $85,000 of equity would probably sell at a much steeper discount...if at all. And selling it would take many days because the buyer would need an appraisal, title report, credit investigation of the borrower, attorney examination of the documents, and so forth.

The Buttes bond has a CCC rating from Standard & Poors. They define CCC as "predominantly speculative with respect to capacity to pay interest and repay principal in accordance with the terms of the obligation."

What rating has Standard & Poors given to the seller second mortgage? None. They don't rate such small bonds. And if they did, this seller second would score about a JJJ...if there was such a rating.

Clearly, the little old lady would be ***better off*** with the highly liquid Buttes bond which she could sell for $56,375 in cash. The seller second leaves her with an unlisted (on any stock exchange), unrated (by any credit rating company), mostly unsecured, bond signed by some nobody who is probably not personally liable on it.

Will the authorities prosecute the mortgage deal?

I said the authorities would almost certainly prosecute...and probably get a conviction... in the Buttes bond deal. What about the no money down seller second...with the exact same payment pattern...and ***more*** risk?

I doubt that the authorities would do anything. Why not? Because the disparity between the value of the Buttes bond and the equity is clear. But the disparity between the value of the seller second and the equity is ***un***clear.

Anyone who thinks about it for more than a few seconds will recognize that the Buttes bond is a better deal. Which makes the seller second even more unconscionable than the Buttes deal. But few people think about it for more than a few seconds. Result? Seller mortgages proliferate. Bond scams are rare.

Peddling junk bonds

Making a loan and buying a bond are synonymous. In fact,the word "bond" often appears at the top of one of the documents you sign when you borrow money. "Bond" and "note" mean the same thing.

When a savings and loan gives you a mortgage loan, they are really buying your bond for the amount of the loan. And when a seller makes you a mortgage loan, they, too, are buying a bond issued by you.

On Wall Street, bonds are divided into two categories: investment grade and junk bonds. Investment grade means a Standard and Poors rating of BBB or better or a Moody's rating of Baa or better. Lower than that is a junk bond. In the Moody's system, junk bonds have ratings of Ba. B, Caa, Ca, or C. Here are the yields on corporate investment grade bonds in May of 1985.

Aaa 11.72%
Aa 12.30%
A 12.70%
Baa 13.15%

You can see that the yields are similar to mortgage yields...on professionally originated first mortgages. The typical junk bond seller second not only deserves a Jjj rating, it also carries a ***lower*** interest rate than an Aaa rated corporate bond. Amazing.

Merrill Lynch will sell you a junk bond if you want. When Merrill Lynch sells someone a junk bond, they make the bond buyer sign a ***letter of indemnity.*** In that letter, the buyer swears that Merrill Lynch informed him of the high degree of risk inherent in junk bonds and that the buyer insists on buying it anyway. Then, if the bond issuer defaults, and the bond buyer tries to sue Merrill Lynch, Merrill Lynch trots out the letter of indemnity and says, "We warned you."

High leverage seller mortgages are junkier-than-junk bonds

I think it's obvious that seller mortgages are ***junkier than junk bonds***. And when a "creative finance" guru sends you out hunting for sellers who will agree to sell you a property with little or no money down, he is telling you to peddle junkier-than-junk bonds...almost door-to-door. And they usually recommend doing this in low-income neighborhoods. Where the least sophisticated folks live.

Below-market interest rates

Most investors think the low interest rates they get on seller loans are a good deal.

No way. Those low rates are a quid pro quo for a higher price. As I said earlier in Reed's Rules, you ***always*** pay market interest rates when you finance real estate. In a seller financed deal, the difference between market rates and the seller's rate is hidden in a higher price for the property...and therefore a higher loan amount than if a market rate loan had been obtained and all cash paid to the seller.

There is no free lunch. There are no below-market interest rates.

Rarely require appraisal

Institutional lenders almost always require an appraisal. If they have a strong relationship with the borrower...and/or the loan-to-value ratio is quite low...they might just make a windshield appraisal. But in the typical case, they want a formal appraisal.

Sellers, on the other hand, feel they ***know*** what the property is worth. I've never heard of a seller requiring an appraisal. They don't ***want*** to know that the property is worth less than their selling for. And they certainly don't want the ***buyer*** to know.

You may ***want*** an appraisal. To make you feel better about the price you're paying.

Here are the reasons to ***not*** want an appraisal:

1. Too-low appraisal
2. Cost
3. Delay

Conservative appraisal

Sometimes, the appraiser appraises the property ***low***. Because he's conservative. Or because he's incompetent. Sometimes the appraiser comes in low because he ***was told to***. I know a guy who appraised for a major bank. When the bank wanted to cut back on mortgage loans, he and his fellow appraisers were told to appraise low.

That enabled the bank to maintain the facade that they were still in the market. And it enabled the loan officers to avoid responsibility for turning down the loan. Like Flip Wilson's Geraldine saying, "The Devil made me buy this dress," they could claim, "The appraiser made me turn you down."

Whether the too-low appraisal is due to conservatism or incompetence or deceit, the result is the same. You don't get the loan. So one of the legitimate reasons to prefer seller loans is that you don't have to worry about too-low appraisals.

Cost

The buyer typically pays for the appraisal. Even when it's done by the lender's in-house staff. Bank of America currently charge $150 to $200 for a home mortgage appraisal. In 1983, I paid $2,000 for an M.A.I. appraisal of a 37-unit apartment building and $3,000 for an M.A.I. appraisal of a 25-unit apartment building. (No reason for the difference in prices. . . just different M.A.I.s.)

Whether it's $150 or $3,000, it's better to avoid the expense and seller financing is the way to do that. Your ***true*** leverage in a deal is ***not*** your down payment divided by your purchase price. It's your down payment ***plus other costs*** divided by the ***fair market value*** of the property.

By eliminating the significant appraisal cost, you ***increase*** the true leverage. Although seller financed properties typically sell for ***more than true fair market value***. So what you gain in cost elimination you may lose in higher price.

Delay

Formal appraisals take time. Especially the income property/M.A.I. type appraisal. The 37-unit appraisal I mentioned above took about a month to get. The 25-unit appraisal was done on a rush basis and took only a couple weeks.

Delay can be an important factor. In '83, I was doing an exchange. I agreed to buy the 25-unit building in August. . . with a November closing. . . and a new Federal Home Loan Mortgage Corporation mortgage required.

But that 25-unit did not use up all the money I had coming out of the 37-unit I was exchanging out of. So in September I had to look for another building to buy. Because the time til the November closing was short, I told the Realtors that I could only look at deals where the financing would come from the seller. Because there simply was not time to be sure that the appraisals and such required in an institutional loan would get done before closing.

If you are the seller

If you are the seller, you can sometimes save appraisal delay by getting the appraisal done ***before*** you put the property up for sale. FHA and VA have a formal program for doing this. You ***might*** try it with an income property. Order an M.A.I. appraisal in advance. But that's a little chancy. . . because the lender in question may insist on ***another*** appraiser or appraisal.

Whether you are selling a home or an income property, getting an appraisal in advance has two other benefits in addition to saving processing time. It helps prevent you from making the costly mistake of ***asking too much*** for the property. Which causes even more delay than appraisers. And the appraisal is an excellent ***selling tool.*** Show it to the buyer to assure him that the property is worth what you're asking.

Little or no credit check

Sellers who are inexperienced in real estate or lending rarely make a credit check when they take back a loan. They go on appearance. ***Experienced*** sellers...like income property owners...typically ***will*** do a credit check.

When I'm a guest on radio and tv talk shows, I frequently get calls from people with bad credit who want to know how to get a mortgage so they can buy real estate. I'm inclined to tell them to drop dead. I have no respect for people with bad credit.

But the standard advice the "creative finance" crowd gives to such people is to buy real estate using existing assumable loans and seller financing. In fact, one of the come ons the "creative finance" guys use to get you to come to their seminars or buy their tapes is that they are going to tell you how to buy real estate with no money down ***"even if you have bad credit!"***

Full disclosure

In my opinion, that's unethical advice. In many states...like California...a ***seller*** has a duty under the law to disclose all material facts about the property to any prospective buyer. A ***real estate agent*** has a duty to disclose all material facts...like the buyer's poor credit history in a seller-financed deal... to the seller.

I know of no ***law*** which requires the ***buyer*** who is not a real estate agent to disclose a poor credit history to a seller in a seller financed real estate purchase. But I think common decency requires it. And symmetry. If the ***seller*** is required to tell the buyer that the furnace is bad, then the buyer ought to be required to tell the seller that his credit is bad.

The seller may make the loan even *knowing* about bad credit

In many cases, a seller will find out that a buyer has bad credit and ***still*** sell to that buyer and take back a mortgage. Why? Because, being inexperienced in mortgage lending, the seller thinks the fact that the loan is secured by a mortgage on the house is adequate security by itself. That is nonsense unless the loan-to-value ratio is ***very*** low...like 40%.

With a 40% loan-to-value ratio, the seller would almost certainly get his principal, interest, and expenses even in the worst case of a resisted foreclosure. But if the loan-to-value ratio is more normal, the probability of loss by the lender is very high in the event of a default by the borrower.

So if you have poor credit, shame on you. But the fact is you ***can*** buy real estate and get mortgages through assumptions and seller financing. I think you have a duty to make full disclosure to the seller of your credit history. If you do that...and he still wants to make the loan...take it. And use it as an opportunity to restore your credit by making all the payments as agreed.

What agents should do

To the real estate agents reading this book, I say this. ***Always*** obtain a credit report...at your own expense if necessary...when a seller is considering taking back a mortgage. If the report is less than AAA, tell the seller ***not*** to do the deal.

If the seller ***insists*** on going ahead, the ***least*** you should do is get the seller to sign a waiver or letter of indemnity. That waiver would say something to the effect that, "I am about to do something very stupid...namely extend a large amount of credit to someone with a bad credit history. My agent has warned me ***not*** to do this in no uncertain terms. So I will not hold him responsible in any way."

That's the ***least*** you should do. The ***right*** thing to do, in my opinion, is to tell the seller you will walk away from the deal if he takes back a high loan-to-value ratio mortgage from a buyer with bad credit. That would mean no commission. But it would also mean no lawsuit. And it might mean that the seller...upon having trouble with that buyer in the future...would become the biggest booster you ever had.

But that's unlikely. Virtue is its own reward. And the satisfaction of knowing you did the right thing is probably all you'll get for your trouble. That's what I would do if I were an agent again. But I know there are only a handful of real estate agents in the whole country who have the character to walk away from a commission in such a situation. Pity.

Credit check applies to subject tos also

Sellers should do a credit check on a buyer even if there will be no seller loan ***if the buyer will be buying subject to an existing loan.*** That's because the ***seller's*** credit is at stake. If the payments are not made on that first mortgage, the ***seller's*** credit history will be marred in many cases.

If the seller is ***personally liable*** on the first mortgage, the seller may actually have to pay a deficiency judgment to the lender if the buyer defaults on the first mortgage. A deficiency judgment is possible when the proceeds of the foreclosure sale are not enough to pay off the loan, interest, and foreclosure charges.

Not a problem in an assumption

This is ***not*** a problem in an assumption. In an assumption, the buyer applies to the lender to assume...not buy subject to... the loan. The first mortgage lender checks the buyer's credit. If the lender approves, the buyer signs a note and mortgage to the lender.

In an assumption, the ***seller*** is ***not necessarily*** off the hook. I sold a duplex on an assumption once. I had bought the property no money down VA. Prior to selling it, I contacted the VA and asked how I should handle the sale to make it a valid assumption.

They sent me credit applications for my buyer to fill out and words which had to be placed in the deed from me to the new buyer/borrower. I required the buyer to ***assume*** my loan...not buy subject to it. And I required him to provide credit information to the VA and otherwise cooperate with their efforts to approve his assumption of the mortgage.

It's not very hard to get a lender to agree to an assumption. Having ***two*** borrowers on the loan is better than one. But it ***is*** hard for the seller to get a ***release from liability.*** And that's what I wanted in my VA deal. If you get a release from liability, you ***are*** off the hook.

About two years after the sale I received a letter from the VA informing me that I ***had*** been released from liability. By the way, that did ***not*** rejuvenate my VA ***eligibility***. The only way to get that back would be for my old loan to be ***paid off***...or for my buyer to be a veteran and substitute ***his*** eligibility on that loan.

The legitimate reason for avoiding a credit check

There is one legitimate reason for wanting seller financing so you can avoid a credit check. That's delay. Credit checks take time...although not much. If you have good credit and seek seller financing only to get a quicker finance commitment, that's a proper use of this advantage of seller financing. But if you had ***bad*** credit, and use seller financing to avoid being found out, you are behaving unethically.

You can use the credit check as an *offensive* weapon

The credit check isn't all negative, you know. If your credit history is ***good***, a credit report showing that can be a powerful tool. It can convince a wavering seller to make the loan.

I recently did a deal in which the other party claimed he did not have enough security for a small loan he was making to me. He wanted a second mortgage on my home. I said no. But when my credit report came back, he settled for my paying just two payments in advance. So use a strong credit report as a selling point...especially when ***security*** is the issue the seller is hung up on.

Rarely an origination fee

Institutional lenders hit you with a whole bunch of fees: points, origination fees, credit application fees, lender's attorney fee, recording fees, escrow fees, tax service fees, etc. They got a million of them.

Except for getting you to pay their attorney's fee for drawing up the seller loan documents, most sellers charge no fees at all. They're nuts to do that. But they do.

Is that a good deal for you, the buyer? Probably. It reduces the cash you need up front. But harking back to Reed's Rules, you always pay market interest rates when you finance real estate.

In fact, the fees the institutional lenders charge are an important part of their yield. So roughly speaking, the fees you save on seller financing...like the interest you save...are built into the higher price you pay for a seller financed property...and the higher loan amount you agree to pay.

But avoiding loan origination fees by using seller financing is a legitimate way to increase your true leverage. True leverage, you'll recall is your down payment ***plus*** all related fees and costs divided by the fair market value. Eliminating thousands of dollars worth of fees will increase your true leverage even if all or part of the unpaid fees are hidden in a higher price.

Often porous documentation

Institutional loan documents are almost always well-written...from the institution's standpoint. But sellers go to the family attorney for their documents. And he tells his secretary to use the documents from the last loan he did...just change the names, dates, amounts, and so forth. Of course, the last loan was based on the one before that and so forth.

Where did the attorney's ***first*** set of loan documents come from you ask? Either from a forms book or from another attorney. These things get handed down and handed down for years with little or no review or updating. The attorney in question typically does few such loan documents. So he gets little or no experience enforcing them in the event of default.

The bottom line is that many, maybe most, loan documents drawn up by run-of-the-mill attorneys are poorly written. That, in turn, means you're more likely to get ***in*** a clause favorable to you...or leave ***out*** an ***un***favorable clause...if the lender is a seller.

Example

I was the real estate salesman on a seller financed deal in the early '70s. The seller owned the house free and clear. And had a terrible time selling it because it was in rough shape. It probably was not mortgageable through an institutional lender.

So the seller offered to take back a mortgage. I did not try to talk him out of it for two reasons. Back then, I saw nothing wrong with seller financing. And I was not the listing agent and my company was not the listing broker. So I was not supposed to communicate directly with the seller.

I found the buyer. The seller's agent had his attorney draw up the mortgage and note. It did not contain a due-on-sale clause at all. I did not notice at the time because I was just a little old 26-year old real estate agent. I figured if an ***attorney*** drew up the documents, there was nothing more to say.

About a month after closing, my buyer got an attractive job offer in another state. And came to me to sell the property. I asked to see his mortgage documents, as I routinely did on all listings. And I discovered that there was no due-on-sale clause.

So I listed it as having an ***assumable*** mortgage. Since the buyer had just moved in with 20% down, the loan-to-value ratio was much more attractive than most assumptions.

The real estate broker who had the listing when I sold it before saw the listing when it hit the MLS book...and noticed the word "assumable." "What are you doing advertising that loan as assumable?" he asked when he called me. *"Those sellers won't allow that loan to be assumed."*

"They have no say in the matter," I told him. "The loan documents do not contain a due-on-sale clause."

"They don't contain a clause saying the loan is assumable, either," he said.

"Don't have to. If there's no clause, it's assumable."

About then he recalled from his pre-licensing training that I was right. 'Oh,'' was his final word on the subject.

Another example

I bought an apartment building from a guy who took back a second. His real estate broker's partner was an attorney. That attorney drew up the second mortgage documents. They contained a due-on-sale clause, all right. But it was so tortured and amateurish in its wording that it was of questionable enforceability. Furthermore, it was too narrow from the seller's standpoint. It failed to prohibit explicitly or implicitly lease options or land contracts.

The law construes ambiguities in contracts most strongly against he who prepared the document...the seller in this case.

***You* draw up the documents**

I recommend that ***you*** or ***your attorney*** draw up the loan documents. Typically the seller demands that you pay the attorney's fees for drawing it up. To keep those attorney's fees under control, it's better that ***your*** attorney do it. It also offers you an opportunity to draw the documents the way ***you*** want them.

Most sellers will understand your desire to control attorney fees. And most will welcome any opportunity to shed some of the administrative load the deal requires. That is, if ***you*** take care of the loan documents, that's one less thing for the ***seller*** to have to take care of.

If the seller is concerned about what you put into the documents, you can simply remind him that he and his attorney will have ample time to review the document and change any part they don't like. In fact, it's far better to ***write*** the documents than it is to simply ***read*** it. Both the seller's eyes and his attorney's eyes tend to glaze over reading a long legal document. That causes those eyes not to see everything that's there. Plus the ***reading*** mind does not see ***omissions***...like leaving out a due-on-sale clause...which the ***writing*** mind would have thought about. Another example would be inserting the words "or more" after the amount of the monthly payment. Those words mean no prepayment penalty and no lock-in.

The ethics of drawing the documents to your liking

There are ethical considerations here. Let's say the seller agrees to let you or your attorney draw up the documents. The main contents of the loan documents will be agreed on in the purchase agreement. With perhaps a ***verbal*** understanding at the eleventh hours on a few minor points. The written and verbal agreements you have with the seller ***must be faithfully recited in the loan documents.***

In other words, if the seller says he wants a due-on-sale clause in the loan...and you agree...it would be unethical to then prepare documents with no due-on-sale clause and hope he won't notice. However, if the due-on-sale clause were ***not discussed***, then it would ***not*** be unethical to leave it out.

By the same token, I believe it is ethical to ***add*** clauses favorable to you. But only if the clauses you add were ***not discussed*** with the seller and if they ***do not conflict with and supersede*** clauses which ***were*** discussed.

So I think it's OK to ***add*** clauses favorable to you or leave ***out*** clauses ***un***favorable to you. But only if doing so does not change the deal you made with the seller prior to drawing up the loan documents.

Different ethical code for real estate agents

If you are a real estate agent participating in the commission on the deal, different ethical rules apply. You may ***not*** add clauses favorable to the buyer or leave out clauses unfavorable to the buyer. On the contrary, you must ***prevent*** that from happening...or at least make urge the seller to have the documents drawn up by a competent attorney to prevent additions or omissions unfavorable to the seller. You must do this ***even if you are also the buyer*** in the deal.

Rarely a prepayment penalty

Prepayment penalties can be a problem when you plan to refinance the property soon. For example, some techniques involve raising the building value shortly after buying it, then refinancing or selling to a buyer who gets a new loan. A prepayment penalty in an existing loan can mess up that plan.

But with institutional lenders, it's hard to avoid a prepayment penalty. So if avoiding a prepayment penalty is important to you, seek seller financing.

Usually no more than a ten-year term

The one unhidden disadvantage of seller financing is short terms. Most sellers would ***like*** about a three-year term. And most can be talked into a five- to seven-year term. Often, you can get ten years. And sellers have been known to agree to fifteen, twenty or longer terms. You never know until you ask.

The longer the better from the buyer's standpoint.

Distress or "don't wanter" sellers

The "creative finance" crowd says you should scour the countryside looking for "don't wanter" sellers. These are people who are in distress for one reason or another. The whole foreclosure movement is aimed at one variety of distressed seller.

The idea seems to be that. . .if you can find a distressed seller. . .you can buy a dollar's worth of real estate equity for less than a dollar. That, of course, is a good deal. But one feels sorry for the distressed person. . .and feels a bit uncomfortable about profiting from their misfortune. Is there a legitimate profit opportunity in distress sellers? I think not.

Forget distress sellers

In the first edition of this book, I listed all the distress situations you might want to pursue as ways of getting favorable financing terms. I started to rewrite that section for this edition because I was uncomfortable with the ethics of profiting from distress. In the course of trying to delineate the line between ethical and unethical behavior, I came to the conclusion that the line is very fuzzy when it comes to distress sellers. So count me out when the subject of how to get rich by taking advantage of distress sellers comes up.

The basic idea behind distress seller techniques is getting the property for less than its market value. Or, if you agree to pay market value, to pay. . .at least in part. . .with a piece of paper known as a mortgage or trust deed. The ***market*** value of the piece of paper is, of course, far less than the ***face value***. So that is simply another way to buy property for less than market value.

"Real Estate Owned"

Even "Real Estate Owned" by mortgage lenders who have foreclosed gives me ethical problems. Banks and savings and loans who have foreclosed often sell properties for ***less than market value***. Because they do not want to incur carrying costs. And because many bank REO officers are incompetent.

But banks and savings and loans are corporations. They have shareholders. Let's say the market value of the bank's foreclosed properties is $1,000,000. And they sell them to various graduates of seminars on "Real Estate Owned" seminars for $400,000. That means the bank's shareholders got the shaft.

It is probably ***not*** a violation of the ***law*** for a bank or savings and loan employees to sell their employer's assets for 40 cents on the dollar. As long as that employees receives no kickback or favor (direct or indirect. . .as to a friend or relative) from the buyer of the property. But it ***is*** an offense for which the employee would typically be fired.

The employee may be instructed to sell for ***quick sale*** value rather than full fair market value. But the quick sale value of $1,000,000 worth of real estate is more likely $850,000 than $400,000.

I talked to an REO officer

A bank REO officer I interviewed said he's seen foreclosed properties sold by his bank for between 60% and 110% of the appraised value. That's an appraisal made shortly ***after*** the property was foreclosed and shortly ***before*** the foreclosure was sold by the bank. So it's a ***current*** appraisal. He noted that the 60% figure was on especially rough property during especially hard times. He guessed the ***normal*** selling price on his bank's foreclosures was between 80% and 100% of market value. And this was an off-the-record interview so he had no incentive to mislead me.

I asked him if there was a legitimate opportunity for real estate investors to get rich in foreclosures or REOs. He said yes. But that it would not be easy. The buyers would have to be experts on the market, on foreclosure laws, and on renovation. . . since about half of REOs are in bad physical shape.

The advantages of REOs

Note that there is nothing intrinsically wrong with buying real estate from a lender which has foreclosed on it. It only becomes questionable when you are buying the property for significantly ***less than market value.***

If you ***are*** paying ***market value*** or thereabouts, why treat REOs as an especially desirable source of property? You will come across your share of REOs by simply looking for property through normal channels. REOs are often listed with real estate brokerage firms.

The only REO ***advantage*** I see to real estate investors is the opportunity to profit from malfeasance or nonfeasance by employees of the lending institution selling the property. And that's a questionable way to make your million.

Getting properties for their ***quick sale*** value instead of their ***market*** value is nice. But there is no free lunch. In order to buy at quick sale value you must buy quickly. That requires cash. And little time to evaluate the property.

Plus, foreclosed properties are likely to have more than their share of problems. So in the haste to close a quick sale, you will occasionally make a costly mistake. That mistake will wipe out the profits from a number of successful quick sale purchases. There is a ***reason*** why buyers who are willing to close quickly get the properties for 10% to 20% less. There is no free lunch.

Buying foreclosures at or before the foreclosure auction

Attorney David Lane writes a weekly column called "Property and the Law" in the *San Francisco Examiner.* He devoted the September 8th and 15th, 1985 columns to the notion of making money in foreclosures. He told of enormous legal complexity and difficulty in finding out the details of the title status. Inability to inspect the property before purchase.

He noted that the more equity the foreclosed borrower or a junior mortgage holder had, the more likely that person will sue to overturn the foreclosure.

Purchase ***before*** foreclosure is especially hazardous due to the fact that other liens including ***junior*** liens are not wiped out, a real estate commission may be due, and a subsequent bankruptcy of the seller/borrower may invalidate your purchase. In addition, some states have special laws aimed at people who buy homes which are about to be foreclosed. In California, it's called the Mortgage Foreclosure Consultant and Home Equity Sales Contract law. These laws are quite strict and carry severe penalties.

PART FIVE: EXISTING LOANS

10

How And When To Keep Existing Loans

Typical characteristics of existing financing

Existing financing typically has these characteristics

- relatively low loan-to-value ratio
- relatively low interest rate
- little or no front-end fees
- always available (if no enforceable due-on-sale clause)
- often no credit check

These characteristics are not ***always*** present. For example, the loan-to-value ratio may be high. A guy who took my seminar in Dallas said that he routinely made offers to VA buyers in new Dallas subdivisions. They bought with zero down.

As soon as he saw their purchase go into the deed records, he wrote them a letter offering to buy their property. Some would sell to him for one reason or another within a year or so of purchase.

So he got a an assumable VA loan with a below-market interest rate typically. Plus he got a ***high*** loan-to-value ratio because the sellers had put nothing down and were selling within a year or so. Why did they sell to my student? No commission, mainly. And he gave them a fair price.

When is a loan transferrable?

I'll use the word "transferrable" in this chapter instead of "assumable" or "subject to-able." Simpler. Whether a loan is transferrable depends on three things:

- Wording of due-on-sale clause, if any
- state and federal law
- policy of the lender

Due-on-sale clause

If the loan has no due-on-sale clause, it's transferrable.

If the loan ***does*** have a due-on-sale clause, it may be so narrowly worded that you can get around it or it may be unenforceable due to state law.

A poor example

Here's an example of a narrowly worded due-on-sale clause. It comes from a second mortgage on an apartment building I bought. The seller hired an attorney to prepare the loan documents. The clause said

"In the event that the subject property is sold by the obligors, then the amount due on account of principal and interest at that time shall become due in full immediately."

Note that this clause is triggered only if the property is "sold." That leaves open the ***lease-option*** or ***land contract*** routes. You could drive a train through those loopholes.

A solid due-on-sale clause

Remember that I told you FNMA and FHLMC call the tune in home mortgages? They know what they're doing when it comes to writing mortgage documents. Here's ***their*** due-on-sale clause.

"If all or any part of the Property or an interest therein is sold or transferred by Borrower without Lender's prior written consent, excluding (a) the creation of a lien or encumbrance subordinate to this Mortgage, (b) the creation of a purchase money security interest for household appliances, (c)a transfer by devise, descent or by operation of law upon the death of a joint tenant or (d) the grant of any leasehold interest of three years or less not containing an option to purchase, Lender may at Lender's option declare all the sums secured by this Mortgage to be immediately due and payable."

Note that FNMA says "If *all or any part* of the Property or an interest therein is sold *or transferred*..." That's a lot broader than just "if the subject property is sold." FNMA's broader clause thereby covers both sales ***and land contracts.***

Note also subparagraph (d). It says it's OK to lease the property...as long as you don't lease it for more than three years. If you lease it for more than three years, you have triggered the due-on-sale clause.

Furthermore, subparagraph (d) also says that your lease better not contain an option to purchase no matter how long the lease term is. In other words, ***any*** lease with an option to purchase the property triggers the due-on-sale clause.

"Due-on-sale" is a misnomer

When it comes to the due-on-sale clause, you can see that the phrase "due-on-sale" is a misnomer. It's really a ***due-on-sale, land contract, more-than-three-year lease, or lease-option clause.***

Many misnomers are harmless. Not this one. For one thing, the phrase due-on-sale led that seller's attorney to write the sloppy, loophole-ridden due-on-sale clause I cited above. For ***his*** clause, due-on-sale is ***not*** a misnomer.

Another problem is that you have "creative finance" pushers running around the country telling people you can get around a due-on-sale clause by using a land contract or a lease-option. Because the audience has heard the phrase "due-on-sale" many times, getting around the clause with a "non-sale" seems plausible to them. If the clause had a more accurate name, they would not fall for that.

Recent action

In 1982 and 1983, there was a lot of action on the enforceability of due-on-sale clauses. All of it made them ***more enforceable.***

The *de la Cuesta* decision

The *de la Cuesta* decision started things off. On June 28, 1982, the U.S. Supreme Court announced its decision in *Fidelity Federal Savings and Loan Association versus de la Cuesta et al.* Fidelity Federal wanted to enforce a due-on-sale clause it had. De la Cuesta said it was not enforceable due to California's *Wellenkamp* decision.

In *Wellenkamp versus Bank of America,* (21 Cal 3d 943), the ***California,*** not U.S., Supreme Court said that due-on-sale clauses were not enforceable in California. Mr. De la Cuesta said that meant that Fidelity Federal could not enforce its clause.

Fidelity Federal said, "We don't have to answer to the California Supreme Court. We answer to a ***higher*** authority. We're ***federal.***" The word "Federal" in Fidelity Federal Savings and Loan Association denotes that Fidelity had a ***federal*** charter. Savings and loans which do ***not*** have the word "federal" in their name have ***state*** charters.

The U.S. Supreme Court said Fidelity Federal was right. Federally chartered savings and loans do not have to abide by ***state*** law when it comes to due-on-sale enforceability. . . because of an FHLBB rgulation.

FHLBB regulation

The Federal Home Loan Bank Board (FHLBB) regulates federal savings and loans. On July 31, 1976, an FHLBB regulation took effect. It said federal savings and loans can enforce due-on-sale clauses no matter what state law says. The de la Cuesta decision upheld that regulation's superiority over state law.

Due-on-sale was always enforceable in most states

The *de la Cuesta* decision did not affect most states at all. Most states had never doubted the enforceability of due-on-sale clauses. New Jersey's highest court, for example, reaffirmed their enforceability around 1980.

The seventeen states

FNMA has a different mortgage document for each state. On October 23, 1980, FNMA announced that it would no longer make thirty year loans in eleven states:

Arizona	Illinois	New Mexico
California	Iowa	South Carolina
Colorado	Michigan	Washington state
Georgia	Minnesota	

The reason was FNMA attorneys had studied the laws and court decisions in those states and concluded that they might have trouble enforcing due-on-sale clauses there. So they would only make ***seven*** year loans there. Seven years is about the average payoff time when due-on-sale clauses are enforceable.

On January 5, 1981, FNMA added six more states to that list:

Arkansas	Mississippi	Ohio
Florida	New York	Oklahoma

Note that I am not saying that due-on-sale clauses were ***not*** enforceable in those states. Just that FNMA attorneys found something to be nervous about in each of those states. How justified their nervousness was varied from state to state. (FNMA rescinded that policy when the Garn Bill was passed. They will now make 30 year loans in all fifty states again.)

In California, for example, FNMA lawyers' nervousness was totally justified. But when I mentioned South Carolina in an article, I got a letter from an attorney there. He wanted to know what the FNMA attorneys based their nervousness on since he couldn't find the slightest indication that due-on-sale clauses were not enforceable there. I referred him to FNMA. And I'll refer you to them too if you want the specifics for any of these states.

So the *de la Cuesta* decision did not affect the other thirty-three states:

Due-on-sale *Always Was* Enforceable

- Alabama
- Alaska
- Arkansas
- Connecticut
- Delaware
- District of Columbia
- Hawaii
- Idaho
- Indiana
- Kansas
- Kentucky
- Louisiana
- Maine
- Maryland
- Massachusetts
- Mississippi
- Missouri
- Montana
- Nebraska
- Nevada
- New Hampshire
- New Jersey
- North Carolina
- North Dakota
- Oregon
- Pennsylvania
- Rhode Island
- South Dakota
- Tennessee
- Texas
- Utah
- Vermont
- Virginia
- West Virginia
- Wisconsin
- Wyoming

These states were not affected by ***either*** the *de la Cuesta* decision or the Garn Bill.

The Garn Bill

On October 15, 1982, President Reagan signed the Garn Bill into law. The Garn Bill is officially known as the Garn-St. Germain Depository Institutions Act of 1982. The Garn Bill was actually more sweeping than the *de la Cuesta* decision...but it got less media coverage.

The Garn Bill did ***not*** affect the thirty-three states where due-on-sale clauses were always enforceable. Although it did say that such clauses would be enforceable in those states starting October 15,1982...thereby prohibiting the legislatures or courts of those states from following in the footsteps of California, etc.. It was sort of like the Emancipation Proclamation which freed only the slaves in the Confederacy and took effect while the Civil War was still going on.

The seventeen states and the Garn Bill

The Garn Bill did ***not*** say due-on-sale clauses were not enforceable in the seventeen states. Rather it said the law on due-on-sale enforceability of existing mortgages in those states may ***stay what it was on October 15, 1982*** until October 14, 1985.

The courts or legislatures in those states may make due-on-sale clauses in existing mortgages ***more enforceable*** during the period October 15, 1982 to October 14, 1985. But neither the courts nor the legislatures may make due-on-sale clauses in existing mortgages ***less*** enforceable in those states. Although they may pass laws which say that the non-enforceability of due-on-sale clauses will continue beyond October 14, 1985...***but only if the lender does not have a federal charter.***

Furthermore, come October 14, 1985 ***all*** due-on-sale clauses will be enforceable in ***all states.***

And ***all*** due-on-sale clauses in all mortgages ***originated after October 15, 1982*** are enforceable in ***all states.***

The Comptroller of the Currency and national banks

The *de la Cuesta* decision said federal savings and loan regulations took precedence over state law. That implies the same for federal ***bank*** regulations.

Federal savings and loans are regulated by the FHLBB. Federal ***banks*** (the ones with "national" in their names) are regulated by the Comptroller of the Currency.

FHLBB had issued a regulation on July 31, 1976 saying that due-on-sale clauses were enforceable. Unfortunately for the national banks, the Comptroller of the Currency had not issued such a regulation. . .until July of 1983.

The Comptroller's new regulation says national banks in the seventeen states can enforce due-on-sale clauses regardless of state laws starting April 15, 1984.

The National Credit Union Administration

The National Credit Union Administration regulates federal credit unions. On December 8, 1982, NCUA issued a regulation saying federal credit unions could enforce due-on-sale clauses. That regulation will have the same effect as the FHLBB reg, except for the effective date.

FHLMC policy

The Federal Home Loan Mortgage Corporation (FHLMC or "Freddie Mac") is like FNMA. Their policy on enforcement of due-on-sale clauses is that due-on-sale clauses are ***not*** enforceable if they are in loans originated during the following "window periods" in the indicated states:

FHLMC/FNMA Window Periods

State	Window Period	Says Who?
Arizona	7/8/71 - 10/15/82	*Patton v. First Federal S & L,* 578 P 2d 152 was decided March 13, 1978. FHLMC says the Arizona window period started 7/8/71
California	8/25/78 -10/15/82	*Wellenkamp v Bank of America* , 581 P 2d 970
Colorado	7/1/75 - 10/15/82	CO Rev. Stat. Art 38-60-65
Georgia	7/1/79 - 10/15/82	GA Code Ann. Sec. 67-3002
Iowa	7/1/79 - 10/15/82	IA Code Ann. Sec. 535.8
Michigan	1/5/77 - 10/15/82	*Nichols v. Arbor Fed. S & L,* 250 NW 2d 804
Minnesota	6/1/79 - 5/8/81	MN Stat. Ann. Sec. 47.20
New Mexico	3/15/79 -10/15/82	N.M.S.A. Secs. 48-7-11 through 48-7-14
Utah	5/12/81 -10/15/82	UT Code Ann. Sec 57-15-1
Washington	8/19/76 -10/15/82	*Bellingham First Federal S & L v. Garrison,* 553 P. 2d 1090 but enforceable by private mortgage lender *Morris V. Woodside,* 682 P 2d 905

The ***starting*** date for each window period is the result of either a court decision or passage of a state law. For example, California's *Wellenkamp* decision was decided on August 25, 1978.

These window periods are ***not*** law. They represent only the ***opinions*** of FHLMC and FNMA lawyers just as the seventeen states were only the opinions of FNMA lawyers. The Garn Bill does not name "window period states." All the Garn Bill says is that if the law of a state prohibited the enforcement of existing due-on-clauses as of October 15, 1982, it could stay that way until October 14, 1985.

The window periods applied to single-family only in Arizona, Georgia, Iowa, Michigan, Minnesota, New Mexico, and Utah. In California, Colorado, and Washington, they applied to both single-family and multi-family mortgages.

Summary

Here's a chart which summarizes the effect of the *de la Cuesta* decision, the Garn Bill, and the regulations of the FHLBB, NCUAB, and Comptroller of the Currency on the enforceability of due-on-sale clauses.

Due-On-Sale Clause Enforceability

Type of Lender	Loan Origination Date	States	Enforceable?	Authority
federal s&l	prior to 7/31/76	all	probably	FHLBB reg & de la Cuesta
	on or after 7/31/76	all	yes	de la Cuesta
national banks	prior to 10/15/82	the 17	no or maybe until 4/15/84	state law Comptroller
federal credit unions	on or after 10/15/82	all	yes	Garn Bill NCUAB reg.
state s&ls and state banks and all other lenders	prior to 10/15/82	the 17	no or maybe	state law
		the 33	yes	state law
	on or after 10/15/82	all	yes	Garn Bill

Questions on due-on-sale enforceability

Question: "My mortgage has a due-on-sale clause. Is it enforceable?"

Answer: *You need to tell me the **state** where the property is located, the **origination date** of the loan, and the name of the lender. Then I'll look it up on the table above.*

Q: "My lender has changed charters from state to federal since the loan was made. Do I look them up on the table according to what they are ***now*** or what they were ***then***?"

A: *What they were **when they originated the loan**. . . I think. Neither the courts nor the Congress have said. Although Senate Report 97-536 said,*

"The identity of the lender at the time the loan was originated determines whether or not a loan is subject to window period restrictions."

*The lenders say it's what they are **now**. The Realtors say it's what they were **then**. I suspect the courts will agree with the Realtors when they decide a case on the subject. A case is pending involving World Savings and Loan of California.*

Q: "Are wraparounds affected by the *de la Cuesta* decision or the Garn Bill?"

A: *Yes. A wraparound is a loan which includes an assumption or subject to. Since you can only have an assumption where there's either no due-on-sale clause or an unenforceable one, **de la Cuesta** and the Garn Bill apply same as if there were no wraparound.*

Q: "Why do you say 'probably' on whether federal savings and loans can enforce due-on-sale clauses in mortgages originated prior to July 31, 1976?"

A: *Because the FHLBB regulation which **de la Cuesta** upheld said that due-on-sale clauses "continue" to be enforceable. The Supreme Court did not specify any treatment of pre-July 15, '76 loans. As a practical matter, I haven't heard of any federal savings and loans trying to enforce due-on-sale clauses on pre-'76 loans. In fact, they've been reluctant to enforce them on **post-July 15, 1976** loans.*

Q: "Do these developments apply only to owner-occupied single-family?"

A: *No. . . except for a FHLBB regulation which came out on May 10, 1983. The de la Cuesta's bought a $350,000 commercial building. And the purpose of the Garn Bill is to help deposit institutions. So it doesn't allow investors to keep low interest loans either.*

The FHLBB reg of May 10, 1983 says the nine exceptions in the Garn Bill apply only to ***owner-occupied home*** *mortgages. Those nine exceptions say that lenders cannot enforce a due-on-sale clause just because*

1. *The borrower got another, junior, loan*
2. *Borrower got a mortgage to buy household appliances*
3. *Joint tenant died*
4. *Borrower leased the property for three years or less with no option to purchase*
5. *Borrower died*
6. *Transfer to spouse or children of borrower*
7. *Transfer to spouse via divorce or legal separation*
8. *transfer to inter vivos trust*
9. *any other transfer prescribed in FHLBB regulations*

The FHLBB reg essentially says that lenders ***can*** *enforce due-on-sale clauses in those nine instances if*

1. *the clause so states and*
2. *the property is not an owner-occupied home*

There was nothing in the Garn Bill about owner-occupied homes. As a result, real estate attorney John Beck (San Francisco) argues that the portion of the May 10, 1983 FHLBB reg which makes non-owner-occupied property different is an ***invalid regulation.*** *I suspect he's right.*

Q: "Are sellers who took back loans affected?"

A: *They are covered by the Garn Bill. That is, sellers who took back loans in the 17 states can enforce their due-on-sale clauses if the loans were originated on or after October 15, 1982. If the loans were originated before that date in those states, the due-on-sale clause may or may not be enforceable depending on the specifics of the state law.*

Q: "Are loans from federal credit unions affected?"

A: *They're in the same boat as the national banks except that they are regulated by the National Credit Union Administration (NCUA).*

I've seen a number of articles listing ways to get around due-on-sale clauses. I'm familiar with all the techniques they advocate. So don't conclude that I'm ***ignorant*** of the techniques just because I don't ***advocate*** them. Here are the techniques I've heard of and why I think they are not a good idea.

Lease-option

Let's say you're buying a property for $100,000. It has a $60,000 existing 10% loan on it. Payments are $561.65 a month. The mortgage contains an enforceable due-on-sale clause. The lease-option advocates say you should lease the property with an option to purchase. For example, you might write a seven year lease with monthly payments of $561.65 and the buyer having the right to purchase the property at that time for an amount equal to what the loan balance will be then.

From a numerical standpoint, that's identical to buying subject to the loan. It would probably even be treated the same as buying subject to for tax purposes.

Would that deal violate the FNMA due-on-sale clause? You're darned tootin. Remember that subparagraph (d) of the FNMA due-on-sale clause said any lease of more than three years or any lease containing an option to purchase would violate the clause. This example deal is a default on both the lease ***term*** (seven years is more than three) and the ***option***.

Keeping the fire insurance in the seller's name

Bob Bruss is probably the biggest advocate of the lease-option technique. He's the nationally syndicated real estate columnist and author of the book *The Smart Investor's Guide To Real Estate*.

I asked Bob why he didn't think the lease-option violated subparagraph (d). He said there was a good chance that it did. . .but pointed out there have been no court decisions he's aware of on the subject. And that he's been using the technique since 1970 and has never had a lender try to enforce a due-on-sale clause.

Furthermore, he said the ***main*** reason for the lease-option was to ***conceal*** the "sale" from the lender. He always tells his readers to keep the fire insurance in the seller's name to make sure the lender doesn't find out about the transfer. In other words, Bob relies on the ***concealment*** which results from the lease-option and fire insurance trick. He does ***not*** believe that the lease-option legally defeats the due-on-sale clause.

No decisions but unambiguous language

Bob is probably right about no court decisions affirming the lease portion of the FNMA due-on-sale clause. But I don't see the need for any. The language of the clause is clear as a bell. It says the lender can call the loan if you lease the property for more than three years or lease option it for any term.

The only way I can see a court not enforcing that language would be on grounds of some overriding consideration like consumer protection. The California Supreme Court, for example, would probably allow lease-options for the same reason it allowed Wellenkamp to buy subject to a loan with a due-on-sale clause.

But I doubt the U.S. Supreme Court would go along. After all, they just shut down states prohibiting enforcement of due-on-sale clauses with their *de la Cuesta* decision. If they allowed people to accomplish the same thing with lease-options, the *de la Cuesta* would be rendered overturned as a practical matter. Buyers and sellers would be doing lease-options all over the place.

In other words, the doctrine of substance over form would apply. The U.S. Supreme Court thinks due-on-sale clauses should be enforceable. They're not about to let anybody get around that decision simply by using a facsimile which goes by another name. . .especially one which is taxed like a sale.

Relying on concealment

I would not rely on concealment to protect me from a due-on-sale clause. It would be too easy for the lender to find out. For one thing, the seller might rat on you for some reason. Or someone else who knew about the deal and got mad at you.

Or the fire insurance might get fouled up. An insurance company clerk might send the bill to the seller at the property address. If the seller had moved more than a year ago, the post office would return the bill to the insurer. The insurance company might then contact the lender.

Or the lender could simply make an effort to check on who's occupying a property or who rents are being paid to. Wouldn't take much effort it seems to me. Looking up the supposed-to-be owner in the phone book. Knocking on the door. Etc.

Instant balloon payment

What does it mean if your concealment is penetrated? Instant balloon payment. You've turned over your down payment money to the seller. You paid a price which reflected the below-market interest rate on the loan. And now the lender says they want the whole thing paid off. . .immediately! That can be a very serious problem. Too serious in my opinion. That's why I would not buy a property in which an existing loan was in default (by virtue of the sale or lease-option or whatever) and rely on concealment.

Lease-options are a lousy way to buy

Setting aside the due-on-sale problems for a moment, I think lease-options are a lousy way to buy property. Getting title insurance on an option is tough even ***without*** the complication of the lease. According to the January-February 1985 *Lawyers Title News*, in a number of states, options ***may not be recorded***. In those states, you probably cannot get title insurance for your option at all.

Even if you can get title insurance, it will not protect you against liens placed on the property ***after*** the option is recorded. Your equity in the option is the difference between your option price and the fair market value of the property.

But the seller can confiscate all or part of that equity by mortgaging the property to the hilt and allowing such additional liens as those for back taxes, unpaid water bills, mortgage payments in arrears, mechanics liens, etc. You can protect yourself to an extent by insisting on paying the mortgage and other bills yourself. But that won't protect you from such nonsense as the seller "creating paper" secured by your equity and using it as down payment money on another property he's buying.

The title insurance policy will also not protect you in the event of bankruptcy of the seller prior to exercise of the option.

The foreclosure technique

Let's say you want to buy a property with an attractive first mortgage. You want to keep the mortgage, but it has an enforceable due-on-sale clause. So instead of ***buying*** the property, you ***loan money to the present owner***. The money you loan is secured by a second mortgage on the property.

The present owner doesn't make his payments to you on time. So you foreclose. By outbidding the other bidders, if any, you become the owner of the property. The first mortgage is intact because, say the advocates of this technique, a foreclosure of a junior loan does not trigger a due-on- sale clause.

I don't think you'd have a snowball's chance in Honduras of winning in court on that one. It's such a blatantly transparent attempt to defeat a due-on-sale clause that you'd probably not only lose but also be reprimanded by the judge for insulting his intelligence.

The FHLBB regulation dated May 10, 1983 also throws a possible monkey wrench into this technique for non-owner-occupied property. It said lenders could not enforce due-on-sale clauses if the borrower "further encumbers" the property. But the reg said that lenders ***could*** enforce due-on-sale on a further encumbrance if the due-on-sale clause so stated and the property was not an owner-occupied home.

That would mean that anyone who tried the foreclosure technique would put the loan in default as soon as he put the second on the property. . . before he got to the foreclosure. Again, that portion of that reg may well be illegal. But it's mere existence is another strike against the foreclosure technique.

The land contract technique

Since the deed remains with the seller until the loan is paid off in a land contract, many believe that the land contract is a way of getting around an enforceable due-on-sale clause. As I told you earlier, the FNMA and most other well-written clauses ***include*** land contracts in their definition of default. Some people acknowledge that but say that a land contract coupled with keeping the fire insurance in the seller's name will successfully ***conceal*** the transfer from the lender.

Maybe.

Also, land contracts add ***many risks*** to the buyer's position that are not present in a sale. I would never use a land contract unless I was buying a property in an area where land contracts are the ***rule*** for seller financing. . . like parts of the Midwest and Northwest. And even then I would only use a land contract in the way that they are commonly used there. . . as normal seller financing. Not as a device to get around a FNMA-like due-on-sale clause.

Owner name change techniques

The remaining techniques I've heard for getting around enforceable due-on-sale clauses involve changing the name of the owner. . .then selling the "name." You change the name of the owner by transferring title to a corporation, trust, or partnership. The lender couldn't object to that, so the argument goes, because the same ***people*** still own the property. Then after a period of time, you sell the corporation's stock or you sell your interest in the trust or partnership. No deed changes hands.

I believe the lender ***could and would*** object to the transfer to a corporation, trust, or partnership. They could argue that it represents a sale and therefore triggered the due-on-sale clause.

In a consumer case, the judge or jury might allow it if the same people still owned the corporation, trust, or partnership. But either the judge or the lender's attorney is likely to ask you what the purpose of the transfer is. "I remind you that you are under oath."

So how are you going to answer that question? Are you going to commit perjury by lying? I trust not. Are you going to tell the court that you did it in order to get around an enforceable due-on-sale clause? That's not perjury. Nor is it likely to help your case.

And the notorious FHLBB May 10, 1983 reg had something to say about this technique, too. Remember that exception number eight in the Garn Bill pertained to inter vivos trusts. It said that lenders could not enforce a due-on-sale clause just because you transferred a property to such a trust. But the FHLBB reg adds that the borrower must ***occupy*** the property in question (which again may be an illegal regulation) and the borrower must not refuse

"to provide the lender with reasonable means acceptable to the lender by which the lender will be assured of timely notice of any subsequent transfer of the beneficiary interest or change in occupancy. . . "

In plain English, the trust technique will not trigger a due-on-sale clause ***only*** if it's an owner-occupied home and the borrower promises in writing to notify the lender if he rents the property out or sells his interest in the trust.

I said I agree with John Beck that the FHLBB's owner-occupant differentiation is probably an illegal regulation. But I do ***not*** feel the same way about the FHLBB's requirement that borrowers promise to notify lenders when their beneficiary interest in a trust is transferred. I suspect that the courts will agree with the FHLBB on that one. The owner-occupant clause goes ***beyond*** the Garn Bill. But the trust transfer clause ***conforms*** to the Garn Bill letter and spirit and strengthens lenders in the way that the Garn Bill intended.

I suspect the first guy who used this technique to get around a due-on-sale clause did so in 1702 in England or somewhere. When the lender discovered that the clause had been gotten around, he wrote an article about for *Bankers Journal* or some similar publication. The other readers underlined it and passed it to their attorneys who dutifully inserted language to prevent it in the loan documents. And they added a paragraph to their policy manuals telling their employees not to approve such transfers. And ever since, those clauses and policies have been a part of loans in the western world.

I said earlier that loan officers were often process-oriented and security-conscious and all that. But I didn't say they were stupid.

I have been hearing these name change techniques advocated for getting around due-on-sale clauses since a 1974 "creative finance" seminar I attended. An audience of investors will generally respond to them by thinking, "Hey, now ***there's*** a good idea." An audience of lenders will generally respond with laughter.

The name change techniques are mainly ***concealment*** tactics. I doubt any court would allow them. Furthermore, they leave the buyer in a much riskier position regarding title and so forth, than a straight sale.

Finally, corporations, trusts, and partnerships are not benign. They are treated differently for ***tax*** purposes when it comes to filing returns and benefits like exchanges. Keeping an existing loan is only ***one*** effect (and a dubious one at that) of switching to those forms of ownership. There are many other effects. . .most of them bad.

Lender policy

As a practical matter, the lenders are usually less hard-nosed than they are entitled to be by law. . .on home mortgages at least. They sometimes don't do anything. More often they either raise the interest rate to current market or they offer a "blended rate." A blended rate is a compromise between market and the rate on the old loan.

There is no law requiring lenders to offer blended rates. Or even a law requiring them to accept ***market*** rates. They can demand total payoff if they want.

Foreclosure optional not mandatory

Remember that the typical due-on-sale clause does not ***require*** the lender to call the loan due. It just gives him the ***option*** to do so.

Nor is it against the law to violate the due-on-sale clause. But it ***is*** against the law to not pay off the loan ***if*** you violate the due-on-sale clause ***and*** the lender demands pay off.

Consumer lenders don't like bad publicity

I have been amazed since the de la Cuesta decision at the restraint of the federal savings and loans. At the time of the decision, nearly all mortgage lenders were in dire financial straits. Their lobbyists in Washington were clamoring for federal bail outs.

But when the Supreme Court handed the federal savings and loans an opportunity to solve much of their problem, the lenders shrank from doing so.

Lender lobbyists are quite willing to pressure Congress to raise taxes on a machinist in Dubuque to improve the lenders' financial position. But just don't expect the lenders to send that same machinist a letter calling his loan due. Basically, the lenders want money but they don't want to be the ones to collect it.

The net result is that federal savings and loans either did nothing or offered blended rates in the wake of the *de la Cuesta* decision. They ***could have*** demanded market interest rates on every transferred loan originated in those seventeen states after July 31, 1976.

Commercial lenders aren't such soft touches

Commercial lenders are a whole nother smoke. When Big Bucks Federal Savings and Loan forecloses on Mr. & Mrs. Littleman's home, the evening news is there with their cameras. The sobbing Littleman's appear on that night's newscast. Then they cut to the panelled, plush office of Mr. Gotrocks, the savings and loan president. "We have a negative yield spread on loans like the Littleman's. We have to make a profit. That's why we had to foreclose."

The next day, two thousand citizens move their accounts out of Big Bucks. That's why s & l executives pussyfoot around when it comes to the enforcement of home mortgage due-on-sale clauses.

But don't expect sellers or commercial mortgage lenders to behave that way on income property mortgages. Ain't gonna be no TV cameras there when your ***investment*** property gets foreclosed. Not even if you sob, "How am I going to make my goal of a net worth of $750,000 by year end if they foreclose on me." You'd have a better chance of getting on TV if the fire department rescued your cat from a tree.

Some lenders will even get tough on a single-family home mortgage. . .if you don't live in the property. In the eyes of the lenders, media, and courts, non-owner occupants are "speculators."

When to preserve existing financing

You preserve existing financing whenever that plus other available financing is better than all new financing. As a general rule, existing financing is worth preserving when it equals 30% or more of the property value.

There are two problems with ***always*** preserving existing financing whenever the interest rate is below-market:

- annual constant
- higher cost of seconds

The annual constant goes up

The annual constant is the annual debt service payments divided by the loan balance. For example, if your payments are $24,000 a year and the loan balance is $215,000, the annual constant is 11%.

On a 30 year self-amortizing loan, the annual constant is usually slightly higher than the interest rate. For example, the monthly payments on a 30 year, $250,000 mortgage at 13% are $2,765.50. Annually that's 12 x $2,765.50 = $33,186. On closing day, the annual loan constant would be $33,186/$250,000 = 13.27%.

I said the interest rate was 13%. So why isn't the constant 13%, too? Because each payment includes some amortization. The amortization adds about .27% in this case.

With each passing month, the amount of principal goes up and the loan balance goes down. At first, amortization is slight. But it accelerates. The increase in the principal portion of the payment and the decrease in the loan balance means that the ***constant*** goes up every month, too. This table shows the annual constant at each five year point in a 30 year, 13% $100 loan.

Constant increases over time

Year	Payments	Balance	Constant
5	$13.27	$100.00	13.27%
10	$13.27	$97.27	13.64%
15	$13.27	$93.22	14.24%
20	$13.27	$85.76	15.47%
25	**$13.27**	**$72.01**	**18.43%**
30	**$13.27**	**$46.67**	**28.43%**

This is one reason why you don't see many 30 years loans with five, ten, or fifteen years left. . .except on single-family owner-occupied homes where the equity buildup represents a retirement program.

From a ***cash-outlay*** standpoint, old loans are expensive in spite of their low interest rates. If you refinanced, even at a higher rate, your ***payments*** would ***drop***.

Interest rates only tell ***part*** of the story. The constant tells the rest.

Seconds are more expensive

In the typical deal, you will be financing 70% to 80% of the purchase price. Existing financing rarely covers that high a percentage of value. So preserving existing financing means you must also have ***secondary*** financing. If it's from the seller, the interest rate will probably be low. . .although you're really paying ***market*** interest via an inflated price.

If you go to a third party lender for your secondary financing, you'll pay market rates either in the form of points or actual market face interest rates on the loan.

It has always seemed to me that only the loan-to-value ratio mattered in the lender's risk. In other words, a second mortgage which, when added to the first, equals 75% of value seems as risky to me as a first mortgage of 75% of value.

The lenders don't see it that way. They say seconds are riskier. Whether they're right or not, they ***charge more*** for seconds in most cases. (FNMA charges the ***same*** for seconds on homes and conventional firsts.)

So keeping the low interest first may be more expensive

Let's say you are buying a $1,000,000 building. It has an existing, assumable loan of $350,000 at 9% with monthly payments of $2,900. You're putting down 25% or $250,000. So you need additional financing of $1,000,000 - $350,000 - $250,000 = $400,000.

Second mortgages cost, say, 15%. And they'll accept a 30 year amortization schedule (although they usually want the loan to balloon in three to ten years). So the payments on the second will be

n	360
i	15/12 = 1.25
PV	400000
PMT	5057.78

That gives you ***total*** payments on the two mortgages of $2,900 + $5,057.78 = $7,957.78.

Let's further say that you can get a ***new first*** mortgage for 13.5%, 30 years. Payments on that would be

n	360
i	13.5/12 = 1.125
PV	750000
PMT	8590.59

So the comparison is

Preserve existing first and get new second	$7,957.78
New first	$8,590.59
Difference	$ 632.81

So in this case, you'd be better off keeping the first and getting a new second than getting a new first. But not by much...just $632.81 a month or a $632.81/$7,957.78 = 8% payment increase. If the front end charges for the new second were high...or there were other considerations, you might prefer the new first. And if the existing first were a little smaller, say $300,000, you'd be better off with the new first. Then the payments on the new second would be

n	360
i	15/12 = 1.25
PV	450000
PMT	5690.00

$5,690 + $2,900 = $8,590...the same as the new first payment.

Investors often get dazzled by the low interest rates on existing financing and try to preserve them at all costs. There is no prize for the guy with the lowest interest rate. The name of the game is after-tax return on equity. Lowering your monthly payments ***improves*** return on equity. And the road to lowest payments sometimes leads to paying off low interest, assumable existing mortgages.

How to legitimately get two "first" mortgages on the same property

Defeasance is a technique I've never read about in any real estate finance book. That's unusual. Most real estate finance techniques are as old as the hills. Even those which "creative finance" gurus say are ***new***. You rarely come across a new one.

I came across this one in the May 22, 1985 ***Wall Street Journal.*** Here's the actual case history from the article.

Lazard Realty Inc. is the real estate investment affiliate of Lazard Freres & Co., a Wall Street investment banking firm. A Lazard Realty partnership owned 11,000 apartment units in 26 properties in Maryland and Pennsylvania. The apartments had old, low interest rate mortgages on them.

Lazard wanted to refinance. But they did not want to pay ***second mortgage*** interest rates. And they did not want pay off their low-interest first mortgage either. So how could they have their cake and eat it, too?

Defeasance

By defeasance. The first mortgages had a total balance of $74,000,000. Lazard bought a bunch of government securities whose yields and maturities matched the payment pattern on the first mortgages. By government securities they mean

Treasury bonds
Treasury notes
Treasury bills
Stripped Treasury issues
Treasury zero coupon bonds
Federal agency bonds like Government National Mortgage Association (GNMA) issues.

The interest rate on the government securities was 10%. Since ***market*** interest rates were higher, the government securities sold at a ***discount.*** Specifically, Lazard bought government securities with a ***face*** value of $74,000,000 for only $62,000,000. That $12,000,000 discount is the whole reason for defeasance in this case.

They did this as part of a deal with the Federal National Mortgage Association (FNMA). FNMA loaned Lazard $260,000,000. The loan-to-value ratio on that $260,000,000 was about 75%. The interest rate on the $260,000,000 was a ***first*** mortgage interest rate. . .three percent lower than Lazard would have had to pay if they had gotten a ***second*** mortgage.

Second mortgage lender had the safety of a first mortgage

Since the $260,000,000 loan was a 75%-of-value ratio, the total value of the 11,000 apartment units was $260,000,000/75% = $347,000,000. The $260,000,000 loan was ***legally*** a second mortgage. Because the $74,000,000 first mortgage was still recorded as a lien against the property. But FNMA was willing to give a ***first*** mortgage loan-to-value ratio and ***first*** mortgage interest rate because the government securities Lazard bought were placed in an irrevocable trust. FNMA was the beneficiary of that trust.

Also, FNMA was willing to do it because the ***title insurance company***, Lawyers Title, agreed to issue a title insurance policy which guaranteed that FNMA would, in effect, get ***first*** mortgage priority. So the idea had to be sold to ***both*** FNMA and Lawyers Title Insurance.

The mortgage payments on the first mortgage would be paid by the interest and principal payments made by the government on the government securities. In other words, the payments on the first mortgage are now ***guaranteed*** to be made by the ***U.S. government.*** So FNMA has no worry about the first mortgage payments ever being in default. Because their normal concern about being a second is eliminated by the trust containing the government securities. That's why FNMA was willing to give Lazard a loan-to-value ratio and an interest rate as if the $260,000,000 loan were a first mortgage.

A 96% loan-to-value ratio!

The total loans recorded against the 11,000 apartments are now $74,000,000 + $260,000,000 = $334,000,000. That's a $334,000,000/$347,000,000 = ***96% loan-to-value ratio!*** Furthermore, Lazard's partnership gets loan proceeds of $260,000,000 - $62,000,000 = $198,000,000. That's $12,000,000 ***more*** than they would have gotten if they had simply paid off the old first and gotten a new first of $260,000,000.

The reason for the $12,000,000 is that when you pay off a mortgage, you have to pay it off at *face* value...unless the lender offers to let you pay it off at a discount as an incentive to pay it off. But in Lazard's case, the first mortgage lender *refused* to allow a discount payoff.

Lazard *sort of* paid it off by buying the government securities to make the payments on the first mortgage. But they bought those government securities at a $12,000,000 *discount* ($62,000,000 versus $74,000,000). Lazard no longer makes mortgage payments on the first. The trust of government securities takes care of that.

Discount for prepayment makes more sense but...

If the first mortgage lender had offered to let Lazard pay the $74,000,000 loan off at a $12,000,000 discount, Lazard could have accomplished the same thing by doing that and getting a new first mortgage. But the first mortgage lender refused.

That's typical. Because mortgage lenders are usually public companies. And the Financial Accounting Standards Board (FASB) and regulators let them carry mortgages on their balance sheet at *face* value. Shame on the FASB and regulators for that. Lenders should be required to carry mortgages on their books at *market* value. But since they carry them at *face* value, agreeing to a discount for prepayment forces the lender to "take a loss."

Both Lazard and the existing first lender could have made more

In fact, the lender *suffered* the loss the moment the market interest rate rose above the interest rate on the mortgage in question. If the first mortgage lender in the Lazard case *had* been required to carry that $74,000,000 mortgage on their books at *market* value, I'd guess that'd be about $55,000,000. Lazard could defease the loan using $62,000,000 of U.S. government securities.

It would have made sense for both the lender and Lazard to split the difference.

Lazard: "Look, Mr. Lender, you're carrying this on your books at $55,000,000. And I can defease you [keep it on your books at $55,000,000] for $62,000,000. Why don't we split the difference by you allowing us to pay you off at $58,500,000?"

That would enable Lazard to save $15,500,000 instead of $12,000,000. And it would raise the lender's shareholders' equity by $3,500,000.

But alas, the FASB and regulators would rather perpetuate the fiction of book value (to cover up the weakened financial condition of mortgage lenders). So the shareholders of the first mortgage lender and Lazard's partners lose out on $7,000,000 (or whatever the actual figure is) they could have easily had.

By using defeasance, Lazard, in effect, paid the first mortgage off at a discount...whether the first mortgage lender liked it or not. But now the first mortgage lender is stuck with that low interest mortgage for many more years.

Legally, the property is leveraged to 96% of its value. Although for the second mortgage lender's purposes, the first mortgage no longer exists. Lazard's not making payments on it any more. And FNMA's not worried about the first being foreclosed, thereby jeopardizing their second.

Requirements for defeasance

Defeasance makes sense when the following are present:

1. Existing loan with assumable below-market interest rate.
2. Existing lender refuses to allow payoff at an adequate discount.
3. New lender will make second mortgage at first mortgage interest rate and loan-to-value ratio if made the beneficiary of a securities trust.
4. Securities acceptable to the new lender may be purchased at a discount.

Lenders often offer such prepayment bonuses in letters to mortgage borrowers during times of high interest rates. Although the discounts institutional lenders offer are almost always too small.

The FNMA deal shows that it is possible to use defeasance in deals involving ***institutional*** money. So, in theory, your local savings and loan should be willing to do what FNMA did in the Lazard deal. In practice, ***some*** institutional lenders and title insurance companies will agree to this. But only after a lot of explaining. Other institutional lenders and title insurance companies will refuse to do it simply because it ain't in the policy manual.

What if there's an enforceable due-on-sale clause?

An enforceable due-on-sale clause in the existing first mortgage could cause a problem. For example, in the FNMA/Lazard deal, if Lazard sold the properties and triggered a due-on-sale clause, the first mortgage lender would demand immediate payment of the $74,000,000 balance. FNMA could sell the bonds. But that would only yield $62,000,000. ***Less*** if interest rates had gone up in the interim.

One way to deal with that would be to require the borrower to make up any shortfall. In the FNMA/Lazard deal, the $12,000,000 short fall would be about the same size as a prepayment penalty. $12,000,000 is about five percent of the $260,000,000 mortgage. Prepayment penalties of five percent are common. If the lender can rely on the borrower to pay a 5% prepayment penalty, they can rely on him to pay a 5% bond trust shortfall. Although in a sale, there are ***sale proceeds*** and the lender has the power to ***compel*** the borrower to pay the prepayment penalty out of those proceeds.

But as I noted, if interest rates go ***up***, the shortfall will be ***bigger*** than $12,000,000. Perhaps so big that the borrower cannot come up with the money. You might be able to rig up some hedge in the interest rate futures market. But I suspect the new lender would simply refuse to participate in a defeasance deal if the existing first mortgage contained an enforceable due-on-sale clause.

Financial Accounting Standards Board issued guidelines on defeasance

Exxon Corporation announced that it had done a $515 million defeasance deal on July 6, 1982. Then a number of others were done. As a result of questions about how to report such transactions, the FASB and Securities and Exchange Commission (SEC) put a moratorium on defeasance for companies under their jurisdiction. That was lifted 18 months later. At that time, FASB issued Statement of Financial Accounting Standards (SFAS) No. 76 on the subject of "Extinguishment of Debt..."which is defeasance.

The main FASB restriction is that the bonds used must be backed by the ***full faith and credit of the U.S. government***. That means companies regulated by the SEC may only claim to have extinguished a debt if the bonds in the trust are issued by the U.S. Treasury or by federal agencies which are backed by the full faith and credit of the U.S. government...like GNMA.

Selling defeasance to local lenders and title people

It ain't gonna be easy to sell a local savings and loan on making a second mortgage on first mortgage terms because you've set up a bond trust to cover payments on the first. For one thing, it ain't in the policy manual. For another, they may fear that this could be done ***to*** them on a property where ***they*** hold a below-market interest rate first mortgage.

It also ain't gonna be easy to sell the idea to a local title insurance company if the lender insists that the title insurance company guarantee that they are protected. I called a couple of title companies near my home to see what they thought. I got nowhere.

One asked where the Lazard properties were. I told him Maryland and Pennsylvania. He said California law would prohibit it. A California attorney I talked to said no California law that he's aware of prohibits defeasance. The title officer just seized on the fact that the deal was done outside of California as a way of dismissing it. You'll probably run into the same kind of not-in-the-policy-manual mentality.

Another title officer I talked to said it sounded like a ***mechanic's lien bond***. If there is a mechanic's lien on a property, and you want to mortgage or sell that property, the mechanic's lien must be lifted. One way is to pay it off. But you can also get it off the title by posting a mechanic's lien bond. Indeed, that is an analogous situation.

But that title officer referred me to their in-house attorney and he said no. He said the California state law which allows mechanic's liens to be released on posting of a bond is quite specific and limited to mechanic's liens only. He further said that he would not do as Lawyers Title Insurance company did in the Lazard/FNMA deal. That is he would not guarantee FNMA that they would not be junior to the first mortgage.

Finance techniques that work in the real world

Most "creative finance" gurus load you up with techniques which do not work in the real world because you can't get lenders to go along. I'm not going to do that. I think defeasance is a great technique. It's legal. It's ethical. It puts money in your pocket...or more accurately converts the benefit of future low interest rate payments to a lump sum of cash now.

But finding a mortgage lender who will go along with it ***will not be easy***. To convince them, point to the Lazard/FNMA deal. Neither Lazard nor FNMA do dumb or illegal deals. You should probably bring with you copies of the following:

• *Wall Street Journal* May 22, 1985 real estate column describing the Lazard/FNMA deal (You can probably get a photocopy at your local library.)

• SFAS No. 76 "Extinguishment of Debt" (Send $5 to FASB Order Department, P.O. Box 8888-B, Stamford, CT 06904.)

• "Refinancing Through Mortgage Defeasance" by Evan Marks in the summer 1985 issue of *The Real Estate Finance Journal* (Warren, Gorham & Lamont). Evan Marks is the Lazard Realty vice president who did the FNMA deal.

• This book.

Your argument with the would-be second mortgage lender would go something like this.

"Mr. Lender, I know this is an unusual finance technique which you've never seen before. But look at these references. This is the ***Wall Street Journal****, not "Creative Finance Monthly." And the companies involved in the deal were the Federal National Mortgage Association, Lawyers Title Insurance Company, and Lazard Realty, an arm of Lazard, Freres & Co., one of Wall Street's establishment investment banking companies. These are not a bunch of far out kooks taking wild risks. Finally, the Financial Accounting Standards Board has issued guidelines showing how to report defeasance deals. FASB is one of the most conservative organizations around. They are frequently criticized for taking way too long to analyze an issue before taking a stand. If all these guys see no problem with defeasance, why should Podunk Savings and Loan conclude defeasance is unacceptably risky?"*

Sellers and defeasance

Most ***sellers*** should be willing to agree to a first mortgage loan-to-value ratio and interest rate even though they are a second...if they are the beneficiaries of a bond trust like FNMA was with Lazard. So that suggests defeasance is a technique you could make good use of with sellers if not with institutional lenders.

Unfortunately, I can't see how it would work with sellers. The problem is sellers are ***soft money*** lenders. A ***hard money*** lender is one who writes a check for the amount of the loan. A soft money lender is one who makes a loan by agreeing to ***defer*** receipt of money due him. Soft money lenders include sellers who take back mortgages and real estate agents who accept a note for their commission. Hard money lenders are banks, savings and loans, etc.

But in order to use defeasance, you must have ***hard money*** with which to buy the bonds at a discount. A seller mortgage provides no hard money. So where would you get the money to buy the bonds? If you have it in your bank account, you can get a better return by investing it in real estate. The return on defeasance is only about what you'd get on a wraparound mortgage...12% to 14% or so. Defeasance becomes much more attractive only when someone else, like a savings and loan, puts up the money.

So defeasance is only feasible when a hard money lender is making a new loan. This could be in a refinancing with no change of ownership or in a sale where the buyer is getting a new, hard money mortgage.

Tax ramifications

I'm not sure what the tax ramifications are. Defeasance is relatively new. So there are no court decisions on real estate defeasance *per se*. My best guess is that you may continue to deduct the interest payments on the first mortgage. But you must include the interest on the bonds in your income. Since you purchased the bonds at a discount, the interest income for tax purposes is, roughly speaking, the ***yield*** on the bonds at the price you paid for them. Not the ***face*** interest rate. This is the original issue discount rule which is required by sections 1271-1273 of the Internal Revenue Code.

In the alternative, if the law said you were relieved of the loan obligation, the discount on the bonds would be the same as the discount you get from a lender for early payoff. On ***non***-business property, like your residence or a vacation home which you do not rent out, that discount is ***ordinary income***. Or at least that's what IRS said in Revenue Ruling 82-202. You ***can*** and should use defeasance on non-business property when the opportunity presents itself.

On ***business*** property, you have a choice. This was established in the Bankruptcy Tax Act of 1980. Don't let the word "bankruptcy" throw you off. The names of laws are often misleading. According to Internal Revenue Code section 61(a)(12), "income from discharge of indebtedness" (prepayment discount) is ordinary income. But "qualified business indebtedness" is ***not*** ordinary income unless you choose that it be. So says Internal Revenue Code section 108(a)(1)(C).

Section 108(c) says you can choose to reduce the basis of the property ***instead*** of counting the amount of the discount as ordinary income in the year of the pay off. This would take effect the year ***after*** you paid the loan off at a discount. If it was a $12,000 discount, for example, you would reduce the basis of the property by $12,000. That, in turn, would lower your depreciation deductions for that and later years. And, if you sold the property, it would increase your gain. Furthermore, the gain due to the basis reduction is ***recaptured*** as ordinary income on sale.

Unless you are in the zero bracket even including the discount in your income for the year, choosing the reduce-basis alternative is best.

Summary on preserving existing financing

Existing, below-market interest rate mortgages with balances greater than 30% of the sale price are usually worth preserving if you're a ***seller***...because they increase your property's value. The only value to a ***buyer*** of below-market rate existing assumable financing is the ability to ***reduce front-end fees, avoid credit checks, and speed the deal.*** Whatever the buyer saves in interest payments when he buys subject to, he gives up in additional purchase price.

Accordingly, if anyone is going to go through gyrations to preserve existing financing, it ought to be the ***seller***, not the buyer. So techniques which weaken the buyer's claim to title to the property aren't worth the risk.

If the loan contains an enforceable due-on-sale clause, you ought not try to get around it. It is unlikely that ***any*** of the techniques you hear for getting around enforceable due-on-sale clauses would survive a trial. And relying on concealment is just too dangerous given the consequences of discovery.

Below-market interest rate, assumable financing is ***not*** the best choice *per se*. You should always compare it to the alternative of getting an entirely ***new*** mortgage...especially when the balance on the existing loan is 30% or less of the sale price.

11
How And When To Refinance

I'll define refinancing as financing of real estate by its current owner. It seems to me that refinancing also implies that he will ***remain*** the owner. I own an extensive real estate library. . .including many books on real estate finance and a couple of real estate dictionaries. Do you know I could only find ***two*** books which defined the word "refinancing."

The best, *Fundamentals of Mortgage Lending* by Marshall Dennis, defined it as

The repayment of a debt from the proceeds of a new loan using the same property as security.

I disagree with the word "repayment." Seems to me that when the owner of a free and clear property gets a new loan on it he is refinancing.

Reasons to refinance

There are several reasons to refinance:

1. To pay a balloon payment
2. To take advantage of better market terms
3. To make the property more marketable
4. To take advantage of other investment opportunities

Balloon payments

If a pending balloon payment is your reason for refinancing, get to work ***early***. Remember that one of Murphy's Laws is

Everything takes longer than you think.

Eighteen months before the balloon payment due date would be about the latest you'd want to start looking for your new financing. It can be very difficult to find financing for real estate.

The liquidity hierarchy

Here's a financeability hierarchy. . .in order of ease of financing.

1. FHAable single-family owner-occupied homes
2. VAable single-family owner-occupied homes (if you're a vet)
3. FNMAable single-family owner-occupied homes
4. Jumbo (more than FNMA limits) owner-occupied homes
5. Tenant-occupied single-family homes
6. Large (more than $1,000,000) income properties
7. Small income properties

Properties outside major metropolitan areas are harder to finance than properties within major metropolitan areas.

FHAable means that the loan amount is within FHA limits. Call your local HUD office or a mortgage company that originates FHA mortgages to find out what those limits are. Last I heard, it was $67,500 unless you were in a "high cost area." HUD has a list of "high cost areas."

VAable means that the loan amount is within VA limits. VA does not have a stated limit per se. But if you call a mortgage company that does VA loans they will tell you the practical limits.

At the time I'm writing this, FNMA's limit on owner-occupied single-family homes is $133,250 (50% higher in Alaska and Hawaii).

Jumbo home loans are those above FNMA's limit. Tenant-occupied single-family homes are eligible for FHA loans (lower loan-to-value ratio than owner-occupied FHA) and conventional loans.

It may seem paradoxical that ***large*** income properties are easier to finance than ***small*** ones. . .in view of the fact that the easiest homes to finance are the smallest. The reason is that home loans are made by formula. Income property loans are made on a case-by-case analysis.

Because the analysis costs about the same regardless of the size of the income property, lenders shy away from small inocme properties. And those that ***will*** make the loans charge a minimum fee which makes financing of small income properties more expensive per thousand dollars. For example, when I got a FHLMC apartment loan of $450,000, Norwest Mortgage charged me $8,000. . .their minimum fee. If the loan had been for $800,000 or more, their fee would have been 1%.

Better market terms

When mortgage interest rates drop, people think about refinancing to take advantage of the new rates. Newspaper and magazine stories tell their readers rules of thumb as to when it makes sense to refinance. They usually say two or three percent.

I like to give action-oriented guidelines like that whenever I can. But the decision to refinance is not that simple. There are two main considerations:

1. Transaction costs
2. Future financing

Transaction costs

Refinancing is expensive. You generally have most of the same costs you have when you ***buy*** a building.

- Title insurance for lender
- Lender's attorney's fee
- Recording fee
- Origination fee
- Points
- Appraisal fee
- Escrow fees
- Settlement room fee
- Mortgage insurance initial premium
- Credit report fee
- Tax service fee
- Termite inspection fee
- Engineer inspection fee (on income property)

Plus, there are frequently costs attached to paying off the ***old*** mortgage.

- Prepayment penalty
- Reconveyance fee
- Payoff statement fee
- Forwarding fee

And in some cases, the old loan is ***locked in.*** That means you may ***not*** pay it off. . . with or without paying a prepayment penalty. My FHLMC apartment building mortgage, for example, is locked in for the first five years. And there's a prepayment penalty thereafter.

To find out exactly what costs you will have due to paying off the old loan, read the old loan documents and contact that lender. Make sure you ask, "Are you sure there are ***no other costs***?" Because they tend to tell you about the big costs and dismiss the others as "standard." Standard or not, you need ***all*** the costs in order to decide whether to refinance.

Three-year payback

The costs of refinancing are an ***investment***. You ought to get a three-year payback on that investment. In other words, it the refinancing costs $6,000, you ought to save at least $6,000/3 = $2,000 per year in interest with the new mortgage.

Make sure you attribute some value to your time. Refinancing not only takes money. It also takes time. Ten hours is probably a pretty good estimate. Figure out how much your time is worth and multiply it by ten.

Include both the costs of the new loan and the costs of paying off the old loan in your "investment." Here's an example using my current home mortgage.

Example

The original loan terms were

Amount: $320,000
Interest rate: 13% fixed
Term: 30 years
Origination date: February 1, 1984
Monthly principal and interest payment: $3,604.84
Prepayment penalty: None

Since I have no prepayment penalty, the only cost of paying off the mortgage should be the cost of generating and recording the deed of reconveyance. A deed of reconveyance is the document which says a trust deed has been paid off. In states where mortgages are used, the document which removes the mortgage from the property has another name. In either case, it has to be recorded. The recording fees are typically in the $5 to $10 range. And the lender will probably hit you up for another $25 or $50 for something or another.

So we'll say it costs $45 to pay off the old loan.

The cost of the new loan

The loan balance as of August 1, 1985 was about $318,500. Here's my best guess at the costs of the new loan using the figures from when we got the current loan.

Title insurance	300.00
Recording	6.00
Application fee	100.00
Loan fee (2 points)	6,370.00
Tax service fee	40.00
Credit report	35.00
Escrow fee	400.00
Appraisal fee	200.00
Subtotal	$7,451.00
Plus payoff costs	45.00
Total	$7,496.00

To meet the three-year payback criterion, the annual interest savings would have to be at least $7,496/3 = $2,498.67. On a loan amount of $318,500, that'd be $2,498.67/$318,500 = .00785 or .785%. So if we can get a new loan at 13% - .785% = 12.215%, we should refinance.

Should you wait until rates go down even further?

No. Do ***not*** wait for rates to go down even further. Remember that Reed's Rule of Finance Number 10 says that "Interest rates are totally unpredictable."

I don't care how many times you hear the "experts" say rates will drop farther, forget it. Those guys who predict interest rate movements are charlatans. No one knows. *No one*!

Whenever refinancing makes sense, you should refinance. If rates ***do*** fall farther, do the calculation again. It may make sense to refinance a ***second*** time. Sure, I know it's much more expensive to refinance twice than to refinance once. But if you wait, rates may go ***up*** instead of down. In which case you blew an opportunity to earn 33.3% on your money (A three-year payback is a 33.3% return on your investment in the transaction costs).

Tax ramifications

Home mortgage interest is deductible if you itemize. So are points on a mortgage on your principal residence if the ***purpose*** of the loan is to "***purchase or improve***" the residence. Points on a refinancing just to lower your interest cost are therefore ***not*** deductible. So you might consider borrowing ***more than*** the balance of the existing loan so as to generate net proceeds which you use for some improvement. (Section 461(g)(2) of the Internal Revenue Code)

On other property like a vacation home or rental property, you must amortize (like straight line depreciation) points over the life of the loan.

Prepayment penalties are deductible as interest. On both homes and investment property.

All the other loan fees must be amortized over the life of the new mortgage on business or investment property. On personal use property like a principal residence or vacation home which is not rented out, you cannot deduct or amortize the other loan expenses.

Use *after*-tax numbers

Above, I calculated the three-year payback using ***before***-tax numbers. You really ought to use ***after***-tax numbers. That is the ***after***-tax transaction costs and the ***after***-tax interest savings. In the 50% bracket, for example, a one percent interest savings ***before***-tax is only a 1/2% savings ***after***-tax.

To convert the cost of the refinancing to its after-tax equivalent subtract any tax savings you get the year you refinance from the before-tax cost of refinancing. For example, in a refinancing for improvement of your personal residence, you could deduct points. In my example above, the points were $6,370. For someone in the 50% bracket, that'd be 50% x $6,370 = $3,185.00.

But the other costs would be nondeductible. So the after-tax refinancing cost would be the before-tax total of $7,496 less $3,185 = $4,311. To achieve a three-year payback, you'd have to save $4,311/3 = $1,437 per year after taxes. In the 50% bracket, that's $1,437/50% = $2,874 before taxes. Or $2,874/$318,500 = .902%.

What if it were an investment property?

If the property in question were an investment property rather than a personal residence, the refinancing cost would be entirely nondeductible. That means the before-tax and after-tax refinancing cost would be the same. However, you would be deducting the prorata share of the refinancing cost every year over the life of the loan. So your ***annual*** benefit from refinancing would be juiced up by the tax savings resulting from amortizing the refinancing cost over the life of the loan.

Let's say you got a 30-year loan with a 10-year balloon in the example above. That would allow you to deduct the $7,496 refinancing cost at a rate of $7,496/10 = $750 a year. In the 50% bracket, that'd save you 50% x $750 = $375 per year. A three year payback would require savings of $7,496/3 = $2,498.67 per year. You're getting $375 from the amortization deductions. So you'd only need to get $2,498.67 - $375 = $2,123.67 from the after-tax interest savings.

That would be $2,123.67/50% = $4,247.33 ***before***-tax. Or $4,247.33/$318,500 = 1.334%. So if my home were an investment property, and I were in the 50% bracket, I'd need to get a new loan at 13% - 1.334% = 11.666% to achieve a three-year payback.

Summary on when to refinance for lower interest rate

To summarize in case you didn't follow that, I needed a .902% lower interest rate to justify refinancing a home mortgage with deductible points. And I needed a 1.334% lower interest rate to justify refinancing an investment property. Both figures assume the costs set forth in the example above and a taxpayer in the 50% bracket.

As you can see, the two or three percent rule of thumb you often read in the newspapers is too high. My rule of thumb would be 2% on a refinancing with nondeductible points; 1% with deductible points; and 1.5% on an investment property. I'll remind you that my example did ***not*** have a prepayment panalty. If you ***do***, the numbers change dramatically.

PART SIX: PAYMENT TECHNIQUES

12

Payment Pattern Variations

The five pattern variations

As I told you earlier in the book, there are five variations on the payment pattern:

- level
- ascending
- descending
- intermittent
- combination of above

Fixed or "if"

And as I told you earlier, your duty to make payments can be fixed or contingent. When it's contingent, the amount of one or more payments...or whether you make any payments at all... is dependent on some event.

The five payment variations and whether any given payment is fixed or "if" cover ***all*** the payment techniques in existence. Real estate investors are more familiar with specific technique names like wraparound or graduated payment mortgage. And I'll use those as I explain them. But it will help you understand real estate finance if you keep in mind that every technique you've ever heard of or will ever hear of is just another permutation of the five payment variations and fixed or "if."

If techniques

If techniques are used when either the lender or the borrower is very concerned about some uncertainty in the deal. For example, lenders are hot to force adjustable rate mortgages (ARM) down our throats lately. An ARM is an if loan. It contains a clause which say if such and such an interest rates goes up, so will the interest rate on your mortgage. That, in turn, will increase either your monthly payments or your balloon payment or both.

Sometimes if loans are made because the ***borrower*** is uncertain. In 1978, Californians passed Proposition 13. It lowered property taxes from an average of 2.3% of value to 1% of value. That, in turn, ***raised*** the value of income property. . .because income property is worth its net income divided by the going capitalization rate.

Example

If you owned a $1,000,000 California building ***before*** Prop 13, it's taxes would have been $23,000. But ***after*** Prop 13, they'd be $10,000. (Actually, Prop 13 was a little better than that because it rolled taxes back to their '75-'76 level.) If you use a capitalization rate of 10%, that $13,000 reduction in taxes would raise the value of the building by $13,000/10% = $130,000.

Naturally, California sellers immediately did that arithmetic and upped their asking prices. Just as naturally, California government employees went to court to try to overturn Prop 13.

Because of the court suit, buyers were understandably reluctant to pay extra for Prop 13 benefits. And sellers refused to seel for pre-Prop 13 prices. What to do?

John Stanfill, then of Coldwell-Banker, a real estate brokerage firm, responded with "earn-out second trust deeds." An earn-out second trust deed is an if loan. In this example, the buyer and seller would do the deal as if it were $1,000,000. But an additional trust deed (mortgage) was signed.

It said that the buyer would pay additional cash down and additional monthly payments ***if*** Prop 13 were upheld by all pertinent courts. Typically there would be a five year deadline. In other words, if the courts did not overturn Prop 13 by the fifth anniversary of the closing, the deal would then be restructured as if the sale price had been $1,130,000.

In fact, the California Supreme Court upheld Prop 13. So the buyers who signed earn-out second trust deeds had to pay.

Buyers should seek if loans more often than they do

I think buyers should seek if loans more often than they do. The only restraint is the market. Sellers will take fixed loans over if loans when they have a choice. But if the seller has no other offer, he may well except your if loan.

"If" loans reduce risk

Investors are constantly looking for ways to increase their yield and reduce their risk. If loans reduce risk. That's why you should try to get them more often.

Right now, many Sunbelt markets are overbuilt. And many more buildings are still under construction! That creates an unusual uncertainty. In the September issue of the *Real Estate Investing Letter*, I had an article in which I suggested using earn-out seconds when buying in an overbuilt market. I picture this kind of conversation between buyer and seller.

Buyer: "Your price is based on gross ***scheduled*** income. But you've got a twenty percent vacancy rate right now. I'm not going to pay for income that isn't there."

Seller: "A year ago I had a 4% vacancy rate. I'm not going to give you a ***permanent*** low price just because of a ***temporary*** vacancy problem."

Buyer: "Tell you what I'm gonna do. You give me a price which reflects your ***current collections***. I, in turn, will agree to pay you more later if the vacancy problem does indeed turn out to be temporary. In other words, the payments on the second mortgage will vary according to the vacancy rate. If the vacancy problem is as temporary as you say, the payment reduction will only be temporary. But if the vacancy problem is as long-lasting as I fear, I'll still be able to make the payments."

How to avoid "if" loan arguments

The main problem with if loans is telling whether the event the payments are tied to occurred. For example, in the case of Prop 13, the California Supreme Court upheld it in a decision. But in some subsequent decisions, the Court allowed some of its liberal friends to circumvent Prop 13. Do those circumventions mean a buyer doesn't have to pay off on the earn-out second? Probably not. Because the circumventions involve other taxes. I've heard of no ***property*** tax increases which violate Prop 13. But you can see the kinds of problems which can arise in an if loan.

From a buyer's standpoint, the ideal if clause would tie payments to the buyer's own cash flow. The problem is the buyer has ***control*** over what that cash flow is. And the buyer would have incentive to overspend because any money he didn't spend would go to the seller.

Net income is also a problem because of arguments over the property amortization period for capital expenditures. . .or whether a particular expenditure was necessary at all.

"Rockford Files"

If clauses tied to net income usually give the recipient of the payments the right to have audits done. That puts the buyer and seller in the same position as a taxpayer and an IRS auditor. A "60 Minutes" segment in recent years featured James Garner.

He was suing a TV production company over an if clause. He had agreed to do the TV series "Rockford Files" in part for a share of the net income. The show was successful. It wasn't cancelled. Garner quit. And it's now in syndication. Yet Garner has never received a dime of net income. The producers claim that they never ***made*** any net income. Garner disputes the way they keep the books.

Tie "if" clauses to difficult-to-argue events

To avoid litigation and strife, you should tie if clauses to indexes or events which are difficult-to-argue about. Like the Consumer Price Index. Or a regional vacancy rate reported by the government or some outside third party. Had I been a California seller in the post-Prop 13 era, I'd have spelled out the circumstances under which I was due my additional money in ***great detail.***

What event or index you tie your payments to is a function of what risk you're trying to reduce. For example, in the high vacancy/overbuilding situation, a regional vacancy rate index published by the government would probably be best.

Arbitration rather than litigation

If you must use an arguable event or figure, you'd better specify that disputes will be settled by arbitration. Both you and the other party are likely to be affluent. Most real estate investors are. So you can afford the better, swifter justice of arbitration.

The courts are run by the government. Same as the post office or motor vehicle department. So if you use them, you'll have to stand in long lines like everybody else. And you'll have to pay lawyers. . .a lot. By specifying arbitration, you give yourselves the right to avoid the morass of socialized justice.

Arbitration is a good idea in general. Not just for if clauses. Here's the way an arbitration clause was worded in a purchase agreement I recently signed.

"If a controversy arises which relates in any respect to buyer's or Seller's rights to any deposit paid pursuant to this contract or the payment of commissions as provided for herein, Buyer, Seller, and Broker(s) agree that such controversy shall be settled by final, binding arbitration in accordance with the Commercial Arbitration Rules of the American Arbitration Association and judgment upon the award rendered by the Arbitrator(s) may be entered in any court having

jurisdiction thereof. Only attorneys at law licensed to practice in the State of California shall be nominated as Arbitrators. The unsuccessful party shall pay the costs of arbitration. The provisions of California Code of Civil Procedure Section 1283.05 shall be applicable to such arbitration."

Fixed and "if" combinations

An obligation does not have to be either fixed or contingent. It can be both. The typical adjustable rate mortgage is both. These days, most adjustable rate mortgages have a 5% cap. In other words, the interest rate can go up or down if the interest rate it's tied to moves. That's an if clause. But no matter where the interest rate index goes, the interest rate on the mortgage cannot go beyond 5% more or less than the original rate. That 5% cap is a ***fixed*** payment clause. So an adjustable rate mortgage with a cap (the only kind of adjustable you should consider) is combination of fixed and if obligations.

There are at least four variations of fixed/if combinations:

- caps or ceilings
- floors or minimums
- start dates
- stop dates

The adjustable rate mortgage has both a floor and a cap in most cases. (Some ARMs have no floor and some have no cap.) The earn-out second I described in the Prop 13 example had a stop date...five years. The payment was contingent on an event...but only for five years. At that point, it became fixed.

So if you meet resistance pushing for an if clause, you might compromise by suggesting a cap or floor or time limit.

Remember you payment pattern objectives

Remember that you have two objectives when it comes to payment patterns.

- lowest present value
- strong probability that you can make the payments

The other guy wants the ***highest*** present value...if he understands time value of money. His desire to get the highest present value makes him want the highest possible payments and want them as soon as possible. You want the ***lowest*** possible payments. And you want them to be ***delayed*** as long as possible.

The best compromise is to match the payments to your income pattern. Your income pattern is typically ascending. So loans with ascending payment patterns like the graduated payment mortgage, make the most sense. Your income pattern also includes sale proceeds. So balloons which fall due ***after*** you expect to sell also make sense.

Where there is a high degree of uncertainty, an if clause can help you make sure the payment pattern fits your income pattern.

Accruing interest

Accruing interest is one of the most important finance techniques for real estate investors today. With today's high prices, if you buy a building with all new, institutional financing, you'll almost certainly have negative cash flow. Negative cash flow is unacceptable.

With ***seller*** financing, the negative cash flow will probably be ***less***. But that's still unacceptable. The ***main*** way to achieve positive cash flow in today's market is by accruing interest.

Example

I bought a 12-unit apartment building in 1975. The seller wanted to take back a $10,000 8% second mortgage. I had no trouble with those terms. But I didn't have any money for the payments.

At first, the seller tried to convince me I was underestimating the net income. I wasn't and I told him so firmly. Either because he knew I was right, or because he saw no point in continuing to argue, he dropped that line.

I finally said, "I can afford to pay you ***$19*** per month interest only on that loan but not a penny more." I figured that would be the end of the deal. But to my surprise, the seller went into the other room with his agent then came back and offered me the following:

- ***no*** payments at all for three years
- balloon payment of three years simple interest only on the third anniversary (8% x $10,000 = $800 x 3 = $2,400)
- no payments at all for the next two years
- balloon payment of two more years simple interest plus the $10,000 principal on the fifth anniversary ($800 x 2 = $1,600 + $10,000 = $11,600).

I accepted. Without realizing it, I had offered an accruing interest deal. The seller got the 8% interest he wanted. It's just that the interest ***accrued*** or built up for the first three years. Result? I had $800 per year more positive cash flow that I would have if I had not accrued interest. My down payment in that deal was $17,500 so $800 was about 5% worth of return. And the seller got his 8%. . .albeit on the third anniversary. (I sold the property and paid off the loan on the third anniversary.)

I ran into one of my seminar graduates a year or so after a seminar. He thanked me for pushing accruing interest because he had since done a deal using it and it worked out well.

So your ***first*** choice is to negotiate such a low seller interest rate that you can pay it and still have positive cash flow. But since the sellers want a higher rate in the typical deal, keep the idea of accruing interest handy.

Remember that interest accrued is not interest avoided. Accruing interest is the same as negative amortization. Accruing interest substitutes negative amortization for negative cash flow. There is a slight present value advantage to doing that (if you use a discount rate higher than the loan interest rate). But negative amortization is not much more fun than negative cash flow. In the typical highly leveraged rental house deal, the negative amortization would ***equal or exceed*** the increase in value. That means the investor's equity would ***decrease*** each year.

Watch out for state law

Accruing interest is a technique where a local mortgage attorney is important. Many states have laws prohibiting ***interest on interest***. In the deal I just described, I paid ***simple*** interest. So the seller did not earn interest on interest. But he also earned less than 8% as a result. Getting $12,400 back after three years is only a 7.4% return. If ***compound*** interest had been the deal, the seller would have received 1.08 x $10,000 = $10,800 x 1.08 = $11,664 x 1.08 = $12,597.12 instead of $12,400.

Minimize or eliminate principal payments

If you can't accrue interest, at least try to avoid making principal payments. Loans where you make payments but not on principal are called ***interest only*** loans. I have one now on an apartment building. The seller took back a $42,652.64 second at 9% interest only with a five year balloon. That means I pay him $42,652.64 x 9% = $3,838.74/12 = $319.90 a month.

An interest only loan saves only a small amount over an amortized loan. If my interest only loan were amortized over thirty years, the payments would be

n	360
i	9/12 = .75
PV	42652.64
PMT	343.19

So by going interest only, I save $343.19 - $319.90 = $23.29 a month. No big deal. But every little bit helps.

Plus, principal payments are ***not deductible***. So the ***after***-tax cost of an interest payment is less than the after-tax cost of a principal payment unless you're in the zero percent bracket.

Split funding

They're big on split funding in Texas...especially syndicators. In split funding, the normal 25% down payment is split in two or three pieces. The buyer pays, say, 12.5% at closing and another 12.5% on January 2nd of the next year.

Some "creative" fiance pushers trot split funding out as a way to achieve high leverage. I'm not impressed.

25% down is not high leverage. The fact that it was 12.5% down for a year or six months or whatever means little.

In virtually every deal you ever do except your first, you will be exchanging up. (I'm assuming you're following the advice in my book, *Aggressive Tax Avoidance For Real Estate Investors.*

If you do a simultaneous exchange, ***all*** of your equity in the old property goes into the new one immediately. How do you reconcile split funding with that?

Split funding and exchanging CAN be combined

You ***can*** combine split funding and exchanging. But it's tricky. For example, you could refinance a property and use the refinance proceeds for payment number two of your two split payments. Then you exchange into the property in question as payment number one. Finally, you take the refinance proceeds out of the bank a year or whatever later and make the second of the split down payments.

But what's the point of all that hassle? Refinancing takes time and money. For what advantage? So you can brag that you bought a property for 12.5% down?

Suppose the split funding called for the second payment to be made a ***week*** after closing? Could you brag that you bought that property for 12.5% down, too?

Split funding is for unusual situations only

You should only use split funding where that ***payment*** pattern matches your ***income*** pattern. And when is that? Not often. Maybe if you were due for an inheritance in a year you could exchange or buy into the property now then use the inheritance to make the second payment. Or if you were due some other lump sum payment.

But do ***not*** use split funding when the second payment would come from sale proceeds on an investment property. That's because you should exchange. And you cannot exchange into a property you already own.

Split funding is nothing more than a shell game used by syndicators to inflate first year tax benefits. It is not a meaningful leverage technique. It's too short lived. It makes you "Queen For A Day" then brings you back to reality in six months or a year. It's more likely to require extraneous gyrations than match your income pattern. Use split funding only when it matches you income pattern.

Kickers

A kicker gives the lender a share of the property's profit. Either part of the increases in cash flow or part of the increase in value or both. A kicker is an "if" clause. It says, "If the cash flow increases, the lender will receive 50% of the increase," or some such.

Investors don't like kickers...because they don't like sharing what was traditionally ***entirely*** theirs. Some investors get emotional about kickers.

I don't like them. And I've never agreed to one. But there's nothing inherently wrong with them. Typically, they appear when money is hard to get and expensive. In those situations, they may be the ***best deal*** available. And that's the way to analyze them. If the deal is worth doing even with the kickers, and you can't get an otherwise equal or better loan with***out*** a kicker, accept the kicker.

If the kicker is in the form of an option to purchase all or part of the mortgaged property, a can of legal worms is opened. It's called "clogging the equity of redemption." That's an old English legal concept. Basically, it says that the law does not like mortgages which make the borrower do something ***other*** than just pay principal and interest to get the mortgage removed from his property.

To increase the probability that the option is valid, the lender must make it a ***separate*** transaction, ***pay*** for the option, and record it ***before*** the mortgage is recorded. Claiming that the making of the loan is the consideration for the option may invalidate the option because of clogging.

Shared Appreciation Mortgages

The shared appreciation mortgage or SAM is an example of the kicker principle being applied to home mortgages. In a shared appreciation mortgage, the lender typically gives a below-market interest rate in return for a share of the appreciation in price of the house.

Because SAMs have below-market interest rates, they enable you to acquire more real estate than you would be able to acquire using market rate financing. That's good. But because the lender gets a large chunk of your appreciation, your overall return ***may*** be reduced. I say "may" because the SAM improves your cash flow during the holding period. You'd have to do the numbers to see whether the improved cash flow is equal to or better than the reduced proceeds when you dispose of the property.

So a SAM allows you to give up yield in return for more safety. I would rather achieve that end through a lower loan-to-value ratio.

Shared appreciation can mean a balloon

If you are considering a loan with an appreciation kicker, SAM or the commercial equivalent, watch out for hidden balloons. Often appreciation kickers require sale or refinance after a certain number of years. That is a balloon payment. Treat it as you would any other balloon payment. In other words, don't agree unless it's at least seven years away.

Tax ramifications of kickers and SAMs

Revenue ruling 83-51 said that the lender's share of appreciation would be taxed as interest. That's what you want as a borrower. Since this is new, there have been no court decisions. In that ruling, the taxpayer was a ***cash basis*** taxpayer. He could only deduct the appreciation/interest when he actually paid it. Rulings are not necessarily law.

If the loan is not a shared appreciation mortgage on a prime residence, how the deal will be taxed is open to question. The doctrine of substance over form will generally decide. It it walks like equity, talks like equity, and associates with equity, it's equity. . .even if you call it a loan.

Lenders get interest no matter how well the property does. Owners' returns depend on how well the property does. Owners have no guarantees. With kickers, you have a hybrid. The lender's return is ***partially*** guaranteed. But it's also partially dependent on how well the property does. Is it a loan? Or a partnership?

If it's a loan, all non-principal payments to the lender are deductible as interest and ordinary income to the lender. But if it's equity, payments to the "lender" are ***not*** deductible. That would be a very unpleasant surprise for the taxpayer/borrower. In his book, *Federal Income Taxation of Real Estate* (Warren, Gorham, & Lamont), Gerald Robinson cites three cases in which the taxpayer/borrower won (got to deduct the kickers as interest):

- *Dorzback v. Collison,* 93 F Supp. 935
- *Stevens Brothers & Miller-Hutchinson Co.,* 24 TC 953
- *Farley Realty Corp..* 279 F 2d 701

But whenever the lender's return is dependent upon property performance, IRS might claim the debt is really equity, deny the deduction, and win in court. As the "creative finance" pushers say, "See your accountant or attorney." And make sure the guy you see really knows this stuff. By reading over the various cases in which the taxpayers won and lost, he can give you an indication as to what you'd better do to improve your chances of surviving a challenge. . . and the probability of challenge.

James Burnes, a Newport Beach, California attorney, wrote a comprehensive article on this subject in the Spring '85 ***Journal of Real Estate Taxation*** ("The SAM—A Joint Venture, Relationship Between Debtor and Creditor, or Both?").

There was also a list of possible problems in "A Look At Shared Appreciation Mortgages" in the March-April 1985 issue of *Lawyers Title News.* It listed

- State usury laws
- State unconscionability laws
- State laws prohibiting interest on interest
- Enforceability of due-on-sale clause in some states
- Doubt as to whether lender's appreciation share has same lien priority as original loan amount vis a vis liens put on the property during the mortgage term

SAMs are a legal can of worms.

Mortgages which are convertible to equity

The main difference between mortgages with kickers and SAMs is that convertible means the lender has the ***option*** to convert. In kickers and SAMs, the equity type benefits are ***automatic*** rather than optional. Also, kickers and SAMs give the lender the ***benefits*** of appreciation or increased cash flow, but not the burdens of ownership, like the risk of negative cash flow or negative appreciation. Once a mortgage has been converted to equity, the former lender now owner can be hurt by reverses in property performance.

I recommend that you ***not*** agree to borrow money which is convertible to equity in your property.

Annuity techniques

Some finance techniques make use of annuities. These say that someone receives money for the rest of his life. These are usually used when a senior citizen is involved.

Sometimes senior sellers ask for or are offered ***payments for life***. That's OK. . . as long as ***you*** are not the one obligated to make the payments. Whenever you get involved in an annuity situation, shift the obligation of making the payments to an insurance company by purchasing an annuity.

The reason is the law of averages. In order for you to analyze such a deal, you have to forecast the date of death of the payee. You can use mortality tables. But when only ***one*** person is involved, the tables could be very wrong. The more people in the group, the more accurate the tables.

In other words, if ***agree*** to make the payments, and the payee turns out to be Methuselah, you got a bad deal. But if you shift the problem to an insurance company by buying an annuity, ***they*** have to worry about him turning out to be Methuselah. And they don't really care because for every Methuselah, someone else dies young.

The older the seller, and the less concerned he is about his heirs, the more sense an annuity makes. You can get annuities which keep paying until one person dies or until ***both*** a husband and wife die. Call a life insurance agent for specifics.

Life estate techniques

A life estate says that someone gets some property for the rest of their life. Typically, they get the right to live in the property for the rest of their life.

If you purchase the remainder estate (the right to get whatever right the life estate guy had), you benefit when the life estate owner dies. If he has the right to live in the property til he dies, you own that right when he dies.

Again, in order to tell what to pay for the remainder estate, you have to predict when the life tenant (as he's called) will die. And as with annuities, mortality tables can be way off when only one individual is involved.

To shift the risk of a Methuselah to a life insurance company, you'd have to buy an annuity tied to the ***seller's*** life but making ***you*** the beneficiary or recipient of the payments. This is theoretically possible because your remainder estate gives you an insurable interest in another person's life. You'd need to find an insurance company willing to do an unusual deal in order to invest in a remainder estate. Annuity payments you receive are taxable.

Non-cash payments

Another set of payment pattern techniques involves making payments which are not in cash. One is the gold coins technique. That's the one where you pay for something with old U.S. gold coins. Since the coins are "legal tender", the argument goes, the seller can report them on his income tax at their ***face*** value. Of course their market value is much higher.

Since that will wipe out the seller's tax liability, he'll sell to you much cheaper.

Forget it. The courts will laugh in your face. As they did in the case of *Cordner v. U.S.,* 45 AFTR 2d 80-1655. The coins will be taxed at their ***market*** value.

Other non-cash payments

You may produce some product or service which you can use as payment for real estate that you buy. If you pay for real estate in part or completely with goods or services, you are bartering.

If you provide a ***service*** and receive property instead of cash, you will be taxed on the fair market value of that property at the time you receive it. . .at ordinary income rates [IRS reg. section 1.61-2(d)]. If you provide ***property*** (like a product you produce) and receive property (like a building you want to acquire), you have done an ***exchange***. A tax-free exchange if it meets all the requirements (See my book *Aggressive Tax Avoidance For Real Estate Investors* for details.) A partially or completely taxed exchange if it does not.

If the seller receives services in return for property, ***I think*** he must count the fair market value of the service as ordinary income and he may deduct his ***basis*** in the property to find his gain. Although there was one case in which a guy got to deduct the ***fair market value*** of the property he gave up instead of his basis. And he was able to claim the income represented by the services he received as long-term capital gain. (*McDougal*, 62 TC 720)

So once again, we have a technique which "creative finance" pushers toss out without a breath of tax ramifications. . .yet the tax laws are relevant and quite complex.

The only reason I can see to make any payments in a form other than cash is when the recipient of the payments represents ***incremental*** sales of your products or services. In other words, if you can sell the products or services to someone else, do so and pay cash for the real estate. But if you ***can't*** sell them to someone else, and the seller is willing to "buy" them with his property, by all means barter.

Remember that barter is ***not*** a tax avoidance technique. . .unless you can pull a *McDougal.*

Shared equity financing arrangements

The shared ***equity*** financing arrangement is not to be confused with the shared ***appreciation*** mortgage. In the shared ***appreciation*** mortgage, the lender ***claims*** to be a lender and hopes he will not be declared a partner. In the shared ***equity*** arrangement, the guy who eventually gets a share of the equity admits to being a partner up front.

In shared equity, one guy puts up all or part of the down payment. But he doesn't ***live in*** the property. the other party lives in the property and puts up part or none of the down payment. The occupant pays a fair market rent to the investor/non-occupant for the use of the investor's part of the property. The investor reports that rent as income and deducts his operating expenses, interest payments, if any, and depreciation.

The shared equity arrangement was a creature of the tight money times of the early eighties. Its legal status was clarified by the Black Lung Benefits Act Of 1981. Now Section 280A (d)(3)(C) of the Internal Revenue Code says that if the arrangement is set up as I described above, the investor's tax deductions will be OK.

The advantage for the investor of a shared equity arrangement is the tax deductions during the holding period and a share of the appreciation down the road. The advantage to the buyer/borrower is that he gets a house he could not otherwise have afforded. Note that the shared equity arrangement is really a partnership, not a mortgage. As such, it is not leverage. Although there typically ***would*** also be a mortgage, the shared equity arrangement itself is not a mortgage.

I recommend that you regard the shared equity financing arrangement as a last resort.

Real estate columnist Bob Bruss says you should only use shared equity with family members. I agree. Shared equity is a partnership. And you should only form partnerships with people you are extremely compatible with. You may want to read "Partnerships Are Easy To Start But Not Easy To Keep Going" in the April 15, 1985 *Wall Street Journal.*

Some real estate gurus advocate using shared equity with strangers as a way to take care of negative cash flow in rental house investing. In this system, the "tenant" is an owner-occupant who pays all the expenses and mortgage payment. He or she gets part of the appreciation in value of the house. The investor who puts the deal together gets the rest.

I don't see why the occupant would pay 100% of the carrying costs but accept less than 100% of the appreciation. If they do the same deal with***out*** the investor they get 100% of the appreciation, too.

Daddy Mac

Family Backed Mortgage Association, Inc. (FBMA) of Oakland, California offers a parent-child sale leaseback program. As far as I know, the Daddy Mac name stands for nothing. It's just a take off on Fannie Mae and Freddie Mac types of nicknames in the real estate finance industry.

In Daddy Mac, FBMA helps you arrange a shared equity financing arrangement in which the parents own part of the home and their child or children owns the rest and leases the parents portion. FBMA vp Katie Canon says the program works best when the parents are in the 35% or higher tax bracket and the child in the 30% or lower tax bracket. That's because the parent can use the depreciation deductions. And the child doesn't miss the interest and property tax deductions.

Laws pertaining to gifts to children are pertinent but they are beyond the scope of this book.

Variable rate mortgage

Variable rate mortgages or VRMs are largely obsolete. There was a brief period when lenders first got nervous about fixed-rate loans. They asked the regulators for help. The regulators responded with the VRM. The interest rate and payments on a VRM were allowed to fluctuate with some external interest rate. But there was a limit of 2 1/2% on how much higher it could go than when it started. And they typically could only go up at a rate of 1/2% per year.

Essentially, the lenders decided the VRM was too tame. It was replaced by the ***adjustable*** rate mortgage or ARM. The main difference is that ARMs allow negative amortization, and larger, faster changes in interest rates. Some ARMs have no cap at all.

So you probably cannot get a ***new*** VRM. But you may encounter an assumable VRM out there somewhere. For most purposes, a VRM is the same as a fixed-rate mortgage. Because of the severe restrictions on changes in rates and payments.

Before taking one on, just figure the worst case payment increase and see whether you can afford it. The worst case would be the maximum rate and payment the loan could go to. But don't forget that the speed at which it can get to that rate is restricted. What matters is not whether you can afford the worst case ***now***. But whether you can afford each step up in rate and payment ***when it occurs***.

VRMs are taxed the same as regular mortgages.

ARMs which are convertible to fixed-rate

One twist on the ARM is an ARM which you may convert, at your option, to a fixed-rate mortgage within a certain time period and at a specified or indexed rate. That is a useless option.

Reed's Rule of Real Estate Finance # 10 says, "Interest rates are totally unpredictable." That means fixed rates could sky rocket right after you close. In which case, you would ***never*** want to convert to a fixed-rate because your ARM with its 5% cap would be lower.

Interest rates are totally unpredictable. So you should simply "convert" to a fixed-rate before you start. That is, don't get an ARM to begin with.

Rollover rate mortgages

Rollover rate mortgages or RRMs are another creature of the early anti-fixed-rate loan movement among lenders. An RRM is nothing more than an adjustable or variable rate mortgage. The main difference is ***slower*** changes in rate. . . typically every three to five years. But bigger rate and payment increases allowed. . . like 5% at once or even no limit at all.

The proper way to analyze the RRM is to run the worst case numbers and see whether you can afford it. If you can't, don't accept an RRM. If you can, compare the worst case to the other alternatives you have and pick the best.

Why the *worst* case?

You may be wondering why I say to analyze adjustables, variables, and rollovers on a ***worst*** case basis. Why not a ***most probable*** case basis?

Because interest rates are ***totally*** unpredictable. You cannot use "most probable" because you have no basis whatsoever for assigning probabilities to any interest rate possibilities.

That another Reed's Rule you should write on the blackboard 100 times. ***Interest rates are totally unpredictable.***

Most people think interest rates ***are*** predictable. Tune into "Wall Street Week" any Friday night and you're likely to hear some "expert" give his interest rate prediction. Is he full of baloney?

Yep. Anyone other than the Chairman of the Federal Reserve who predicts interest rates is a charlatan. A charlatan is someone who claims to have knowledge which he does not in fact have. Future interest rates are unknowable. So people who claim to know what interest rates will do in the future are claiming to know the unknowable.

But don't rates always go down just before presidential elections?

Cynics point to the "fact" that interest rates always go down before presidential elections as evidence that rates are somewhat predictable. The *fact* is that interest rates exhibit no such pattern.

The interest rate for conventional existing home mortgages was 9% in 1975, a non-election year. In 1976, an election year, it was also 9%. The interest rate for mortgages in 1979 was 11%. In election year 1980, it was 14%. So if you had been gambling on the "fact" that interest rates always drop in an election year, you'd have lost.

In the April 29, 1985 *Business Week* there was an article on mortgages ("How To Lighten A Heavy Mortgage"). In it, Data Resources economist Robert A. Gough said, "If you can get a 13% fixed[-rate mortgage], I'd say do it. . . You're not going to see rates of 12.5% by the end of this year." *Business Week* was so impressed they featured that quote in a large print box in the middle of the article.

Yesterday's *Wall Street Journal* (August 21, 1985) says FHLMC fixed-rate mortgages were yielding 12.01% and FNMA fixed-rate mortgages were yielding 11.625%. Borrowers pay about .375% more to cover servicing. So economist Gough was simply wrong. If an economist with enough credentials to get quoted in *Business Week* doesn't know what he's talking about regarding future interest rate movements, what makes little old you think ***you*** know?

In the Spring of 1984, Wharton Econometrics predicted mortgage interest rates would be 16% come December 1984. At the same time, Chase Econometrics said mortgage rates would be 17% in early 1985. In fact, the mortgage interest rate ended up at about 13% in the December '84 through February '85 time period. And these turkeys ***charge*** people money for these predictions!

On October 15, 1984, the Chief Economist of the U.S. League of Savings Institutions forecast that the home mortgage interest rate would vary between 12.75% and 14.5% in 1985. Wrong. It varied from about 11.8% to about 13% as of August 29, 1985.

The July 2, 1984 *Wall Street Journal* showed the interest rate forecasts 20 of the top economists in the country had made at the beginning of 1984. They were only forecasting ***six months*** ahead. Predicting the 6/29/84 30-year Treasury bond rates. ***All 20 were wrong!*** Their forecasts ranged from 9.5% to 12.5%. The actual rate was 13.64 on 6/29/84.

And what of the greatest forecaster of them all...Henry Kaufman of Salomon Brothers? He said interest rates would rise sharply in '84. They did not. He said the Consumer Price Index would be gong up at an annual rate of 7% by the end of '84. It did not. In fact, ***nobody*** knows what interest rates will do. Not Henry Kaufman. Not Robert Gough. Not Wharton Econometrics. Not Chase Econometrics. Not the Chief Economist of the U.S. League of Savings Institutions. Not me. And not you. As a result, you have no business agreeing to an adjustable rate mortgage whose worst case you could not afford.

You can't afford an uncapped adjustable

Uncapped adjustable, variable or rollover mortgages are ***totally unacceptable***. That's not an emotional response. It's just common sense.

You shouldn't agree to a mortgage in which you cannot afford to make the payments, right? Since the beginning of time, lenders would refuse to let you even try. They make you fill out an application form and they verify your income and credit history, etc. All of which makes sense.

So now the lenders are eager for you to sign up for uncapped adjustable rate mortgages. Aren't these the same guys who refused to let you take on a mortgage you couldn't afford before?

Can you afford an uncapped adjustable rate? Who knows? I just said interest rates were totally unpredictable. That means you don't know what they'll be...and the lenders don't know what they'll be...and Henry Kaufman doesn't know what they'll be.

The "if" loan with the BIG IF

Adjustables, variables, and rollovers are "if" loans. If rates go up, so will either your monthly payments or your balloon payment. You can probably afford a jump from 12% to 14% or even 17%. But what if goes to 18% or 22%?

You probably can***not*** afford those rates. Will the lenders loan you floating rate money? You bet.

Can you afford the loan if the rate goes up a lot? No way.

Like I said, uncapped adjustables, variables, and rollovers are totally unacceptable.

The "Growing Equity Mortgage"

In a growing equity mortgage (GEM), your payments increase according to a fixed schedule...like a graduated payment mortgage. But **all** of the payment increase is applied to **principal reduction**.

That means the annual constant goes up faster than with a traditional level-payment, self-amortizing mortgage. I wrote an article on the growing equity mortgage in the *Real Estate Investing Letter* in February '83. In it I compared one GEM with a traditional mortgage. Both started with annual constants of 13.27%. But five years later, the GEM constant was 16.33% versus only 13.45% for the traditional mortgage.

That's undesirable because it makes you want to refinance to get a lower constant. And refinancing costs money. So while the GEM doesn't **say** you have to refinance it in three to five years, the payment structure is such that you almost have to.

GEMs are not as popular as their proponents had hoped. Alan Crittenden, editor of the *Crittenden Report,* said in 1983 that borrowers didn't care for the GEM so it was dying from lack of interest.

The analysis I did in that February '83 article said that a GEM would slightly depress your return in the first few years. . . **dramatically** depress it with each additional year. So if you only hold the loan for a short period, a GEM isn't much different from a traditional loan. But the longer the holding period, the more onerous the payments become. So the GEM is a sneaky way of giving you a short term loan. If a short-term loan is all you want, there's little wrong with it.

Graduated payment mortgages

There are two categories of graduated payment mortgage loans (GPM):

- FHA/VA
- all others

The FHA/VA GPM is a standard program for home buyers. They offer five plans. The bottom line is that you pay **less** than normal in the beginning of the loan; **more** than normal later on.

You pay less in the early years because the lender not only loans you the money to buy the house, it **also** loans you a little more money each month to make the monthly payments. As a result, the amount you owe goes up each month. That's negative amortization. It's also one way to use the principal of accruing interest which I described earlier.

The advantages of the FHA/VA GPM are that it enables you to afford a bigger mortgage, and therefore a bigger house, than you could afford with a traditional mortgage. The theory behind the GPM is that it better fits the income pattern of the typical home buyer. The typical young home buyer's income goes up as the years goes by. So why not have his payments go up too?

I said matching the payment pattern to your income pattern is one of your prime goals in selecting a payment pattern. So the GPM is a good idea because it does just that.

FHA GPMs are more expensive. A FNMA news release dated August 26, 1983 shows a traditional FHA/VA yield of 13.6% versus a yield of 14.1% on the FHA/VA GPM. But it may be worth it. I like the FHA/VA GPM.

PLAM

PLAM stands for Price Level Adjusted Mortgage. In a PLAM, the mortgage balance is adjusted for inflation. Which causes the loan to have a low interest rate. . . like 3% or 4%. Unfortunately for would-be PLAM lenders, this may violate federal prohibitions against "gold clauses." A PLAM would be similar to requiring a mortgage's terms and repayment schedule to be stated in ounces of gold instead of dollars. And that's not allowed.

"Why?" you ask. Good question. No ***good*** reason. Just a political one. Politicians use inflation to avoid having to vote for tax increases. If gold clauses were allowed, part of the economy could exempt itself from this political game. Then the politicians would have to vote for tax increases again.

Note that PLAMs would have transferred most of the profits real estate investors made during the post-World War II era to the lenders. Because we made our money not from appreciation. . . but from the ***combination*** of assets (properties) which appreciated and liabilities (mortgages) that did not. An investor who owned real estate ***free and clear*** since 1945 would have about the same buying power now as then. Only ***leverged*** investors gain from inflation.

Non-FHA/VA GPMs

There is no standard for the non-FHA/VA GPMs. Last week, I negotiated a purchase of an apartment building in which the interest rate on the loan increased 1/2% every two years. That's a GPM.

GPMs make sense for investors for the same reason they make sense for home buyers...the payment pattern matches the income pattern. That is, the rent on the typical building goes up each year.

I think virtually all seller loans should be GPMs. When I was in Dallas shopping for apartments last week, the asking terms of nearly every seller would have put me about $10,000 under water (negative cash flow). But they were willing to negotiate down to terms which would permit a small positive cash flow in the first year. One property I bought has a seven year, 10% interest only loan.

Seems like I'd be better off for both cash return and safety if I'd instead gotten him to agree to say, 9% the first year, 9 1/2% the second year, 10% the third year, 10 1/2% the fourth year, and 11% thereafter. The mortgage amount was $585,000 so one percent less the first year would reduce the payments by $5,850. Every little bit helps.

Nine percent is about as low as you can get anyone to go these days. That's because nine percent is the current IRS minimum. If you go below nine percent, IRS will tax the deal as if the interest rate were ten percent.

So make it a practice to find out what interest rate and term the seller wants. Then chop it down to nine percent for the first year. Escalate every year or two to the point where it's as far **above** what he originally wanted as nine percent was **below** it.

Skip payment option

Some consumer lenders made headlines a few years ago by offering loans in which the borrower had the option to skip a couple payments. In that context, the idea was a gimmick. But it **could** have merit.

As always, the principal is **match the payment pattern to the income pattern**. There are situations in which skipping one or more payments could make sense in investment real estate. For example, you might take over an existing loan with a balloon payment several years out. Since that balloon payment affects your net income pattern, skipping payments on the **new** loan you're negotiating makes sense.

For example, your payments on a new seller wraparound are $50,000 a year. And there's a $50,000 balloon payment due in the fourth year. To produce the cash necessary to pay that balloon, you and the seller might agree that no payments will be due to **him** that year.

If some uncertainty looms...like overbuilding...you might negotiate for the option to skip, say, six monthly payments whenever you want. You'd probably have to agree to accrue interest during that time, thereby increasing the balloon payment.

I don't see many instances where skipping payments is appropriate. But there are some. So you ought to keep it in mind as an alternative.

Seasonal payment patterns

Some buildings have seasonal income patterns. When I owned buildings in New Jersey, I used to do better in the summer. That's because I paid for the heat but not the air-conditioning.

In Texas in my master metered (owner pays all utilities) buildings, it was just the opposite. I paid for both the heat and air-conditioning. But the air-conditioning was much more expensive. So my buildings made much more profit in the winter.

In keeping with the admonition to match the payment and income patterns, why not negotiate a seasonal payment pattern?

Instead of, say, a $1,000 a month, pay $500 a month from May through October and $1,500 a month from November through April. The total would be the same...$12,000 for the year. But the payment pattern would better fit the net income pattern (of a master metered Texas building).

This would make sense for **any** abnormal expense...even a once a year lump like workers compensation premiums or annual property taxes. As long as the seller gets the same total at the end of the year, what does he care?

I think **all** buildings with seasonal net income patterns ought to have seasonal payment patterns on any seller financing. There's no reason why institutional lenders couldn't do the same...except you probably can't convince the policy manual crowd of the wisdom of it.

Prepayment bonus

You've heard of prepayment **penalties**. Institutional and professional lenders like them because they hold out the possibility of an even better yield than they bargained for. Also, having gone to the trouble to make the loan, they want it to stay made.

But institutional lenders sometimes offer to waive their prepayment penalties. . . and even to pay prepayment **bonuses**. They do that when the interest rate on the loan is below market. In some cases, the lenders send a letter to all borrowers with below market mortgages making the offer. In other cases, you have to ask.

If you plan to prepay a mortgage which is below market, you **ought** to ask. But **don't tell them you plan to prepay anyway.** If the lender thinks you're going to prepay, they have no incentive at all to offer a bonus. So you must keep your plans to prepay a secret. But if the lender thinks your decision to prepay will hinge on how good the bonus they offer is, you may get a good deal.

Getting a prepayment bonus in this fashion is the same as buying back your own loan at a discount. If the lender would rather have cash than the loan, they have to sell it at a discount to someone. Why not to the borrower?

Prepayment bonuses from sellers

Sellers, on the other hand, are usually reluctant lenders to begin with. "You say you want to prepay? By all means!" is their likely response.

In the typical negotiation, you want a long term, like ten years. And the seller wants a short term, like five years. Instead of just compromising on seven years, you should also ask for a prepayment bonus if you pay it off ***before then.*** That increases the probability the seller will get an earlier payoff. . . or so you can explain to the seller. I think all buyers ought to ask for prepayment bonuses in the mortgage documents when using seller financing.

Wraparounds

The word wraparound is one of the most misunderstood in real estate finance. One buyer I was negotiating with went ape when I suggested using a wraparound. When I drew him out I learned that **balloon** payments were his bugaboo. He had just gotten into trouble with a wraparound with a short fuse. Now he was terrified of wraparounds.

I've also met people who thought wraparound was synonymous with land contract. Not so. You can have a wraparound mortgage or a wraparound land contract or a wraparound trust deed. Actually, a wraparound trust deed is more often called an all-inclusive trust deed. You can even have a wraparound lease. Although they're usually called subleases.

So keep in mind that the word wraparound is an **adjective** not a noun.

Misconception # 2: wraps don't increase yield

The other major misconception about wraps is that they increase the lender's yield. Baloney! They do no such thing. In fact, wraps are meaningless. That's right. Meaningless.

It's true that the lender's yield is higher than the interest rate on the wrap. Here's an example.

Existing Loan: Original balance $400,000.00
- Interest rate 9%
- Term 30 years
- Monthly payments $3,218.49
- Current balance $374,561.77

Wrap: Amount $600,000.00
- Interest rate 10%
- Term 30 years
- Monthly payments $5,265.43

The seller in this case is making a $600,000 loan. But only $600,000 - $400,000 = $200,000 of that money is his. The other $400,000 belongs to the existing first mortgage lender. The seller collects $5,265.43 each month then sends $3,218.49 to the first lender, pocketing the $2,046.94 difference.

$2,046.94 x 12 = $24,563.28 and $24,563.28 is a greater than 10% return on $200,000. In fact, it's $24,563.28/$200,000 = 12.28%. That, supposedly, is the "magic" of wraparounds. The buyer pays ten percent, but the seller earns a 12.28% return on his money. Isn't that wonderful?

Not really. Why not just have the buyer buy subject to the first and have the seller take back a second at 12.28%? The buyer's payments would be

first $3,218.49
second $2,046.94
total $5,265.43

The buyer's total payment is the same and the seller's yield is the same. So why bother with a wraparound?

There are only two reasons:

- psychology
- excess loans over basis

Psychology

Most buyers would prefer a 10% wrap to a 9% assumption and a 12.28% second. That doesn't make any sense. But it's a fact. I guess they don't like the "high"12.28% interest. Why they prefer 10% to 9% on the first escapes me. But that's the way many people think in real estate. So wraps are meaningless. But they're also harmless. So if the psychology of the situation calls for it, by all means use a wrap.

Just keep in mind that wraparounds are the most overrated finance technique there is. They are nothing more than a complicated way of doing a second mortgage. And one of Reed's Rules is, "Simple is better than complex."

I covered the excess loans over basis aspects of wraps in the tax ramifications chapter so I won't cover it again here.

Wraparounds are very controversial in legal circles. Although you'll never hear a word about the controversy in "creative" finance circles. There are many articles about wraps in legal and accounting journals. Controversies involve state usury laws, recording fees, and taxes, as well as the excess loans over basis controversy. Wraps are much more complex than the "creative" finance crowd leads you to believe.

Balloon payments

Seven years. That's about all I have to say on balloon payments. I said it earlier in Reed's Rules. You ought not agree to a balloon payment which falls due in less than seven years if the balloon is so large that the money must come out of the property. Smaller balloons which you can pay out of your checkbook or via quickly obtainable loans can fall due anytime you have the money to pay them. But seven years is the magic number on big balloons.

Where, you ask, did I get seven years? The way to survive and prosper in real estate is to hang on for a complete cycle. Real estate, you'll recall, is a cyclical business. The cycles last from four to seven years. If you hang on for a full cycle, you'll almost certainly make money. The way to hang on for a full cycle is to avoid being forced to sell the property before the cycle is up. That means avoiding big balloon payments sooner than seven years.

Rapid amortization mortgages

Rapid amortization mortgages are mortgages which self-amortize in less than 25 to 30 years. Typically, you pay them off with equal monthly payments. . . no balloon payments. . . in seven to 15 years. In May of 1985, FNMA reported that approximately 15% of the loans they purchased from lenders were 15-year self-amortizing mortgages. David Glubetich, owner of Impact Publishing and author of the book, *Real Estate Turnaround Formulas* has also been pushing rapid amortization mortgages.

Are they a good idea?

No.

They are at best a psychological trick you play on yourself. . . not unlike joining a Christmas Club to help save money to buy Christmas presents.

Leverage is good or it isn't

If you don't like leverage, don't borrow. If you ***do*** like leverage, why would you want to amortize a loan rapidly. Amortizing a loan is paying it back. When you agree to a rapid amortization mortgage, you are borrowing money and then paying it back as fast as possible. That is schizophrenic behavior.

The good deal is supposed to be the interest you save. Why not save it ***all*** by paying cash to begin with? Some say they couldn't ***afford*** to pay all cash to begin with. Maybe. Maybe not.

If you're just starting out trying to buy your first home, you probably cannot afford to pay all cash. But if you are a real estate investor with $75,000 or $100,000 in cash to spend, you ***can*** buy properties free and clear. And if minimizing your interest expense is your goal in life, buying free and clear is the way to do it.

The whole idea behind this book is that the overall return on real estate is greater than the interest rate on mortgage money. Therefore, borrowing magnifies return. Amortization is the ***opposite*** of borrowing. Amortization ***depresses*** return.

To pay ***down*** a mortgage or other loan is the same as investing ***in*** that loan. If you think 12% or whatever of ordinary income is a great return, invest in mortgages not real estate. The interest rate on your mortgage is exactly the rate of return you're earning whenever you make an amortization payment.

Why not just avoid prepayment penalties?

A rapid amortization mortgage ***obligates*** you to pay large amortization payments. Why not just get a loan with no prepayment penalty? Or a loan which allows prepayment of up to 20% per year or some such? Why ***obligate*** yourself to make higher payments? And thereby risk your credit?

With no prepayment penalty, you can accomplish the same thing. . . ***if*** you have the cash available. But you don't ***have*** to if you don't have the cash or want to spend it on something else.

Smaller property

Also, if you insist on a rapid amortization mortgage, you will have to buy a ***smaller*** property than if you got a 30-year loan. That's because you and the property can only afford a certain payment level. Rapid amortization mortgages have higher payments. So you will not qualify for as large a mortgage with a high payment, rapid amortization mortgage as you would with a low payment, 30-year mortgage.

Weekly and bi-weekly payment patterns

Paying the mortgage weekly or every other week instead of monthly are other forms of rapid amortization. And, like 15-year mortgages, they are just useless gimmicks. Weekly and bi-weekly payments amortize the mortgage more rapidly than monthly payments because they arrive at the weekly or biweekly payment amount by assuming there are four weeks in a month. There are, in fact, 4.3 weeks in a month.

A $1,000 a month payment is $12,000 a year. But a $250 a week payment is 52 x $250 = $13,000 a year. And a $500 payment every other week is 26 x $500 = $13,000. So, in this example, you are paying $1,000 extra per year. That lowers your interest expense and amortizes the loan more rapidly. But so does just sending $1,000 extra in each year if you have no prepayment penalty.

"Money back" deals

A payment pattern variation which has appeared lately is the "money back" deal. You buy a house for a $100,000 and the seller...typically a builder...gives you a $100,000 bond which matures in 30 years.

Is that a good deal? Are you getting the house for free? A zero coupon $100,000 bond (no interest payments) which matures in 30 years is worth about $3,400 according to a Jane Bryant Quinn article on the subject. If the house is worth $100,000 - $3,400 = $96,600 or more, it's a good deal. But you aren't getting the house for free by any means. And in most cases, the house is worth ***less*** than $96,600...otherwise, why would the builder fool around with the zero coupon bond?

Note that you must ***disclose*** the fact that you are receiving a zero coupon bond to any lender who's financing the purchase. And that the lender will deduct the market value of the bond from the purchase price and base their loan on the ***net*** purchase price. That will force you to make an additional down payment equal to the market value of the bond.

Note also that you will not ***get*** the interest you earn on the bond until it matures 30 years hence. But you have to pay ***tax*** on that interest ***now*** and each and every year of those 30 years. So say the Original Issue Discount rules contained in the Tax Reform Act of 1984.

If tax exempt bonds are used, the interest on the portion of the mortgage which financed the purchase of the bonds is ***not deductible.*** That's because section 265 of the Internal Revenue Code says you cannot deduct interest on money borrowed for the purpose of purchasing a tax-exempt bond.

If you sell a property combined with a zero coupon bond, you may be violating state securities laws. The State of Louisiana issued a cease and desist order against one zero coupon home sale program. The bottom line? This technique is nonsense.

Free and clear ownership

If owning a building free and clear excites you, either start out that way or get a mortgage with no prepayment penalty and pay it down as rapidly as you wish. But do ***not*** get fooled into thinking there is any ***return on investment*** reason for rapid amortization. There absolutely is not. Rapid amortization mortgages only make sense as a forced savings plan for people who want to save but do not have the willpower to do so. If you suffer from that psychological deficiency, rapid amortization mortgages are for you.

Payment patterns summary

If you go to a seminar on "creative" real estate finance...or read a book on the subject, you'll encounter a zillion techniques involving payment patterns. Most are simply variations on the same theme.

About all you can accomplish by fiddling with the payment pattern is a better match between income and outgo. That's worth doing in most cases. But it's hardly a cure for high interest rates.

One way to match income and outgo patterns is "if" loans. When the income is uncertain, the only way to match is to make the outgo uncertain, too. Try to pick events which are hard to argue over.

Interest accrued is not interest avoided. But accruing can be helpful...as a means of matching income and outgo.

Uncapped adjustables, variables, and rollovers are financial Russian Roulette. Don't play.

Virtually all seller loans ought to be graduated payment loans. Property income is graduated. Therefore graduated payments are a better match then level payments.

If your income pattern is seasonal, your payment pattern should be, too. . . at least on seller loans.

You should ask for a prepayment bonus clause in all seller loans. And you should ask institutional lenders for prepayment bonuses whenever the loan interest rate is below market. Just make sure they think your paying off the loan will depend on the size of the bonus.

PART SEVEN: SAFETY TECHNIQUES

13 Collateral Techniques

The three Cs

Remember the three Cs? Credit. Capacity. And collateral.

This chapter is about collateral. Real estate finance techniques which involve pledging property as security for the loan.

Remember the three questions lenders want answered?

- How much do I get?
- When do I get it?
- How sure am I to get it?

The chapter on payment pattern techniques covered the "how much" and "when" questions. This chapter covers *part* of the "how sure" question. The other parts of the "how sure" question are the other two Cs—-capacity and credit. I'll cover them in the next chapter.

Two aspects of collateral

There are two aspects of collateral:

- The property pledged
- The security instrument

The property is self-explanatory. It can be ***real*** property or ***personal*** property. Like a car.

The security instrument is the piece of paper that says the lender can take the property if you don't make the payments. In a secured loan, there are ***two*** things to sign:

- Note
- Security instrument

The note is an IOU. It states the amount of the loan and the payment pattern. The security instrument is the paper that says if you don't pay the note as agreed, the lender can take a designated property. A mortgage or trust deed is a security instrument.

Actually, when I use the phrase security instrument, I mean it in a broader sense. To me land contracts and leases are also security instruments. Technically, those are sort of notes and security instruments combined. I'll just define a security instrument as an agreement which is

- used in conjunction with financing
- and which identifies a particular piece of property.

Value

The whole idea behind a secured or collateralized loan is that the lender is protected by being able to sell the pledged property if the borrower doesn't make the payments. Obviously, that only works when the value of the pledged property is equal to or greater than the loan balance.

Then there's the question of how value is defined. Lenders often talk about ***market*** value. That's the same value you and I talk about as real estate investors. Lenders will tell you they'll loan up to such and such percent of value.

But the value lenders are concerned with primarily is ***not*** market value. They only use that term to speak the same language as we borrowers. The value they care about is ***quick sale*** value. In other words, if they have to foreclose, seize the property, or whatever, how much are they going to get for it. Same thing applies to car loans. The banks look the car up in the Blue Book. . .and loans against the ***wholesale*** not ***retail*** value.

So they want to know what it'll sell for if they have to sell it fast. They also take into account the costs of foreclosing or seizing the property and the costs of carrying it between the time they take title and the time they sell it.

So if you get into a negotiation with a lender and the debate centers on collateral, keep in mind the lender's perspective:

- quick sale value
- foreclosure costs
- carrying costs

Property life and loan term

Different properties have different lives and value-over-time patterns. Cars tend to wear out in five to ten years. And their value typically goes down every year. The same is true of most other types of personal property like computers or copiers or whatever.

Buildings, on the other hand, last indefinitely if maintained. And land, so they say, is indestructible. In any event, real property tends to ***appreciate*** rather than depreciate over time as long as it's maintained.

Since the quick sale value of the property has to equal or exceed the loan balance, loan terms on personal and real property are different. Personal property only lasts five to ten years. So loans secured by personal property have short terms.

Personal property depreciates rapidly in value. So loans secured by personal property amortize rapidly. . .to keep the loan balance at or below the quick sale value throughout the term of the loan.

Makes sense, doesn't it?

Financing real estate with personal property loans

What does ***not*** make sense is financing real estate with personal property loans. Yet that's one of the techniques you hear at "creative" finance seminars.

Remember my talking about the loan constant? On an interest only loan, the constant and the interest rate are the same. The constant on a ten percent interest only loan is 10%.

The constant and the interest rate are ***almost the same*** on a thirty year loan. For example, the constant on a 13.5% thirty year loan is 13.75%. . .the .25% difference being the principal portion of the first year payments.

But on a short-term loan, like the short-terms used on loans secured by personal property, the constant is ***much higher*** than the interest rate. For example, on a 13.5% five year loan, the constant is 27.61%.

That means a $10,000 13.5% 30 year loan on real estate would require payments of $1,375 a year. But a $10,000 13.5% 5 year loan secured by personal property would require payments of $2,761 per year.

In the typical real estate deal, you've got negative cash flow with a 13.75% constant. Try changing that to a 27.61% constant and you'll ***really*** see some negative cash flow.

If negative cash flow were a spectator sport, this would be a philosophical discussion. But negative cash flow means you have to come up with money to pay the building's bills and loans from some source other than the property's income. If the negative cash flow is not too bad, that money can come from your salary or savings. But if it gets too high, you'll lose your property, your equity, and your shirt.

You rarely use personal property loans in real estate

Remember the principal of matching the payment pattern on any loan you get to the income pattern of the property being financed. The payment pattern on a personal property loan sure as heck doesn't match the income pattern of the typical real estate investment.

But don't rule out loans secured by personal property all together. Sometimes, you ***can*** use a personal property loan and still match the income pattern.

Although their annual constants are worse, personal property loans do have some advantages over real property loans:

- quicker
- little or no transaction costs

And they have one characteristic which is neither an advantage nor a disadvantage. They're usually for smaller amounts than mortgages.

When to use personal property loans

Personal property loans are short-term, quick, cheap on transaction costs, for small amounts, and require high payments to pay back. So when do you use them?

When you own some valuable debt-free personal property. . .and you need a small amount of money quickly. . .for a short term. . .and you can afford to make the high payments.

When might that be? Suppose you plan to sell a property. But not until next year. However you've also got a small balloon payment to make on the loan the seller took back when he sold you the property five years ago. That payment is due in two weeks. You need a small, quick loan. And you only need it for a year. Furthermore, after owning the property in question for five years, you've got a substantial positive cash flow. . .more than enough to make the high constant payments on a personal property loan.

So what would you do? Disdain personal property loans because they have high constants? Go out and apply for a new mortgage? Pay an appraisal fee, and a credit application fee, and points, and recording costs, and closing fees, and title insurance premium? And hope the lender can somehow get it all done in two weeks?

That wouldn't make sense. In this case, a personal property loan would probably make the most sense. So don't rule any type of loan out or in. Just recognize that there's a time for every loan. If it fits the situation, use it. But make sure it fits. Using a loan secured by personal property for part of your initial down payment on a leveraged real estate investment would be an example of a situation which does ***not*** fit.

Remember to match the payment pattern to the income pattern.

Personal property check list

Here's a list of personal property to make sure you don't overlook any. You can ***borrow*** against this stuff. But that's not all. You can also ***sell*** it. . . via garage sale or ad in the paper or to a wholesaler. Or you can use it as all or part of your ***down payment.***

However, if your basis in the personal property you give does not equal the market value of the personal property you receive, you may have to pay tax. That would be a ***partially taxed exchange.***

"Paper" (a mortgage or trust deed or unsecured note) may ***not*** be exchanged tax free. "Evidences of indebtedness" are specifically excluded from tax-free exchanges by Section 1031(a)(2)(C) of the Internal Revenue Code.

And if you buy "paper" at a ***discount*** and trade it for real estate worth more than you paid for the "paper," you have a ***capital gain.*** A short-term capital gain (ordinary income) if you owned the "paper" for six months or less when you get rid of it. That gain is the difference between the fair market value of the property you receive and your basis or cost of the "paper" you use for payment. And the tax is payable for the year you dispose of the "paper." IRC Section 1001(b).

- car
- truck
- recreational vehicle
- boat
- other vehicles or motorized equipment
- savings account
- certificates of deposit
- stocks and bonds
- jewelry, gems, precious metals
- trust of which you are beneficiary (borrow against only)
- office equipment
- accounts receivable
- stereo equipment
- video recording equipment
- insurance policy cash value
- vested pension benefits
- appliances
- furniture
- tools
- ladders
- books
- mortgages or trust deeds on which you are the lender
- options
- your right to rent or royalty income
- art
- guns
- furs
- oriental rugs
- collections (stamps, coins, records, etc.)

Beware the Rule of 78s

Loans secured by personal property sometimes have prepayment penalties. One common one is the rule of 78s. Under that system, the lender is entitled to disproportionate interest in the early part of the loan. On a twelve payment loan, the lender gets 12/78 of the total finance charge with the first payment, 11/78 with the second payment, and so forth. So if you prepaid in the fourth month, you would owe 12/78 + 11/78 + 10/78 + 9/78 = 42/78 of the total finance charge.

If the loan were $10,000 and the interest rate 14%, the total finance charge would be $1,400. 42/78 of that is $753.85. . .which is a lot of interest to pay on a $10,000 loan you only had for four months. Twenty-two percent on an annual basis to be exact. That's a hefty prepayment penalty you should watch out for.

The formula for the Rule of 78s is

Interest for this month = Total interest over life of loan x number of months remaining/sum of the month's digits for the entire loan term

It's called the Rule of 78s because the sum of the month's digits on a one-year loan is 12 + 11 + 10 + 9 + 8 + 7 + 6 + 5 + 4 + 3 + 2 + 1 = 78.

Revenue Ruling 83-84 said you could not use the Rule of 78s for tax purposes. Revenue Procedure 83-40 says the Rule of 78s is OK for tax purposes if the loan in question self-amortizes in five years or less.

Mortgage or trust deed

Your state uses either mortgages or trust deeds. I don't know of any that use both. Trust deeds are common in the West. Westerners claim that trust deeds are better for the lender. . .quicker foreclosure or some such. Who cares?

If you're in a trust deed state, you use trust deeds. If you're in a mortgage state, you use mortgages. When in Rome, finance as the Romans do. If you try to use a trust deed in a mortgage state you're just going to make trouble for yourself. The benefits, if any, of a trust deed over a mortgage are far outweighed by the disadvantages of using a foreign security instrument. Because there's very little case law on trust deeds in a mortgage state, it's extremely hard to tell what your legal rights are.

You say you want to know whether a particular state uses mortgages or trust deeds? Call a Realtor.

The main thing I want to say about mortgages and trust deeds is that they are what you should be using in virtually ***all*** your real estate financing. Exotic security instruments like land contracts and lease-options add nothing to most deals. . .and they have ***many*** disadvantages.

Think of real estate finance like carpentry. Carpenters mainly use hammers and saws. Of course, there ***are*** all sorts of other oddball tools, like froes (for splitting shingles), for doing once-in-a-lifetime jobs. But if a "creative" carpenter seminar giver ever told a room full of carpenters that froes were the solution to all their troubles, he'd be laughed out of the room. Yet that's exactly what the "creative" finance pushers do when they advocate exotic financing instruments.

Notes and mortgages or trust deeds are the hammers and saws of real estate finance. You should use exotic security instruments about as often as carpenters should use froes.

Blanket mortgages

A blanket mortgage is about as useful as an appendix transplant. A blanket mortgage is one which covers two or more separate properties. The obvious substitute for it is separate mortgages on each property.

Why would you ever use a blanket instead of separate mortgages? Beats me.

One reason might be to make the total package big enough to interest lenders with high minimum loans. For example, many lenders will not consider loans of less than a million dollars. But they might consider a blanket on two properties which totals a million or more. Then again they might also consider two ***separate*** mortgages which total a million too.

Another reason to do a blanket might be to save on transaction costs. But about the only cost you'll save is the credit check fee. Typically $25 to $100. Big deal. Whether you do separate or a blanket, you'll still have to pay to have each property appraised. That costs hundreds of dollars on a single-family house; thousands on an income property.

Subdivisions

Actually, I'm overstating the case a bit on blankets. There ***is*** one situation where they make sense. Subdivision.

A builder buys a large parcel for subdivision. He plans to chop it into a hundred lots and sell them separately. In that case, you ***can*** make just one appraisal. . .on the original parcel. And using a blanket mortgage instead of a hundred separate mortgages saves a substantial amount on document preparation and recording fees. But unless you're a subdivider, you can pretty much forget blanket mortgages.

Release clauses

If you ***do*** use a blanket mortgage, beware the release clause. A release clause says how much of the loan you have to pay off to get each property released from the mortgage.

There's no law that says there has to be a release clause in a blanket mortgage. And if there is no release clause, the lender can require you to pay off the ***entire*** balance just to release one property from the mortgage.

For example, you might have a $60,000 property and a $40,000 property with a $75,000 blanket mortgage on both. You decide to sell the $40,000 property. When the escrow company contacts the lender for the payoff amount to release the $40,000 property from the mortgage, the lender says, '$75,000.'

It'd be tough to pay off a $75,000 mortgage with a $40,000 sale, wouldn't it? But unless you had a release clause put in the mortgage at the outset, the lender ***could*** legally demand payoff of the entire amount. . .and ***would*** if the loan were at a below market interest rate.

Wording of the clause

All right. So you're smart enough to demand a release clause. Is that all you need to know? Nooooo, sir.

Lenders have ways to make the release clause almost as bad as no release clause at all. Typically, they want you to pay off a disproportionate part of the loan balance to release one property. In the example above, the release clause might say that either property will be released upon payoff of at least 75% of the outstanding balance of the loan.

That's no fun either. To sell the $40,000 property you'd have to pay off 75% x $75,000 = $56,250. That's better than paying off the entire loan. But it's also hard to do with just $40,000 coming in.

Also, make sure the mortgage ***payment*** is reduced accordingly. Otherwise you may have to continue making the full payment even though the mortgage is half paid off. That would result in the ***term*** of the loan being reduced. You want the ***payment*** reduced, not the term. And make sure you don't have to pay a prepayment penalty to get a parcel released.

Proportional release clause

What you want is a proportional release clause. The $40,000 property is 40% of the total. So the lender ought to release that property if you pay off 40% of the loan. Right?

Seems right to me. But lenders typically resist that. They claim the $60,000 property may have deteriorated in value since it was purchased. Not likely. But many lenders lie when it suits their purpose.

The most the lenders will typically give is either an ***almost*** proportional release clause. . .or an appraisal release clause. An appraisal release clause says you have to get a new appraisal when you want release. Then they'll allow you to get release of one property according to its then percentage of the value of all the properties covered by the blanket.

That's a proportional release clause. But given the cost of appraisals (I just paid $2,000 for one on a 37 unit and $3,000 for one on a 25 unit), an appraisal release clause can be as bad as a disproportionate clause.

You'll have to run the numbers in the particular case, but an almost proportional clause may be the best you can get. In the $60,000/$40,000 example above, the lender might have agreed to a 50% release on the $40,000 property and a 70% release on the $60,000 property.

In other words, you'd have to pay off half the loan balance to obtain release of the $40,000 property. Half of $75,000 would be $37,500. Not much fun. But at least the $40,000 coming in covers it (if no other sales costs). And you'd be left with a $60,000 property with only a $37,500 mortgage on it. Your overall leverage would drop from $75,000/($40,000 + $60,000) = 75% of value to $37,500/$60,000 = 62.5% of value.

The ***best*** way to get proportional release is to not do a blanket mortgage to begin with. Get a ***separate*** mortgage on each property. Then you can sell each without hassle or loss of leverage.

Adjacent and contiguous release clause

Don't you just love that subheading? I'm surprised more "creative" finance pushers haven't discovered that phrase and built an hour's worth of seminar around it.

An adjacent and contiguous release clause is the kind commonly used in subdivision blanket mortgages. It's an anti-checker board device.

The best laid plans of builders oft times go awry. And when they do, lenders often have to foreclose. Add to that the fact that home buyers tend to select lots all over the place. The first home buyer wants lot 6 on the southwest side of the development. The second guy wants lot 74 on the northwest side. And so on.

Now suppose the lender has to foreclose after half the lots are sold. And the lots that were sold are all over the place. The parcel which is left would likely look like a checker board with all the red squares cut out. Try putting that on the market and selling it. Try explaining it in your sales brochure. Or try to have your sign painter draw the boundaries on your for sale sign.

The "adjacent and contiguous" means the builder can select any lot he wants to be released...once. Thereafter, all future lots to be released must be adjacent to previously released lots. That way, if there's a foreclosure, the lender's piece is one contiguous lump instead of a perforated checker board.

Adjacent and contiguous mean the same thing. That phraseology comes from the same legal profession that brought you "cease and desist" for "stop."

Ground leases

The best way to think of a ground lease is as a mortgage taken back by the guy who sold you the land. That will give you a more accurate mental image than the exotic phrase "ground lease" conjures up.

There are two kinds of ground leases:

- unsubordinated
- subordinated

Just as there are two kinds of mortgages...senior and junior.

The vast majority of ground leases are subordinated. For the same reason the vast majority of seller mortgages are subordinated. The buyer and seller want a new mortgage. And the new mortgage lender is not about to be junior to someone else.

Unsubordinated ground leases

Actually, lenders will make mortgage loans on unsubordinated ground leases just as lenders will sometimes make high leverage loans. When there is a high credit guarantee present. One lender I interviewed said the only unsubordinated ground lease they have ever mortgaged had Stanford University as the borrower. Presumably they would do similar deals with such borrowers as the state or federal government.

It is also possible to do an unsubordinated ground lease deal if the ground lessor will agree to waive his right to ground rent in the event the tenant defaults on the mortgage. The property's net operating income needs to equal or exceed the ground rent for the lender to agree to that. Of course, waiving the right to ground right rent in the event of default on a mortgage is tantamount to subordination.

Advantages of the ground lease

In a mortgage, only interest is deductible. In a ground lease (on business or investment property), the entire lease payment is deductible.

Since there is no down payment is a lease, a ground lease is 100% financing of the land. In a purchase, the buyer would typically be required to make a down payment. So ground leases are often thought of as leveraging devices. Since sellers can take back 100% financing if they want, I see no such distinction. Maybe it's easier to sell the idea of a ground lease to a land owner than to get him to sell on a nothing down basis.

Tax ramifications of ground leases

You cannot ***exchange*** out of or into a ground lease unless it has at least 30 years remaining. Revenue Ruling 60-4.

The lessee ***can*** claim depreciation on buildings on leased ground. But complicated rules apply.

If the ***recovery period*** of the building or other improvement is ***less than*** the remaining lease term, you can ***depreciate*** the property as if you owned it. But if the remaining lease term is ***less than*** the recovery period, you must ***amortize*** the cost over the remaining lease term.

If the lease is ***cancelled or terminated*** before the end of the term, you may deduct the unamortized or undepreciated portion that year.

If the lease contains ***options to renew***, the lease term may or may not include the renewal periods for tax purposes. The more probable the tenant will exercise the option to renew, the more likely the IRS and courts will require the renewal period be included in the lease term for calculating amortization or depreciation. See Section 178 of the Internal Revenue Code for details. I don't want to turn this into a book on ground leases.

This is a good time to remind you that exotic finance techniques usually come with enormous complexity. "Creative" finance gurus and newspaper writers often ballyhoo exotic techniques as saviors. In fact, exotic techniques are difficult to sell to the other parties involved and dangerous as regards where you stand legally with them. That's why Reed's Rule of Real Estate Finance Number 2 says, "Familiar is better than exotic."

Land contract

When you buy a property the normal way you get "legal and equitable title." That means you get to use it, sell it, live on it, improve it, etc. And you receive a copy of a deed signed by the seller.

When you buy a property on a land contract, you get only "equitable title." That means you get everything ***but*** the deed.

A land contract is like a mortgage except that instead of receiving a mortgage cancellation when you pay off the loan, you get the deed. By selling on a land contract, the seller is saying, "Here's the property. But I'm keeping the deed until you finish paying me off."

Why use land contracts?

Far as I can tell, the original reason for using a land contract was that it left the lender in a stronger position if the borrower didn't make the payments. Instead of foreclosing, the lender just repossessed the property. The buyer/borrower was like a tenant who didn't pay his rent.

Other names

Before I go any farther, I'd better list the synonyms for land contract. Land contract is probably the most misunderstood phrase in real estate...and the one which goes by the most different names in different parts of the country.

It's also called "contract for deed," "installment sale contract," "contract of sale," "agreement to convey," and others. I was shocked to see "agreement of sale" defined as a land contract in the book *The Language of Real Estate*. The guy who wrote that book is a resident of Hawaii. And they do indeed use the phrase "agreement of sale" to mean land contract.

But where I'm from originally, New Jersey, an agreement of sale is a purchase agreement.

In the West generally, the word "contract" alone means land contract. But in Texas, a contract is a purchase agreement...or any other agreement on anything. Same in New Jersey.

Regional popularity

Not only do the names change dramatically around the country, so does the popularity. Land contracts are common in the northwest and midwest. In fact, people there think ***all*** seller financing is done on land contracts. To them, seller financing and land contracts are synonymous. Lately, Californian investing in the Northwest have dismissed the notion of using a land contract and trust deeds are used more as a result.

Try to use a land contract in New Jersey and people head for the exits.

Disadvantages

The disadvantages to the buyer are many and serious. For starters, you don't get the deed. Sure, you've got a piece of paper that says the seller has to sign over the deed when you pay off the loan. But what if he doesn't?

You can sue. But that's no fun.

What if the seller is out of the country when you're ready to pay off? Or in a mental institution? Or dead?

Land contracts often contain restrictions that a deed would not. Restrictions that would make it hard for you to sell.

Theoretically, you can sell a property you own under land contract. But who's going to buy it? Not me. And not most investors. To sell it, you'd probably have to give a super deal.

Theoretically, you can borrow against a property you own under land contract. But from whom? Not the vast majority of lenders.

What if the seller encumbers the property after he sells it to you? Or gets into some trouble and goes bankrupt? Or loses a court suit and has a lien slapped on the property? Legally, he's still the owner even though you paid your down payment and made all your monthly payments on time.

And what about the fact that you lose the property and any equity you have after just one missed payment? With a mortgage or trust deed, the lender has to sell the property at auction and give you any excess proceeds. With a land contract, you lose everything.

I hope I've talked you out of land contracts. They may be OK in the Northwest. Although I doubt it. I asked one Realtor there about the various disadvantages and he said those problems ***do*** occur. I thought maybe they had eliminated them somehow.

As I've said several times, most "creative" finance pushers advocate land contracts. That's because they're heck bent on giving you as many "new" techniques as possible. This book is not the Razzmatazz Real Estate Finance Book. It's *Sensible Finance Techniques For Real Estate Investors*. Land contracts are ***not*** sensible in the vast majority of cases.

Albert Winnikoff is the author of *How To Make A Fortune in Real Estate: The Land Game* (Wilshire Book Company). In it he says, "I know of no experienced land buyers who will enter into a land contract except with the federal or state government."

Excess loans over basis

I won't go into it here because I covered it in the tax ramifications section. But where a seller has an excess loans over basis tax problem, a wraparound land contract may solve it. In that case, you may find the advantages of agreeing to a land contract outweigh the disadvantages.

One word of warning, though. If you agree to accept a land contract, make use of an experienced land contract attorney. How do you find one? Call a Seattle real estate broker...like Cain and Scott.

"But I don't live in Seattle," you protest. Call a Seattle real estate broker...no matter where you live. Cause the Northwest or Midwest is about the only place you're going to *find* an experienced land contract attorney. Ask the broker if he'll send you a copy of a land contract used there. Pay him for his trouble if necessary.

Total pay off not necessary

A land contract need not say that you don't get the deed until you pay off the entire loan. It may say you get the deed when your equity reaches 25% of the price or some such. And the remaining balance of the loan become a mortgage or trust deed.

The various books I have on real estate finance say that land contracts were often used when the buyer made an unusually small down payment. When his equity reached the level of a normal down payment, he got a normal deed and mortgage.

Usury laws still apply in some states

There used to be a lot of state usury laws on mortgages. Then, the Depository Institutions Deregulation and Monetary Control Act of 1980 and Housing and Community Development Act of 1980 preempted usury ceilings on federally related residential mortgages. But a land contract is not a mortgage. So it may still come under state usury laws. You need to check with an experienced mortgage attorney in your state.

Sale leaseback

In a sale leaseback, the seller and the tenant are the same. You own a property. You sell it. And in conjunction with the sale, you sign a lease making you a tenant in the property you formerly owned.

Or you can be the investor...the guy who buys the property and leases it back to the seller.

Sounds simple. In fact, it can be enormously complicated. The pertinent tax laws alone are complex.

Like refinancing

A sale leaseback is a form of refinancing. The property owner could go to a lender and ***borrow*** the money he needs. So why not do that instead of a sale leaseback?

One reason is taxes. Typically, the seller's basis for depreciation purposes is quite low. If he ***borrows*** he money, he can buy new real estate and fix his tax problem without having to pay any tax.

But what about his lender? The lender will receive no benefit but interest income...which is taxed at ordinary rates. (Actually, there are special tax rules for taxation of deposit institutions so their ordinary income tax is not the same as yours.)

Borrower gets part of tax benefits

Let's say you do a sale leaseback instead of borrowing the money you need. The buyer's depreciation basis will be his cost. So a $500,000 building might have a $100,000 depreciation basis to you (because you bought it for $200,000 some years ago) but a $500,000 basis to the new owner. Because the new owner can depreciate the building, he gets part of his yield from tax benefits.

So a straight lender would get just interest. But a sale leaseback buyer gets both rent and depreciation deductions. As a result, the sale leaseback buyer can afford to let you pay less in rent than you would have had to pay in interest...yet he'll still get an equal or better yield than the lender would have gotten.

In other words, ***you*** can't use the potential tax benefits locked up in your building. Neither can a lender. But a sale leaseback buyer can. And he can share those benefits with you in the form of rent which is less than the interest would be on a comparable amount of money.

According to an item in the December 4, 1980 *Wall Street Journal*, the sharing of tax benefits can make the cost of sale leaseback financing up to three and a half percent lower than debt financing. Also, the ***entire*** rent payment is deductible for you. Only the ***interest*** portion of debt service is deductible.

Sale means capital gains tax

Of course, if you sell...leaseback or not...you have to pay tax on any capital gain. So although you may share in some of the new owner's tax benefits through lower rent, you'll have to ***pay*** some tax on the sale. With straight refinancing, you save the capital gains tax but pay more in interest than you would have in rent.

But if the lease is for 30 years or more, the sale-leaseback is a section 1031 tax-free exchange. So says Regulation Section 1.1031(a)-1(c)(2)

Financial statement aspects

Public corporations like leases. That's because ownership of real estate forces them to include depreciation in their earnings. We real estate investors ***love*** depreciation deductions...because they're paper expenses which reduce our taxes and therefore raise our after-tax cash flow. But public corporations are judged on their "earnings." Earnings are what a real estate investor would call taxable income.

In other words, public corporations want their taxable income or earnings to be as high as possible! So they'd rather ***lease*** the real estate they need than own it.

Also, mortgages show up on their balance sheet as liabilities. Leases only show up as footnotes...if at all. So sale leasebacks are a technique public companies sometimes use to mislead the stock market as to their earnings and net worth.

Repurchase options

The seller/lessee often wants to add a provision allowing him to buy the building back at the end of the lease. That's a good way to run afoul of the walks/talks/associates rule...the doctrine of substance over form.

Remember I told you that leases and options are often used to finance a property where the borrower wanted a loan but needed to not ***call*** it a loan for some reason. If you structure a lease-option properly, it is almost exactly the same as a mortgage.

That's why the courts insist on examining what it ***is***...not just what you call it.

So if it walks like a lease, talks like a lease and associates with leases, it'll be taxed and otherwise viewed as a lease. But if it walks like, talks like, and associates with mortgages, it'll be taxed as a mortgage.

The legal term for this specific situation is "equitable mortgage." If a court says that the seller/lessee has an equitable mortgage, he must ***foreclose*** to get the property.

The key phrase is "market value." If the sale price, rent, and option price are market value...or as close to accurately estimating market value as the parties could come at the time, it'll be treated as a sale leaseback-option by the courts. But if the sale price, rent, or the option price are ***below*** market value, the courts will probably treat it as a loan.

Golden States Lanes v Fox, 42 Cal Rptr 568. *Narver*, 75 TC 53.

Subordination clauses

You hear a lot of rot about subordination clauses in "creative" finance seminars. Usually, they suggest that you get a subordination clause in a mortgage which you persuade a seller to take back. The subordination clause supposedly allows you to refinance a mortgage senior to the seller loan, thereby raising your leverage.

For example, you buy a $100,000 building. You buy subject to a $40,000 first mortgage and the seller takes back a $35,000 second. But "creative" financier that you are, you slip a subordination clause into the second mortgage. It says you can get a new first or second mortgage, in which case, the seller's mortgage will continue to be the most junior lien.

So in this example, you go out and get a new $75,000 first. That combined with the seller's $35,000 second means you've ***mortgaged out*** to the tune of $10,000 ($75,000 + $35,000 = $110,000 - $100,000 = $10,000). Isn't that neat? Aren't you glad you paid $400 to learn that trick?

It's a bunch of nonsense.

Enforceable subordination clauses

There ***is*** indeed such a thing as a subordination clause. Usually, you get the lender in question to sign it when you want to refinance. And the lender typically either refuses...demanding that you pay off the loan instead...or he exacts a heavy price for his cooperation.

If you had gotten the subordination clause in the original loan...back when the seller was eager to do the deal...you'd probably have less onerous terms. So why not do as the "creative" finance pushers say?

You ***can*** do as the "creative" finance pushers say. It's just that it's a lot more complicated than they tell you.

Title companies and lenders

Normally, liens rank according to first come, first served. In other words, a mortgage put on a property in 1981 is senior to one placed on the same property in 1983. A subordination clause attempts to reverse that.

But think about who you have to convince. In the example above, you go to an institutional lender and say, "I'd like a new first mortgage of $75,000 on my property." The lender says sure and orders a title report... to make sure they are the first mortgage to be placed on the property.

The title commitment says there are already two mortgages on the property: the $40,000 first and the $35,000 seller second. "Fine," says the lender. "We'll make the loan as long as you pay off these two existing mortgages first."

"I'll pay off the first," you say, "but I don't have to pay off the second. It's got a subordination clause. So your new loan will be a first."

"Is that so?" says the lender. Then the lender turns to the title company and says, "Will you guarantee that we're a first?"

The title company will probably say, "Yes, if the second mortgage holder signs a subordination agreement drawn up by our attorney." Then you protest that the second mortgage holder has ***already*** signed a subordination agreement...in the original mortgage document. To no avail. The title company insists the seller sign ***their*** subordination agreement or no deal.

Of course, that puts you in pretty much the same position as if you had no subordination clause in your mortgage to begin with.

I've never heard a "creative" finance guru acknowledge the need to sell some finance techniques to the title insurance company. That's an oversight. Many "creative" finance techniques require active involvement of title company executives who are willing to do an unusual deal.

Specific versus future subordination agreements

The problem lies in the difference between ***specific*** and ***future*** subordination agreements. Subordination agreements which apply to specific new loans are generally enforceable and accepted by the courts, the lenders, and the title insurors.

But subordination clauses which apply to some future, unknown mortgage are a whole 'nother smoke. The courts don't like them. The lenders generally wouldn't rely on one in a million years. Ditto the title insurors. That's the part the "creative" finance pushers don't tell you about.

Put simply, most ***future*** subordination clauses are unenforceable...not worth the paper they're written on...meaningless.

Handy v Gordon, (55 Cal. Rptr. 769) is one case in which a vague subordination clause was found unenforceable. Although some vagueness ***was*** allowed in *Stockwell v Lindeman*, (40 Cal. Rptr. 559).

An enforceable future subordination clause may be possible

I suppose it's possible to write an enforceable future subordination clause. But the key is probably to make it highly specific. Furthermore, you probably need to go to the lender and title insuror you plan to use for that future loan, and ask them how they want the subordination clause worded. If they don't flat reject the whole idea, they'll probably want the entire, filled-in, proposed mortgage and note attached to the subordination agreement.

That raises the problem of what the interest rate will be. If it's a future mortgage we're talking about, who knows what the rate will be? You might make it a floating rate... tied to some interest rate index. But that would probably blow the enforceability.

Obviously, a subordination clause has the potential to dramatically increase the subordinate lender's risk. Or to put it another way, to dramatically reduce the value of the lender's loan. In the example above, the seller starts out with a $35,000 loan at an altitude of 75% of value. But after subordination, he has a $35,000 loan at an altitude of 110% of value. Clearly, the market value of that loan would drop as a result of that increase in loan-to-value ratio...if the 110% loan were marketable at all.

If you plan to rely on a future subordination clause, you'd better get the top subordination clause attorney in your state to draw it up. (No one specializes in subordination clauses. You'll need a second mortgage attorney or some such.) And even after getting the best attorney, you'd better pray that the lender, title insuror, and courts continue to be satisfied with it until you've got your new loan.

There have been court decisions in which senior lenders suffered total or partial loss of seniority (moved from being a first mortgage to being a second mortgage) as a result of simply ***modifying*** the terms of the senior loan...let alone subordinating an existing loan. *Gluskin v. Atlantic S. & L.*, (108 Cal. Rptr. 318).

To sum up, you can pretty much forget about clauses which subordinate a mortgage to some future new mortgage.

There is a place for subordination

I don't mean to suggest that subordination is a technique you never use. ***Specific*** subordination is alive and well and often very sensible and useful.

There are two instances where specific subordination agreements can be obtained and make sense:

- to be improved property
- lender willing to sign new subordination agreement

To be improved property

Frequently, both the seller and the buyer know a property being sold will be significantly improved immediately after the sale. Raw land sold to a developer is one example. Property in need of renovation is another.

In those cases the buyer usually needs to obtain a mortgage to finance the improvements. If the seller is taking back a mortgage, that forces the loan to finance the improvements into a junior position. Since junior loans are more expensive and harder to get, that may be unacceptable to the buyer.

In that case, a specific subordination agreement is desirable and possible. Since the new loan is to be obtained in the immediate future, a sufficiently specific agreement can be drawn to satisfy the courts, lender, and title insuror.

Typically, the lender agreeing to subordinate insists on a clause which requires the buyer/borrower to put the proceeds of the loan into the property in the form of specific improvements. That's somewhat superfluous. Because the new lender will also require that the money go into the improvements. And will typically dole it out in stages as the improvements progress.

You can get wording for a ***probably*** enforceable subordination clause in the book, *Construction and Development Financing* by Richard Harris. Although Harris and I both recommend that would-be senior lenders ***not*** rely on a subordination clause in an existing, to-be-junior loan. The would-be senior lender should get the to-be-junior lender to sign a ***new subordination agreement***. Better yet, get the existing lender to wipe out the existing loan and create a new second mortgage to be recorded after the new first mortgage is recorded.

Approach an existing lender

If you plan to refinance a property, subordination of an existing loan can increase your refinance proceeds. The refinancing in question may be only a refinancing...or it may be a refinancing in conjunction with a sale.

On any refinancing, there are three routes you should consider regarding existing mortgages:

- pay off, perhaps at a discount
- subordination
- refinance via junior mortgage
- defeasance

Discount pay off

As I said elsewhere in the book, lenders will often let you pay off their loan at a discount. That happens when they think they can get a better return on the money elsewhere...or just need the money. And when they think offering you a discount will persuade you to pay it off.

If they have a due-on-sale clause in the mortgage, and they know you are planning to sell or refinance, they know it would be unnecessary and foolish to offer any discount whatsoever. So, keeping plans to sell or refinance a secret is an absolute necessity when you hope to get a discount payoff

By the way, mortgage holders are not the only lien holders who might agree to a discount pay off. Holders of other liens like the IRS, water department, contractors, etc. may be willing to settle for less than face value. It doesn't hurt to ask. I presume that this would only apply to a ***purchase*** since an upstanding citizen like yourself would never have liens on his property.

Note also that you have to do this negotiating ***before*** you buy the property. ***After*** you buy the property, you have to pay the liens off at full face value. In order for your negotiating to succeed, the lien holder must believe that if they do not agree to a discount payoff, that you will decide not to buy the property and they'll end up with even less or with nothing at all.

Asking for subordination

Let's say you own a property worth $100,000. It has an existing first mortgage of $38,000 and a seller second of $20,000. You're selling the property. The buyer will put 25% down or $25,000. That leaves a gap of $17,000.

Many sellers would take back a third mortgage for that amount. Not you I hope. Don't ever take back a mortgage. If you follow that advice, you're left with three alternatives:

- get a new first for $75,000 and pay off the existing first and second
- get a new third for $17,000
- get a new first for $55,000, paying off the existing first and subordinating the existing second

If you get the new first, you're asking the lender to go about as high as they go on non-owner-occupied properties. 75% of value. There's a chance they might refuse to go above 70% of value...or that the appraisal might come in under $100,000. A low appraisal would mean the new first mortgage lender would loan less than the $75,000 you need.

Getting a new third is easier said than done. Not many lenders make third mortgages. And the few that do expect to be paid a lot.

Getting a new first of $55,000 would be no sweat. That's only 55% of value...well below virtually every lender's maximum loan-to-value ratio. Even if the appraisal is five or ten percent low, your buyer will have no trouble.

In fact, with such a low loan-to-value ratio, you can probably find some ultra conservative lender who'll give your buyer a below market interest rate.

But in order to get a new $55,000 first, you'll have to persuade the holder of the existing $20,000 second to subordinate. That means he'll have to sign a subordination agreement prepared by the lender or title company.

"What's in it for me?"

The second mortgagee ***may*** agree to subordinate without making any demands at all. His loan-to-value ratio after subordination will only be 75%. . . which is not bad. He probably started out at 75% or thereabouts when he sold it to you.

More likely, he'll ask, "What's in it for me?" Or, "If I do that for you, what will you do for me?"

He's within his rights. At present, his loan has an altitude of 58% of value. If he subordinates to any loan, he increases his risk and decreases the resale value of his mortgage. So he's not being unreasonable to ask for something in return for subordinating.

Risk and reward

Remember that the lender is interested in risk and reward. Or yield and safety to put it in lender terms. So in order to obtain subordination, you need to give the lender more yield or more safety or both.

To do that, just look over the payment pattern and security techniques in this book. In the payment pattern category, you might agree to a sooner balloon or a higher interest rate in return for subordination. In the security category, you might offer him an additional mortgage on another property you own.

Give as little as possible in either category.

Run the numbers

Subordination is not necessarily the ***best*** course. It depends on what you have to give up to obtain subordination. . .and what the other alternatives will cost. If the lender you want to subordinate is too greedy, either pay off his loan, or put on a new, more junior loan. But if the lender's price for subordinating is sufficiently reasonable that it's the cheapest course of action, pay him.

Moving the mortgage

Another way to accomplish the same thing as subordination is moving the mortgage. The fancy legal term is ***substitution of collateral.*** Moving the mortgage is simpler.

In the example above, if you or your buyer own another piece of real estate, you might be able to persuade the second mortgage holder to ***move*** his mortgage to that property.

For example, you own a home worth $95,000 and you're selling that $100,000 investment property. The home has a $34,000 first mortgage on it. The second holder on the investment property refuses to subordinate to the new first. So you offer to give him a $20,000 second on your house if he'll agree to remove the $20,000 second from your investment property. Again, that clears the way for the new $55,000 first you need.

The collateral you substitute does not have to be other real estate. It can be bonds or other personal property.

In fact, you could easily get ***more*** than $55,000. That, in effect, would be a cheap way to refinance some equity out of your home. Because individuals like the holder of the second rarely charge all the points and such that institutional lenders do.

If you moved the second to your home and your buyer got a new $75,000 first, your cash proceeds would be $25,000 down + ($75,000 - $38,000) = $62,000. But if you paid off the second, your cash proceeds would only be $25,000 down + ($75,000 - $38,000 - $20,000) = $42,000. In effect, you've sold your property ***and*** gotten a new second on your home.

Additional collateral

I've just covered subordination and substitution. How's about addition. When you ask the second mortgage holder to ***move*** the mortgage (substitution of collateral), he may say, 'How about if I do ***both***?''

In other words, he'll agree to subordinate ***and*** to accept a mortgage on your home or some other property. So he's got a higher altitude mortgage on the investment property you're selling. That makes him less safe. But he gets an additional mortgage on your home. That makes him more safe. On balance, he may figure he's better off subordinating under such circumstances.

You could use a blanket mortgage as the security instrument for providing additional collateral. Just remember to get a proportional to value release clause. As I said earlier, institutional lenders are a pain when it comes to release clauses. But you can probably get an individual to agree to a proportional to value release clause. In this example, you might say that either property will be released from the mortgage if half the balance is paid off.

You can use the ***additional collateral*** technique in practically ***any*** real estate finance situation. It doesn't have to be a subordination situation like the one in this example.

Give him your worst property

Whenever you use the moving the mortgage or additional collateral techniques, give him your worst. If you have more than one other property, try to move the mortgage to the worst. By worst, I mean the one with the ***least liquid*** equity. That would be ***hard-to-finance property*** like raw land or vacation homes. Or property which is ***already leveraged*** up to 75% or higher.

The appraisal

Which property you pledge as collateral is important. But so is what that property is worth. In real estate finance, what the property is worth is determined by an appraisal.

Appraising, like lending, is an art, not a science. Furthermore, an appraisal is an opinion. So there is a range of possible outcomes...all of which are "correct." It is in your interest to have the appraisal come out at the top of the range of correct values. And it is ethical for you to try to make that happen.

Just as lending often turns on such non-scientific, non-business criteria as whether you have rapport with the loan officer, so does appraising. That brings me to the Three Cs of Appraisals.

The Three Cs of Appraisal

You've already learned the Three Cs of Credit. Now you're going to learn the Three Cs of Appraisals:

- Cookies
- Coffee
- Comparables

I got that from real estate columnist Bob Bruss. Cookies and coffee refer to the fact that it doesn't hurt to be nice to people...including appraisers.

When I was a real estate salesman, my broker taught us to always ***meet the appraiser***. In our typical deal, the buyer needed a new mortgage. And the mortgage lender required an appraisal. We were supposed to look up comparable sales which were favorable to the value we were seeking and give them to the appraiser.

And we were supposed to go through the property with the appraiser. The theory being we could help him if need be. And that by going through the property with him he would get to know us. It's harder for someone to give bad news, like a low appraisal, to someone he knows than it is to send it to some faceless name on a form.

Appraisers need information

Appraisers need information to do their appraisal. On a single-family home, they typically have to fill out a two page, legal size form. On an income property, they typically have to fill out a multi-page form as well as a full narrative appraisal.

What information do they need?

Here are the FHLMC forms. The first two pages are for a single-family home; the last four, for an apartment building.

Your mission is to help the appraiser fill out the forms. . . to make it as easy as possible for him to fill out the forms. Of course, it may not be a FHLMC appraisal *per se*. No matter. The FHLMC forms ask for essentially the same information an appraiser needs to do a narrative or any other kind of appraisal.

There's a book on this subject: *How To Fill Out a Fannie Mae-Freddie Mac Appraisal Report, Small Residential Income Property* by Henry S. Harrison (Collegiate Publishing Company, New Haven, CT). Must be pretty good. It has sold 10,000 copies.

Comparables

Some aspects of appraisal forms are judgmental. . . like ***which*** comparables do you use? You should give the appraiser those which are on the high side. . . but within reason.

Like most other humans, most appraisers have a lazy streak. They'd rather use the comps you've gotten than dig up new ones. But appraisers are rarely stupid. So the comps you hope to persuade them to use have to be reasonably comparable to the subject property.

And remember that a comp is more than, "I heard the building around the corner sold for $275,000." You have to give the appraiser hard, detailed facts about the property if you expect to have any effect. "But," you say, "hard detailed facts about sales are hard to come up with."

I know. That's one of the main reasons appraisers make as much money as they do. I told you at the beginning of the book that I'd tell you how real estate finance is done. I didn't say it'd be easy.

Advocacy

I took a couple of Appraisal Institute courses years ago. The instructors told us repeatedly that we were not to be ***advocates***. A lawyer is an advocate. He pushes his client's case as hard as he can. The judge, on the other hand, is ***not*** an advocate.

Every time I write an article or book telling people to try to influence appraisers I get nasty letters from appraisers saying that's improper advocacy. Not true. The appraisers are correct to try to avoid being influenced. . . just as judges are. But they are ***wrong*** to say that ***everybody*** has to be a judge.

Lawyers try to influence judges with their arguments and evidence. That's proper. By the same token, it's proper for you as a buyer or seller to try to prove your case to an appraiser.

It ***is*** improper to try to persuade an appraiser to violate his duty to those who rely on the accuracy of the appraisal. Bribery and other attempts to establish conflicting interests are clear examples of improper attempts to influence. But ***every*** attempt to influence is not improper.

It's true that appraisers may not act as advocates. But you most certainly can.

Holdbacks

You'd like to get the appraiser to say the property is worth more than you're paying for it. . . and get a larger loan accordingly. Unfortunately, most lenders base their loan on the appraised value or sale price, ***whichever is lower.***

But there is one way to get even those lenders to accept a value greater than your sale price. That's where you promise to make some improvement to the property shortly after closing. If you're a cosmetic renovator, making improvements shortly after closing is your ***normal*** pattern.

These are called "holdbacks." Typically, the lender holds back a portion of the loan until you complete the promised improvements. Appraisers will often appraise these proposed im-

RESIDENTIAL APPRAISAL REPORT

File No.

To be completed by Lender

Borrower | Census Tract | Map Reference
Property Address
City | County | State | Zip Code
Legal Description
Sale Price $ | Date of Sale | Loan Term yrs | Property Rights Appraised ☐ Fee ☐ Leasehold ☐ DeMinimis PUD
Actual Real Estate Taxes $ (yr) | Loan charges to be paid by seller $ | Other sales concessions
Lender/Client | Address
Occupant | Appraiser | Instructions to Appraiser

NEIGHBORHOOD

Location	☐ Urban	☐ Suburban	☐ Rural
Built Up	☐ Over 75%	☐ 25% to 75%	☐ Under 25%
Growth Rate ☐ Fully Dev.	☐ Rapid	☐ Steady	☐ Slow
Property Values	☐ Increasing	☐ Stable	☐ Declining
Demand/Supply	☐ Shortage	☐ In Balance	☐ Over Supply
Marketing Time	☐ Under 3 Mos.	☐ 4–6 Mos.	☐ Over 6 Mos.

Present Land Use ___% 1 Family ___% 2–4 Family ___% Apts. ___% Condo ___% Commercial
___% Industrial ___% Vacant ___% ___
Change in Present Land Use ☐ Not Likely ☐ Likely (*) ☐ Taking Place (*)
(*) From ___ To ___
Predominant Occupancy ☐ Owner ☐ Tenant ___% Vacant
Single Family Price Range $___ to $___ Predominant Value $___
Single Family Age ___ yrs to ___ yrs Predominant Age ___ yrs

	Good	Avg.	Fair	Poor
Employment Stability	☐	☐	☐	☐
Convenience to Employment	☐	☐	☐	☐
Convenience to Shopping	☐	☐	☐	☐
Convenience to Schools	☐	☐	☐	☐
Adequacy of Public Transportation	☐	☐	☐	☐
Recreational Facilities	☐	☐	☐	☐
Adequacy of Utilities	☐	☐	☐	☐
Property Compatibility	☐	☐	☐	☐
Protection from Detrimental Conditions	☐	☐	☐	☐
Police and Fire Protection	☐	☐	☐	☐
General Appearance of Properties	☐	☐	☐	☐
Appeal to Market	☐	☐	☐	☐

Note: FHLMC/FNMA do not consider race or the racial composition of the neighborhood to be reliable appraisal factors.
Comments including those factors, favorable or unfavorable, affecting marketability (e.g. public parks, schools, view, noise) ___

SITE

Dimensions ___ = ___ Sq. Ft. or Acres ☐ Corner Lot
Zoning classification ___ Present improvements ☐ do ☐ do not conform to zoning regulations
Highest and best use: ☐ Present use ☐ Other (specify) ___

	Public	Other (Describe)	OFF SITE IMPROVEMENTS		
Elec.	☐	___	Street Access: ☐ Public ☐ Private	Topo	___
Gas	☐	___	Surface	Size	___
Water	☐	___	Maintenance: ☐ Public ☐ Private	Shape	___
San.Sewer	☐	___	☐ Storm Sewer ☐ Curb/Gutter	View	___
	☐ Underground Elect. & Tel.		☐ Sidewalk ☐ Street Lights	Drainage	___

Is the property located in a HUD Identified Special Flood Hazard Area ☐ **No** ☐ **Yes**
Comments (favorable or unfavorable including any apparent adverse easements, encroachments or other adverse conditions) ___

IMPROVEMENTS

☐ Existing ☐ Proposed ☐ Under Constr. | No. Units ___ | Type (det, duplex, semi/det, etc.) | Design (rambler, split level, etc.) | Exterior Walls
Yrs. Age: Actual ___ Effective ___ to ___ | No. Stories ___
Roof Material | Gutters & Downspouts ☐ None | Window (Type): ___ ☐ Storm Sash ☐ Screens ☐ Combination | Insulation ☐ None ☐ Floor ☐ Ceiling ☐ Roof ☐ Walls
☐ Manufactured Housing
Foundation Walls
☐ Slab on Grade ☐ Crawl Space

BSMT
___% Basement ☐ Floor Drain Finished Ceiling ___
☐ Outside Entrance ☐ Sump Pump Finished Walls ___
☐ Concrete Floor ___% Finished Finished Floor ___
Evidence of: ☐ Dampness ☐ Termites ☐ Settlement

Comments ___

ROOM LIST

Room List	Foyer	Living	Dining	Kitchen	Den	Family Rm.	Rec. Rm.	Bedrooms	No. Baths	Laundry	Other
Basement											
1st Level											
2nd Level											

Finished area above grade contains a total of ___ rooms ___ bedrooms ___ baths. Gross Living Area ___ sq. ft. Bsmt Area ___ sq. ft.

INTERIOR FINISH & EQUIPMENT

Kitchen Equipment: ☐ Refrigerator ☐ Range/Oven ☐ Disposal ☐ Dishwasher ☐ Fan/Hood ☐ Compactor ☐ Washer ☐ Dryer ☐
HEAT: Type ___ Fuel ___ Cond. ___ AIR COND: ☐ Central ☐ Other ☐ Adequate ☐ Inadequate

Floors ☐ Hardwood ☐ Carpet Over ☐ ___
Walls ☐ Drywall ☐ Plaster ☐ ___
Trim/Finish ☐ Good ☐ Average ☐ Fair ☐ Poor
Bath Floor ☐ Ceramic ☐ ___
Bath Wainscot ☐ Ceramic ☐ ___
Special Features (including energy efficient items) ___

ATTIC: ☐ Yes ☐ No ☐ Stairway ☐ Drop-stair ☐ Scuttle ☐ Floored
Finished (Describe) ___ ☐ Heated
CAR STORAGE: ☐ Garage ☐ Built-in ☐ Attached ☐ Detached ☐ Car Port
No. Cars ___ ☐ Adequate ☐ Inadequate Condition ___

PROPERTY RATING

	Good	Avg.	Fair	Poor
Quality of Construction (Materials & Finish)	☐	☐	☐	☐
Condition of Improvements	☐	☐	☐	☐
Room sizes and layout	☐	☐	☐	☐
Closets and Storage	☐	☐	☐	☐
Insulation—adequacy	☐	☐	☐	☐
Plumbing—adequacy and condition	☐	☐	☐	☐
Electrical—adequacy and condition	☐	☐	☐	☐
Kitchen Cabinets—adequacy and condition	☐	☐	☐	☐
Compatibility to Neighborhood	☐	☐	☐	☐
Overall Livability	☐	☐	☐	☐
Appeal and Marketability	☐	☐	☐	☐

Yrs Est Remaining Economic Life ___ to ___ Explain if less than Loan Term

FIREPLACES, PATIOS, POOL, FENCES, etc. (describe) ___

COMMENTS (including functional or physical inadequacies, repairs needed, modernization, etc.) ___

FHLMC Form 70 Rev. 7/79 ATTACH DESCRIPTIVE PHOTOGRAPHS OF SUBJECT PROPERTY AND STREET SCENE A FNMA Form 1004 Rev. 7/79

VALUATION SECTION

COST APPROACH

Purpose of Appraisal is to estimate Market Value as defined in Certification & Statement of Limiting Conditions (FHLMC Form 439/FNMA Form 1004B). If submitted for FNMA, the appraiser must attach (1) sketch or map showing location of subject, street names, distance from nearest intersection, and any detrimental conditions and (2) exterior building sketch of improvements showing dimensions.

Measurements		No. Stories		Sq. Ft.
____	x ____	x ____	=	____
____	x ____	x ____	=	____
____	x ____	x ____	=	____
____	x ____	x ____	=	____
____	x ____	x ____	=	____
____	x ____	x ____	=	____

Total Gross Living Area (List in Market Data Analysis below) ____

Comment on functional and economic obsolescence: ____

ESTIMATED REPRODUCTION COST – NEW – OF IMPROVEMENTS:

Dwelling ____ Sq. Ft. @ $ ____ = $ ____

____ Sq. Ft. @ $ ____ = ____

Extras ____ = ____

____ = ____

Special Energy Efficient Items ____ = ____

Porches, Patios, etc. ____ = ____

Garage/Car Port ____ Sq. Ft. @ $ ____ = ____

Site Improvements (driveway, landscaping, etc.) = ____

Total Estimated Cost New . . . . = $ ____

	Physical	Functional	Economic	
Less Depreciation	$	$	$	= $ ( )

Depreciated value of improvements . . . . = $ ____

ESTIMATED LAND VALUE . . . . = $ ____
(If leasehold, show only leasehold value)

INDICATED VALUE BY COST APPROACH . . . $ ____

MARKET DATA ANALYSIS

The undersigned has recited three recent sales of properties most similar and proximate to subject and has considered these in the market analysis. The description includes a dollar adjustment, reflecting market reaction to those items of significant variation between the subject and comparable properties. If a significant item in the comparable property is superior to, or more favorable than, the subject property, a minus (-) adjustment is made, thus reducing the indicated value of subject; if a significant item in the comparable is inferior to, or less favorable than, the subject property, a plus (+) adjustment is made, thus increasing the indicated value of the subject.

ITEM	Subject Property	COMPARABLE NO. 1		COMPARABLE NO. 2		COMPARABLE NO. 3	
Address							
Proximity to Subj.							
Sales Price	$		$		$		$
Price/Living area	$ ☐		$ ☐		$ ☐		$ ☐
Data Source							
Date of Sale and Time Adjustment	DESCRIPTION	DESCRIPTION	+(–)$ Adjustment	DESCRIPTION	+(–)$ Adjustment	DESCRIPTION	+(–)$ Adjustment
Location							
Site/View							
Design and Appeal							
Quality of Const.							
Age							
Condition							
Living Area Room Count and Total Gross Living Area	Total / B-rms / Baths; Sq.Ft.	Total / B-rms / Baths; Sq.Ft.		Total / B-rms / Baths; Sq.Ft.		Total / B-rms / Baths; Sq.Ft.	
Basement & Bsmt. Finished Rooms							
Functional Utility							
Air Conditioning							
Garage/Car Port							
Porches, Patio, Pools, etc.							
Special Energy Efficient Items							
Other (e.g. fireplaces, kitchen equip., remodeling)							
Sales or Financing Concessions							
Net Adj. (Total)		☐ Plus ☐ Minus	$	☐ Plus ☐ Minus	$	☐ Plus ☐ Minus	$
Indicated Value of Subject			$		$		$

Comments on Market Data ____

INDICATED VALUE BY MARKET DATA APPROACH . . . . $ ____

INDICATED VALUE BY INCOME APPROACH (If applicable) Economic Market Rent $ ____ /Mo. x Gross Rent Multiplier ____ = $ ____

This appraisal is made ☐ "as is" ☐ subject to the repairs, alterations, or conditions listed below ☐ completion per plans and specifications.

Comments and Conditions of Appraisal: ____

Final Reconciliation: ____

Construction Warranty ☐ Yes ☐ No Name of Warranty Program ____ Warranty Coverage Expires ____

This appraisal is based upon the above requirements, the certification, contingent and limiting conditions, and Market Value definition that are stated in

☐ FHLMC Form 439 (Rev. 10/78)/FNMA Form 1004B (Rev. 10/78) filed with client ____ 19 ____ ☐ attached

I ESTIMATE THE MARKET VALUE, AS DEFINED, OF SUBJECT PROPERTY AS OF ____ 19 ____ to be $ ____

Appraiser(s) ____ Review Appraiser (If applicable) ____

☐ Did ☐ Did Not Physically Inspect Property

FHLMC Form 70 Rev. 7/79 Forms and Worms, Inc. 315 Whitney Ave., New Haven, CT 06511 REVERSE A FNMA Form 1004 Rev. 7/79

APPRAISAL REPORT—RESIDENTIAL INCOME PROPERTY

This Form may be used for appraisal of income producing properties provided the loan requested does not exceed $750,000.

TO BE COMPLETED BY LENDER

Borrower/Client ______ File No. ______
Property Address ______ Map Reference ______
City ______ County ______ State ______ Zip Code ______ Census Tract ______
Legal Description ______

Current Sale Price (if applicable) $ ______ Date of Sale ______ Loan Requested $ ______
Terms of Sale ______
Property Rights Appraised ☐ Fee ☐ Leasehold (attach completed Lease Analysis FHLMC Form 461)
Lender ______ Lender's Address ______

Instructions to Appraiser: The purpose of this Appraisal is to estimate the current Market Value of the Subject Property. The Definition of Market Value is as set forth in Certification And Statement Of Limiting Conditions (FHLMC 439).

Note: FHLMC/FNMA do not consider the racial composition of the neighborhood to be a relevant factor and it must not be considered in the appraisal.

Other Information: ______
Appraisal requested from ______ Date ______ 19 ____ By: ______

Items 1, 2, 4, 5 & 6 are required. Attach additional items and check box if items are considered appropriate for this appraisal or are requested by Lender.

1.☐ Descriptive photographs of subject property
2.☐ Descriptive photographs of street scene
3.☐ Photographs of ______
4.☐ Sketch or floor plan of typical units
5.☐ Owner's current certified rent roll if existing, or pro forma if proposed or incomplete
6.☐ Owner's income and expense statement 19 ____ , or pro forma income and expense statement
7.☐ Map(s) ______
8.☐ Plot plan or survey
9.☐ Qualifications of Appraiser
10.☐ Lease Analysis FHLMC Form 461 (required if leasehold interest appraised)
11.☐ Summary of reciprocal agreements with other owners for use of parking, driveways, recreational facilities, private streets, (required if applicable)
12.☐ ______
13.☐ ______

NEIGHBORHOOD

Location . . . . ☐ Urban. . . ☐ Suburban . . ☐ Rural
Built-up . . . . ☐ Over 75% . . ☐ 25% to 75% . ☐ Under 25%
Present land use: . . . . ____% Condominiums ____% 1-Family ____% Apartments
____% Commercial ____% ______
Change in present land use . . ☐ Not likely . . ☐ Likely(*) ☐ Taking Place(*)
(*)From ______ To ______
Property values . . . . . ☐ Increasing . . ☐ Stable . . . ☐ Declining
Housing demand/supply . . ☐ In balance . . ☐ Shortage . . ☐ Oversupply
Predominant occupancy . . ☐ Owner . . . ☐ Tenant . . ____% Vacant
Condominium: Price range $ ______ to $ ______ Predominant $ ______
Age ______ yrs. to ____ yrs. Predominant ______ yrs
Single Family: Price range $ ______ to $ ______ Predominant $ ______
Age ______ yrs. to ____ yrs. Predominant ______ yrs
Typical apartment: Type ______ No. Stories ______
No. Units ____ Age ____ yrs. Condition ______
Rent Levels: ☐ Increasing ☐ Stable ☐ Declining

OVERALL RATING	Good	Avg	Fair	Poor
Employment Stability				
Adequacy of Utilities				
Convenience of Schools				
Police and Fire Protection				
Recreational Facilities				
Property Compatibility				
Protection from Detrimental Conditions				
General Appearance of Properties .				
Appeal to Market				

	Distance	Access or Convenience
Public Transportation		
Employment Centers		
Shopping Facilities		
Grammar Schools		
Freeway Access		

Estimated neighborhood apartment vacancy rate ____ %, ☐ Decreasing ☐ Stable ☐ Increasing. Rent Controls ☐ No ☐ Yes (comment on page 4 if Yes)

Describe any incompatible land uses and overall property appeal and maintenance level ______

Describe any oversupply of units in area by type and rental ______

Describe any shortage of units in area by type and rental ______

Describe potential for additional units in area considering land availability, zoning, utilities, etc. ______

Is population of relevant market area of insufficient size, diversity and financial ability to support subject property and its amenities? ____ If yes, specify.

Describe any probable changes in the economic base of neighborhood which would favorably or adversely affect apartment rentals (e.g. employment centers, zoning)

General comments including either favorable or unfavorable elements not mentioned (e.g. public parks, view, noise, parking congestion) ______

SITE

Dimensions ______ Area ______ Sq. Ft. or Acres
Zoning (classification, uses and densities permitted) ______
Present improvements ☐ do ☐ do not conform to zoning regulations.
Highest and best use: ☐ Present use ☐ Other (specify) ______

	Public	Comm.	Individual
Electricity	☐	☐	☐
Gas	☐	☐	☐
Water	☐	☐	☐
Sanitary Sewer	☐	☐ Sep. Tnk.	☐

☐ Underground Electricity & Telephone

Street ☐ Public ☐ Private
Surface ______
☐ Storm Sewer
☐ Curb & Gutter
☐ Sidewalk ☐ Alley
☐ Street Lights

Ingress and Egress (Adequacy) ______
Topography ______
View Amenity ______
Drainage and Flood Conditions ______

Is the property located in a HUD Identified Special Flood Hazard Area? ______

COMMENTS (including any easements or encroachments or any nonconforming use(s) of present improvements) ______

FHLMC Form 71B—Rev. 8/77 Page 1

DESCRIPTION OF IMPROVEMENTS

☐ Existing Approx. Year Built 19___ ☐ Proposed ☐ Under Construction ☐ Elevator ☐ Walk-up No. of Stories_______ ☐ Row or Townhouse

No. of Bldgs._______ No. of Units_____ No. of Rooms______ No. of Baths______ Parking Spaces: No.____ Type ______

Basic Structural System______ Exterior Walls______ Roof Covering______

Interior Walls______ Floors______ Bath Floor and Walls______

Insulation______ Adequacy______ Adequacy of Soundproofing______

Heating: ☐ Central ☐ Individual Type______ Fuel______ Condition______

Air Conditioning: ☐ Central ☐ Individual Describe______ Adequacy and Condition______

Elevator(s): Number______ Automatic______ Adequacy and Condition______

Security Features______

Kitchen cabinets, drawers and counter space ☐ Adequate ☐ Inadequate

☐ Range/Oven ☐ Fan/Hood ☐ Dishwasher ☐ Disposal

☐ Refrigerator ☐ Washer ☐ Dryer ☐______

Hot Water Heater(s)______

Plumbing Fixtures______

Electrical Service______

Recreational Facilities______

OVERALL PROPERTY RATING	Good	Avg.	Fair	Poor
General appearance of property				
Quality of construction (materials and finish) .				
Condition of improvements				
Rooms size and layout				
Closets and storage				
Plumbing—adequacy and condition				
Electrical—adequacy and condition				
Amenities and parking facilities				
Appeal to Market				

Effective Age______**Yrs. Estimated Remaining Economic Life**_____**Yrs.**

COMMENTS: (Special features, functional or physical inadequacies, repairs needed, modernization, etc.)______

COST APPROACH

LAND SALES (complete ONLY if appropriate for this appraisal)	Zoning	Area	Sales Price	Date	Price per Sq. Ft. or per Unit	
1.		¢	$		$	Per
2.		¢	$		$	Per
3.		¢	$		$	Per

Comments & Reconciliation______

Estimated Land Value $______

APARTMENT BUILDING(S)—ESTIMATED REPRODUCTION COST NEW

______ x ______ = ______ sq.ft. x ______ (Stories) = ______ sq. ft. x $ ______ $______

______ x ______ = ______ sq.ft. x ______ (Stories) = ______ sq. ft. x $ ______ $______

______ x ______ = ______ sq.ft. x ______ (Stories) = ______ sq. ft. x $ ______ $______

OTHER IMPROVEMENTS______ . . . . $______

______ . . . . $______

______ . . . . $______

TOTAL ESTIMATED COST NEW OF IMPROVEMENTS . . . . . . $______

LESS DEPRECIATION______ . . . . ______

DEPRECIATED VALUE OF IMPROVEMENTS . . . . $______

ADD—ESTIMATED LAND VALUE . . . . $______

INDICATED VALUE BY THE COST APPROACH (IN FEE SIMPLE) . . . . $______

IF LEASEHOLD DEDUCT VALUE OF FEE INTEREST (ATTACH CALCULATIONS) . . . . . . $______

INDICATED VALUE BY THE COST APPROACH (LEASEHOLD) . . . . $______

COMPARABLE RENTAL DATA

ITEM	COMPARABLE No. 1	COMPARABLE No. 2	COMPARABLE No. 3
Address			
Proximity to subj.			
Rental survey date			
Brief description of property improvements	No. Units___ No. Vacant___ Age___ yrs	No. Units___ No. Vacant___ Age___ yrs	No. Units___ No. Vacant___ Age___ yrs
Individual unit breakdown	Rm. Count (Tot BR b) / Size (Sq.Ft.) / Monthly Rent ($ ¢ Rm)	Rm. Count (Tot BR b) / Size (Sq.Ft.) / Monthly Rent ($ ¢ Rm)	Rm. Count (Tot BR b) / Size (Sq.Ft.) / Monthly Rent ($ ¢ Rm)
Utilities, furniture and amenities included in rent			
Comparison to subject including rental concessions, if any			

MONTHLY RENT SCHEDULE SUBJECT

Utilities included in actual rents: ☐ Water ☐ Gas ☐ Heat ☐ Electric ☐ Air Conditioning ☐______

Utilities included in forecasted rents: ☐ Water ☐ Gas ☐ Heat ☐ Electric ☐ Air Conditioning ☐______

No. of Units	Unit Rm Count Tot.	BR	b	Total Rooms	Sq. Ft. Area Per Unit	No. Units Vacant	ACTUAL RENTS Per Unit Unfurnished	Furnished	Total Rents	FORECASTED RENTS Per Unit Unfurnished	Furnished	Total Rents	Per Sq. Ft. or Room
							$	$	$	$	$	$	¢ $
TOTAL									$			$	

FHLMC Form 71B—Rev. 8/77

MARKET APPROACH

ITEM	SUBJECT	COMPARABLE No. 1	COMPARABLE No. 2	COMPARABLE No. 3
Address				
Proximity to subject				
Map code				
Lot size				
Brief description of building improvements	No. Units: ______ No. Vac.: ___ Year Built: 19 ____	No. Units: ______ No. Vac.: ___ Year Built: 19 ____	No. Units: ______ No Vac.: ___ Year Built: 19 ____	No. Units: ______ No. Vac.: ___ Year Built: 19 ____
Quality				
Condition				
Recreational facilities				
Parking				
Tenant appeal				
Unit breakdown	No. of Units / UNIT ROOM COUNT: Tot. BR b	No. of Units / UNIT ROOM COUNT: Tot. BR b	No. of Units / UNIT ROOM COUNT: Tot. BR b	No. of Units / UNIT ROOM COUNT: Tot. BR b
Util. paid by owner				
Data source				
Price	$ ☐ Unf. ☐ F	$ ☐ Unf. ☐ F	$ ☐ Unf. ☐ F	$ ☐ Unf. ☐ F
Sale–Listing–Offer				
Date of sale				
Terms (Including conditions of sale and financing terms)				
Complete as many of the following items as possible using data effective at time of sale				
Gross Annual Income	$	$	$	$
Gross Ann. Inc. Mult.(1)				
Net Annual Income	$	$	$	$
Expense Percentage (2)	%	%	%	%
Overall Cap. Rate (3)	%	%	%	%
Price per unit	$	$	$	$
Price per room	$	$	$	$
Price gross bldg. area	$ /sq. ft. bldg. area	$ /sq. ft. bldg. area	$ /sq. ft. bldg. area	$ /sq. ft. bldg. area

(1) Sale Price ÷ Gross Annual Income (2) Total Annual Expenses ÷ Total Gross Annual Income (3) Net Annual Income ÷ Price

RECONCILIATION: ______

INDICATED VALUE BY MARKET APPROACH $

INCOME APPROACH

INCOME	
Total Monthly Apartment Forecasted Rents	$______
Other Monthly Income (Itemize) ______	$______
Total Gross Monthly Forecasted Income	$______
Total Gross Annual Forecasted Income	$______
Less Forecasted Vacancy and Collection Loss (____%) .	$(______)
Effective Gross Annual Income	$______
Less Forecasted Expenses & Replacement Reserves . . .	$(______)
Net Annual Income from Total Property	$______
Less Return on and Recapture of Depreciated Value of Furnishings ($ ______ @ ______ %) . . .	$(______)
Net Annual Income from Real Property	$______
Capitalized as follows:	

*Real Estate Taxes ☐ Actual ☐ Est. Tax Rate Per $100 $______
Total Assessed Value $ ______
Comments: ______

EXPENSES	ACTUAL	FORECASTED
Real Estate Taxes*	$______	$______
Other taxes or licenses		
Insurance		
Unsubordinated ground rent . . .		
Fuel		
Gas		
Electricity		
Water and sewer		
Trash removal		
Pest control		
Maintenance and repairs		
Interior and exterior decorating . .		
Cleaning expenses and supplies . .		
Management (Off-site)		
Res. Mgr. salary & apartment . . .		
Janitor(s) salary & apartment . . .		
Miscellaneous		
______		
REPLACEMENT RESERVES		
Carpeting and drapes		
Ranges and refrigerators		
Dishwashers and disposals		
Individual heating & AC units . . .		
______ . . .		
TOTAL EXPENSES & REPL. RES. .	$______	$______

INDICATED VALUE BY INCOME APPROACH . . . . $______

FHLMC Form 71B–Rev. 8/77

Page 3

General Comments (including comments on any items rated poor or fair) ______

CONDITIONS AND REQUIREMENTS OF APPRAISAL (include required repairs, replacements, painting, termite inspections, etc.): ______

RECONCILIATION AND VALUE CONCLUSION

Indicated Value by the Cost Approach . . . . $______

Indicated Value by the Market Approach . . . $______

Indicated Value by the Income Approach . . . $______

FINAL RECONCILIATION: ______

I certify, that to the best of my knowledge and belief, the statements made in this report are true and I have not knowingly withheld any significant information; that I have personally inspected subject property, both inside and outside, and have made an exterior inspection of all comparable sales listed herein; that I have no interest, present or contemplated, in subject property or the participants in the sale; that neither the employment nor compensation to make said appraisal is contingent upon any value estimate; and, that all contingent and limiting conditions are stated herein. ☐ Certification and Statement of Limiting Conditions (FHLMC Form 439 Rev. 9/75) applies (☐ On file with client ☐ Attached).
As a result of my investigation and analysis, my estimate of Market Value of the subject property as of ______ 19__ is ....

$ ______

Date ______ Appraiser ______
If applicable, complete the following

Date ______ Appraiser ______

Date ______ ☐ Supervising or ☐ Review Appraiser ______
☐ Did ☐ Did Not Physically Inspect Property

FOR LENDER'S USE ONLY (completion optional)

Loan Recommended: $______ @ ______%. Term ______yrs. Principal & Interest $______/mo. $______ /annually
Subject to: ______

Borrower's Cost or Purchase Price $______ Appraised Value $______ Loan to Appraised Value ______%
Loan: Per Unit $______ Per Room $______ Per Sq. Ft. of Building Area $______
Gross Annual Forecasted Income $______ Gross Annual Income Multiplier ______ Overall Capitalization Rate ______%
Forecasted Annual Expenses and Replacement Reserves $______ (______ % of Gross Annual Forecasted Income)
Break-even Point (this loan): (Annual Exp. & RR $______ + Annual P&I pymts $______) ÷ (Gross Annual Income $______) = ______%
(All financing) : (Annual Exp & RR $______ + Annual P&I pymts. for all financing $______) ÷ (Gross Annual Inc. $______) = ______%
Borrower's Return on Appraised Equity: (Net Annual Inc. $______ (–) Annual P&I pymts $______) = $______(1)
(Appraised Value $______ (–) Loan Amt. $______) = $______(2)
$______ (1) ÷ $______ (2) = ______%
Comments or Committee action ______

FHLMC Form 71B–Rev. 8/77

provements at cost or higher before closing. To them, it's the same as appraising a to-be-built building. . . a common appraisal assignment.

Choosing an appraiser

Sometimes the ***lender*** chooses the appraiser. Some even have staff appraisers. But other times, ***you*** get to choose. My wife an I just bought a house. We got a construction loan, standby loan commitment, and a permanent loan. In each case, the bank/lender sent staff appraisers out.

This year we also sold one apartment building and bought another (actually it was an exchange). In each case, new loans were required. . . and appraisals. And in each case, ***I*** got to choose the appraiser. The lenders said only that they had to be MAIs or SRPAs.

We picked the first one on price. He wanted $2,000. Others wanted $3,000 or more. The loan officer actually selected him subject to approval. Naturally, she chose someone with whom she had worked successfully before. And he appraised the property for $740,000 in spite of a sale price of $665,000.

The second appraiser was highly recommended by the loan broker. It was for a FHLMC apartment building mortgage. The loan broker had previously worked for FHLMC. He said FHLMC was particular about how the appraisal was done. And this appraiser had done the appraisal on other FHLMC loan applications which had resulted in approvals. Also, we needed the loan commitment in record time. The loan broker assured me that this appraiser would work fast in recognition of our deadline.

To make a long story short, I went along with the loan broker's recommendation. I paid the appraiser $3,000 (even though I had just gotten a larger building appraised for $2,000 by an MAI). He appraised it for $650,000 even though the sale price was $600,000. He met the short deadline. And I got the loan.

Hang-ups, experience, relationships, skills

Appraiser vary according to specialty. They also vary according to hang-ups. I remember one always discounted houses where he could see the roof as he drove up (due to the lot being below street level). Another told a syndicator friend of mine, "You San Francisco guys are overpaying for property out here in Sacramento. I know what the properties are ***really*** worth." That appraiser did ***not*** get the assignment.

I just mentioned that I used an appraiser with successful FHLMC experience.

Look for an appraiser by talking to real estate agents, mortgage brokers, loan officers, attorneys, fellow investors. Try to talk to the appraiser in question before you give him the assignment. Look for

- experience with the property type and lender
- rapport with you
- absence of hang-ups that might hurt your value
- price
- speed if important

Further information

As part of your general real estate education, you ought to buy and read the latest edition of the book, *The Appraisal of Real Estate* (American Institute of Real Estate Appraisers, 430 North Michigan Avenue, Chicago, IL 60611).

Cross-collateralization and cross-default clauses

Cross-collateralizaton can be used when there are two or more loans between the same borrower and lender. It means that if you default, the lender may foreclose on any or all of the properties pledged as security. A cross-default clause makes a default on ***one*** loan a default on ***all*** the loans relating through the cross-default clause. As a borrower, you should resist these clauses.

Sunset clauses

Most real estate loans are ***over***-collateralized after the first couple years. That is they have more equity protecting them than they need. That's a waste of debt-carrying capacity. So try to get "sunset" clauses when it comes to collateral.

For example, the borrower is released from personal liability on the third anniversary of closing or when the loan-to-value ratio drops to 70% or some such. These "sunset" clauses can be used to release additional collateral...to convert a land contract to a deed and mortgage...and so forth. So give what collateral you must to get the loan. But keep in mind that while the lender may need all the collateral they're demanding as of closing day, they probably will ***not*** need that much collateral throughout the life of the loan.

14
Character And Capacity Techniques

The Three Cs of credit are collateral, character, and capacity. The previous chapter covered finance techniques related to collateral and ways of pledging collateral as security for a loan. These chapter covers the other two Cs: character and capacity.

Remember that it's not just ***your*** character and capacity that matter. Rather the character and capacity of ***everyone who promises to pay the loan***. That leads me to one category of character and capacity techniques—-co-signers.

Co-signer techniques

The word "co-signer" conjures up images of parents co-signing on a lease or mortgage to help their young, adult children get started. That's OK. But when ***I*** use the word "co-signer," I'm thinking of a much broader group.

Individuals like parents can be co-signers. But so can the government. ***FHA and VA mortgage insurance*** are essentially co-signing by the government for part of your loan. (Technically, FHA and VA only insure the top portion of a loan, not the entire amount.)

Likewise, ***private mortgage insurors*** are co-signers. So are banks when they write ***letters of credit.***

Others who might co-sign include anyone who's interested in seeing you get the loan you seek.

That includes

- sellers
- tenants
- real estate agents
- people who will get all or part of the financing proceeds
- your accountant or attorney
- your employer
- anyone on the People Check List (see index)

When to use a co-signer technique

The following conditions need to be present for co-signing to make sense:

- Lender feels your character and/or capacity are inadequate
- Lender feels that the combination of your character and capacity and the co-signer's character and capacity ***are*** adequate
- Co-signer feels your character and capacity combined with any benefits he'll receive warrant the risk he'll be taking by co-signing.

More to the point, you use the co-signer technique when you're turned down for a loan. Or when a loan officer tells you before-hand that you won't be approved.

Mortgage insurance

There are two kinds of mortgage insurance:

- government
- private

Government mortgage insurance is commonly referred to as FHA and VA. FHA has a zillion different programs. VA several. You should be interested in VA even if you're not a veteran...because you can assume or buy subject to a loan which was originally put on the property by a vet.

Private mortgage insurance is just a civilian version of FHA and VA...with less bureaucracy...and more fees.

FHA

It's very difficult to get information on FHA programs. Call an FHA office and you'll get recordings, busy signals, no answers, and clerks who'll tell you such and such program doesn't exist...when it does. Making it even tougher is the fact that the programs change fairly often. So what's a prospective FHA borrower to do?

I just dialed FHA in San Francisco. I got a recording which told me their office hours (8:15 through 4:45...not bad) and told me to call another number. I did. The lady who answered cut me off in mid-sentence with, "Would you please hold?" She didn't wait for an answer. When she came back, she promised to send me a booklet on FHA programs.

Offices of the Department of Housing and Urban Development in major cities have libraries where you can go to get information. They also have brochures...although often either out-of-stock or out-of-date.

Mortgage brokers are good information sources

You generally get FHA and VA loans through mortgage brokers. They act as sort of interpreters between the public and the bureaucrats. Very necessary interpreters. In my opinion, their man function is to make the bureaucrats do the job they're supposed to do without prodding. However, the fact is they have to be prodded.

In some Latin American and other foreign countries, corrupt bureaucracy is pervasive. As a result, there are small businessmen who get paid to obtain various government approvals and documents. In the U.S., mortgage brokers who specialize in government loans perform much the same function. Except that bureaucratic sloth rather than outright corruption are the reason.

Because it's their livelihood, mortgage brokers ***have to*** know the details of the programs they work with. And they'll be glad to tell you about them if they think you might lead to a commission.

Limitations of mortgage brokers

But mortgage brokers are only *limited* information sources. For one thing, the ***commercial*** mortgage brokers generally have minimum fees in the $5,000 to $10,000 range. That, in turn, means large minimum property sizes. Like a hundred units. Even though some programs have much smaller minimums officially. For example, the 223f FHA program for financing of existing apartment buildings applies to properties with five or more units. But you probably cannot find a mortgage broker with 223f experience who'll work on less than 75 units or so.

Mortgage brokers who work on ***home*** loans generally do ***not*** have a minimum that would affect you.

The other problem with relying on mortgage brokers for FHA and VA information is that they know what they need to know to make a living. But they do ***not*** have encyclopedic knowledge of all HUD and VA programs. So there might be some oddball program which will help you. . . but which your mortgage broker doesn't know about.

It's like "orphan diseases." Those rare diseases which have too few victims to support cure research by private industry or charities. Some HUD programs are "orphans" in that they benefit such a small number of people that neither the bureaucrats nor the mortgage brokers bother to learn about them.

BNA's *Housing and Development Reporter*

So where do you find out about these orphan programs? Try the Bureau of National Affairs. Their *Housing and Development Reporter* (HDR) covers FHA programs, including single-family, mobile home, multi-family, and home improvement loans. It also covers VA programs. And even has a brief section on private mortgage insurance.

The Housing and Development Reporter costs over $500 a year. It consists of a *Current Developments* volume and three reference volumes. The *Current Developments* volume is a sort of weekly newsletter covering changes in laws and programs relating to housing. You can subscribe to *Current Developments* only for a couple hundred less.

The reference volumes contain the text of laws and regulations pertaining to housing. FHA, VA, The Real Estate Settlement Procedures Act, Truth-in-Lending, etc. When there's a change in a law or regulation, they send you a new page and tell you to tear out the old one.

You may be turned off by the relatively high price. I have two comments on that. One is, see if you can find *HDR* in a local library. My county library does ***not*** have it. Nor does the San Francisco Business Library or the Oakland Business Library or the San Francisco Library documents section or the San Francisco Law Library.

The other comment is compare the *HDR* price with the size of the deal you're trying to do. Is $500 too much to spend to get the information you need to do a $100,000 deal? Or a $500,000 deal? Or whatever? If you can't find it in your area, as I've been unable to do in the San Francisco area, it may well be worth the $500. You'd probably pay an attorney or mortgage broker that much without blinking.

Characteristics of government insured loans

Government insured loans generally have the following characteristics:

- red tape
- strings
- low limits (on less than five units)
- below market interest rates

- points
- high loan-to-value ratios
- no prepayment penalty
- long term
- transferrable

Red tape

If you haven't been through it, words cannot describe the frustration of obtaining a government insured loan. I suspect some go through smoothly. Especially on new homes where everything's pre-approved except the buyer's credit. But my experience with government insured loans was that getting one was like crawling naked over one mile of broken glass.

At the beginning of your career, it's often worth it. Because of the high loan-to-value ratio and below market interest rate, the loans are especially helpful to beginners. Furthermore, a beginner's time is less valuable so it can be cost effective for him to do the mortgage equivalent of standing in line at the motor vehicle department.

But I can't see applying for a government insured loan after you've "arrived." Unless you're into masochism.

Actually, there may be times when it makes sense. Like when it's the only alternative. The 223f program is the one I have in mind. It's for apartment buildings. And might be worth going after in some cases.

Co-insurance

I understand the government tried an experimental program. They delegated the authority to approve 223f loans to certain approved mortgage brokers. In other words, the mortgage broker decides whether or not you get the loan. And whatever the mortgage broker says is OK with FHA.

The purpose of that is to eliminate government red tape. Sounds good to me. Although I'm sure the brokers have to meet a zillion requirements...which are in themselves red tape. But it sounds like a step in the right direction.

Low limits

The maximum FHA loan limit tends to be behind the times. The limits vary around the country. Here in the San Francisco area the maximum FHA single-family loan is $90,000. That's at or below the median home price in the area. So on less than five-family buildings, you have to buy in the bottom half of the market to use FHA.

VA has no limit *per se*. But as a practical matter, they don't go much higher than FHA.

Points

The FHA/VA interest rate ***used*** to be set by the Secretary of Housing and Urban Development. He usually set it below market. But as of November 30, 1983, the FHA rate floats with the market. The VA rate is still set by the government.

Also, under the old rules, the buyer could only pay one point. The seller had to pay the rest. In fact, the buyer paid all of them in the form of a higher price. Under the new rules, who pays how many points is up to the buyer and seller.

Rainier Bancorp in Seattle offered FHA loans with interest rates ranging from 11.5% to 13.5%. Fixed rate, thirty year loans. You could have whichever interest rate you want between 11.5% and 13.5%. However, the farther the interest rate you pick is below market, the more points you and/or the seller will have to pay.

I think the new rules are great. As I said elsewhere in the book, I am dead set against seller financing. But I very much like seller buy downs. The floating FHA rate and programs like Rainier Bancorp's make it easy for the seller to do full or partial buy downs.

High loan-to-value ratios

VA will insure loans up to 100% of value. FHA will insure up to 95% plus $500 (that's a derivative of the actual formula). On non-owner-occupied property, FHA will go up to 85% of value. VA doesn't do non-owner-occupied. Although they ***will*** insure up to a four-unit building in which only one unit is owner-occupied.

No prepayment penalty

I've never heard of an FHA or VA loan with a prepayment penalty. When there's no prepayment penalty, you can win, but you can't lose, on interest rate movements. If rates go ***up***, you've got a locked-in rate.

But if rates go ***down***, you can refinance the loan. In fact, you can even replace it with another FHA or VA loan at a lower interest rate.

There ***is*** a ***practical*** prepayment penalty. . . the transaction costs of refinancing. But if rates fall enough, it's worth it to pay those costs.

Most conventional loans have prepayment penalties. That's to eliminate the heads-I-win, tails-you-lose effect of no prepayment penalty. Some conventional loans even have lock-ins. That means you ***can't*** pay them off at all for a certain period. In reality, a lock-in is a sort of negotiated prepayment penalty. The lender will typically let you prepay. But they'll ask you to pay whatever penalty they think you'll bear.

None of that with government insured loans.

Long terms

Government insured loans are usually for thirty years. Some even go for 35 or 40 years.

The longer the better if you're a borrower. But it's no big deal. The payments on a $100,000 thirty year loan at 13.3% are $1,129.70 a month; on a similar forty year loan, $1,113.95. . . a $15.75 a month reduction.

So forty years is better than thirty. . . but not much. Then again, every little bit helps.

Transferrable

There are no due-on-sale clauses in FHA or VA loans. That ***is*** a big deal. A fixed rate loan protects you from interest rate increases as long as you own the property. But it doesn't do beans for you when you sell if it has an enforceable due-on-sale clause.

Most conventional home loans do. Due-on-sale clauses are less common in income property loans.

If interest rates go ***up***, your property value goes ***down***. . . ***unless*** it has a transferrable loan with a fixed-rate.

Actually, it's more technically correct to say that your ***equity*** still goes down in value. . . unless the loan-to-value ratio is 75% or more. But at least the portion of value represented by the fixed-rate, transferrable mortgage is unaffected by an increase in interest rates.

They've talked about charging more, maybe a half percent for assumability in FHA and VA loans. If they put that into effect, pay it.

Assumability or transferability protects the loan portion of your property value from adverse interest rate movements. That's a very valuable aspect of FHA and VA insured loans.

FHA programs (HUD actually)

Here's a brief description of the HUD programs currently available. You could write a whole book on them. I'm not going to. See BNA for that. Either the aforementioned *Housing & Development Reporter* or their *Guide To Federal Housing Programs* (Edson and Lane, BNA Books). Edson and Lane are the authors of the *Guide* and the editors of *HDR*. You can also get information from the booklet *Programs of HUD* published by HUD.

• 203(b) One- To Four-Family Home Mortgage. This is the standard FHA program for financing houses.

• 203(i) same thing but for "outlying areas."

• 235 Homeownership Assistance For Low- And Moderate-Income Families. Interest subsidy. Only available in some areas after September 30, 1983. Definition of "low- and moderate-income" varies from area to area.

• 221(d)(2) Homeownership Assistance For Low- And Moderate Families. Like 203(b). No income limits but low limits on mortgage size. My HUD brochure says there's a $36,000 loan limit in "high cost areas." Can be used to rehabilitate substandard housing, buy a home, or construct one. Displaced households get special terms.

• 223(e) Housing In Declining Neighborhoods. For purchase, rehab, or construction of housing in "older, declining, but still viable urban areas." Don't invest in declining neighborhoods at all. . . with or without this mortgage insurance. That doesn't mean you should never use this program. Just make sure you only use it on neighborhoods which are on the rise. And even then, I don't recommend such investments. They are highly speculative and risky.

• 237 Special Credit Risks. For low- and moderate-income folks with lousy credit. Very low, loan limit—-$21,000 in "high cost areas." That "high cost" loan limit sounds like a contradiction in terms.

• 234 Condos. Sort of a 203(b) for condos.

• 213 Co-ops. Sort of a 203(b) for co-ops.

• Title I Mobile Homes. Max loan is $22,500; $35,000 if two or more modules. Max term is 20 years and 32 days????

• 207 Mobile Home Parks. To finance rehab or construction of mobile home parks. Loan limit of $9,000 per space; 15,750 in "high cost areas."

• 207 Multifamily Housing. For construction or rehab of apartment buildings. Rents are controlled by the federal government. Although their control is lenient and can be eliminated by paying off the loan. No prepayment penalty.

• 223(f) Existing Multifamily Housing. Most FHA programs are of little help to a real estate investor. That's ***not*** true of 223(f). You ***may*** find this one useful. It's for purchase or refinancing of existing apartment buildings. As with most multifamily HUD programs, you need to have at least five units. In this program, the building has to be at least three years old, too. Some mortgage brokers specialize in this one. Up to 35 years. Federal rent control but not as bad as the typical municipal control. . . can be eliminated by prepayment. Last I heard you could get up to an 85% loan-to-value ratio. And they'd even let the seller take back an additional 7 1/2% of value. . . unusual for a HUD loan. There are mortgage brokers who specialize in this one. It's good to ask a prospective mortgage broker how many of the type loan you seek he has successfully obtained. You'll be surprised how often the answer is, "None."

• 221(d)(3) and (4) Multifamily Rental Housing For Low- And Moderate-Income Families. For construction and substantial rehab of low rent apartments or co-ops.

• Title I Home Improvement Loans. Limit of $17,500 on a single-family house; $8,750 per unit on an apartment building but not more than $43,750 for the whole building. Term of 15 years and 32 days??? Unsecured if under $2,500.

• 203(k) Rehab Mortgage Loans. Up to $12,000 a unit; $17,400 in "high cost areas." Total debt on property cannot exceed what you could get on a 203(b) mortgage. 20 years. Has to be at least ten years old unless major construction defects or casualty loss.

• 241 Supplemental Loans For Multifamily Projects. For improvements to buildings which already have FHA mortgages. Also available for buildings with non-HUD financing...*if* they want to use the money to "expand housing opportunities, to provide fire or safety equipment or to finance energy conservation improvements."

• 245 Graduated Payment Mortgage. Five different plans. Same as 203(b) except for payment pattern. If you've owned a home in the last three years, you have to make a larger down payment than with 203(b).

• Title X Land Development. To prepare raw land for residential home building. That is, install water, sewer, streets, lights, sewer, etc.

• 238(c) Housing In Military Impacts Areas. Gawd, I hate it when people used the word "impact" other than as a noun. Only available when the effect of the military on the community in question renders a mortgage otherwise uninsurable (by FHA)??? I don't know what that could mean.

• 222 Homes For Servicemen. Small subsidy but otherwise like 203(b) program.

• 201 Flexible Subsidy. For troubled apartment buildings with HUD loans. They ought to call this the "good money after bad" program.

Don't rely on any of the information I've given you on these programs. It may be out of date. Check the current edition of *HDR* to be up to date.

Geographic variation in utilization

You would think HUD programs are used uniformly across the country. Not true. Some regional HUD offices do far more volume than others on a particular program. Especially the apartment building programs.

Does that mean you should move to the high volume areas?

No.

But it might be a good idea to call one of the high volume regional offices for advice. You may have trouble getting help as Joe Homebuyer. But your mortgage broker or your local HUD employee might be more successful. Plus you may be able to motivate a HUD guy at your local office who's trying to discourage you by pointing out the volume done in Denver or wherever. Finally, you may be able to contact a fellow investor in the high volume region...one who got the kind of loan you're looking for...and who might send you photocopies or other helpful material.

VA loans

Eligible veterans can buy a house with as little as zero down. Actually, they can buy up to a four-family building...as long as they live in one unit. They can even buy a *five*-unit building if they team up with another veteran-occupant. Six units if there are ***three*** veterans and so forth.

I'm generally anti group ownership. So I recommend against teaming up with other veterans or anybody else...regardless of the VA rules.

The VA insures the top part of the loan ($27,500). But that's not the maximum loan. Lenders will make 100% VA loans on properties up to $110,000. Up to $135,000 if the veteran puts more down.

Veterans can get an unlimited number of VA loans. Used to be a once-in-a-lifetime deal. But they can only have one VA loan outstanding at a time.

If a vet allows the guy who buys his home to buy subject to the loan, he cannot get another VA loan until that loan is paid off. Unless the guy who buys his home is also a veteran. In which case, they trade eligibility.

A vet can, however, ask the VA to ***relieve him from liability*** on the loan when he sells his house and lets someone else take over the loan. Contact the VA before the sale for details.

I did that some years ago. The VA required me to put certain language in the deed. They also required a credit application from my buyer and that he sign documents in which he promised to pay the loan. Two years after closing, I got a letter from the VA saying I had been relieved of liability on that loan.

Without such a release, the vet remains liable to make the payments even though he sold the property.

The VA normally only ***insures*** loans. But they will actually ***make*** a loan if the vet lives in an area where mortgage money is not available. Those loans have a lower limit.

Vets with service-connected disabilities can get grants for modifying their home to accommodate their handicap.

To find out if you're eligible, call the VA. The rules vary depending on when you were in the service and under what circumstances. A loan officer I just talked to said, "The vets all know whether they're eligible or not."

Widows of vets who died as a result of their service can also get VA loans. If they remarry, their eligibility is suspended. It returns if and when the new spouse dies or the marriage is annulled or they are divorced??? Sort of like restoration of your virginity, I guess.

You can get a VA loan to buy or refinance an existing or new home, condo, or mobile home. Some states have programs for veterans. Make inquiries of your state government and/or local Realtors and mortgage brokers for information.

VA loans for non-vets

If you're not a vet or a vet's unmarried spouse, you can still get a VA loan. Not a ***new*** VA loan. But you can buy subject to or assume an existing VA loan. That might occur due to running across one when you're looking for property. Or you might deliberately look for properties with VA loans on them.

The mortgages are recorded in the county courthouse. You could systematically search the mortgage records for VA loans. Then send the buyer/borrowers a letter offering to buy their house. Most won't be ready at that time. Tell them to put your letter with their deed so they remember to get in touch with you if they ever do think of selling. Point out that they'll have no commission to pay.

Some investors have done this and acquired a large number of rental houses with less than normal down payments. They also save on closing costs since the typical VA assumption or subject to has no loan transaction costs. This technique is as applicable to FHA loans as to VA.

Remember that leverage is not the be all and end all of real estate investing. You ***can*** acquire a bunch of rental houses by buying subject to FHA and VA mortgages. But I don't think you ***should***. I think single-family rental houses are a poor investment. Income properties are better. You only buy rental houses at the beginning because they're all you can afford. When you can afford to buy bigger, do so. Even though you can't assume VA loans at that level. (You ***can*** find some FHA subject tos at the income property level.)

Farmers Home Administration

The third government mortgage insurance agency is the Farmers Home Administration (FmHA). FmHA differs from FHA and VA in that you deal directly with them for a loan. . .instead of with a mortgage lender who in turn deals with FHA and VA. But, ultimately, FmHA's money comes from private investors who want federally insured mortgages.

FmHA is a subsidiary of the Department of Agriculture, not HUD. You can get information on FmHA programs from the FmHA or BNA's *HDR*. Here's some general information.

The property in question has to be in a "rural" area. Last definition I saw said "any area outside a city of 50,000 or more and its immediately adjacent urbanized areas with population density of more than 100 persons per square mile.'' The definition changes from time to time so you need to check whether the property in question is eligible.

FmHA's Business and Industrial Division (Don't ask me what that has to do with farmers' homes. I'm just a writer.) makes loans which preserve or create jobs. FmHA also has a Rural Housing program.

Loan term on home loans is 33 years. The loans are only for low- or moderate-income people so you have to poor mouth to get one. Can be used for buying as new or used home or refinancing. FmHA also has a program to finance senior citizen (age 62 or older) apartments for low- or moderate-income people.

FmHA also has programs for

- Farm ownership
- Farm operating
- Farm emergency
- Irrigation and drainage
- Soil and water conservation
- Recreation enterprise
- Repair and rehabilitation
- Farm labor housing

FmHA is another program I don't recommend. Generally, I don't think farms or farm property are real estate investments. That's not to say that everybody agrees with that. Nor do I deny that some of the people who thought farm land was a real estate investment have made money at it. Certainly a lot of farmers became rich owning farm land.

But I still say don't invest in farm land. And don't invest anywhere but major metropolitan areas. Just because there's a program doesn't make the eligible property a good investment.

Warning on government loan programs

In recent years, some ''creative finance'' gurus have glommed onto government loan programs. Specifically, they have advocated using government loan programs to generate tax-free cash. This has upset the people who run those loan programs.

They are particularly upset about gurus who advocate cashing out on renovation loans. That is, you apply for a $100,000 renovation loan then get the work done for $75,000 and put $25,000 in your pocket. I suspect that is ***not*** against the law ***if it is done in good faith***. That is if you really believed the work would cost $100,000 when you applied for the loan...then were fortunate enough to get it done cheaper.

The problem is it looks bad on its face. At best, you must have done a sloppy job of estimating the cost originally. At worst, you and the contractor who supplied the bid used in the loan application conspired to defraud the government.

Since the only way to ***legally*** keep excess cash is if it occurs ***unintentionally, advocating*** doing that seems to be *ipso facto* improper because advocating it takes it out of the ***un***intentional category and puts it in the ***intentional*** category.

If you did more than one deal in which you pocketed money not needed for renovation, the government would have additional evidence that you are lying in the initial application.

The laws you violate by lying to the lender about your renovation costs are Title 18 United States Code sections 1001 and 1014 (false statements to federally related entities). You might also be charged with violating sections 371 (mail fraud), 1341 (conspiracy), and 1961 through 1964 (racketeering). Those Code sections are explained in detail elsewhere in this book.

Federal regulations relating to specific loan programs may give rise to other violations of the law. For example, section 201.6(b) of the Title I Property Improvement Loan program says

''The proceeds of a loan shall be used only to finance alterations, repairs, and improvements...''

Section 201.8(a)(2) says the borrower and improvement contractor must sign a certificate that the borrower has not been given or promised a cash rebate, bonus, or commission on either this or future work.

Private mortgage insurance

So much for the ***government*** mortgage insurers. ***Private*** mortgage insurers (pmi) are at least as important...maybe more so.

The typical private mortgage insurer will insure loans up to 90% or 95% of value...on owner-occupied properties. Front end charges are usually higher than on conventional mortgages. And you have to pay 1/4% extra for the mortgage insurance premium. The front end fees are not much different than on FHA/VA with two exceptions: The ***buyer*** pays all and there are no points to equalize the yield with market because it's already at market. (That doesn't mean you won't pay ***any*** points. You just won't have to pay any due to the mortgage interest rate being below market.)

As a result of the buyer paying all the fees, sellers generally regard pmi buyers as equivalent to conventional buyers. Actually, pmi buyers are slightly less desirable because the pmi requirements are stiffer than conventional lenders as a rule. That increases the processing time and the probability that the buyer will be turned down.

PMI for income properties

Most people are aware that you can get private mortgage insurance on one- to three-family homes. But did you know that there are a couple of companies which issue private mortgage on income properties. United Guaranty Commercial Insurance Company (UGCI) is one. They're at P.O. Box 21945, 1327 Beaman Place, Greensboro, North Carolina 27420 (800-373-0232). The other is Commercial Loan Insurance Corporation (CLIC). CLIC is a subsidiary of Mortgage Guaranty Insurance Corporation (MGIC or "magic"). You can contact them at MGIC Plaza, Milwaukee, WI 53202 800-558-9900.

These two companies only do ***first*** mortgages. By using them, you can get the loan-to-value ratio up above what it would otherwise be...maybe 80% or 85% instead of 70% to 75%. But they will not go as high on commercial property as private mortgage insurers will on owner-occupied homes.

The fact that they ***will*** go up to 80% or 85% doesn't mean it's *easy*. They have strict requirements regarding debt coverage ratios and so forth. Often their debt coverage ratios prevent the borrower from getting as high a loan-to-value ratio as their policy on loan-to-value ratios would allow.

UGCI insures the top 20% of a loan. That reduces the lender's exposure on an 80% loan-to-value ratio loan, for example, to the equivalent of a 64% loan-to-value ratio. UGCI will consider a surprisingly broad range of property types

- apartments
- office buildings
- shopping centers
- mobile home parks
- nursing homes
- restaurants
- motels
- industrial parks
- light manufacturing facilities
- warehouses
- medical clinics
- special purpose properties
- recreational facilities

CLIC has four different programs in which they insure the top 10%, 15%, 20% or 25% of the loan.

You do not deal direct with CLIC or UGCI. They deal only with mortgage lenders. You deal with mortgage lenders. But you should know about CLIC and UGCI. If a loan officer says, "We'd like to make the loan, but it exceeds our policy on loan-to-value ratios." "No sweat," you respond. "We can get commercial private mortgage insurance."

The loan officer may have forgotten about pmi. Or he may have been hoping that you had never heard of it. One loan officer told me that they used pmi on income properties only when they wanted to do a loan which exceeded their normal policy. But if they didn't want to do the loan at all, pointing out the existence of loan insurance wouldn't change their minds. So at least your asking the loan officer why he can't use mortgage insurance will smoke out whether he really wants to do the loan or not.

Lease insurance

CLIC used to write insurance policies on commercial leases. No more. Too many claims. As far as I know, no one currently writes commercial lease insurance. There is one organization that, in effect, writes ***residential*** lease insurance—-the federal government.

You may recall that when I started this section on mortgage insurance I labelled it a "co-signer" technique. ***Lease*** insurance is an ***indirect*** co-signer. With lease insurance, the insurer does not insure that you'll pay the ***mortgage***. They insure that the tenant will pay the ***rent***.

But if the lender is convinced that you'll make the mortgage payments as long as you receive the rent payments, you've got a deal.

The federal government's residential "lease insurance" is more commonly known as the "Section 8" program. In it, the federal government subsidizes a portion of a low-income tenant's rent. That, in effect, makes them partial co-signers on the lease.

You can sometimes get "lease insurance" from the seller. I put it in quotation marks because it's not an insurance policy *per se*. If there is some question about the tenant's living up to the lease terms, you may be able to get the seller to guarantee. He could co-sign on the lease(s). Or you could use an if loan. . . in which your payments were contingent on one or more of the tenants completing living up to their lease. A variation on this is called a "cash flow guarantee."

"Credit" tenants

The word "credit" sometimes has a special meaning in real estate finance. You hear people say things like, "They're a credit-oriented lender." or "They like credit tenants."

If you're not familiar with the term, you may wonder what other kind of lender there is. . . lenders who want tenants with ***no*** credit?

That's not what they mean. In that context, the word "credit" means that the tenant in the building has such a high credit rating that the real estate aspects of the deal are of little or no importance. The opposite of a "credit" deal would be a "real estate" deal.

The typical apartment building loan is a real estate loan. The lender looks carefully at the property and the market for apartments. But what if it was an office building and IBM was gong to lease it for twenty years? Why should the lender spend a lot of time checking out the property and the market for office space when IBM says in writing that they'll pay the rent payments no matter what?

The IBM building would be a "credit" deal. The lesson for you is that credit deals are easier to finance. In fact, leases with credit tenants are sometimes called "bond leases." That's because the lease is more like a bond than a lease. A long-term lease to IBM is like a long-term bond from IBM. Which do you think would be easier to borrow against, an office building rented to a bunch of nobody tenants, or an IBM bond which you are willing to turn over to the lender as security for the loan. Borrowing against a building which is long-term leased to a credit tenant is not too much different from borrowing against a savings account.

Note that the lender will want to ***check the credit*** of any long-term tenants the loan will be based on. And the lender will have its attorneys examine the ***wording of the long-term leases.*** If a long-term lease contains an ***easily exercised out*** for the tenant, it's ***not*** really a long-term lease.

If you are leasing space to a long-term tenant at the same time you are applying for a mortgage on the property, make sure the lender approves both the tenant and the lease wording ***before*** you sign the lease.

You'll have the ***worst of both worlds*** if you have a long-term credit tenant. . .and the low rent that usually means. . .and lenders refuse to make you a good mortgage loan because they don't like the wording of the lease. Be extremely careful about the wording of long-term leases. Whether you are buying a property with existing leases or writing a new lease.

I won't try to list the clauses lenders don't like here. Instead I'll refer you to paragraph 3.05 of *The Law of Real Estate Finance* by Madison and Dwyer. There begins an excellent discussion titled "Analysis of Shopping Center and Other High-Credit Leases by Permanent Lender."

Bonds and insurance

In many loan situations, bonding companies will increase the lender's safety. Bonds are mainly used in construction lending. That would include renovation.

Construction bonds guarantee performance or payment of subcontractors and suppliers. If more than one bond is involved, it's best to use ***one*** bonding company for all of them. The American Institute of Architects has a standard form (A311) which you might want to use. The character and capacity of the bonding company are important. A.M Best publishes ratings of insurance companies. Dun and Bradstreet rates corporate credit. Either of those reference books is probably in a library near you. It might be a good idea to attach a photocopy of the bonding company's rating to the mortgage application when you are using a bond to help get the loan. Industrial Indemnity Company insured investor notes against default in a limited partnership deal done by Van Kampen Merritt, Inc., an Illinois investment banking firm. That backing gave the partnership's borrowing a AAA rating. The AAA rating, in turn, enabled them to get a loan with an interest rate 1% lower than the loan they were refinancing. And, I presume, 1% lower than the then market interest rate for the same notes if they had ***not*** been insured.

Financial Guaranty Insurance Corp. insured $200 million of notes sold by Coast Savings and Loan Association of Low Angeles. That also got a AAA rating for the notes and saved 1/2% interest.

Sunset clauses

As with releasing collateral after the risk of the loan has declined, you can use "sunset" clauses to release guarantors, mortgage insurors, or bonding companies. You want to be able to release mortgage insurors and bonding companies as soon as possible so you can stop paying their premiums.

A sunset clause would allow you to drop a guarantor or other character/capacity requirement after a certain number of years or after reaching a certain loan-to-value ratio.

Good terms from lender; but not from tenant

In some cases, you can even get 100% leverage on a credit leased building. And the terms tend to be easier than on real estate loans. The point is you should always try to make ***whoever*** your tenants are look as good as possible to the lender. In other words, do your best to convince the lender that your tenants have lots of character and capacity.

Now having heard how easy it is to finance buildings leased to credit tenants, you may feel you ought to buy such buildings. Not so fast. Keep the big picture in mind.

Credit tenants ***know*** they're credit tenants. They know their presence in your building and their signatures on your lease make your building more valuable and more easily financed. That's why lots of landlords try to get them as tenants. So credit tenants negotiate hard on the ***lease*** terms. In other words, the lender giveth and the tenant taketh away.

I don't like long-term leases as investments. . .unless you're retired from real estate. Long-term leases, as I said, are like bonds. Bonds are have very little upside potential. (Theoretically they can go up when market rates go down. But as a practical matter, most bonds and many leases have clauses which allow the debtor or lessee to get out when rates or rents go down.) On the other hand, if interest rates go up, bond holders get killed. And if market rents go up, and you're stuck with a long-term lease, everybody's building but your goes up in value.

So, yes, buildings leased to credit tenants are easy to finance. But ease of finance is not the only criteria for a good investment. Yield is also very important. And you will typically get a relatively low yield from buildings leased to credit tenants.

Multiple borrowers

As a general rule, the more borrowers the more merrier the lenders become. In other words, it's easier for two people to get a loan than one, easier for three than two, and so forth. The reason is increased capacity. Having a partner/borrower adds his debt-carrying capacity to yours.

Again, I see more important issues than finance. I don't like group ownership. It complicates your life considerably without enough benefits to offset the disadvantages.

So I want to point out the financial advantages of multiple borrowers. But not leave you with the impression that group ownership is therefore a good idea.

Bank as co-signer...the letter of credit

A bank will 'co-sign' on a loan for you...for a fee...and only if they feel it's safe. The device banks use to do that is a ***letter of credit***. (Federal savings and loans may not issue letters of credit.)

Getting a letter of credit is as hard as getting a loan. Or at least it should be. However, some lenders behave as though a letter of credit were somehow less than a loan. So as a practical matter, it is often easier to get a letter of credit from a bank than it would be to get a loan for the same amount.

A letter of credit is a co-signer technique. If you run into a lender who's concerned about whether you're going to make certain payments, a letter of credit is one of the techniques you should consider.

FSLIC Credit Enhancement Bonds

You probably haven't heard of FSLIC Credit Enhancement Bonds. The FSLIC hadn't even heard of them when I called to ask about them. But you ***may*** hear about them in the future. And I want this to be a no-stone-unturned book. So here's the explanation.

FSLIC is the Federal Savings and Loan Insurance Corporation. They insure savings and loan deposits up to $100,000 like FDIC does for banks. If the FSLIC insures your deposits, you are willing to accept a lower interest rate than you would from, say, a mortgage to an apartment builder.

But apartment builders would like to get lower interest rates. So they started thinking,"How can we the FSLIC guarantee to get us some cheap money?" And E.F. Hutton came up with a way to sort of do that in a deal they did with U.S. Shelter Mortgage.

Hutton rounded up investors to buy certificates of deposit (CDs). Let's say $10,000,000 worth. With each investor keeping his share below $100,000 in order to be fully insured. The CDs had the same payment pattern as a ten-year mortgage an apartment builder wanted. The interest rate was more or less the same as you would normally get on a ten-year insured investment. But part of the interest ***accrued***. That lowered the builder's monthly payments. Also, part of the interest was ***contingent***. That is, it depended on how well the building did.

Hutton took that deal to a savings and loan as a package. That is they said something to the effect of, "Here are depositors who wish to deposit $10,000,000 in your institution. They want ten-year CDs with the following payment pattern. And here is an apartment developer who wants a mortgage with the same payment pattern. If you accept the deposits and make the loan, you will get a fee and a spread on the interest rate."

Thus did the apartment builder sort of benefit from the FSLIC guarantee. Another similar deal was done by Murray Savings in Dallas. And these are the only FSLIC Credit enhancement bond deals which have been done according to Jerry Chautin of Trust Realty Funding, Inc., Atlanta.

My wife happens to be a former FDIC bank examiner. I asked her about this. She said it did not sound acceptable. She said the FDIC did not care for "linked deposits." That is, deposits which are linked to the making of a loan. Because it inspires lenders to lower their loan standards for the loan in question.

And if the loan goes sour and takes the institution with it, FDIC would have to pay up. FDIC does not like being made an indirect co-signer on loans. Especially loans made at lower standards. Presumably, FSLIC's feelings on the subject would be similar to FDIC's.

Obviously the loan ***must*** be a better deal for the borrower than a regular loan. Otherwise, why would he go to all this trouble and expense? E.F. Hutton gets about five or six points for doing this.

So I recommend that you ***not*** get involved with FSLIC or FDIC Credit Enhancement Bonds. They surely violate the ***spirit*** of the laws pertaining to deposit insurance. And they may violate the ***letter*** as well.

Character and capacity in general

Whenever you seek a loan...whether from an individual like a seller or from an institution...you should try to convince the lender that the character and capacity are adequate or more than adequate. Remember that includes not only ***your*** character and capacity, but also the character and capacity of all your

- co-borrowers
- individual co-signers
- mortgage insurors
- tenants
- letter of credit issuers

You generally establish ***character*** with ***credit reports*** and ***personal relationships***. You establish ***capacity*** with ***financial statements*** in their various forms including income tax returns, private audited statements, annual reports, 10K's (corporate financial disclosure statements).

Appearances can count

Capacity can also be ***implied***...by the way you dress, the car you drive, where you live, the cosmetic impressiveness of offices, annual reports, luxury accessories, etc. A good loan officer will demand financial statements and ignore appearances. But not all loan officers are good.

I don't mean to suggest that you should try to fool loan officers with fancy clothes and such. Nor do I want to give spendthrifts justification for extravagance. One good suit is all you need to impress a loan officer. However you should not neglect such details. Lest you or your co-signer weaken the effect of strong financial statements by making a bad impression.

PART EIGHT
HOW TO MANAGE YOUR MORTGAGE

15
How To Manage Your Mortgage

How to manage your mortgage

Most real estate finance books focus almost entirely on ***getting*** loans and occasionally on paying them off. But they rarely mention what happens ***between*** getting the loan and paying it off. There's some money to be made or saved there. So I'll cover it.

Mortgage insurance premiums

When the loan-to-value ratio is higher than 75% to 80%, lenders generally require mortgage insurance. Either private mortgage insurance or FHA or VA. On FHA and private mortgage insurance, the borrower must pay an insurance premium. You pay one year's worth at closing. And one month's worth every month thereafter.

These premiums are substantial. $100 to $500 per year on the typical home mortgage. My wife and I were paying $768 a year recently.

A Federal National Mortgage Association memo to its lenders dated October 10, 1984 said those lenders had the option to cancel mortgage insurance if the loan-to-value ratio dropped below 80% of the ***original purchase price*** or 80% of the current appraised value.

In other words, you can cancel your mortgage insurance if you owe 80% or less of the original purchase price with***out*** an appraisal. But you have to get a new appraisal if your loan-to-value ratio is still ***above*** 80% of the original purchase price.

FHLMC's *Sellers' and Servicers' Guide*, Volume 2 says

"Mortgage insurance cancellation: original borrower, owner-occupied property

*If the borrower so requests, the Servicer **must** cancel mortgage insurance if the following conditions are met:*

***(a) Loan-to-value ratio.** The unpaid principal balance of the mortgage has been reduced to 80 percent or less of*

- *the lessor of the original purchase price or the property's original appraised value, or*
- *if there are indications that the value of the property has declined since the original appraisal, the lesser of the original purchase price or the property's value as estimated by a Servicer-approved appraiser within 60 days of the request for cancellation of insurance, using the applicable Freddie Mac appraisal form, or*
- *if 7 years or more have passed since the closing of the mortgage, the property's value as estimated by a Servicer-approved appraiser within 60 days of the request for cancellation of insurance, using the applicable Freddie Mac appraisal form."*

The FHLMC policy goes on to say you must never have been more than 30 days late in the last 12 months on a ***fixed-rate*** mortgage or the last 24 months on an ***ARM or GPM***. And there must not have been any other default.

For ***non-owner-occupied*** property, original borrower, the policy is the same except that the required loan-to-value ratio is ***65%*** not 80%. Non-owner-occupied property is investment property. Like a rental house or duplex rented to others.

For property being sold where the mortgage is being assumed or bought subject to, the insurance may be cancelled if the loan balance is less than 80% of the ***sale price*** or appraisal, whichever is less.

Section 6421 of FHLMC's policy states

*"Upon cancellation of mortgage insurance, the Servicer **must***

- *discontinue collection of related premiums,*
- *make any necessary adjustment to the borrower's escrow account and the escrow portion of the monthly installment amount, and*
- *advise the borrower, in writing, of all such adjustments."*

FHLMC will ***not*** allow cancellation of ***FHA*** mortgage insurance.

Other lenders have their own individual policies on cancellation of mortgage insurance.

Some lenders are, themselves, pocketing the mortgage insurance premium. Which is not illegal as long as it was agreed to by you at closing. But you can see why they are reluctant to "cancel" the "policy" in those cases. According to an article in the February 27, 1985 *Wall Street Journal*, a spokesman for the U.S. League of Savings Institutions said there are "no sound reasons" for lenders to insist on mortgage insurance when the loan balance has dropped to 80% or less of the market value. You may wish to photocopy that article and use that quote in small claims court if your lender balks.

Loan-to-value ratio drops for three reasons

There are three reasons why the loan-to-value ratio drops after you buy the property:

1. Appreciation
2. Amortization
3. Improvement

How to get the lender to cancel

When you think your loan-to-value ratio has dropped below the 75% to 80% level, you should write your mortgage lender a letter requesting that they cancel the mortgage insurance coverage and refund the unused premium to you.

The letter should state your opinion of the value of the property and any basis you have for that opinion. . .like comparable sales, receipts for improvements you've made, median sale price statistics from the local MLS book versus the same statistics when you bought the property.

In some cases, the lender will simply cancel the policy. That's what happened to us. They charged us a $15 fee. Made us sign a form. And a couple weeks later we got a check for $421.16. . .the unused premium for the year.

If the lender resists

Many lenders will resist. They may throw up discouraging road blocks like requiring a new appraisal or demanding that you fill out a whole new credit application and pay substantial fees.

Whether they have the ***right*** to do such things is questionable. For starters, you should read the note and mortgage or trust deed to see if it contains any wording about cancellation of mortgage insurance. Our home trust deed is a FNMA/FHLMC standard form for California. It mentions that the lender will collect the mortgage insurance premium monthly and pay the annual amount to the insurer. But it says nothing about cancellation of that policy.

If there is no language in the documents about cancellation of the mortgage insurance, a standard of ***reasonableness*** should apply. Lenders are entitled to fees like the $15 my wife and I paid to cover the cost of processing the change. But they are not entitled to hundreds of dollars in my opinion. After all, if you move, virtually all your other creditors and periodicals will change your address in their records for ***free***. Why should mortgage lenders get $300 "transfer fees?"

Getting an appraisal

The lender may require an appraisal. That's not unreasonable if there's any question about whether your loan-to-value ratio is low enough to cancel. If you've owned the home ***ten years***, an appraisal requirement is probably harassment. But if you've only owned it a couple years, it's a legitimate request.

There are appraisals and appraisals. When you ***applied*** for the mortgage, the lender probably got a $150 to $200 appraisal. If a $150 to $200 appraisal was good enough then, it ought to be good enough now. A requirement that you get an MAI appraisal. . .which is typically much more expensive. . .is probably out of line.

I have a three-year pay back criterion. If an expenditure will pay for itself in three years or less, I'll do it. Since annual mortgage insurance premiums are $100 to $500 per year, an appraisal fee of $150 to $200 falls well within the three-year payback criterion. An MAI appraisal, however, might not.

If the lender insists on an MAI or other expensive appraisal, you may want to protest.

The wisdom of fighting with lenders

Americans are used to raising Cain with businesses that do them wrong. We complain about bad service. We threaten to take our business elsewhere.

Before you do that with a mortgage lender, be advised that there's less "elsewhere" in mortgage lending than in, say, dry cleaning. In small apartment building loans, for example, FHLMC is about the only game in town. So it would ***not*** be a good idea to read FHLMC the riot act if you'll ever need another apartment building mortgage.

Not only are mortgage lenders rare some times. They also talk to each other. If you borrow from lender A, then switch to lender B, lender B will call lender A to ask about you. If the answer includes an unpleasant incident in which you gave lender A a hard time, lender B may decide they don't need your business.

So think twice before you read your mortgage lender the riot act. You may need them in the future. This is ***less*** true with single-family home mortgage lenders. There are lots of them. And they have a retail image to uphold. They don't like to see stories in the paper that they done a borrower dirty.

Income property lenders don't much care about such things. Because the press is less likely to cover a landlord who was done dirty. And also because business borrowers are less skittish than consumers.

Sometimes you should fight

If your mortgage lender either flat refuses to consider cancelling mortgage insurance. . .or makes unreasonable requirements, it may make sense to fight.

First you write a letter which states just the fact, ma'am. Don't use adjectives or rant and rave. Just say value is X, loan-to-value ratio is Y, that's less than 75% or 80% (whichever was the trigger point when you got the loan), therefore the mortgage insurance policy should be cancelled. Give any evidence you have regarding the value.

If an unreasonable requirement has been made, explain why you think it's unreasonable and state what you think a reasonable requirement would be.

Then climb the chain of command. I usually go to the supervisor of the person who turned me down. Then if the supervisor also turns me down, I go to the chief executive officer of the company. Return receipt requested is not a bad idea.

If he turns me down, I start sending letters to

- FNMA or FHLMC if they hold the loan
- government regulators
- local media
- national media

Each time, I send a copy to the chief executive. The chances of regulators or media actually doing something about a $400 mortgage insurance premium dispute are small. But they ***might***. That fear tends to worry the chief executive. He's liable to look up from his desk and see Mike Wallace and a "60 Minutes" camera crew pouring into his office. "Is it true that you refuse to cancel unneeded mortgage insurance policies on thousands of home mortgages?"

When all else fails, go to ***small claims court***. Follow the local procedures. And sue for the amount of the annual premium. It's like in Judge Wapner's "People's Court" on TV. Tell the judge why you think you're right. Show him the policy that required you to get the mortgage insurance in the first place because your loan-to-value ratio was above 75% to 80%. Then show him the evidence that it is no longer is above 75% to 80%. And show him the letters you sent trying to persuade the lender to cancel the insurance. I think there's a good chance you'll win.

Learning how to get your mortgage insurance cancelled isn't going to make you rich. But it will get you back the amount you paid for this book and more. Every little bit helps.

Refinancing will do it

In some cases, it may make sense to refinance to get rid of the mortgage insurance premium. That would be when your letters and small claims suit failed...and there's little or no prepayment penalty. Again, the three-year payback criterion would apply. If you can refinance without mortgage insurance for three times the amount of the annual mortgage insurance premium or less, do it.

You may be due a refund when you pay off an FHA loan

When you pay off an FHA mortgage which is at least 12 years old, either due to sale or refinancing or making all 360 payments or cancellation of the insurance by the lender, you are due a refund of part of the mortgage insurance premium. This is called a "distributive share." It is the "profit" made by the FHA on your loan. FHA is not allowed to make a profit.

You do ***not*** have to be the original borrower to get the refund. In fact, the refund goes to the borrower of record 90 days before the insurance is terminated. To get the refund, contact the guys you send the payments to. They need to submit HUD Form 2344 ("Lender's Request for Termination of Home Mortgage Insurance') to HUD. HUD will send you a claim form which you sign and return. Then you'll get your check.

You do ***not*** get a refund when you sell the property and the loan is assumed or taken subject to. Only when it is paid off and HUD is not required to pay a mortgage insurance claim. If the loan is foreclosed, you may still be due a refund if HUD does not lose any money.

If you got your FHA loan in 1984 or later, you paid the entire mortgage insurance premium for the 30 years up front. If one of ***those*** mortgages is paid off, you are entitled to a ***refund of the unearned premium.*** When the entire premium for the life of the loan was paid up front, the loan need not be at least twelve years old when paid off to generate a refund.

For further information, contact HUD, Director of Mortgage Insurance Accounting and Servicing, OFA, Attention: Insurance Operations Division, Washington, DC 20410. Give them your FHA case number.

Impound accounts are your money

The other thing you gotta do every year is make sure the money going into and out of the impound accounts was proper. I mentioned elsewhere in the book that I discovered one of my mortgage lenders had secretly bought a hazard insurance policy with my impound account money...even though I had already bought insurance with my own money.

This year, my hazard insurance policies were cancelled twice. That causes premiums to go back and forth between the lenders and the hazard insurance companies. Also this year, my insurance agent billed both me and the lenders for an increased premium. And we ***both*** paid. The agent claims they refunded the lender's payment back to the lender. OK. Now I have to make sure the money got back into my impound account.

That's ***your*** money in that impound account. And somebody else, namely the lender, has the power to spend it on your behalf. That's dangerous. Whenever somebody else has the power to spend your money, you'd better watch them very carefully. Do most mortgage borrowers watch them very carefully?

Are you kidding? Most mortgage borrowers only look at their annual mortgage statement to get the tax information off it. They almost never check the figures. That'd be like not balancing your bank account each time you get a statement.

It's not a mystery

Your annual mortgage statement is ***not*** an impenetrable mystery. Nor are the people who prepare it infallible or always trustworthy. They make mistakes. They cheat you to throw some business to an insurance agent friend. Or they ***up*** your payment in a year when your property taxes went ***down*** and your insurance premium stayed the same.

Go over the mortgage statement every year and keep studying it until you know where every penny went and why. You should even check the amortization figure. One loan I had they put the wrong interest rate into the computer.

If you can't understand it, call the lender and ask them to explain the part you don't understand. Don't give up until you ***do*** understand it. What you don't understand, and the lender assures you is OK, may well be a lender mistake or wrongdoing. If the lender cannot give you a satisfactory explanation, demand a refund of the overcharge. If you don't get it, go to small claims court. Then they'll have to explain it so the judge can understand it.

When to pay down a loan

You have two kinds of loans: those with significant transaction costs and those with***out*** significant transaction costs. Mortgages almost always have significant transaction costs. Credit card balances and personal loans rarely do.

You should put your cash in a money market checking account or CD until you need it. That way you earn interest on it.

However you should ***not*** put money into an interest bearing account if you have any loans outstanding at a higher interest rate than the deposit earns...except when paying off the loan and reborrowing it has significant transaction costs.

Example

My present situation is probably somewhat typical. I have three mortgages with interest rates ranging from 10% to 13.25%. But one is locked in (no prepayment of any amount allowed). The other two are neither locked in nor have prepayment penalties. But there would be significant transaction costs if I wanted to reborrow the money after I paid them off. In the case of the 10% mortgage (from a seller), I'd also have to pay a higher interest rate on the reborrowing.

I also have on my balance sheet several non-real estate loans. A couple car loans, an education loan (my wife's graduate school), and a personal loan. The education loan is at a below-market interest rate, 7%, and cannot be reborrowed. The car loans have a preferential rate, 13.34%, due to my wife working for the lender. But they're still pretty high. And the personal loan is 16.9%.

Last month, the money market checking account I keep most of our money in earned 5.95%. So why am I paying rates of 7% to 13.25% to borrow money when I have money in the bank at only 5.95%? Good question.

Since the car loans and personal loan can be paid off and reborrowed almost without transaction costs, I plan to do just that next time I pay the bills. It is insane to have money in the bank earning 5.95% and loans outstanding on which you are paying ***more than*** 5.95%. By paying ***off*** those loans, you are, in effect, ***investing*** the money at the loan interest rate.

So why should I invest the money at 5.95% when I can invest it at 16.9% or 13.34%? Whenever you have a nickel in your pocket, you ought to pay off a nickel's worth of principal on any loans you have. . . as long as they don't have significant prepayment or reborrowing costs.

When there are significant prepayment or reborrowing costs

If there are significant prepayment or reborrowing costs, it ***might*** still make sense to pay all or part of the loan off. The key question is when do you think you will want to reborrow that money.

Let's say you have a $100,000 mortgage at 12% with no prepayment penalty. But reborrowing it would cost $4,000. If you have $100,000 in cash, should you put it in a money market fund earning 5.95%? Or pay off the 12% mortgage. For the moment, we'll ignore the third possibility of investing in real estate.

If you put the $100,000 in a money market fund, you lose 12% - 5.95% = 6.05%. Or $6,050 per year. I said it would cost $4,000 to reborrow that mortgage. So if you know that you will not be reborrowing it for at least $4,000/$6,050 = 66% of a year or .66 x 12 months = 8 months, you should pay off the mortgage. If, however, you think you will need to reborrow the money sooner than 8 months from now, you should put the $100,000 in the money market fund.

So the formula is

transaction costs/annual interest savings = number of years which must transpire before reborrowing.

What about below-market interest rate loans?

In the case of a below-market interest rate loan, the calculation is a little trickier. Because one of the transaction costs is the higher interest rate you'll have to pay on the reborrowing.

Take my wife's education loan, for example. Since it's at 7%, we have a negative spread compared to our 5.95% money market. But if we needed to reborrow that money, we'd have to pay 16.9% for a personal loan. The opportunity to get a student loan is no longer available to us. The loan balance is $2,000. So we're losing 7% - 5.95% = 1.05% x $2,000 = $21 a year. But if we need to reborrow the $2,000 at 16.9%, it'll cost us $338 a year, which is $338 - $140 = $198 more than now. If you just figure one year's worth of that $198 as the transaction costs, the number of years we'd have to be sure we wouldn't need that $2,000 would be

$198/$21 = 9.43 years

Am I sure I won't need to reborrow that $2,000 in the next 9.43 years? No, I'm not. It doesn't matter anyway. The loan only has four more years to run. So we don't pay off the 7% education loan even though we have a negative spread between it and our money market account.

But never make that decision without doing the numbers. People get enamored of below-market interest rate loans. You have to keep in mind that below-market interest rate loans are nice. But it's nothing but stupid to pay ***any*** interest rate if you don't need the loan. And if you'll have an equal amount of money in the bank the whole remaining term of the loan, you do ***not*** need the loan.

Put it on your computer

You should calculate this time-til-reborrow figure regularly. I put it on a Visicalc spreadsheet in my computer. Here's what it looks like.

Time-Til-Reborrow Calculation

Lender	Chase	Crocker	Crocker	Harvard	
Balance	8000.00	5500.00	11600.00	2000.00	
Rate	16.90	13.34	13.65	7.00	
Prepay Cost	0.00	0.00	0.00	0.00	
Reborrow Cost	0.00	0.00	0.00	0.00	
Security	none	Chevy	Buick	none	
Market Rate	16.90	13.65	13.65	16.90	
Rate Step-Up	0.00	0.31	0.00	9.90	
Annual Step-Up $	0.00	17.05	0.00	198.00	
Transaction Costs	0.00	17.05	0.00	198.00	
Money Market Rate	5.95	5.95	5.95	5.95	
Savings If Pay Off	876.00	406.45	893.20	21.00	
Time-Til-Reborrow	0.00	0.04	0.00	9.43	years
Annual Payment	2995.80	2274.24	3993.72	697.20	
Annual Constant	0.37	0.41	0.34	0.35	

Watch the constant, too

Note that I've calculated the annual constant on each of these loans at the bottom of the page. And that they have pretty high constants compared to mortgage loans. A new mortgage has a constant about 1/4% higher than the mortgage interest rate. For example, a 12% mortgage has about a 12.25% constant. Our car loans and unsecured loans, in contrast, have constants ranging from 34% to 41%. That means we're paying a lot of principal with each payment...which is typical of unsecured loans and loans secured by personal property like cars.

High annual constants crimp your cash flow. If you need cash flow, consider replacing high constant loans with lower constant loans. Generally that means longer term loans. You can sometimes get unsecured loans or car loans restructured for a longer period of time. That will reduce the constant. Or you might refinance a piece of real estate with a new first or second mortgage. Either one will have a lower constant than the typical unsecured or personal property loan.

In our case, for example, we could refinance some real estate at, say, 13% for 30 years to raise the $8,000 + $5,500 + $11,600 = $25,100 needed to pay off our car and personal loans. The annual payments on that loan would be $3,331.87. Compare that to the $2,995.80 + $2,274.24 + $3,993.72 = $9,263.76 we're now paying. The result would be $9,263.76 - $3,331.87 = $5,931.89 in additional annual cash flow.

ARM calculations

If you have an adjustable rate mortgage, you must check the rate calculations. I've seen a number of newspaper stories which reported that mortgage lenders are making errors in calculating adjusted rates. As a result, borrowers are unwittingly paying hundreds and thousands of dollars of overcharges.

The California Association of Realtors (CAR) said in June 1985 that it was getting scattered reports of erroneous ARM calculations. One of the reports came from CAR's own staff attorney, William Pfeiffer. His ARM was incorrectly calculated to say his payment had to go up $120 a month instead of the correct $30. The July 1985 issue of *Changing Times* had an article titled "Don't Let Your Lender Twist Your ARM" which chronicled a number of errors. The Massachusetts Department of Banks made a spot check of ARM interest rate change notices and found numerous errors.

One reason for the errors is that lenders deliberately used complicated formulas which concealed accumulations from periods when the interest rate on the loan lagged behind the index the loan was tied to. They also often use interest rate indexes which are not published. Or indexes which are hard to find. For example, the index to which most ARMs are tied is the one-year Treasury security index. That's published only in *USA Today*.

Whenever you receive notice of an interest rate change in your mortgage, check the calculation. If you can't come up with the same figure as the lender, ask them to explain. If you do not understand their explanation, demand that they use ***your*** figure. If they refuse, try small claims court again. Let them explain their figure to the judge.

Make sure you get the interest rate index your loan is tied to from a source ***other than*** the lender. Get it from the Federal Reserve Bank or the *Wall Street Journal* or the Federal Home Loan Bank Board or whoever publishes it. Do ***not*** accept your lender's word as to the index figures.

How to pay off a balloon payment

Do ***not*** make a balloon payment by sending a check for the balloon amount to the lender. Arrange instead to close the deal through a title company or escrow company. Then the title or escrow company will make sure the lender signs the necessary papers to have the mortgage removed from your property.

If you just send the lender the payment, you may need to go through all sorts of gyrations to get the mortgage removed. Because the lender may cash your check then not send the required papers. They may even do so ***deliberately*** to extort money out of you. Knowing that the legal alternatives to paying them a bonus will be more expensive.

PART NINE
HIGH LEVERAGE

16
High Leverage

High leverage

By high leverage I mean higher than institutional lenders will go on a conventional loan. That generally means

80% of value on an owner-occupied single-family home
75% of value on an investment property.

Most real estate investors want ***higher*** loan-to-value ratios. And most investors think the institutional lenders are unreasonable and overly conservative to refuse to loan more than 75% to 80%.

As I said earlier in the book, that's not true. The lenders know what they're doing. While real estate equity above 75% to 80% of value may have meaning to the ***owner*** of the property, it is largely meaningless to a ***lender.***

Why high altitude equity is only a mirage to a lender

Real estate equity above the 75% to 80% level is a mirage to a professional lender. He knows that if he tries to grab it in a foreclosure, it's like a man dying of thirst on the desert reaching for the water in a mirage pond. He grabs only air.

That's because in a foreclosure, three forces confiscate that 20% to 25% equity before the lender can lay a hand on it.

1. Sagging real estate values
2. Owner neglect
3. Foreclosure costs

The equity eaters

Foreclosure is only likely when the value of the property in question has sagged. If there is significant equity in a property, the owner will usually sell it rather than let it go into foreclosure. It's generally only when there is very little equity that the seller walks away or is unable to sell the property. The sagging value may be due to a generally soft market. Or due to mismanagement of the property in question.

Runzheimer Reports on Relocation is a newsletter for relocation managers of major corporations. Those are the guys who buy your home if you're transferred by your employer and cannot sell it yourself. Runzheimer did a survey of 79 relocation managers and found houses sold by relocation companies typically went for 3% less than appraised value if they sold in less than 120 days. If they took 120 days or more, they sold for 15% or more below appraisal. Plus, 56% of the firms offered buyers "refurbishing allowances," 55% paid buyer's closing costs, 47% were willing to buy down the interest rate, and 18% took back mortgages.

Owner neglect...or even vandalism...is another value-reducing force. At the time the loan was originally made, the property was almost certainly in good shape. But ***keeping*** a property in good shape takes money...and motivation. People who get foreclosed are almost always short of both money and motivation to spend money on the about-to-be-foreclosed property.

Vandalism

In some cases, the borrower gets mad at the foreclosing lender. And actually ***vandalizes*** the property out of spite.

Foreclosure costs

Finally, there are the foreclosure costs. On the date the property is sold at auction, the mortgage payments are typically six months or so in arrears. That's six months of interest, six months of property taxes, and six months of insurance premiums...all of which have to come out of the foreclosure sale proceeds. If the lender receives a deed in lieu of foreclosure, and sells through a real estate agent, he has to pay a 6% or 7% commission.

In addition, the borrower/property owner has probably not paid his utilities bills. By foreclosure time, the utilities have typically been turned off by the utility companies. If any of the turned-off utilities provide heat, air-conditioning, electric, etc. for the tenant's apartment or non-residential space, the turn-off has probably caused the tenant to move out or be on the verge of moving out. In freezing weather, pipes may have burst.

Suppliers and subcontractors have typically not been paid in the months before foreclosure. And they have slapped materialmen's liens and mechanics' liens on the property. Then there are the attorney fees, filing fees, court costs, process server fees, and so forth.

When you add up all these things, it's easy to see why lenders are ***not*** being ultraconservative when they insist on at least 20% to 25% borrower equity. So there's no padding in the usual 20% to 25% down payment requirement. That's about as far as lenders can go without suffering unacceptable losses.

Above 75% to 80% of value is "unsecured"

The best way to understand how to get high leverage is to think of the portion of a loan above the 75% level on a rental property and above the 80% level on an owner occupied home as *unsecured*. Technically, it *is* secured in a high loan-to-value ratio loan. But for *practical* purposes, it is not.

So when you seek a high leverage loan, you're really looking for a ***secured*** loan on the first 75% or 80% of the value and an ***un***secured loan on the rest. So this chapter on high leverage is really about finding those "unsecured" loans.

Equity is to a mortgage lender what a deductible is to an insurance company

Most laymen don't realize it, but the insurance and lending industries are very similar. They often use the same terminology like "underwriting," "loss," "risk," "liability," "bond," and so forth. And sometimes they use ***different*** terms which cover the same concept. For example, what the mortgage industry would call a "blanket" mortgage, the insurance industry would call an "umbrella." Both mean including more than one property in one deal. And the word "equity" in mortgage lending is similar to the word "deductible" in insurance.

Insurance companies have deductibles for two reasons:

1. To reduce the ***number and size*** of claims and losses
2. To give the policyholder **incentive** to avoid losses.

By the same token, mortgage lenders have found that the main reason for mortgage defaults is not lack of money to make monthly payments. It is lack of ***equity*** to create the ***incentive*** to make the payments. In other words, when a borrower concludes he has little or no equity in a property, he figures, "Why should I bust my butt managing the place and sending money to the mortgage lender?" And he walks away from the property.

In insurance, if you have a $1,000 deductible and you suffer an $800 loss, the insurance company loses nothing. By the same token, if you own real estate with an 80% loan-to-value ratio loan on it, and it drops in value by 10%, the lender suffers no loss. But if the insured's loss ***exceeds*** the deductible, or the borrower's loss in value ***exceeds*** his equity, the insurance company or lender suffers.

A lender who makes mortgage loans to borrowers who have no equity in the property is like an insurance company who writes policies with no deductibles. Such lenders and insurance companies would quickly go bankrupt.

Character and capacity or imprudence

You get unsecured loans by either convincing the lender that your deal offers so much character and capacity that they don't ***need*** any more sub-75%-of-value collateral...or by finding a lender who will make an imprudent loan. As I said in the seller loan chapter, there are some sophisticated lenders who will make imprudent loans. And if they're smart enough to know better, you can't be blamed for taking advantage of their imprudence. I covered finding imprudent sophisticated lenders in the seller loan chapter. In this chapter, I'll concentrate on the techniques which offer the lender mucho character and capacity.

Can you get an unsecured loan? Sure you can. You probably have a couple on your balance sheet right now. From credit card loans. Or maybe a bank personal loan. But those loans are not very ***big*** compared to the real estate loans you have or plan to get.

That's because the amount of money you can borrow on an ***un***secured basis is much less than you can borrow on a ***secured*** basis. Roughly speaking, you can borrow about 10% of your net worth on an unsecured basis. No collateral. Just your character and debt-carrying capacity providing the lender's safety. Although unsecured loans require shorter terms like three to five years. Only governments and major corporations can borrow long-term unsecured money.

So if you have a net worth of $750,000, you can borrow about $75,000 unsecured...for three to five years. That's enough to buy one median priced house.

If you have a net worth of $100 billion, you can get an unsecured loan big enough to let you buy just about any piece of real estate there is. Now I know ***you*** don't have a net worth that big. But the ***U.S. government*** does. And they not only borrow hundreds of billions on an unsecured basis. They'll also lend their awesome borrowing capacity to ***you.***

The government does that through various ***mortgage insurance programs***. For example, a bank will loan you up to 100% of the value of a home you plan to occupy...if the VA guarantees the loan. As I said above, that's a *secured* loan to the tune of 80% of the property value...and an "*un*secured" loan for the other 20%.

Why is the bank willing to make that 20% "unsecured" loan? Because the United States government in the form of the Veterans Administration is co-signing. The bank will loan the U.S. government all the unsecured money the government wants at mortgage interest rates.

Where to get the extra character and capacity you need

The character and capacity you need to convince the lender to make the above 75%-of-value or "unsecured" loan can come from

- agree to personal liability
- bring in partners who will agree to personal liability
- mortgage insurance like FHA, VA, or private mortgage insurance
- surety bonds as in construction lending
- high credit tenants like government agencies or investment grade corporations on long-term leases

You can legitimately get a high leverage loan only if the borrower(s) or other person(s) or entity(ies) which agree(s), directly or indirectly, to pay the loan has character and capacity so large that they would qualify for the above-75%-to-80% portion of the loan on an *un*secured basis.

That's a long sentence. Let me now break it down to explain it.

By saying "borrower(s) or other person(s) or entity(ies)," I mean to include you, your partners, co-signers, mortgage insurors, surety bond companies, etc. Anyone or any organization which promises to pay the loan or part of it.

By saying "indirectly," I mean to include ***long-term tenants***. As I said in the chapter on character and capacity techniques, a properly written, long-term lease signed by a high credit tenant enables you to get higher than normal loan-to-value ratios.

For example, if you have a properly written long-term lease with IBM, IBM is indirectly agreeing to pay the mortgage. Because if you default on the loan, the lender or other new owner after foreclosure can simply get the money to cover the mortgage payments from IBM's rent check (assuming it's enough to cover both the mortgage payments and operating expenses).

Do mortgage insurance agencies and companies have the character and capacity to borrow huge sums on an unsecured basis? You bet. They do it all the time. Do high credit tenants like IBM or the State of Texas have the character and capacity to borrow huge sums on an unsecured basis? You bet. They also do it all the time.

So you can buy property with a less than normal down payment if the property in question is quite small in relation to your net worth. Or, barring that, you can buy property with a less than normal down payment if the government or IBM or some such provides the lender with direct or indirect security.

High leverage deals involving new institutional money

Most high leverage finance techniques rely on ***seller financing***. But many involve a combination of seller financing and a new loan from an institution like a bank or savings and loan. And some high leverage techniques rely ***totally*** on new loans from institutions.

It is possible to legitimately do a high leverage deal involving new institutional money. As I said earlier, when someone who is promising...directly or indirectly... to pay the loan has so much financial strength that they would qualify for the loan in question on an *un*secured basis. Like a buyer with a big net worth buying a little property. Or an owner-occupant home buyer with mortgage insurance. Or a conventional loan on a property leased on a long-term basis to a high credit tenant.

But if such financial strength is ***not*** present, a high leverage deal involving new institutional money is almost certainly ***fraudulent***.

Institutional lenders don't do high leverage deals

Institutional lenders generally will not make a loan on a purchase where the buyer is also getting secondary financing or borrowing all or part of the down payment. It's not just ***their*** loan-to-value ratio institutional lenders care about. They also care very much about ***your*** loan-to-value ratio.

That's because they know from experience that the less equity you have, the greater the probability that you will default. And the greater the probability that the institutional lender will suffer a loss...even though their loan is at only 75% or 80% loan-to-value. FNMA did a study which found that loans with 10% to 19% down were ***three*** times riskier than loans with 20% or more down. And loans with less than 10% down were ***five*** times riskier than loans with 20% or more down.

When you apply for a mortgage, institutional lenders ask you

- what price you're paying
- how much you're putting down
- and where you are going to get the down payment from.

If you say you will have secondary financing ***above*** the 75% to 80% loan-to-value ratio...or that you are borrowing any part of the down payment on an ***un***secured basis...the lender will almost certainly turn you down.

FNMA's new, tighter standards

Due to increased foreclosures and the spread of "creative financing," the Federal National Mortgage Association announced tighter standards on August 5, 1985. FNMA only buys 11.5% of the home mortgages in the U.S. But virtually all lenders want to be ***able*** to sell their loans to FNMA, so virtually all lenders comply with FNMA rules.

1. If less than 10% down, total housing expense must not exceed 25% of gross income and total housing expenses plus installment debt payments must not exceed 33%.
2. No ARMs without interest rate caps.
3. No ARMs with graduated payments.
4. No buydowns greater than 3% of the sale price if less than 10% down. No buydowns greater than 6% of the sale price if 10% or more down. All payments by seller to buyer are considered buydowns. And any payment by seller of costs normally paid by buyer are buydowns. No buydowns on ARMs.
5. Co-borrower must be member of borrower's immediate family and must take title to the property. If less than 10% down, co-borrower must also ***occupy*** the property.
6. Buyer must make at least a 5% down payment from his own funds. ***Gifts*** cannot be the source of that 5%.
7. No investor or second home loans on which negative amortization is possible.
8. No refinancing on which negative amortization is possible.

No. 6 is interesting. They're saying equity is not enough. It has to be ***your*** equity. Your own hard-earned money. Apparently FNMA has observed an easy-come-easy-go phenomenon. That is, if the down money to buy the house came from a gift, the borrower has more of a tendency to walk away than if the same amount of money came out of his own earnings.

You usually have to lie to get new institutional money for high leverage deals

So in the vast majority of cases, in order to do a high leverage deal with new institutional financing, you must ***deceive*** the institutional lender. You must make them ***think*** their loan is the only loan you're using to buy the property.

It's not nice to fool Mother Nature. It's also not nice to fool a federal agency or a federally insured deposit institution. In fact, it's a violation of Title 18 United States Code Section 1014. If you look at the FNMA mortgage application elsewhere in this book you'll find that Code section mentioned where you sign your name certifying that all statements made in the application are true.

Title 18 United States Code Section 1014

Here's the pertinent wording of Title 18 United States Code Section 1014

Whoever knowingly makes any false statement or report, or willfully overvalues any land, property or security, for the purpose of influencing in any way the action of. . . any Federal intermediate credit bank, or any division, officer, or employee thereof, . . . a Federal Home Loan Bank, the Federal Home Loan Bank Board, the Home Owners' Loan Corporation, a Federal Savings and Loan Association, a Federal land bank, a small business investment company, a Federal credit union, an insured State-chartered credit union, any institution the accounts of which are insured by the Federal Savings and Loan Insurance Corporation, any bank the deposits of which are insured by the Federal Deposit Insurance Corporation, any member of the Federal Home Loan Bank System, the Federal Deposit Insurance Corporation, the Federal Savings and Loan Insurance Corporation, or the Administrator of the National Credit Union Administration, upon any application, . . . purchase, purchase agreement, commitment, or loan, or any change or extension of any of the same, by renewal, deferment of action or otherwise, or the acceptance, release, or substitution of security therefor, shall be fined not more than $5,000 or imprisoned not more than two years, or both.

The plain English translation of that is you can get two years in prison and a $5,000 fine if you make a false statement to a lender who has any connection with the Federal government. That's for ***each count***. In other words, if you make ***two*** false statements, you can get ***four*** years in prison and a $10,000 fine.

People really do go to jail for this stuff

Earlier in the book I told you that two guys who tried to buy President Reagan's house pleaded guilty to this crime. One got the max. The other got the max fine but only one year in jail.

A San Francisco condo converter recently got ***thirty years*** in the federal prison at Texarkana, Texas for making false statements to a federally insured deposit institution (Bank of America) in connection with mortgage applications. His 26-year old daughter also pleaded guilty to making false statement to a federally insured deposit institution. She got fined $2,000 and put on probation for five years.

And I told you of a couple from my neighborhood who recently got indicted by a San Francisco Federal grand jury on multiple counts involving mortgage loans and at least one no money down deal.

Between October 1, 1984 and March 31, 1985, the HUD Inspector General opened 429 investigations involving false statement allegations. On January 28, 1985, two Camden, New Jersey real estate company officials were convicted on 15 counts of making false statements, conspiracy, and mail fraud. A third had pled guilty earlier. As did one of the property buyers. The false statements were in purchase agreements, loan applications, inflated home repair costs, and settlement statements. Two received five years in prison, one a three-year prison sentence, and the property buyer had not been sentenced as of March 31, 1985.

On February 14, 1985, a federal grand jury indicted a VA Fee Appraiser in New Jersey on nine counts of making false statements to HUD and one count of conspiracy.

On March 22, 1985, three Marysville, Washington home builders pled guilty to submitting false statements to HUD. These were nothing down deals. Here's an exact quote from the HUD Inspector General's report.

"The three were charged with reporting down payments of 15 to 20% as required for non-occupant, HUD-insured investor loans, when in fact, they made no down payments. They defaulted on 76 loans..."

A Lombard, Illinois couple who owned a real estate firm submitted numerous false statements to HUD and the VA. He got two years in prison and five years probation; she got five years probation.

A Pennsylvania man and his partner submitted seven different Title I home improvement loan applications to seven different lenders on the same property. They received suspended prison sentences, probation and were required to make $30,000 restitution.

A San Antonio man left some of his liabilities off three property improvement loan applications. He got two years in prison and was order to pay restitution of $13,992.

Twenty-five people were indicted for making false statements on loan applications to three Dallas savings and loans. At least four of the 25 were indicted for listing real estate they owned at inflated values. These charges were the result of plea bargaining. So it is reasonable to suppose that they were threatened with more severe charges.

Geraldine Ferraro ran for vice-president in 1984. That threw the spotlight on her husband, John Zaccaro, a real estate investor and broker. He pleaded guilty to a misdemeanor charge of second-degree "scheming to defraud" in a real estate loan application to purchase apartment buildings.

He was charged under ***state***, not federal law. For stating that his net worth was $21.64 million when he "well knew" that it was $4 million. And for altering a copy of an appraisal by changing the date and addressee. And for submitting a false purchase agreement which showed a price of $15.5 million when in fact the purchase price was $11.98 million. He pleaded guilty to the first two charges and the third was plea bargained away. Zaccaro claimed he could successfully defend himself on the charges. But that he pleaded guilty to spare his family the publicity of prolonged legal proceedings. His real estate license was suspended for three months. And he was sentenced to 150 hours of community service. He could have received one year in jail and a $1,000 fine.

The May 12, 1985 issue of *Housing and Development Reporter* told of a Florida real estate developer whose conviction for "knowingly and willfully concealing the true purchase price" of a building he was buying was upheld by the Circuit Court of Appeals. He applied for a $2,225,000 loan on a building he was buying for $1,613,000. In that case, he was charged with a violation of Title 18 United States Code section 1001. That section says

Whoever in any matter within the jurisdiction of any department or agency of the United States knowingly and willfully falsifies, conceals or covers up by any trick, scheme, or device a material fact, or makes any false, fictitious or fraudulent statements or representations, or makes or uses any false writing or document knowing same to contain any false, fictitious or fraudulent statement or entry, shall be fined not more than $10,000 or imprisoned not more than five years, or both.

Note that section 1001 is a lot like section 1014...except that the punishment is more severe. So be advised that cheating a little on a mortgage application ain't spit ball. I've sat through "creative finance" seminars where they tell you how to mislead lenders to get the loan you want. And I've read "creative finance" books which tell you how to deceive institutional lenders regarding the amount of your down payment. You may have thought that if it's in a nationally known seminar or book, it must be OK.

Wrong.

Consumers are very protected in most areas of life. Go into a car dealership and you'll find all sorts of rules and regulations to protect you. The same is true in a restaurant or toy store or furniture store. But when you go to a ***seminar*** or ***book store***, you're on your own, baby. Because book stores, book publishers, seminar givers, and book authors come under the First Amendment. That's the one which says "Congress shall make no law...abridging the freedom of speech, or of the press..."

That means seminar speakers and book authors have the right to advocate a fraudulent "creative finance" technique and say that it is ***not*** fraudulent. Sounds amazing, doesn't it? But that's exactly what the Constitution says. You can say or print ***anything*** you want...as long as it's not libelous, an invasion of someone's privacy, or plagiarism.

Conspiracy and mail fraud, too

People who do high leverage deals involving new institutional money are probably guilty of ***three*** crimes...not just one. They are

- making a false statement to a federally insured deposit institution
- conspiracy
- mail fraud

The guys who tried to buy President Reagan's house in Pacific Palisades were ***convicted*** of making a false statement. But they were also ***charged*** with conspiracy and mail fraud. The U.S. Attorney dropped the conspiracy and mail fraud charges in an apparent plea bargain to get the defendants to plead guilty of making a false statement.

My neighbors who were indicted were indicted for both making a false statement and mail fraud. If you lie to a lender, there's a good chance you'll be charged with conspiracy and mail fraud, too. Here's how those crimes are defined in the United States Code.

Title 18 United States Code Section 371. Conspiracy to commit offense or to defraud United States

If two or more persons conspire...to defraud the United States, or any agency thereof in any manner or for any purpose, and one or more of such persons do any act to effect the object of the conspiracy, each shall be fined not more than $10,000 or imprisoned not more than five years, or both.

If, however, the offense, the commission of which is the object of the conspiracy, is a misdemeanor only, the punishment for such conspiracy shall not exceed the maximum punishment provided for such misdemeanor.

Who might the "two or more persons" be? You and a partner...as was the case in the Reagan house deal. Or you and the seller...since he receives the loan proceeds in a falsely obtained mortgage.

Title 18 United States Code Section 1341 Mail Fraud

Whoever, having devised or intending to devise any scheme or artifice to defraud, or for obtaining money or property by means of false or fraudulent pretenses, representations, or promises...for the purpose of executing such scheme or artifice or attempting to do so, places in any post office or authorized depository for mail matter, any matter or thing whatsoever to be sent or delivered by the Postal Service, or takes or receives therefrom, any such matter or thing, or knowingly causes to be delivered by mail according to the direction thereon, or at the place at which it is directed to be delivered by the person to whom it is addressed, any such matter or thing, shall be fined not more than $1,000 or imprisoned not more than five years or both.

Plain English translation: If you ***mail*** any of the papers which make false statements to a federally insured deposit institution, you add up to $1,000 to your fine and up to five years to your prison sentence. Or to put it another way, if you plan to do high leverage deals with new institutional financing, ***hand carry*** your application material to the lender. You'll get out of prison sooner.

You might even be charged with racketeering

If you commit mail fraud ***twice***, you can also be convicted of ***racketeering***. No kidding. Racketeering activity is defined in Title 18 United States Code section 1961. Mail fraud is specifically named as a racketeering activity. In order to be convicted for racketeering, you must be guilty of a "pattern of racketeering activity." A "pattern" is defined in subsection 5 of the law as "...at least two acts of racketeering activity...[within ten years]."

The penalties for racketeering are severe. Up to a $25,000 fine and/or twenty years in prison! I'll bet they didn't mention that at the "creative" finance seminar.

One more thing about racketeering. Only the government can charge you with violations of the other federal laws. But ***your fellow citizens***...like sellers and lenders...can file suit against you under the racketeering law. Section 1964 (c) of Title 18 says

Any person injured in his business or property by reason of violation of section 1962 of this chapter may sue therefor in any appropriate United States district court and shall recover threefold the damages he sustains and the cost of the suit, including a reasonable attorney's fee."

That's triple damages. Lots of incentive for an attorney to take the case on a contingency basis (no fee unless he wins).

How to guarantee you're not violating these laws

There is a simple way to make sure you're not violating the law against making false statements to federal agencies or federally insured deposit institutions when you do a high leverage deal. Tell the lender the ***truth, the whole truth, and nothing but the truth*** about the loan-to-value ratio.

There's nothing wrong with asking a lender to loan money in a high leverage deal. As long as you ***tell*** them it's a high leverage deal. As I say elsewhere in the book, I once did a deal with a 75% of value first mortgage from a savings and loan and a 10% of value second mortgage from the seller. But this was fully disclosed to the lender. They did the deal because of their relationship with the seller and his promise to put the sale proceeds in that s & l. And because the loan-to-value ratio still wasn't too bad at 85%.

Examples of probably fraudulent techniques

The following techniques...when used in conjunction with new institutional financing...probably violate the law against making false statements to federal lenders or federal mortgage insurors...unless the lender were told the ***whole truth*** about the deal.

- Money borrowed for purpose of deposit verification
- New 75%-of-value first and seller second
- Paying off existing loans at a discount
- Refinance which is in fact part of a sale
- Using vacation loan for down payment
- Credit card down payment
- "Changing your mind" about the source of the down payment between loan application and closing
- Substantial rebate from seller to buyer
- "Paper" down payment
- Simultaneous borrowing from more than one institution even if unsecured
- Using home improvement loan for down payment
- Unsecured financing from seller or other private lender

Again, there's nothing wrong with any of the above ***if they are fully disclosed to the lender.*** You only run the risk of a making-a-false-statement conviction if statements you make in conjunction with the mortgage application do not give the lender a true picture of the deal.

Cash at closing deals

In the "arms race" of real estate seminar land, the latest I-can-top-your-seminar technique is techniques which not only allow the buyer to purchase a property for nothing down...the buyer puts cash in his pocket at closing! It is next to impossible to do that legally.

The California Department of Real Estate says it believes failure to make mortgage or tax payments after closing such a deal shows the deal was entered into with fraudulent intent. Some

California district attorneys have filed criminal charges against buyers who bought property in a deal in which they got cash at closing then walked away from the property.

And the California Department of Real Estate has advised California real estate agents that failure to properly advise the sellers of the dangers in cash-at-closing sales may result in either disciplinary action by the Department of Real Estate or a lawsuit by the seller or both.

Lenders will almost always refuse to make a mortgage which results in the borrower pocketing excess loan proceeds. As a result, you'd almost always have to lie to the lender to get such a loan. That's a felony. Multiple felonies if you use the mail or have a partner.

The legitimate high leverage techniques

Here are the legitimate techniques for achieving high leverage with ***new*** mortgages.

- VA or FHA owner-occupied purchase or refinance
- FHA non-owner-occupant purchase or refinance
- Private mortgage insurance
- Seller take back by ***sophisticated*** seller
- Buyer is personally liable on the loan and can qualify for amount of loan above 75% loan-to-value ratio on an *un*secured basis
- Co-signer who is personally liable on the loan and can qualify for amount of loan above 75% loan-to-value ratio on an *un*secured basis
- Property leased long term to high credit tenant
- Subordination by ***sophisticated lender*** of existing mortgage to new first mortgage
- Substitution of collateral agreed to by ***sophisticated*** lender where resulting loan-to-value ratio on substituted collateral will be above 75%
- Additional collateral agreed to by ***sophisticated*** lender where resulting loan-to-value ratio on all collateral will be above 75%
- Loan based on ***future*** value after projected value-increasing action.

Here are the legitimate techniques for achieving high leverage with ***existing*** mortgages.

- Assumption or subject to of high leverage mortgage on which seller does ***not*** have personal liability
- Assumption or subject to of high leverage mortgage on which a ***sophisticated*** seller ***does*** have personal liability.

Note that I have restricted the technique to ***sophisticated*** sellers or lenders ***only*** whenever the high leverage technique in question results in increased risk to that party.

Portfolio versus property leverage

Earlier in the book, I noted that the loan-to-value ratio on your ***entire portfolio*** is the only way to evaluate your leverage. Many so-called no money down techniques give you a 100% loan-to-value ratio as to the acquisition of a ***single property*** but only slightly increase your ***portfolio*** loan-to-value ratio...like getting a second on a property with a lot of equity and using the loan proceeds as down payment on another property.

It is possible to achieve a high loan-to-value ratio on your entire portfolio ***early in your career.*** For example, if you are a veteran and buy your first property with a no-money-down VA mortgage, your entire portfolio has a 100% loan-to-value ratio. If you then move out and buy another duplex with an FHA, owner-occupied loan, your ***portfolio*** loan-to-value ratio would be up in the 90% to 95% range...assuming your VA property had appreciated a little.

High *portfolio* loan-to-value ratios are harder to achieve as you get bigger

But the more property you own, the ***harder*** it is to keep your ***portfolio*** loan-to-value ratio high. That applies not only to little old you. It also applies to high credit entities like governments and IBM. The higher ***their*** loan-to-value ratio gets, the harder it is for ***them*** to borrow, too. The whole ***reason*** they have high credit is because they do ***not*** have high loan-to-value ratios.

New York City is big. And for years they had a top credit rating. But they borrowed and borrowed and borrowed. As a result, they had an undeclared bankruptcy in the mid-seventies. And could only borrow the money they needed by getting the federal government to co-sign. The government bailout of New York City in the mid-seventies took the form of loan guarantees. Ditto Lockheed and Chrysler which had borrowed too much and thereby killed their ability to borrow more without federal government guarantees.

If *any* government or corporation increases its loan-to-value ratio, Moody's and Standard & Poors bond rating services will, after a point, lower their credit rating. . .from AAA to AA and so forth. Each lowering ***increases*** that entity's cost of borrowing. Ultimately, their rating would be so low that their bonds (loans) would be unsaleable. In other words, no one would loan them any more money. Too high a loan-to-value ratio.

Little guys find it easiest to achieve a high portfolio loan-to-value ratio

So paradoxical as it may seem, ***little*** guys find it easiest to achieve high loan-to-value ratios across their entire portfolios. . .except, of course, for ***fraudulent deals*** in which lenders are ***misled*** as to the loan-to-value ratio of the borrower.

Bank of America recently fell prey to one of those when they took a $95 million loss on bad mortgages on apartment buildings in Texas. Bank of America ***thought*** the loans were secure because they had ***appraisals*** showing decent loan-to-value ratios and because they had ***mortgage insurance***. But the appraisals were inflated and the mortgage insuror failed to pay Bank of America's claims.

Large investors can achieve high leverage on their entire portfolio in some cases

A ***large*** investor ***could*** achieve a high loan-to-value ratio on his entire portfolio using some of the legitimate techniques listed above. For example, if he owned only ***post offices*** leased long-term to the federal government, mortgage lenders would probably loan him as much as the lease payments could cover.

But long-term leases wipe out one of the main benefits of leverage. . .magnification of appreciation. There ain't no appreciation on a long-term leased property. . .unless there are escalation clauses which raise the owner's ***net*** income. (Escalation clauses which raise the ***gross*** but not the net add nothing to building value.) The owner only gets the benefit of appreciation in property value when the long-term lease nears its end. But then it's a ***short-term*** lease. And can no longer be highly leveraged.

And high credit tenants don't like to pay much rent. So what you ***gain*** in leverage through magnified tax benefits, you may ***lose*** in reduced appreciation and cash flow. There is no free lunch.

Tax benefits *are* magnified in high-credit, long-term leased property

Note that you ***would*** still get magnification of the ***tax*** benefits on a highly leveraged property leased long-term to a high credit tenant. Although watch out if the tenant is a ***tax exempt*** entity like a government or charity or non-profit organization. The Tax Reform Act of 1984 restricted the depreciation deductions you are allowed to take on property leased long-term to such entities.

Lots of sophisticated sellers willing to make dumb loans

You could also be a large investor with a high loan-to-value ratio across your entire portfolio if you could find a lot of those sophisticated sellers I described earlier. . .and persuade them to make high leverage. . .and therefore dumb from their standpoint. . .loans to you. Such sellers ***can*** be found. Because emotion and ego cloud the judgment of even sophisticated people. And emotion and ego run high in real estate deals.

Lots of high leverage, no personal liability subject tos

Another legitimate way to achieve a large, high leverage portfolio would be to specialize in buying only properties with high loan-to-value ratio, assumable, mortgages on which the seller is not personally liable. When the seller ***is*** personally liable, you'd have to make sure he was sophisticated. . . which puts you back in the lots-of-sophisticated-sellers-willing-to-do-dumb-deals category.

This strategy works in areas with lots of VA and FHA home mortgages. The ***dis***advantage is that these are mostly on single-family homes. And the economics of single-family rental homes are such that they typically have much worse cash flow than apartment buildings and such. So the ***good news*** is that you can achieve a high leverage portfolio by buying lots of homes with FHA and VA mortgages. The ***bad news*** is that it's hard to get enough rent to pay the mortgages on such properties.

So what you ***gain*** in leverage through magnified appreciation and tax benefits, you may ***lose*** in negative cash flow. There is no free lunch.

Is this the way to create wealth?

Bob Allen is the author of the best-selling books *Nothing Down* and *Creating Wealth*. In those books, he rarely runs the numbers out. That is, he rarely shows how you will make a profit on the deal. Rather, there's just a sort of blanket assumption that owning real estate is profitable. Therefore, the more you buy, the more profit you make.

It ain't that simple.

One of the rare occasions in which he ***does*** run the numbers out is on page 163 of *Creating Wealth*. There he tells of buying a property for $52,000. He bought subject to a $32,000 FHA mortgage. And the seller took back a second for $19,000. The other $1,000 was Allen's down payment.

The interest rate on the seller second was 11%. But there were ***no monthly payments***. That is, the 11% interest accrued into a balloon payment due on the fifth anniversary of the purchase. By then, Allen admits, the second mortgage would have grown from $19,000 to $32,849 due to the interest accruing at 11%. And the first mortgage would be paid down to about $30,000. That means the total loans on the property at the end of the five years would be $30,000 + $32,849 = $62,849.

The appreciation rate better be high

So what's the property worth then? Allen assumes 10% appreciation per year. And comes up with a value after five years of $85,000. At which time he refinances to pay the balloon payment.

But what if the appreciation rate is ***not*** 10%? What if it's 4%? If the property is worth $52,000 on day one and appreciates at 4% per year, it'll be worth $63,265.95 in five years. That's only $63,265.95 - $62,849 = $416.95 more than the loan balances on that date! And although you may be able to avoid paying a commission on the sale of the property, closing costs would almost certainly wipe out that $416.95.

Note that Bob Allen is from the Salt Lake City area. According to Jane Bryant Quinn's July 8, 1985 *Newsweek* column, the appreciation rate in Salt Lake City for the year ending in March of 1985 was ***minus*** two tenths of a percent.

Can't refinance if only 4% appreciation per year

Refinancing ain't gonna work unless, it's a single-family home, you are an owner-occupant veteran, and you can refinance 100% of value. But even then, what's the point? You put out all the effort, $1,000 down payment, and closing costs required to buy, manage, and refinance the property for five years for what? Some tax deductions? And maybe a little positive cash flow. You may well find it more profitable to spend those five years working part-time shoveling french fries at McDonalds.

And when you factor in the fact that you probably ***overpaid*** in order to get a $1,000/$52,000 = 2% down deal, the numbers look even worse.

Note that Allen considers the possibility that "the market is bad in five years." It doesn't have to be bad. Four percent appreciation isn't bad...unless you have very high leverage.

Sell to *another* nothing down buyer?

Allen's recommended solution in the event of a "bad" market five years hence is to sell the property on a "nothing down" basis. Specifically, Allen has the after-five-years buyer buying the property for $85,000 (Because no money down buyers pay 34% more than market value, I guess. $85,000 is 34% more than $63,265.95.). The buyer gets a new $65,000 mortgage from an institutional lender, and Allen, as seller, takes back a $20,000 second.

I got a couple questions about that solution:

1. How are you gonna get an $85,000 appraisal if, as in my 4% appreciation example, the value only goes up to $63,265.95?
2. What answer will the after-five-years buyer give the institutional lender to the question, "How much are you putting down?"

Seems to me that if the appreciation rate is only 4% per year...giving a $63,000 value...you will ***not*** get a bank appraiser to agree to an $85,000 appraisal...regardless of what the purchase agreement says. And it also seems to me that if the nothing down nature of the sale is ***disclosed*** to the institutional lender, they will ***not*** approve the loan. If the nothing down nature of the deal is ***not*** disclosed to the institutional lender, how do the buyer and the seller avoid violating the laws against making a false statement to a federal agency or federally insured deposit institution and conspiracy?

Walk away from the property

Another alternative Allen cites is "to give the property back to the seller." In other words, a deed in lieu of foreclosure. I will point out that investing $1,000 plus closing costs plus five years of management effort into a property, only to give the property back to the seller, is hardly a way to "create wealth."

I will also point out that the FNMA/FHLMC mortgage application (reproduced elsewhere in this book) has on its front side the question,

"Have you ever had property foreclosed or given title or deed in lieu thereof?"

If you follow Mr. Allen's advice to "give the property back to the seller," you will henceforth answer "yes" to that question. That question also appears on most other mortgage applications. If you answer, "yes," you will generally be turned down. At the very least, you will be required to explain the circumstances. If you are able to get future institutional mortgages at all after giving a property back to the seller, it will only be when lenders are flush with funds.

Finally, I will point out the ***tax*** consequences of giving the property back to the seller. For tax purposes, foreclosure or deed in lieu of foreclosure is considered a ***sale*** of the property. With the amount of the debt that is forgiven being the sale price. As with any sale, you must compute your gain and pay tax on it. What's your gain in this example?

Your taxable gain if you walk away

Let's say that $45,000 of the original $52,000 purchase price was depreciable improvements and $7,000 was undepreciable land. And we'll assume that you bought the property in January of 1985. Under the ACRS table in effect then, you'd have deducted 9% the first year, 9% the second, 8% the third, 7% the fourth, and 7% the fifth. That's a total of 40%. Forty percent of $45,000 is $18,000. So your adjusted basis after five years would be $52,000 - $18,000 = $34,000.

Your "sale price" is $63,265.95. Your adjusted basis is $34,000. So your gain is $63,265.95 -$34,000 = $29,265.95. If you used accelerated depreciation, as I have assumed in this example, you'd have to pay ***recapture***. Recapture means that you must pay tax at ***ordinary income tax rates*** on the excess of the depreciation you claimed over what you ***would have*** claimed if you had taken straight line depreciation.

In this case, the annual straight line depreciation deduction would be $45,000/18 years = $2,500. Five years worth of that would be 5 x $2,500 = $12,500. In fact, you claimed $18,000 of depreciation. So you had $18,000 - $12,500 = $5,500 of excess depreciation. That $5,500 will be taxed at ordinary income rates. The other $34,000 - $5,500 = $28,500 of your gain will be taxed at long-term capital gains rates (unless you trigger the alternative minimum tax or are a dealer).

If you're in the 30% bracket, giving the property back to the seller will cost you

Recapture: 30% x $5,500 = $1,650
Capital gain: 40% x 30% x$28,500 = $3,420
Total tax: $1,650 + $3,420 = $5,070

Gains tax must be paid even though no sale proceeds

You must pay that $5,070 in income taxes for the year in which you gave the property back to the seller. You must pay it even though there really was no sale. You must pay it even though there were no sale proceeds. And according to the U.S. Supreme Court's *Tufts* decision (51 U.S.L.W. 4518), you must pay it even if the market value of the property at the time you gave it back was ***less than*** the loan balance.

So, yes, you can give the property back to the seller. That won't make you rich. And, in this example, it'll cost you over $5,000 in income taxes.

Lest you think the IRS might not find out...be advised that the Tax Reform Act of 1984 added section 6050J to the Internal Revenue Code. That section requires sellers and other lenders who foreclose or receive deeds in lieu of foreclosure or become aware of abandonment of property they sold to notify the IRS of the details. The same way banks are required to notify the IRS of interest paid to you.

Run the numbers out before you do a high leverage deal

The main point I want to make is that high leverage deals ***may not be a good investment***. The no-money-down movement was born in the late seventies...when appreciation rates were 10% or higher.

When appreciation is 10%, no money down makes sense. But it generally does ***not*** make sense when appreciation rates are 4%. If you run the numbers out for your entire holding period, you'll see this.

So don't accept the notion that real estate is so wonderful that the more you own the better. Do the numbers.

Leverage has a tipping point

There's a tipping point in leverage. Up to that point, more borrowing makes things better. But ***after*** that point, more borrowing ***reduces*** return. Obviously, you should not go past that point.

Howard Ruff says you should either buy real estate with ***all*** cash down or ***no*** cash down. That's very glib. But it's also nonsense. When you start out, you should take advantage of several of the mortgage insurance programs for owner-occupant home purchases. But after that, your down payments should probably be in the 15% to 25% range.

There are two very basic ideas behind leverage. Ideas which many real estate investors either don't know or forget about. Number one: Leverage only has good effects when the percentage return on the investment is greater than the interest rate on the loan used to buy that investment. Number two: You gotta be able to make the payments.

The cap rate is the starting point

If you buy an apartment building or other income property with 25% down, you can either break even or make a small positive cash flow. That is ***not*** true for single-family homes or even two- or three-family buildings as a general rule. With 25% down, the typical one- to three-family rental property would have negative cash flow. That's because income properties have higher capitalization rates than smaller properties

Apartment buildings, for example, typically sell for five to nine times gross income. And they have operating expense ratios (all operating expenses divided by gross income) of 35% to 50%.

Single-family homes, on the other hand, typically sell for 120 to 200 times monthly income. Or 120/12 to 200/12 = 10 to 16.67 times ***annual*** gross. And they have operating expense ratios in the 20% to 50% range. So here's how the cap rates would compare.

Apartments with $100,000 gross annual income would have, say, a 42.5% expense ratio or $42,500 in operating expenses leaving net operating income of $100,000 - $42,500 = $57,500. That same building would sell for, say, seven times gross or $700,000. So the capitalization rate or cap rate would be $57,500/$700,000 = 8.21%. A single-family home with $10,000 a year gross income would have, say, a 35% expense ratio or $3,500 in operating expenses leaving net operating income of $6,500. That home would sell for, say, 13 times gross annual income or $130,000. So the cap rate would be $6,500/$130,000 = 5%.

The cap rate is the cash-on-cash return the property would earn if you bought it free and clear. If you paid $700,000 cash for the apartment building and had no mortgage payments, you'd pocket $57,500 per year for an 8.21% return on your cash investment. The house, free and clear, would only give you a 5% return.

Free and clear overall return must exceed mortgage interest rate

Neither 8.21% nor 5% is greater than today's mortgage rates...even on seller loans or assumptions. Does that mean you are always better off paying all cash? No. But it does mean that the ***cash flow*** portion of your return will always be ***worsened*** by borrowing.

The reason it makes sense to use leverage in real estate is because your ***overall*** return is usually greater than the mortgage interest rate. For example, a free and clear apartment building with an 8.21% cap rate and a 4% appreciation rate generates a total return from cash flow and appreciation of 8.21% + 4% = 12.1%. Can you get mortgages for less than 12.1%? Yes. If you use seller financing or subject tos. Plus, you get additional return from tax savings on your non-real estate income due to depreciation deductions.

But a free and clear house with a 5% cap rate and a 4% appreciation rate only generates a total return from cash flow and appreciation of 9%. That is ***not*** high enough to clear the interest rate you'll have to pay on the mortgage.

Leveraged rental houses OK for high bracket investors

Again there are tax benefits. And if you are in a ***high*** bracket, your overall return will exceed the mortgage interest rate on a single-family rental house...although it would be even better on an income property. So high bracket investors ***can*** magnify their return on a single-family rental house if they use leverage.

Unfortunately, I suspect that most of the no money down seminar attendees and book buyers are ***not*** in high tax brackets. That means that borrowing...whether it be 75% of value or 100% of value will do nothing but ***depress*** their return over what it would have been if they had paid all cash. The only way they are going to make a profit on the deal is if appreciation rates kick way up.

How to calculate the break even point for leverage

Look at what cranking up the leverage does to cash flow. Let's assume you can get an overall mortgage interest rate of 11%. That might be a seller mortgage or wraparound. Or a combination of buying subject a 9% first and a seller second at 12%. Or whatever.

The break even point (cash flow of zero) is the net operating income divided by the mortgage constant. The constant, you'll recall, is the annual principal and interest payments divided by the loan amount. On a 30-year 11% $100,000 mortgage, the monthly payments would be $924.40 or 12 x $924.40 = $11,092.81 per year. So an 11% 30-year mortgage has a constant of $11,092.81/$100,000 = 11.09281%.

With that mortgage, the break even point on the apartment building would be $57,500/11.09281% = $518,353.78. In other words, a $518,353.78 mortgage at 11% for 30 years would require annual principal and interest payments of $57,500...which is the same as the net operating income...so you'd break even.

The break even point on the house would be $6,500/11.09281% = $58,596.51.

Converting to loan-to-value ratios, you hit break even on the apartment building when the loan-to-value ratio hits $518,353.78/$700,000 = 74%. And you hit break even on the house when your loan-to-value ratio hits $58,596.51/$130,000 = 45%. With lower loan-to-value ratios, you'd have ***positive*** cash flow. And with ***higher*** loan-to-value ratios, you'd have ***negative*** cash flow.

Either negative cash flow or negative amortization

When you leverage up ***above*** the break even loan-to-value ratio, you get either negative cash flow or negative amortization (the amount you owe goes up every month). Generally, the "creative finance" gurus tell you that their techniques will ***not*** generate negative cash flow. That's because they generally recommend accruing interest. That's how Bob Allen avoided negative cash flow in that example I did a few pages ago.

But accruing interest simply substitutes negative amortization for negative cash flow. It's like the Fram oil filter commercial...you can pay me now or you can pay me later. Negative amortization has a slight present value advantage over negative cash flow...if you use a discount rate higher than the interest rate on the mortgage. But negative cash flow and negative amortization are six of one and a half dozen of the other for most purposes.

Negative cash flow and negative amortization eat return like Pac Man

The main problem with negative cash flow or negative amortization is that both eat away at the overall return. When that happens, leverage is magnifying return all right. ***But in the wrong direction!***

In the Allen example, the negative amortization ate up virtually all the appreciation if you assume 4% inflation. And look what happens if you leverage my $130,000 house example up to 100% of value or nothing down. The monthly payments on a $130,000 11% 30-year mortgage are $1,238.02, 12 x $1,238.02 = $14,856.24 a year.

You've only got $6,500 of net operating income on that house. So your negative cash flow would be $6,500 - $14,856.24 = $8,356.24 a year. Or if you accrued it, your cash flow would be break even and your negative amortization would be $8,356.24 a year. $8,356.24 is 6.43% of the purchase price of $130,000. So the house would have to appreciate at a rate of 6.43% per year just to keep the negative amortization from eating up not only all the appreciation but also part of the tax benefits.

Little or nothing *in* equals little or nothing *out*

If the house appreciates at *less* than 6.43%...which has been the case since 1979...every day you get another day older and deeper in debt. Since you have to overpay for a property to get it on a nothing down basis, the situation is even worse. Because you start out with ***negative equity*** as measured by an appraisal rather than the zero equity stated in the purchase agreement.

So where's the return? You've got no cash flow, no appreciation that isn't consumed by negative amortization, and your tax benefits are partially consumed by the negative amortization which exceeds the appreciation. Unless the appreciation rate kicks up to where the value exceeds the growing loan balance, you'll be forced to walk away when the balloon payment due date arrives. And that walking away will trigger an income tax liability which will consume all or most of the tax benefits you got during the five-year holding period.

What's the point? You bust your butt to find the rare seller who will sell on a nothing down basis. For five years or so you put up with all the hassles of managing the property. You can't escape without paying IRS. All you get are five years worth of depreciation deductions. Will that make you rich? Is it even worth the time and effort? I think not. I think flipping burgers at Wendy's at $5 an hour for the same number of years would be more profitable.

Buying property with little or no money down is simply a speculation that the appreciation rates of the late seventies might return. If they do not, buying real estate with little or no money down is wheel spinning at best and an actual cash loss at worst.

You might even lose your depreciation deductions

I've got another bit of news you'll never hear at a "creative finance" seminar. If you buy property with little or no money down. . .and no personal liability. . .IRS may say that you are ***not the owner***. That means no depreciation deductions.

How can they do that? The legal doctrine of substance over form. A purchase with little or no money down. . .and no personal liability. . .and a balloon payment. . .resembles a lease option more than a purchase.

An option gives you the ***right*** but not the obligation to buy a property within a certain time period. In a little or no money down deal, the small down payment and transfer of management responsibilities to the "buyer" looks a lot like an option payment and lease arrangement. And the non-recourse balloon payment looks a lot like exercising an option.

Does the "buyer" have the ***right*** to buy the property within a certain period of time? Yes, if he pays the balloon payment. Is he ***obligated*** to make the balloon payment? No. Since he has no personal liability, he can walk away. . .just as an option buyer can walk away and not exercise his option. In the book, *Construction and Development Financing*, author Richard Harris said, "If the seller [who takes back a loan] foregoes the right of personal recourse against the buyer,. . .the transaction approaches the economic and legal equivalent of an option."

In other words, the little or no down payment/no personal liability approach pushes the deal so far in the direction of no risk for the buyer that it may push it outside the realm of a purchase. And if you don't ***own*** the property, you can't depreciate it.

Who says so?

Have there been any IRS pronouncements or court decisions on this? Yes. The IRS warned that it would not accept inflated purchase prices in deals with nonrecourse financing in Revenue Ruling 69-77.

And in the case of *Franklin* (64 TC 752, 544 F 2d 1045 9th Circuit), the court said a taxpayer with inflated nonrecourse debt had ***not*** purchased the property. Rather he only had obtained a ten-year option to purchase it. Therefore no depreciation deductions.

In the Franklin case, the claimed purchase price appears to have been inflated more than in the typical no money down deal. But on the other hand, the taxpayer had made a $75,000 cash down payment. With little or no money down, the courts may not need as much inflation in the purchase price to label the deal a lease-option rather than a purchase.

Or IRS may say the "lender" is really your partner

In the alternative, IRS could say that the "lender" is really your partner. In *The Law of Real Estate Financing* by Madison and Dwyer (Warren, Gorham & Lamont), they list seven criteria which are relevant for deciding whether a lender is a lender or really a partner. One is "In the case of nonrecourse financing, is the loan-to-value ratio reasonably low?" 100% is ***not*** reasonably low. Madison and Dwyer refer readers to the case *Hambeuchen*, 43 TC 77 for an example of where a high loan-to-value ratio, nonrecourse loan contributed to a lender being designated a partner for tax purposes.

Another question they ask to tell a lender from a partner is "Does the transaction have independent economic significance or is tax avoidance the motivating reason for the transaction?" In the numbers I ran above, I showed that the only benefit the owner of a single-family rental house gets is tax benefits. So such investors might have a hard time convincing IRS or a court that they really did borrow any money. No kidding.

One more criteria Madison and Dwyer point to is who bears the risk of decline in property value? In a nonrecourse, nothing down deal, the ***seller*** is the only one who suffers if the property value goes down. The buyer has no money at risk. The seller is left holding the bag.

The tax consequences of the lender being declared a partner

What are the tax consequences of that? What you thought was deductible interest becomes ***non***deductible dividends. That's a biggie, isn't it?

Each partner may claim depreciation...but according to his contribution to the partnership. What was your contribution? Nothing, remember? You did a nothing down deal. So your depreciation deductions are also nothing. The "lender" contributed the property to the partnership, so he gets ***all*** the depreciation deductions. That's another biggie.

Finally, there's the matter of your failure to file partnership tax returns for five years. They charge penalties for that.

High leverage can make sense if appreciation rates are high enough

Note that I assumed 4% appreciation in the numbers above. That gave you a before-tax free-and-clear return of 12.1% on the income property and 9% on the single-family rental house. That makes the use of leverage marginal for the income property owner unless he gets significant tax benefits. And it makes the use of leverage by a low bracket investor insane for a single-family rental house owner. But if that appreciation rate were ***higher***, use of leverage makes sense even for a low bracket, single-family rental house investor.

How might the appreciation rate be higher? One way is if the market in your area picked up. Boston and the New York area have had appreciation rates higher than 4% in recent years. But that is purely speculative. Not investing. No one knows whether high appreciation rates will continue in the Boston or New York areas. Nor does anyone know what the next Boston or New York will be. The nation is littered with the "bodies" of investors who thought they could forecast hot markets.

But there is another way your property might go up in value faster than 4%. Upgrading.

Upgrading means forced appreciation

By upgrading, I mean doing something to the property which increases its value. And not just renovation or other physical changes. I'm talking about everything from zoning changes to selling off excess land to kicking out terrible tenants, etc., etc. I won't go into any more detail here. I'm half finished a book tentatively titled *Techniques for Increasing the Value of Real Estate*. That entire book contains ways to upgrade a property.

Upgrading profitably is far easier said than done. But if you ***can*** upgrade profitably, your appreciation rate will be much higher than 4%. And that means you should use leverage on one- to three-family properties even if you are in a low tax bracket.

Leverage is a no no for low bracket, non-upgrader rental house investors

But according to the numbers as I see them, if you are a low tax bracket investor who does ***not*** have upgrading skills, leverage will ***reduce*** your real estate investment return.

That's a rather shocking difference from what the "creative finance" crowd says. But it's simple arithmetic. Not opinion. The "creative finance" crowd generally does not ***dispute*** these numbers. They simply don't mention them. If you think I'm wrong, do a little five-year projection and show me where I'm wrong. Send it to John T. Reed, 342 Bryan Drive, Danville, CA 94526.

In order to do that, you'll have to assume significantly better cap rates...or significantly higher appreciation rates. To convince me of either of those, you'll need to show me a real world example.

Wonder drug or just useful drug?

When I started out as an investor, high leverage excited me. I was always trying to do high leverage deals. And I *did* do a bunch. But as I got more experienced, my views on high leverage matured and changed.

The public and press frequently refers to a particular drug as a "wonder drug." But medical doctors don't talk that way. They look at the same drug and see its uses, its contraindications (situations when it should ***not*** be used), and its side effects.

That difference between the public's "wonder drug" image and the doctors' more balanced view describes what has happened to me over the years regarding leverage. And I hope it has happened to you as you read through this book. Leverage is a useful investment technique. It almost always magnifies return on investment.

But as with wonder drugs, there are contraindications and side effects. So, like wonder drugs, it should not be used in ***all*** situations. And, like wonder drugs, more is not always better. You can easily take an overdose of leverage.

Contraindications

You should not use ***any*** leverage, let alone ***high*** leverage, when the overall return on the property if it were free and clear is less than the interest rate on the loan. In fact, you shouldn't invest in the property even on a free and clear basis if that's true. Invest in loans instead. You'll get a higher return.

And you should not use leverage which is so high or so structured that you cannot make all the payments.

The too-low return situation occurs on low cap rate properties like one- to three-family rental properties owned by low tax bracket investors. And it occurs on ***any*** property if you ***overpay***. The unable-to-make-payments situation occurs in ***any*** type property or with ***any*** tax bracket if you agree to a loan with an inadequate ***debt-coverage ratio*** to withstand normal dips in net operating income or if you agree to a ***too-soon balloon*** payment.

The myth about lenders not foreclosing if you owe them a lot

The more you owe them, the less likely lenders are to foreclose on you. That's one of the fairy tales you hear at "creative finance" seminars. The most recent time I heard it was in the July 15, 1985 issue of *Forbes*. In an article on fraudulent mortgage applications, one of the borrowers was quoted as saying, "What I think is that if you're on enough paper they can't afford to let you go down."

That always gets a big yuck at the seminars. Now let me tell you what really happens.

When you fall behind on a mortgage, the lender has you by the default clause. The interest, tax, and insurance meters continue to run. And ***new*** meters start to run...like the bank's foreclosure attorney's meter, a court costs meter. If you have any positive cash flow or any equity to speak of, the lender will foreclose. And the bills which have been run up since you stopped making payments will be paid out of the foreclosure sale proceeds.

Workouts

The situation in which the lender ***will*** refrain from foreclosure is called a "workout." Workouts are the kernel of truth which gave rise and credence to the lenders-won't-foreclose-if-you-owe-a-lot myth.

The best straight scoop I've ever seen on workouts is in *Construction and Development Financing* by Richard Harris (Warren, Gorham & Lamont).

It is in the lender's interest to do a workout (renegotiate the loan terms so you are no longer in default), if a couple of factors exist. One is an ***honest, competent borrower***. Another is ***lack of***

equity or cash flow which is adequate to service the debt.

If you've got nothing, the lender may let you keep it

Think logically. If the lender can get the money they need to cover the interest, taxes, and insurance from the property's net operating income, they will foreclose if you don't make the payments. They figure, if ***you*** won't make the payments, the ***property*** will. Alternatively, if you have any ***equity*** in the building, they can force a foreclosure sale and get the loan paid off in full. So why should they hesitate a moment if the cash flow or equity is lying there for the taking? The answer is they shouldn't and they won't.

The workout is not all concessions ***to*** the borrower. Typically, the lender will also demand concessions ***from*** the borrower as part of the renegotiation. Like a mortgage on your home and a lien on your car. Or escrowing of money to pay ***all operating expenses***, not just taxes and insurance. Or subordination of your future profits from the property to the lender's foreclosure expenses prior to the workout and extra administrative expenses after the workout in the event of such changes as an all-operating-expenses escrow account. Or ***personal liability*** if that was not already part of the original deal.

Does this all sound like the barrel of monkeys the "creative finance" gurus described?

If you'll work for nothing, they'll keep you on

Another perspective on the fact that lenders will sometimes agree to a workout rather than foreclose is why should they foreclose and have to manage the property when they've got a chump like you willing to do it for nothing? Remember that they ***will*** foreclose if there is positive cash flow or positive equity. The only time they'll let you stay on in a workout is if there is ***no cash flow or equity***. In which case, you're working for nothing...or at best you're working only for the speculative possibility that some day the property's equity will exceed the mounting debt. That's hardly the road to riches.

Finally, it's absurd to prescribe high leverage as the way to ***prevent*** foreclosure when high leverage is exactly what is likely to ***cause*** you to go into default. The ***proper*** advice is to avoid default in the first place. And the best way to do that is prudent debt-coverage and loan-to-value ratios.

Summary on high leverage

It is difficult to use high leverage without either exceeding prudent debt-coverage ratios or suffering ruinous negative amortization. But it ***can*** be done. By not going too far above the 75% loan-to-value ratio. By upgrading profitably. Etc.

It is also difficult to use high leverage without either making a false statement to a federally insured deposit institution or taking advantage of an unsophisticated seller in an unconscionable way. But it ***can*** be done. By using mortgage insurance. By buying properties leased long-term to high credit tenants. Etc.

The "creative finance" seminars you may have attended and the "creative finance" books you may have read often recommend techniques which are impractical or illegal. They typically omit huge quantities of important information like tax ramifications, ethical considerations, legal problems in enforcing vague subordination clauses, and so forth.

And they usually fail the "Where's the beef?" test. That is, where's the profit? Unless you have unusually high appreciation rates or cap rates, an investment real estate purchase with little or no down payment will almost certainly lose money.

PART TEN: TAKING BACK A LOAN WHEN YOU SELL

17 Why You Shouldn't

Don't take back a loan. . .ever

You should never take back a loan when you sell real estate. Never. I know you've heard many reasons why you should. I know most sellers ***do*** take back loans on income property. And that many home sellers do. . .especially when mortgage interest rates are high. But they're making a mistake. . .a mistake which you should not make.

Taxes are one of the biggest reasons

If you take back a mortgage, you have to pay tax on the sale. "But," you protest, "it's an ***installment sale.***"

Big deal. On a cash sale, you pay the tax in cash. On an installment sale, you pay the tax in installments. Is that supposed to be a good deal?

I've got a better idea. Don't pay ***any*** tax at all. How do you do that? Exchange.

A tax-free exchange and an installment sale are mutually exclusive

Most people think of installment sales and exchanges as two different tax avoidance techniques. Furthermore, most investors know that you can do both an installment sale and an exchange in the same deal.

That's true. So why do I say they're mutually exclusive?

Because when you combine an installment sale and an exchange, the installment sale portion of the deal is not a tax-free exchange. Combining an installment sale and an exchange is like doing two separate deals for tax purposes. The exchange is typically tax-free. But to the extent that you do an installment sale also, you pay taxes.

An exchange is where you go to closing with real estate and leave with real estate (you also typically exchange personal property like refrigerators). But if you go to closing with real estate and leave with real estate ***and*** a note you took back, the note is taxed.

It's called "boot" or "property which is not of like kind."

For more information on exchanges, see my book, *Aggressive Tax Avoidance For Real Estate Investors* (Reed Publishing, 342 Bryan Drive, Danville, CA 94526 $21.95 plus $2.50 for postage and packaging plus sales tax for California residents). There's also a section on installment sales in that book.

Don't sell. Don't do "sales" of any kind...including installment sales. Exchange instead.

Opportunity cost

The reason I say don't do a taxable installment sale is not because I hate taxes. Rather it's because paying taxes reduces your net worth dramatically...and it reduces the amount you have to put down on your next property. That means you have to buy a smaller building than you could have afforded if you had exchanged and avoided the tax. Typically, we're talking about tens of thousands, hundreds of thousands, or even millions of dollars in taxes.

The IRS isn't the only one who reduces the size of your next property. Tying money up in a mortgage does the same thing.

I exchanged out of a property with the following numbers once.

Sale price:	$665,000
Loan balance:	250,000

I sold via a buy down. That is I obtained at my expense a commercial second mortgage for the buyer.

If I had been willing to take back a mortgage, I probably could have gotten the following terms:

Sale price:	$740,000.00
Loan balance:	250,000.00
Down payment:	185,000.00
Second mortgage:	305,000.00

The way I ***did*** the deal, I got $425,000 in cash (actually it was an exchange so the equity moved into the new property not into cash). That enabled me to buy a building worth $425,000 x 4 = $1,700,000.

If I had done an installment sale, I'd have only had the $185,000 down payment ***less the tax payable on that amount*** to use as down payment. Let's just pick a number out of the air for the tax payable...say $30,000. That'd leave $185,000 - $30,000 = $155,000 to put down on my next building. That's enough to buy a $155,000 x 4 = $620,000 building.

So if I do an exchange and refuse to take back a mortgage, I become the owner of a $1,700,000 building and my net worth is unchanged. But if I do an installment sale, my net worth drops by the amount of tax I pay ($30,000 in this case) and I become the owner of a $620,000 building.

That building is less than half the value of the non-installment sale building. As a result, it will have less than half the appreciation, cash flow, tax shelter, and amortization as the $1,700,000 building.

So not only does the installment sale cost me taxes. I also suffer the opportunity costs of owning only a $620,000 building instead of a $1,700,000 building!

"But what if I HAVE to take back a mortgage to sell?"

A lot of sellers feel they ***have*** to take back a loan in order to sell their property. Especially when mortgage interest rates are high.

That's nonsense. You can ***always*** sell for all cash...if the price is right. If you are having trouble selling for all cash, your price must ***not*** be right. Lower it.

Actually, the ***buy down*** is the best idea. Theoretically, you could simply cut the price and get a cash buyer. But I tried it and it didn't work.

A Realtor told me the building I described above would sell for $720,000 if I took back a 75% wraparound at 10% for seven years. But he said, I'd have to drop the price to $600,000 to sell for cash. I dropped the price to $600,000 and listed it with him. The listing expired with no offers.

Then I put it up for sale myself...for $740,000...and I offered a 75% wraparound at 12% for five years. I sold it for $720,000 and agreed to extend the wrap term to seven years. The buyers agreed to a 25% down payment and the 12% interest rate.

I then explained to the buyers that I would not be the lender. Rather I would obtain the loan from a commercial lender. Buying it down if necessary.

I did. I won't go into the details of how it evolved here. But we ended up with a 17%, seven year second mortgage for $219,000 on top of buying subject to the existing first of about $250,000, a change in the price from $720,000 to $665,000, and an increase in the down payment from $180,000 to about $200,000. I had to pay four points to buy the second down to 17% from 18%...the lender's yield.

But note that I sold the building for $665,000 less four points or about $8,400 for a net sale price of $656,900...with no real estate commission. That's $56,600 ***more*** than I was ***unable*** to sell for through a Realtor several months earlier.

In other words, the building I couldn't sell for $600,000 on a get-your-own-mortgage basis sold for $660,000 when ***I*** got the mortgage. Note that the buyers could have saved themselves that $60,000 if ***they*** had bought the building for $600,000 and obtained the mortgage that I ended up getting for them.

And I had offered the building to those same buyers for $600,000 just before I listed it at that price. So they ***turned it down*** when offered for $600,000 with no financing but they ***bought*** it for $720,000...ultimately $665,000...when I offered to go get the financing for them.

The lesson is that buyers don't have the imagination to get their own financing...at least on income property deals. And since they are that unimaginative, you're probably better off offering to buy down a mortgage than offering the property for a low all-cash price.

Taking back a mortgage is self delusion

Sellers take back a mortgage because they're unwilling to reduce the price to what the property's really worth. And because they're unwilling to pay the points and put forth the effort necessary to get a commercial loan for their buyers.

Earlier in the book, I showed you how to calculate the ***true*** price of a property. How to eliminate the smokescreen of below-market interest rate financing...like seller financing. Same thing applies to ***your*** taking back a loan. Your ***true*** sale price is far less than the price on the purchase agreement. The difference is self delusion.

"But don't installment sales save taxes?"

Most investors think installment sales are a tax saving device.

How so? In a sentence, the law says if you do an installment sale, you pay the tax in installments, too. Where's the savings?

The savings is ***supposed*** to be in the ***spreading out*** the income. But is it?

Not if you're in the 50% bracket. The 50% bracket is the highest. For 1984, the 50% bracket is $162,400 for a married couple filing jointly; $81,800 for a single person. If you're in the 50% bracket, each additional dollar of income you receive will be taxed at 50%...whether you receive it this year or next. So why not get it ***this*** year so you can reinvest it?

Only spreads if you're below the 50% bracket

An installment sale will only reduce the rate at which your income is taxed if

- you are in a bracket ***less than*** 50%
- you will ***still*** be in a bracket lower than 50% after adding the installment payments to your other income.

What about averaging?

And what about averaging? Did you know that you can ***already*** spread income out when you get it in a lump? By income averaging. You're allowed to income average for an unlimited number of years. . . as long as you qualify.

You qualify if your income exceeds by more than $3,000 120% of your average income for the last four years. Or to put it another way, you can probably average if this year's income is very much more than previous years. . . which is likely in a year in which you sell real estate.

So the amount you "save" by doing an installment sale is not installment sale versus cash sale. It's installment sale versus ***income averaged*** cash sale. To find out if you'll benefit from an installment sale, you need to figure the tax that way and what it'd be if you sold for all cash and used averaging.

An installment sale spreads income over ***future*** years. That's nice. But you have to ***wait*** to benefit. With averaging, you spread income over ***past*** years. And you get the benefit ***all this year***.

Actually, you can average ***and*** do an installment sale. . . if your income qualifies in any or all of the years you receive installment payments.

I set up a Visicalc computer spread sheet to analyze real estate decisions. (See the Special Report that accompanied the March '83 issue of the *Real Estate Investing Letter* for details) One of the things I had it do was ***always*** figure out what the tax would be with and without income averaging and use the one which was lowest. Unless you've done that very complicated calculation, you don't really know how much tax, if any, averaging is saving you.

Tax benefits of installment sales greatly exaggerated

The tax benefits of installment sales are greatly exaggerated. Many investors save ***no taxes whatsoever*** when they do an installment sale. Although even those people ***think*** they're saving taxes. . . because of the reputation of the installment sale.

Those who ***do*** manage to lower the rate at which the income is taxed even after taking into account averaging save less than they think.

And above all, installment sales only save taxes when compared to ***cash*** sales. I think anyone who does ***either*** an installment sale or a cash sale needs their head examined. Exchange! Exchange! Exchange!

The calculations needed to determine how much, if any, taxes you'll save by doing an installment sale (when compared to a cash sale) are ***extremely*** complicated. In fact, they are ***so*** complicated, I wonder if ***anyone anywhere*** in the United States has actually done the correct numbers.

"But isn't a second a good investment?"

Many of those who take back mortgages believe such loans are good investments. After all, they ***know*** the property. And the yield is higher than a pass book savings account.

Who are they kidding?

Nobody but nobody has money in passbook savings accounts anymore. Their money's in money market accounts. As of December 2, 1983, Merrill Lynch's Cash Management Account was yielding 8.7%.

As I said earlier in the book, all investments are judged on their combination of risk and reward. Let's compare the typical seller mortgage to investments of equal risk. Namely, other seller mortgages.

If you buy discounted second mortgages, what yield can you expect? I suspect you could get in the neighborhood of 20% at present. Furthermore, you could easily limit your purchases only to ***seasoned*** mortgages. A seasoned mortgage is one in which the borrower has been making payments for some time. Seller mortgages are all ***un***seasoned as of closing day.

And you could and should limit your investments in seller mortgages to loans in which ***an independent appraisal*** shows that the borrower has equity equal to at least 25% of the value of the property. That equity protects your investment and increases your security.

Here's a comparison of the typical seller loan versus what you could expect if you bought ***other*** sellers' mortgages at a discount.

Characteristic	You as lender	Other as lender
Interest rate	10-12%	10-12%
Yield	10-12%	20%
Seasoned?	No	Yes
Borrower's equity	10-25%	25%
Independent appraisal?	No	Yes
Credit check?	Maybe	Usually

That's a "good investment?"

Does that look like a "good investment" to you? The yield is ***much*** less than you could get in a ***less risky***, but similar investment.

What if a yield of 10 to 12% were all you wanted? How does the risk of a seller mortgage compare to the risk of investments with comparable yields?

Perusing the December 1983 *Money Magazine* I find

Kemper Money Market Fund	9.3%
USAA Mutual Income Fund	12.6%
Vanguard Fixed In.-High Yield.	14.1%
Franklin U.S.Government Bond Fund	12.2%
Fidelity High Yield Muni Bond Fund	9.8%

So explain to me how an unseasoned, unappraised seller mortgage on a rental property is a "good investment" when it pays the same or lower yield than some of the safest, most diversified money market and bond funds.

In other words, the notion that a seller mortgage paying 10 to 12% interest is a good investment is blatant hogwash. And anyone who tries to "prove" seller mortgages are good investments by comparing them to passbook savings accounts is simply knocking over a straw man.

Seller mortgages offer a combination of risk and reward which is so lousy it's hard to find anything comparable in the market.

What if the buyer doesn't send the payments?

If you take back a loan, the buyer may not make the payments. Most seller/lenders say, "So what? So I get the property back and I get to keep the buyer's down payment."

It doesn't work that way. You don't just "get the property back." You foreclose.

Only someone with no lending experience would regard foreclosure as simply "getting the property back."

The Mortgage Bankers Association (MBA) did an informal survey of 30 of the nation's largest mortgage lenders. Most lenders said they suffered losses of $1,000 to $2,500 per foreclosure plus overhead and resale related expenses. And the typical foreclosure occurred within three years of closing the loan. The average length of time to resell foreclosed homes ranged from one to 15 months. One lender who lost an average of $3,500 on each foreclosure said some properties suffer significant deterioration during the six months it usually takes him to sell the property.

Remember that this is the experience of the nation's 30 largest mortgage lenders. These guys know what they're doing. They require 20% to 25% down or mortgage insurance. They require appraisals and credit reports. And they ***still*** lose $1,000 to $1,500 per foreclosure before resale expenses. What do you think happens to ***sellers*** taking back ***higher*** leverage mortgages with ***no credit checks or appraisals***?

I can't give you statistics on seller loan foreclosures or sellers' losses. Because no one keeps track of them. But we can safely assume they are a heck of a lot higher than the losses suffered by the 30 largest mortgage lenders. And probably higher than HUD's losses.

Foreclosure

I'll guarantee you that some lawyers are going to make money if you foreclose. ***You*** may lose money. But the lawyers involved are going to profit.

Foreclosure is one area of the law in which you must follow procedures ***very*** carefully. Failure to cross a t or dot an i might force you to start over again...with attendant costs and losses.

The legal costs are significant. And you have to pay them whether you get ***your*** money out of the foreclosure or not.

Vandalism

In a foreclosure, the foreclosee is not happy. If the property in question is owner-occupied, the owner/foreclosee will most likely vandalize it out of spite.

If it's ***not*** owner-occupied, it will probably be in bad shape due to neglect and lousy tenants. Keeping a property up takes money. If the foreclosee had money, he wouldn't be getting foreclosed, right? So the typical income property foreclosure involves a property which has been neglected for many months. Neglect means expensive deferred maintenance like leaking roofs, cannibalized uninhabitable apartments, and tenants who don't pay the rent or high vacancies.

So if you ***do*** get the property back in a foreclosure, it won't be the property you sold. It'll probably be a badly neglected, possibly vandalized version of what you sold.

Auction

When you foreclose, you ultimately get the right to force the sale of the property. You do ***not*** have the right to ***take*** the property. Most states require a public auction. The only way you would get the property back is to ***buy*** it back. And in order to do that, you have to outbid all the other buyers.

Typically, there's little or no equity left in the property when it gets foreclosed. In fact, negative equity is common. If there ***is*** any equity, there will be other buyers trying to acquire it...cheap. The net effect of various buyers competing to buy the equity is that you pay market value or some facsimile thereof.

The lawyers are paid first from the foreclosure proceeds. Then the lenders in order of priority. If there's any money left over, it goes to the foreclosee.

So forget the notion that you're going to get a valuable property back when you foreclose. If the owner has any equity, he'll sell before you can foreclose. Foreclosure generally happens only when the owner's equity is already wiped out or so small the effort of selling is not worth it.

Deed in lieu of foreclosure

Sometimes, the owner who's about to be foreclosed will offer you a deed in lieu of foreclosure. That keeps his credit clean...or at least keeps it from getting further sullied by a foreclosure.

Deed in lieu of foreclosure simply means that the owner deeds you the property in return for your releasing him from liability on the loan. It can be advantageous for both parties because it avoids the costs of a foreclosure. And vandalism can usually be forestalled by making the good condition of the property a requirement before the lender will issue the release.

But again, the owner/borrower is not going to deed you a property in which he has equity. That'd be foolish. He'll sell instead. So you're only likely to get a deed in lieu of foreclosure when the value of the property is close to or less than the outstanding loans.

Problems with accepting a deed in lieu of foreclosure

Getting a deed in lieu of foreclosure beats having to go through a full foreclosure from a lender's standpoint. But a deed in lieu of foreclosure is far from the problem-free event most sellers think. Here are the problems.

Title insurance is necessary. That is, a new title insurance policy as of the date you get the deed in lieu. Because when you accept a deed in lieu of foreclosure, you are ***buying*** the property. The fact that you used to own it means nothing. And the fact that you are paying for it by letting the current owner off the hook on a mortgage rather than with cash means nothing. You are ***buying*** the property. And you should always get title insurance when you buy. (Massachusetts buyers rely on title opinions of attorneys instead of title insurance. I don't think much of that system. But when in Rome...)

Borrowers who are in default often ***demand concessions***...even money...for deeding the property to you. You may think that would take a lot of nerve for a guy behind in his payments. True. But many borrowers have the required nerve. Their logic is that a deed in lieu saves you money. Which it often does. They want you to split the savings with them. So they have some bargaining power in spite of their otherwise indefensible position.

Junior liens and bankruptcy

Foreclosure wipes out all junior liens. Deed in lieu ***wipes out nothing*** but the loan held by the lender who's accepting the deed in lieu. By accepting the deed in lieu, you are also ***buying subject to*** those junior liens which would have been wiped out if you foreclosed.

Junior liens might include other mortgages. If you have a second, for example, the borrower may have "created" a third on the property to use as a down payment on another property. Or there may be mechanics liens or water department liens or judgment liens on the property. You're buying subject to all of them when you accept a deed in lieu. And you must pay them or risk losing the property through foreclosure or sheriff's sale by ***those*** lien holders.

If the borrower declares bankruptcy within one year of deeding you the property, the property may revert to the bankruptcy trustee. In that case, you would become just one of the borrower's many creditors. And the bankruptcy law and bankruptcy trustee would decide how much of the bankrupt person's assets you'd get.

Your new title insurance won't protect you. Title insurance policies almost always exclude bankruptcy.

Deed in lieu of foreclosure may not be valid

A deed in lieu of foreclosure can sometimes be declared an "equitable mortgage" by a court. That means the court is saying, "We know you aren't calling it a mortgage. But as far as we're concerned, it still looks like a mortgage to us." If you are judged to have an equitable mortgage instead of a deed in lieu of foreclosure, you still have to foreclose. It would be the worst of both worlds if you paid money or gave some other concession to a delinquent borrower in order to ***avoid*** foreclosure...only to learn that you ***still*** have to foreclose. Plus, it's ***tougher*** to foreclose on an equitable mortgage than a written mortgage.

Commission still due

Finally, borrowers who are in default often put their properties up for sale when they get into financial difficulty. Often listing them with a real estate broker. Since a deed in lieu is a type of sale, a ***commission is generally still due*** to a real estate agent with an exclusive right to sell listing.

The real estate agent might slap a commission ***lien*** on the property or get an ***injunction*** preventing the sale before closing if he suspects he's being cut out. Or if the agent doesn't learn that he's been cut out of his commission until ***after*** closing, the agent may ***file suit***. His main beef is with his client...the former owner. But people who sue generally sue everybody in sight especially when the primary bad guy appears not to have any money.

Deeds in the mail

Most old time income property loan officers have been through times when borrowers sent deeds instead of payments. That's right, the lender opens an envelope from the borrower expecting to find a payment check and instead finds a newly signed deed to the property...deeding it to the lender.

Lenders do not talk fondly of receiving those deeds. Far from it. They shudder at the memory. When they get the deed in the mail...a deed in lieu of foreclosure...it's generally because the properties are experiencing high vacancies and there's not enough income to make the payments.

Talk to an old pro

So if you're considering taking back a loan, talk to an old pro. Someone who makes his living making second mortgage loans on the type property you are selling. Ask him about the risks, the costs of foreclosure, the losses. Ask him if foreclosure means simply getting the property back.

Tax consequences of getting the property back

The lender's ***basis*** in the property after receiving a deed in lieu of foreclosure will be its ***fair market value.***

But the lender will have to pay tax on a ***gain*** if the fair market value of the property ***exceeds*** the lender's basis in the ***loan.*** The lender's basis in the loan is generally the ***loan balance*** unless the loan was purchased at a discount.

And the lender can deduct a ***bad debt loss*** if the fair market value of the property is ***less than*** the principal balance of the loan. But the lender can***not*** deduct a bad debt loss if the loan was not made in conjunction with a ***trade or business***. For example, a loan taken back on the sale of a ***principal residence*** would ***not*** be eligible for a bad debt deduction.

If part of the gain is ***back interest***, it's taxed at ordinary income rates like any other interest. Otherwise, whether the gain is short term or long term capital gain depends on the holding period.

Bad debt deductions are covered by Section 166 of the Internal Revenue Code; gains in deeds in lieu of foreclosure in Section 1038.

18
How To Take Back A Loan

Half take back mortgages

In a poll of its readers, the *Real Estate Investing Letter* asked, "Have you ever taken back a mortgage?"

Half said they had.

Shame on them.

But statistics like that convince me that many of you reading this book are going to take back mortgages in spite of my denunciation of them. That's why I've included this chapter on how to do it right.

Imitate the pros

My advice can be summed up in one sentence: "Imitate the pros."

Most investors do the opposite. They're amateurs. And it shows in the way they take back a mortgage. Here's a comparison.

Item	Seller	Pro
Credit check	rarely	always
independent appraisal	never	always

prepayment penalty	never	usually
late charge	sometimes	always
equity percentage	10 - 25%	25% minimum
standardized documents	rarely	usually
drawn by	any lawyer	specialist
due-on-sale clause	poorly worded	thorough
loan fees	never	always
impound accounts	rarely	usually

Talk to a pro

Before you take back a loan, call a lender who makes the same kind of loans on the same kind of property in the same area as the property in question. Ask

- what is your ***procedure***?
- what ***fees*** and ***other charges*** are there?
- may I have a copy of each of the ***documents*** I would have to sign?

The lender may balk at giving you a copy of their documents. If necessary, offer to pay them for the documents. I wouldn't give them more than five or ten dollars. Because if one lender won't give them to me, another probably will.

Get them from the court house if necessary

If you can't find a lender who'll give you a copy of their documents...or let you make photocopies of them...you can always copy them at the court house. Just go to where they record the mortgages or trust deeds...usually the county court house...and look up a recent mortgage recorded by a local lender. The clerks who work there will help you find one. And they have photocopy machines or services so you can get copies.

Charge the same fees

Lenders get a lot of their return from front end fees...points and straight fees. They also get the borrower to reimburse them for expenses like credit reports, appraisals, and legal fees.

You should, too. Most seller loans include absolutely ***no*** front end fees whatsoever. And sellers rarely charge for credit reports or document preparation. To heck with that. You should charge the same as the pros...for the same reasons...to increase your profit.

Will the buyer/borrower like it? No. But what do you care? Do you need his vote for some elective office you want? He'll probably grumble. But he'll also probably pay it.

So find out what the going rate is for all these charges. And charge ***your*** buyer that rate for each of the usual fees. Do ***not*** try to surprise the buyer with these fees at closing. Tell him when you negotiate the deal. Give ground if you must during the negotiation. But don't give up these fees without a fight.

Missouri and North Carolina regulate loan fees. Maybe other states do too. Check your local law. Usury laws, too. Because some fees are considered interest.

Not just any mortgage

Make sure it's a ***recent*** mortgage. The more recent the better. That's because the state and federal laws pertaining to mortgages change from time to time. Professional mortgage lenders employ attorneys who specialize in keeping up with those changes. And when a change in the law occurs, they immediately modify their documents to comply.

Also, make sure it's a mortgage on the ***same type of property***. That is residential versus non-residential, home versus rental property, and so forth. That's because different laws pertain to mortgages on different kinds of properties. Single family homes in particular come under different laws from commercial properties.

Different laws aren't the only reason to make sure you copy documents form the same property type. Different property types also have ***different problems***. For example, a mortgage on an apartment complex might allow the lender to seize control of not only the building but also the right to use the building's name. That would not be included in a single-family home mortgage.

Also, make sure the loan you copy has the same ***seniority***. That is, if you're going to do a first, copy another first. If you're doing a second; another second. And so forth. Again, the laws vary according to seniority.

For God's sake, don't use a mortgage from another state. You might have a mortgage in your files from a deal you did back when. And you might be tempted to use that mortgage to save yourself the trouble of visiting a lender or the court house. Don't. Variations in ***state*** laws can be dramatic. Plus there's usually a clause which says, "This mortgage will be governed by the laws of the state of such-and-such." It had better be the state in which the property is located.

Type it into a word processor

Once you get hold of a copy of a mortgage to use, type it into a word processor or memory typewriter. If you don't have one, find someone who will lend or rent you one.

Then type it into the word processor, changing the names and amounts as you go. Why do I say type it? After all, you could save time by whiting out the old names, addresses and amounts and typing in the new ones.

I want you to type it yourself...not your secretary...so that you ***know what's in it***. I've learned from experience. If you want to know what's in a legal document, read it in a noisy environment like a closing. If you want to ***really*** know what's in it, read it in a quiet environment like your home when everyone else is asleep. And if you want to know it like you ***ought*** to know it, type it in its entirety. The process of typing will cause you to see things you missed even in your quiet reading.

Prepare it yourself

You ought to prepare the loan documents yourself. Saving the lawyer's fee is only ***part*** of the reason. And a minor part at that.

If you follow my advice to type the documents into a word processor, you've already prepared the documents. So why pay someone else to do it again?

Secondly, I want you to ***know*** what's in those documents. Too many people use attorneys not for their special expertise but rather out of laziness. They're too darned lazy to read the documents so they ask an attorney to do it for them.

What's the attorney supposed to look for? Bogeymen? ***You're*** the only one who knows what your goals and strategy are. Most laymen think attorneys are looking for "bad" clauses. Attorneys will do that...but only if you first ***define*** what's a "bad" clause to you. Most clients don't do that. They simply hand the documents over to be read without instructions. And "badness" is in the eye of the beholder.

Other disadvantages of attorneys

Legal fees aren't the only disadvantage of using attorneys. There are also delays. The attorney's office is an extra stop on everyone's route to closing the deal. And attorneys are notorious for letting important documents sit until they receive an angry "wake up" call from the parties who are waiting for them.

Somebody once defined an attorney as someone who is paid to be his client's S.O.B. To an extent, that's true. Unfortunately, some attorneys...especially inexperienced ones...play the S.O.B. role far more often than is needed. To impress their client, they pick fights with other parties in the deal. These nit picking grandstand plays are the main reasons attorneys have the reputation for being "deal killers."

How attorneys prepare the documents

When you ask an attorney to prepare a note and mortgage he usually does the following. He writes the names, addresses, dates, and amounts on a sheet of paper. If you've asked for some special terms, he writes them down. Then he tells his secretary to get the file on the ***last*** note and mortgage of this type he did. He attaches the notes to those documents and tells his secretary to type a new set replacing the old names, etc. with the new.

If you've asked for a special clause, he'll search through some legal books looking for a sample. Then he'll mark it and tell the secretary to insert it.

If you doubt my version of what they do, carefully read a mortgage and note prepared by an attorney. I'll bet you'll find changes in references...like calling the buyer "Buyer" in some clauses but "Purchaser" in others. That's because some of the sample books used "Buyer;" others, "Purchaser."

In many cases, you'll also find clauses which do not apply to your deal. In his haste, the attorney neglected to tell his secretary to leave them out. This is sloppy legal work. But it's also par for the course. Generally, you will ***not*** find this kind of sloppiness in a Federal National Mortgage Association or Federal Home Loan Mortgage Corporation mortgage document.

If the attorney is simply recycling his last mortgage, why not cut out the middleman? That is, ***you*** do the recycling instead of his secretary. "But," you protest, "How can I get access to the file containing his last mortgage?"

It's at the courthouse, remember? Notes and mortgages are recorded. Attorneys will howl when they read this. If what I'm suggesting became widespread, they'd probably try to ***copyright*** their documents...except for the fact that ***they*** got them the same way...and there are only so many ways to say what a mortgage says...especially phraseology with special meaning like "time is of the essence."

By the way, you may be wondering whether you have to be a lawyer to prepare documents. For ***other people***, yes. But you do ***not*** have to be an attorney to represent yourself. So if you are a party to the documents in question, you can prepare them yourself.

Picking an attorney

If you insist on using an attorney, make sure you get a good one. Use a specialist. Do not use a family lawyer. Or a corporation lawyer. Get a mortgage lawyer. How do you find one? Ask the most successful mortgage lenders in your area who they use. Then call him or her.

If they won't tell you, make a visit to the county court house. The attorney who prepared the documents typically puts his name on the "cover." The court house tells all.

How to use an attorney

Do not use an attorney to read documents you are too lazy to read yourself. Rather read them thoroughly, make note of any legal questions you have, and ask your attorney to both read the documents and to answer your questions. If you take him to closing, give him a specific job...making sure the documents are signed properly and completely. Have him arrive only when necessary and send him home when he's done that job. Don't just have him "spectate" at your expense. Do ***not*** just take him for some vague reason like, "It's good insurance." Attorneys do not insure anybody.

Title people can help

The people who work for title companies can help you, too. They've processed a zillion mortgages. They often prepare the documents. Although I wouldn't recommend that. Because they tend to produce mortgages which are just mortgages. Not tight, well-written mortgages.

Loan criteria, too

Don't just copy the pros' procedures, fees, and documents. Copy their criteria, too. In other words, their credit standards and their equity requirements.

Generally, your borrower ought to have a clean credit history. If the borrower has ***no*** credit history, you should require a co-signer who does.

25% is the minimum down payment you should accept. Most mortgage lenders demand that unless the property is an owner-occupied single-family home.

Green Point Savings Bank in Brooklyn has been making mortgage loans for 50 years without verifying the borrower's income. And they've suffered fewer losses than the average mortgage lender. How can that be, you ask? Because they require a ***25% down payment*** and they ***check credit***. They figure once the borrower has put down 25%, they'll find a way to make the payments. And if they couldn't make the payments, they wouldn't risk the 25%.

Richard Gardiner sold a number of his properties to nothing down buyers in 1979. He later had to take most of the properties sold to investors back. One he foreclosed; the rest via deeds in lieu of foreclosure. He lost $6,000 on one due to neglect of the property, bankruptcy of one of the borrowers, and back real estate taxes.

No change in senior loans

Your second mortgage should prohibit changes in the terms of the first mortgage. Because virtually any change that ***improves*** the position of the senior lender, ***weakens*** your position. Whether it pertains to collateral or guarantees, there's only so much collateral and other money available.

Liquidity

The ***main*** reason you should be careful to imitate the pros is to improve the risk and reward combination of the mortgage you take back. But there's also another reason...liquidity.

You may want to ***sell*** your loan in the future...or borrow against it. If so, you need to originate the loan in a way that pleases the prospective loan buyer or lender.

Professional lenders also want their loans to be as liquid as possible, so imitating them will probably make your loan pretty liquid. But in some cases, you can go a step farther regarding liquidity.

The FNMA program

On November 10, 1980, FNMA announced that they will agree, in advance, to buy seller loans on homes. To get this guarantee, you must originate your loan through a FNMA-approved lender. The FNMA-approved lender will also service the loan (collect the payments, pay taxes and insurance) if you wish.

The buyer/borrower simply applies to the FNMA-approved lender and they originate (create) the loan using FNMA's standard mortgage documents and credit and appraisal guidelines.

If, after closing, you should ever want to sell the loan, FNMA would buy it from you...or you'd be free to sell to another buyer. They'd pay ***face*** value if the loan interest rate were equal to or greater than the then market interest rate. If you're loan interest rate is ***lower*** than the then market rate, they will buy the loan at a discount which brings their yield up to market.

Note that they do ***not*** pay a premium when the loan interest rate is ***above*** market. Theoretically, you're entitled to a premium in such cases. But FNMA doesn't pay one. Probably because the borrower is likely to pay off a loan on which the interest rate is above market.

Contact FNMA for details at 3900 Wisconsin Avenue, N.W., Washington, DC 20016.

You may be able to get a deal like this with other lenders

I know of no formal program like FNMA's. But you may be able to ***informally*** get another lender to do a similar deal. For example, a lender who normally makes second mortgages on income properties might be interested in promising to cash you out on a loan which they originate and service. As with FNMA, your buyer/borrower would apply to the lender and they would process the loan as they normally would.

Even if you can't find a lender who'll promise to buy the loan in the future, you still might want to pay a lender to originate and service the loan for you. They'll almost certainly be willing to do that. After all, that's what they do for a living. And that might be well worth the money.

Prepayment penalty

Most sellers didn't want to take back a loan to begin with. So they'd ***love*** for the buyer/borrower to pay it off early. That's why they almost never put in a prepayment penalty.

Put in a prepayment penalty.

You can tell the buyer that you might consider waiving it to encourage him to prepay. But you want the clause in the loan to enhance its resale value.

And it ***will*** enhance resale value. Professional investors like prepayment penalties. Penalties create the possibility that the lender's yield will be higher than the interest rate on the loan. Or higher than the original yield if the loan is sold at a discount.

According to the Mortgage Bankers Association, prepayment penalties are against the law in

Alabama
Alaska
Illinois
Iowa
Maryland
Minnesota
New Jersey
New Mexico
North Carolina (less than $100,000 mortgage)
Pennsylvania
South Carolina (less than $100,000 mortgage)
Texas
Vermont
West Virginia

Penalty reduces the one-way street effect

A loan with a fixed-rate and no prepayment penalty is a one-way street. If market rates go ***up***, you, the lender, are stuck with a below-market loan. But if market rates go ***down***, the borrower will refinance.

It's rate up, you lose; rate down, the borrower wins.

The only way to ***eliminate*** the one-way street effect is to make the loan ***locked in***. That means the borrower can***not*** pay it off no matter what.

A prepayment penalty only partly offsets the one-way street effect. When the market rate is below the loan rate, the borrower will refinance. The only deterrent is the transaction costs.

Because transaction costs are fairly high in real estate loans, the market rate would have to drop significantly below the loan rate before refinancing would make sense. By adding a prepayment penalty, you increase those transaction costs. That, in turn, lowers the threshold. With a prepayment penalty, the rate has to drop even farther before the borrower will refinance.

Most state laws limit prepayment penalties. If you copy a recent mortgage document from the same state and on the same property type, the lender will probably have the legal prepayment penalty or less in the loan. But that's the kind of thing you would ask an attorney to make sure of if you use an attorney. This is very important. The penalties for exceeding the limits are often quite severe. In fact, I've heard ***forgiveness of the loan*** is sometimes the penalty.

Cross-default clause

If your loan is one of two or more on the property, it should contain a clause saying that a default on ***any*** of the loans is a default on ***your*** loan too.

Due-on-sale clause

Put in a due-on-sale clause. Most sellers do this. The reason is obvious. If market rates are higher than your loan rate, you'd like the loan paid off. Sales, which are fairly common give you that opportunity. . . but only if you have a due-on-sale clause.

Make sure it's a ***thorough*** due-on-sale clause. I've held the FNMA/FHLMC due-on-sale clause up as an example of a good one. But if I were ever to take back a loan, I'd make it even more thorough.

The FNMA clause covers land contracts by saying "transfer of any interest therein." I'd add to that, "including but not limited to a land contract."

I'd also spell out the various name change techniques as constituting default and triggering the due-on-sale clause.

In other words, I'd use the FNMA/FHLMC clause. But I'd also specifically include every "creative" finance technique for getting around due-on-sale clauses as constituting default under my due-on-sale clause.

Late penalties

Put in the maximum late penalty allowed by your state law. You ***got*** to have a late penalty. Most people will pay late regularly if you don't. And all you can do is threaten to foreclose...if you have no late penalty. If your late penalty is higher than allowed by state law, you may be subject to severe penalties.

Again, copying a pro's current mortgage and note on the same property type will pretty much make sure you don't use an overly high penalty. Also, most mortgages include a clause saying that the lender does not want to violate any pertinent law and that if the stated penalty rate exceeds the law, the legal rate is really what they mean.

Personal guarantees

Experienced real estate investors generally prefer to avoid personal liability on a loan. You are probably one of them.

Because sellers are former borrowers, they tend to be sympathetic to their buyer/borrower's request for no personal liability on the loan. Don't be.

If it's at all possible, make the buyer/borrower personally liable. It makes the loan both safer for you and more marketable. So don't give it up without a fight.

As with payment patterns, you can use limits as a compromise if necessary. For example, on a FHLMC apartment loan I got last week, my wife and I are liable for the top 25%. It was a $450,000 loan so we're personally liable for the amount by which the loan balance exceeds $337,500.

You can use dollar limits, time limits, loan-to-appraised value limits, you name it.

Note that personal guarantees are ***hard to cash in on*** as a practical matter. So try to get them. But don't get complacent ***because*** you have a personal guarantee. Note also that many states restrict or prohibit personal guarantees on mortgage loans.

Impound accounts

Impound accounts are called "escrow accounts" in some areas. It's where the lender makes you pay the insurance and property taxes to him. If a senior lender hasn't already done so, you should require your buyer/borrower to send the property taxes and hazard insurance payments to you each month.

It increases your security...and therefore the marketability of your loan. And it gives you cash which you can earn interest on.

Get your tax act together

If you're taking back a mortgage, you probably want installment sale treatment for tax purposes. There's more to it than just taking back a mortgage. I won't go into it here. Because I've written another book which covers that subject. It's called *Aggressive Tax Avoidance For Real Estate Investors* (Reed Publishing, 342 Bryan Drive, Danville, CA 94526 $21.95 plus $2.50 for postage and packaging. CA residents add sales tax.)

The two main issues which laymen would be likely to overlook are ***excess loans over basis*** and ***constructive receipt***. If you don't know the definitions of those phrases...and if you're not familiar with the pertinent laws and court decisions, get my book. Might also be a good idea to run your documents by a real estate tax attorney to make sure the tax treatment is what you want.

Work on the property

The buyer of the property you're selling may plan to have work done to the property. Like grading or construction or renovation. Any of these could result in mechanics liens on the property. In may cases, these liens would have ***priority*** over your mortgage even though they were recorded ***after*** your mortgage. That's because some states feel more sympathy for contractors than they do for mortgage lenders. The book *Construction and Development Financing* by Harris has details on this problem and how to minimize it.

My recommendation not to take back a mortgage goes ***triple*** for to-be-built-upon raw land.

Don't take back a little second behind a big first

Don't take back a loan which is small in relation to the loans senior to it. That's because any payments not made on the senior loans instantaneously consume the equity which is security for your loan. For example, suppose your $10,000 mortgage is a second behind a $500,000 first mortgage. And let's say the total payments on the first. . .counting principal, interest, insurance, and taxes. . .are $6,000 a month.

If the borrower fails to make just ***two*** payments, ***you*** would have to make them to protect your mortgage. But what's the sense of paying $12,000 to save a $10,000 mortgage?

Don't assume that the first is current because your second is

Borrowers sometimes continue making payments on the second after they've quit making them on the first. So you need to contact the first mortgage lender each month to make sure the first is current when you are holding a second or other junior loan. Real estate columnist Bob Bruss had to pay four months back payments on a first once because the borrower had stopped making them. But the same borrower had continued to make the payments on the second to Bob all along!

Don't accept gemstones or other non-building collateral

Some sharpies will try to get you to take back loans secured not by buildings but by raw land, gemstones, corporate or government bonds, etc. Don't do it. The property in question is usually worth only a fraction of the value the sharpie claims. And its very difficult to make sure of the value. The August 20, 1985 *Wall Street Journal* contained a horror story in which 16 banks in five countries were cheated on a gemstone loan.

They made a $45 million loan secured by $90 million worth of gemstones. The value of the gemstones was verified by two Swiss gemologists and a professor of mineralogy at a German University. When the borrower defaulted, they got the stones out and brought in a buyer. He said they were worth $4.5 to $9 million. . .not $90 million. Would ***you*** have gotten three experts to certify the value? Probably not. And even if you had, three experts didn't protect these 16 banks.

If you ***insist*** on doing such a deal, again I say, "Imitate the pros." Call your local bank and ask how much they'd loan on the collateral you're being offered. And ask how they'd establish its value. Then follow their procedure and criteria.

To sum up

If you insist on taking back a mortgage, imitate the pros regarding

- procedures
- fees and charges
- documentation.

And if you want installment sale treatment, read the installment sale section of my book, *Aggressive Tax Avoidance For Real Estate Investors* and/or check your deal with a real estate tax attorney.

PART ELEVEN SUMMARY

19 Summary

The purpose of this chapter is to summarize. No explanations of ***why*** here. Go back to the main part of the book for that.

Leverage is analogous to ***speed*** in a car. The faster you go, the sooner you arrive. . .if you don't crash first.

Determination is more important than fancy techniques.

All finance techniques are variations of ***payment patterns*** and ***security techniques.***

The ***Three C's of Credit*** are

- Character
- Capacity
- Collateral

There are an ***infinite number*** of real estate finance techniques.

You should have a target ***loan-to-value*** ratio and target ***debt-coverage*** ratio.

The appropriate debt-coverage ratio depends on the ***volatility*** of the income source.

High leverage...that is less than 20% down...is for beginners. It's too time-consuming and dangerous for investors with net worths in the multi hundreds of thousands of dollars range.

Learn how to do ***time value of money*** calculations. You can't understand real estate finance unless you do.

All real estate deals have ***one true sale price***. It is that discounted present value or market value of what the seller receives. Whenever below market interest rate financing is involved...either through an assumption or otherwise...the true sale price is less than the stated sale price.

Real estate finance techniques have ***tax ramifications***. Do not employ any finance technique without making sure you understand how it will be taxed.

Reed's Rules Of Real Estate Finance

1. Simple is better than complex.

2. Familiar is better than exotic.

3. You ***always*** pay the current market interest rate when you finance real estate.

4. Face-to-face negotiating is almost always better than through a third party.

5. Real estate is a cyclical business.

6. Don't take back a loan when you sell.

7. Don't agree to a large balloon payment which falls due in less than seven years.

8. Tell the truth.

9. Keep your promises.

10. Interest rates are totally unpredictable.

11. Lenders' loan criteria are inversely proportional to the amount of money they have to lend.

Shop around for loans.

Lending...and therefore borrowing...is an ***art***, not a science.

Rapport with a loan officer can make an enormous difference.

Try to get maximum ***notice*** of defaults and ***time to cure*** in the mortgages you sign.

Most professional ***due-on-sale*** clauses also cover land contracts and lease options.

It generally makes sense to ***preserve existing*** financing when its loan-to-value ratio is 30% or more.

The five ***payment pattern variations:***

- level
- descending
- ascending
- intermittent
- combination of above

Your obligation to make the payment can be ***fixed or contingent***.

You can ***combine fixed and contingent*** obligations via:

- caps or ceilings
- floors or minimums
- start dates
- stop dates

APPENDIX A
RECOMMENDED BOOKS AND PERIODICALS

Books

Aggressive Tax Avoidance For Real Estate Investors John T. Reed (same author as this book). Annual. Reed Publishing.

Alternative Mortgage Instruments Barnett & McKenzie. Warren, Gorham & Lamont.

Apartment Investing Check Lists John T. Reed (same author as this book) HBJ Press. 1979.

The Appraisal of Real Estate Classic. Official text of the AIREA. American Institute of Real Estate Appraisers.

Creative Financing of Real Estate James A. Misko. A "creative" finance book. Institute For Business Planning. 1981.

Essentials Of Real Estate Finance David Sirota. Text book. Real Estate Education Company. 1977.

Everything You Need To Know About Creative Home Financing Frank Coffee. Darned good little paperback book. May be the best real estate finance book. Simon and Schuster. 1982.

Financing Income-Producing Real Estate Britton and Kerwood. Choppy because each chapter is written by a different author, but useful. McGraw-Hill Book Company 1977

Fundamentals of Mortgage Lending Marshall Dennis. Text bookish. Authoritative. Reston Publishing Company, Inc. 1978.

High Leverage Real Estate Investments Oliver Ray Price. Many case history examples to illustrate techniques. Prentice-Hall, Inc. 1978.

Housing and Development Reporter Loose leaf service covering government related real estate programs and private mortgage insurance. Bureau of National Affairs.

How To Fill Out a Fannie Mae-Freddie Mac Appraisal Report, Small Residential Income Property Henry S. Harrison. Collegiate Publishing Company. 1980.

How To Use Interest Rate Futures Contracts Edward W. Schwarz. Dow Jones-Irwin. 1979.

How To Buy An Office Building John T. Reed. Check lists covering all aspects of acquiring an office building. Reed Publishing. 1985.

Interest Rate Futures-Profits & Pitfalls Ben Weberman. 1980.

The Law of Letters of Credit John F. Dolan. Warren, Gorham & Lamont.

Marketing Investment Real Estate Messner, Schreiber, and Lyon. Explains discounted cash flow but very difficult to understand. Realtors National Marketing Institute. 1979.

Modern Residential Financing Methods: Tools of the Trade Stephen R. Mettling. Real Estate Education Company.

Real Estate Finance Dasso and Kuhn. Text book. A bit ivory towerish. Prentice-Hall, Inc. 1983.

Real Estate Finance John P. Wiedemer. Text book. Very academic discussion of finance. Reston Publishing Company, Inc. 1977.

Real Estate Financing Case and Clapp. Text book. John Wiley & Sons. 1978

Periodicals

Crittenden Directory Real Estate Financing Loose leaf directory of lenders who make loans other than home mortgages. You get a weekly newsletter and quarterly updates to the directory. Crittenden Publishing, Inc.

Journal of Real Estate Finance Quarterly. Warren, Gorham & Lamont.

Mortgage Banker Monthly magazine for mortgage bankers. Mortgage Bankers Association of America.

National Thrift News Weekly newspaper for managers of savings and loans. National Thrift News.

Novick's Income Property Finance Report Detailed description of what loans several featured lenders are currently making in each issue. Novick's Income Property Finance Report.

Real Estate Finance Update Monthly newsletter. Warren, Gorham & Lamont.

Real Estate Finance Today Mortgage Bankers Association. Semi-monthly.

Real Estate Finance Federal Research Press. Quarterly.

Real Estate Investor's Monthly The author of this book is the editor and publisher. Covers all aspects of real estate investing by individuals.

Publishers' Addresses

American Institute of Real Estate Appraisers 430 North Michigan Avenue, Chicago, IL 60611

Bureau of National Affairs 1231 25th Street, N.W., Washington, DC 20037

Collegiate Publishing Company, New Haven, CT

Crittenden Publishing, Inc. P.O. Box 1150, Novato, CA 94948

Dow Jones-Irwin 1818 Ridge Road, Homewood, IL 60430

Federal Research Press 65 Franklin Street, MA 02110

McGraw-Hill Book Company, 1221 Avenue of the Americas, New York, NY 10020

Mortgage Bankers Association of America 1125 15th Street, N.W., Washington, DC 20005

National Thrift News 212 West 35th Street, New York, NY 10001

Novick's Income Property Finance Report 111 John Street, Penthouse Floor, New York, NY 10038

Prentice-Hall, Inc. no street address, Englewood Cliffs, NJ 07632

Real Estate Education Company 500 North Dearborn Street, Chicago, IL 60610

Realtors National Marketing Institute 430 North Michigan Avenue, Chicago, IL 60611

Reed Publishing 342 Bryan Drive, Danville, CA 94526

Reston Publishing Company, Inc. 11480 Sunset Hills Road, Reston, VA 22090

Simon and Schuster 1230 Avenue of the Americas, New York, NY 10020

Ben Weberman 80 Park Avenue, New York, NY 10016

John Wiley and Sons 605 Third Avenue, New York, NY 10158

APPENDIX B
DEFINITIONS

Acceleration clause—-Loan clause that says the entire balance becomes due and payable immediately for one reason or another.

Accrue interest—-Allow interest to build up for later payment.

Adjustable rate mortgage—-Mortgage in which the interest rate and often payments rise and fall according to movements in a specified market interest rate index. May or may not be a ceiling on how high the rate can go.

Amortization—-Reduction of a loan via principal payments. The amount by which the balance is reduced.

Annuity—-A series of equal payments received over a period of years.

Appreciation—-Increase in property value.

Assumption—-Buyer agrees with lender to pay an existing loan.

Balloon payment—-Abnormally high loan payment made only once or a few times during the life of the loan. As opposed to a regular monthly payment.

Beneficiary of a trust deed—-The lender.

Blanket mortgage—-Mortgage in which more than one parcel of real property is pledged as security.

Bullet loan—-Loan with a balloon payment.

Buy down—-Payment of points by a seller to a lender to induce the lender to make a below-market interest rate loan.

Call—-Lender's option to require a balloon payment.

Capacity—-Ability to pay.

Capitalization rate—-Net operating income divided by market value of the property. Can also be defined as the before-tax cash flow rate of return you would get if you owned the property free and clear. Also called "cap rate."

Cash flow—-Cash income less cash outlays.

Chinese money—-Seller financing at below-market interest rates.

Co-insurance—-Insurance policy clause which requires the insured to bear part of any loss. . . used to encourage loss prevention.

Collateral—-Assets pledged as security for a loan.

Commitment—-Lender's promise to make a certain loan on certain terms during a certain period.

Comparables—-Similar properties which have sold recently. They show what the property you're financing is worth.

Compensating balance—-Amount required to be in a lending institution as part of a loan agreement.

Constant—-The total annual loan payments divided by the loan balance.

Contract for deed—-Another phrase for land contract.

Conventional loan—-A loan in which neither the FHA nor the VA is involved.

Credit tenant—-A tenant with excellent credit and big league financial strength, like IBM.

Debt-coverage ratio—-The property's net operating income divided by its annual principal and interest payments.

Debt-service—-Principal and interest payments on a loan.

Deficiency judgment—-Court judgment allowing a lender to confiscate a borrower's property other than the property pledged as security for the loan. Obtained when foreclosure fails to produce enough to pay off the loan ***and*** the borrower has agreed to be personally liable on the loan.

Discount rate—-The rate at which you discount a stream of payments to arrive at the present value of those payments. The lender's or investor's opportunity cost is the appropriate discount rate.

Equity—-Property value less mortgage or trust deed balances.

Equity kicker—-Loan clause which gives the lender a share of rent and/or property value increases.

Factor—-Company which buys accounts receivable.

Freddie Mac—-Federal Home Loan Mortgage Corporation

Ginnie Mae—-Government National Mortgage Corporation

Graduated payment mortgage—-Any mortgage with an ascending payment pattern.

Growing equity mortgage—-A graduated payment mortgage in which the additional amount paid is applied to reduction of the principal balance of the loan.

Hard money loan—-Loan from a lender other than a seller or real estate broker who's taking part of his commission in the form of a loan.

Hedging—-Arranging your financial affairs so that interest rate movements create a loss and gain which approximately cancel each other out.

Holdback—-Amount held back by lender when a loan is originated. . . usually to make sure some property improvement is completed.

Hypothecate—-Pledging a loan as security for another loan.

Impound account—-Money held by lender for payment of property taxes and hazard insurance.

Improvements—-The non-raw land part of real estate.

Installment sale—-Sale in which the seller receives at least one payment in a year other than the year of sale.

Interest-only—-Mortgage in which the borrower's payments consist entirely of interest.

Internal rate of return—-The rate of return at which the present value of the income equals the original investment.

Kicker—-See "equity kicker."

Land contract—-Installment sale in which the seller retains the deed until a specified portion of the loan is paid off.

Letter of credit—-Promise by a financial institution to pay a certain amount if a borrower fails to do so.

Leverage—-The use of borrowed money to magnify return.

Life estate—-Right to use a property during one's lifetime.

Liquidity—-The speed and ease with which an asset can be converted to cash.

Loan-to-value ratio—-Loan balance or balances divided by property value.

Lock-in—-Prohibition against prepayment.

Magic—-Nickname for Mortgage Guaranty Insurance Corporation.

Margin—-A sort of security deposit required for interest rate futures trading.

Mortgagee—-Lender.

Mortgagor—-Borrower.

Negative cash flow—-Cash outlays exceed cash income.

Net lease—-Tenant pays all or some operating expenses direct to creditor rather than in the form of rent to landlord.

Net operating income—-Income less operating expenses but before debt service.

Neutron bomb loan—-Balloon payment loan. So called because it financially destroys the people but leaves the building standing.

Nonrecourse—-Lender may not do anything but foreclose if borrower defaults on loan.

Note—-IOU.

Operating expenses—-Property expenses other than those for financing and acquisition.

Operating ratio—-Short for operating expense ratio. The total annual operating expenses divided by the total annual income of the property.

Opportunity cost—-Money lost due to not being able to make a particular investment.

Origination—-Creation of a loan.

Participation—-Same as "equity kicker."

Permanent loan—-Real estate loan other than a construction or interim loan. Almost always longer term than construction or interim loans.

Point—-One percent of the loan amount. Usually paid as a fee or to raise the lender's yield.

Prepayment penalty—-Penalty for paying a loan off before the due date.

Priority—-Seniority of the loan.

Purchase money mortgage—-Seller loan.

Real estate owned—-Financial institution phrase describing property which the institution owns as a result of foreclosure or receipt of deed in lieu of foreclosure.

Release clause—-A clause which describes how the borrower may have the lien on a portion of the collateral removed.

Rollover rate mortgage—-Mortgage in which the interest rate is fixed for an intermediate period like three to five years, then goes to market.

Rule of 78's—-Method for figuring interest which loads much of the interest onto the early years. Like accelerated depreciation does to depreciation deductions. Has the effect of a large prepayment penalty in the early years. Interest allocable to each period is found by multiplying the total interest payable over the life of the loan by the number of periods remaining on the loan at the time the calculations are made then dividing by the sum of the period's digits for the term of the loan. Not allowed for tax purposes unless the loan is self-amortizing and has a term of five years or less.

Sale leaseback—-Sale and lease combination in which the seller remains in the property as the buyer's tenant.

Selling short—-Agreeing to sell something you do not yet own.

Servicing—-Collection of loan payments and payment of property taxes and hazard insurance in some cases.

Shared appreciation mortgage—-Lender gives borrower a below-market interest rate in return for a share of any appreciation.

Shared equity—-Financing arrangement in which an investor puts up all or part of the money for a home buyer who in turn pays rent to the investor and shares the appreciation with him.

Subject to—-Same as assumption except that buyer does not enter into an agreement to pay with lender.

Subordination—-Agreement in which a lender agrees to take a security position junior to a new loan.

Substitution of collateral—-Moving a mortgage from one piece of real estate to another.

Underwriting—-Analyzing the risk of a loan and establishing the interest rate it will require. The act of "bidding" for a loan by a lender.

Usury laws—-Laws which limit the amount of interest a lender can charge.

Variable rate mortgage—-One in which the interest and often the payments vary according to specified market interest rate indexes. Usually has a 2 1/2% maximum cumulative interest rate increase.

Visicalc—-Popular computer spread sheet program.

Wraparound—-Adjective describing a junior loan or land contract in which the borrower makes one payment to the junior lender who in turn makes the payment to the senior lender.

Yield—-Investor's or lender's return.

Zero sum game—-Negotiation in which no party can gain except at the expense of another party.

APPENDIX C
ABBREVIATIONS

AAA—-"Always As Agreed," a top credit rating

ACRS—-Accelerated Cost Recovery System

AIREA—-American Institute of Real Estate Appraisers

AITD—-All-Inclusive Trust Deed (same as wraparound mortgage)

ARM—-Adjustable Rate Mortgage

ATCF—-After-Tax Cash Flow

BNA—-Bureau of National Affairs

BTCF—-Before-Tax Cash Flow

CF—-Cash Flow

CLIC—-Commercial Loan Insurance Corporation

CMB—-Certified Mortgage Banker

C of C—-Comptroller of the Currency

CPI—-Consumer Price Index

DC—-Debt Coverage Ratio

DCF—-Discounted Cash Flow

DMP—-Decision Making Process

DMU—-Decision Making Unit

D/S—-Debt Service

D/T—-Deed of Trust

FDIC—-Federal Deposit Insurance Corporation

FHA—-Federal Housing Administration

FHLBB—-Federal Home Loan Bank Board

FHLMC—-Federal Home Loan Mortgage Corporation

FLB—-Federal Land Bank

FmHA—-Farmers Home Administration

FMV—-Fair Market Value

FNMA—-Federal National Mortgage Association

FSLIC—-Federal Savings and Loan Insurance Corporation

FV—-Future Value

GECC—-General Electric Credit Corporation

GEM—-Growing Equity Mortgage

GNMA—-Government National Mortgage Association

GPM—-Graduated Payment Mortgage

HDR—-*Housing and Development Reporter*

HUD—-Department of Housing and Urban Development

i—-Interest Rate

I—-Income

IOU—-"I owe you"

IREM—-Institute of Real Estate Management

IRR—-Internal Rate of Return

IRS—-Internal Revenue Service

KISS—-Keep It Simple, Stupid

LIC—-Life Insurance Company

LTV—-Loan-To-Value Ratio

MAI—-Member of the Appraisal Institute

MGIC—-Mortgage Guaranty Insurance Corporation

MLS—-Multiple Listing Book

MSB—-Mutual Savings Bank

n—-Number of payments

NAR—-National Association of Realtors

NCUA—-National Credit Union Administration

NOI—-Net Operating Income

NPV—-Net Present Value

PMI—-Private Mortgage Insurance

PMT—-Payment

PV—-Present Value

R—-Capitalization Rate

RAM—-Reverse Annuity Mortgage (a senior citizen refinancing device)

REIT—-Real Estate Investment Trust

REO—-Real Estate Owned

RNMI—-Realtors National Marketing Institute

RRM—-Rollover Rate Mortgage

SAM—-Shared Appreciation Mortgage

S & L—-Savings And Loan Association

s/l—-Straight Line Depreciation

TC—-Tax Court

TD—-Trust Deed

UGCI—-United Guaranty Commercial Insurance Company

USAA—-United Services Automobile Association

V—-Value

VA—-Veterans Administration

VRM—-Variable Rate Mortgage

APPENDIX D
CASH SOURCES

Sometimes you have to scramble

Sometimes in real estate investing, you have to scramble. The cause might be a balloon payment. Or an unusually high vacancy rate. Or an unexpected major repair. Or just general overextension.

Whatever the reason, you need to know how to deal with it. I'll offer you two sections that might help:

- a cash sources check list
- and a general description of "The Full Peanut Butter"

Cash sources check list

The following are sources of emergency cash

- forgotten bank accounts in cities you used to live in
- scholarships, education loans, and grants
- tax refunds (submit amended returns for past years—-see my book *Aggressive Tax Avoidance For Real Estate Investors* for specifics)
- interest on your tenant security deposit account (unless the law requires you to give that interest to tenants)
- excess rent security deposits (sometimes the amount in your rent security deposit account is higher than the total deposits)
- lawsuit settlement—-settle a pending lawsuit now for cash
- cancel unneeded insurance policies (some times investors forget to cancel policies on properties they've sold)
- encourage tenants to pay rent in advance, perhaps by offering a discount
- if you've bought or sold property recently, go over the closing statements with a fine tooth comb looking for errors. Institutions like lenders and title companies will probably give you refunds if you can prove the mistake. Individual sellers and buyers are usually harder to get money out of.
- property tax refunds you may be eligible for as a veteran, homeowner, senior citizen, handicapped person, etc.
- semi-forgotten rainy day accounts, insurance policies, and savings bonds for junior's education, daughter's wedding, 21st birthday, etc.
- cash or travellers checks you've hidden or carry in a secret compartment for emergencies
- settle an estate which you were disputing
- file for reimbursable expenses from your employer or others you've done work for
- file for rebates on things you've bought—-cars, smoke detectors, batteries, etc.
- appeal your property taxes
- recover deposits left with landlords, leasing companies, utilities (To make sure you don't forget about such deposits, put a note about them in your safe deposit box and add them to the asset side of your balance sheet.)
- file insurance claims if you've had a covered loss you haven't bothered to claim
- collect debts you've written off—-take bad checks to police, turn other debts over for collection or collect them yourself. Call the loan you made to your college roommate.
- refund of mortgage impound account excess—-If the balance in your mortgage lender's tax and insurance account exceeds what they need, ask for a refund of the excess.
- send invoices for goods you've sold or services you've performed but haven't billed for yet.
- change your W-4 if you're an employee. That's your withholding instructions to your

employer. You can reduce the amount withheld. But if you underpay your withholding by too much, you'll have to pay a penalty at tax time. See J.K. Lasser's *Your Income Tax* to find the minimum you have to pay to avoid the penalty. If your income has dropped significantly, you may be able to reduce your withholding without any penalty.

- reduce your 1040ES payments if your self-employed. 1040ES payments are the self-employed person's equivalent of withholding.
- rent rooms in your home
- sell property you own and lease it back
- hold a garage sale
- sell an option on property you own

"The Full Peanut Butter"

The Full Peanut Butter is a drastic cut in your standard of living and spending to conserve cash in the event of a financial emergency. . .like those which often occur in real estate finance. The phrase "Full Peanut Butter" refers to a diet of peanut butter sandwiches and milk.

Become the resident manager

Fire the resident manager and take over his job. And his apartment if he doesn't want to stay on a rent-paying tenant. Rent out or sell your house. If you have some sort of work at which you can make more than you would save by becoming the resident manager, keep the manager and do more of the better paying work. Becoming the resident manager only makes sense when the value of your labor falls below that of your resident manager.

"Super manage" your properties

There is a point of diminishing returns in property management. You can always manage the building better, thereby increasing income and reducing expenses. But it takes time and some times money. And there's a point beyond which it's not worth it.

However, when you suffer an economic reverse, the value of your time often drops. That changes the economics of the point of diminishing returns. In other words, the point of diminishing returns moves.

Go over every property expense with a fine tooth comb looking for opportunities for savings. For example, you could reduce the wattage of light bulbs you pay the electric for. Fix leaking toilets and dripping faucets. Rent out what was previously your store room. Reduce the size of your newspaper ad. Fix the roof yourself. Etc.

Slash personal expenses

Tell the maid service to stop coming. Cancel your newspaper and magazines subscriptions. Buy peanut butter, bread, and milk only at the grocery store (or some other equally cheap, marginally nutritious diet). Work while you eat instead of taking time off. Walk, bicycle, or just plain don't go instead of spending money on gas and auto upkeep.

Put your credit cards away. Cancel your cable TV service. Get rid of telephone frills like extensions, leased princess phones, chimes instead of a ringer, extra names in the directory, etc. Get rid of your postage meter (unless driving back and forth to the post office will cost more than the meter rent). Resign from associations to get refunds of dues. Don't replace your stationery. Use blank white paper. Kill monthly payroll deductions for charity or other non-mandatory items. Move back in with Mom and Dad.

Consolidate your bills

Bill consolidation loans are generally considered a poor people's tactic. But then avoiding being permanently poor is what this chapter is about. And there's nothing wrong with the bill consolidation loan. It often makes sense.

In real estate terms, a bill consolidation loan is one in which you substitute low constant money for higher constant money. Typically, the loans you're replacing have short terms and/or high interest rates. The bill consolidation loan has a longer term and perhaps a lower interest rate than at least some of the loans it replaces. In any event, the effect is to reduce your total monthly payments. Generally, the ***amount*** of money you owe overall does not change.

Psychological safety net

I fully realize that this is depressing reading. I'm not ***recommending*** these actions. I'm just reminding you of things you can do if you get into financial trouble.

I've never had to do a full peanut butter. Although in my early years, I was frugal in general and have had to pay some bills from several different checking accounts and run up my credit card lines of credit on a couple of occasions.

But the knowledge that I ***could*** do a "Full Peanut Butter" has always been one of my sources of courage to do real estate deals. That psychological safety net is the main benefit of the "Full Peanut Butter" concept.

Financing real estate is scary. It's usually a big jump in the amount you owe and in your monthly payments. You wonder whether you'll be able to make the payments. You worry.

That's all normal and sensible. As in combat, only the crazy aren't scared. Just keep in mind that if things ***really*** get tough, you can always go on a "Full Peanut Butter."

Index

D

E

F

G

H

I

J

K

L

Q

R

S

T

YOUR OPINION OF THIS BOOK IS IMPORTANT TO ME

At the end of each session of my seminars, I ask the attendees to fill out a "Seminar Evaluation." Mo: seminar givers do that. But few book authors do. I think the book authors are making a mistake. So hereby ask you to send me your comments on this book. I'm interested in both compliments and construc tive criticism. Your compliments provide encouragement and guidance on what you want. And, with you permission, I'd like to use your favorable comments to sell the book. Constructive criticism also helps m make the book's next edition better.

. . . .

BOOK EVALUATION

Circle one: Excellent Good Satisfactory Unsatisfactory

Circle one: Too advanced About right Too basic

What part did you like best? ________________________________

What part did you like least? ________________________________

How can I improve the book? ________________________________

____

____

My promotional material includes brief comments by people who have read the book or taken my seminar and the name, occupation, company (in some cases), and city of the individual who made the comment. I would appreciate any remarks you could give me for that purpose:

____

____

____

____

Name ____________________ Occupation ____________________

Address ____

City ______________________________ State________ Zip________

Feel free to leave blanks if you prefer not to answer all of these questions. I would appreciate receiving your evaluations even if you only fill out one line. The following questions are designed to enable me to get a better fix on who my typical readers are. I will not be offended if you choose not to answer one or more of them however.

How long have you been a real estate investor? ____________________

What is thc total value of your holdings? ____________________

What types of property do you own? ____________________

____

If your comments will not fit on this sheet, feel free to write on the back an on additional sheets. Please send your evaluation to:

Reed Publishing
342 Bryan Drive
Danville, CA 94526

Order Form

TELEPHONE ORDERS
call toll-free 800-544-1016
in MA call 617-491-6562

Please send me:

_____ copies of *AGGRESSIVE TAX AVOIDANCE FOR REAL ESTATE INVESTORS* at $21.95 .... $ _______

_____ copies of *APARTMENT INVESTING CHECKLISTS* at $19.95 .... $ _______

_____ copies of ***HOW TO BUY AN OFFICE BUILDING*** at $19.95 .... $ _______

_____ copies of ***HOW TO USE LEVERAGE TO MAXIMIZE YOUR REAL ESTATE INVESTMENT RETURN*** at $19.95 .... $ _______

_____ copies of *HOW TO MANAGE APARTMENTS FOR MAXIMUM CASH FLOW AND RESALE VALUE* at $19.95 .... $ _______

Sub-total $ _______

Discount: 5% for orders over $50;
10% for orders over $100 $ _______

California residents add sales tax $ _______

Shipping: $2.50 per item $ _______

_____ subscription to ***Real Estate Investors' Monthly***
$96 per year (no sales tax or shipping charge) .... $ _______

TOTAL $ _______

Make check or money order payable to Reed Publishing.

☐ Check enclosed ☐ Visa ☐ MasterCard Card No. ________________________

Exp.
Date _________ Signature ________________________

SEND TO:

Name ________________________

Address ________________________

City ________________________ State _______ ZIP _______

Send your order to:
REED PUBLISHING
c/o Publishers Business Services
P.O. Box 643
Cambridge, MA 02139

Order Form

TELEPHONE ORDERS
call toll-free 800-544-1016
in MA call 617-491-6562

Please send me:

______ copies of *AGGRESSIVE TAX AVOIDANCE FOR REAL ESTATE INVESTORS* at $21.95 . . . . $ _______

______ copies of *APARTMENT INVESTING CHECKLISTS* at $19.95 . . . . $ _______

______ copies of ***HOW TO BUY AN OFFICE BUILDING*** at $19.95 . . . . $ _______

______ copies of ***HOW TO USE LEVERAGE TO MAXIMIZE YOUR REAL ESTATE INVESTMENT RETURN*** at $19.95 . . . . $ _______

______ copies of *HOW TO MANAGE APARTMENTS FOR MAXIMUM CASH FLOW AND RESALE VALUE* at $19.95 . . . . $ _______

Sub-total $ _______

Discount: 5% for orders over $50;
10% for orders over $100 $ _______

California residents add sales tax $ _______

Shipping: $2.50 per item $ _______

______ subscription to ***Real Estate Investors' Monthly***
$96 per year (no sales tax or shipping charge). . . . . $ _______

TOTAL $ _______

Make check or money order payable to Reed Publishing.

☐ Check enclosed ☐ Visa ☐ MasterCard Card No.________________________

Exp.
Date_________ Signature __________________________________

SEND TO:

Name ____

Address ____

City ______________________________ State_______ ZIP_______

Send your order to:
REED PUBLISHING
c/o Publishers Business Services
P.O. Box 643
Cambridge, MA 02139

NOTES

NOTES

NOTES